THE LAVENDER SCREEN

Greta Garbo

THE LAVENDER SCREEN

The Gay and Lesbian Films: Their Stars, Makers, Characters, and Critics

by Boze Hadleigh

A CITADEL PRESS BOOK

Published by Carol Publishing Group

Carol Publishing Group Edition - 1993

A Citadel Press Book
Published by Carol Publishing Group
Citadel Press is a registered trademark of Carol Communications, Inc.
Editorial Offices: 600 Madison Avenue, New York, NY 10022
Sales & Distribution Offices: 120 Enterprise Avenue, Secaucus, NJ 07094
In Canada: Canadian Manda Group, P.O. Box 920, Station U, Toronto,
Ontario, M8Z 5P9, Canada
Queries regarding rights and permissions should be addressed to:
Carol Publishing Group, 600 Madison Avenue, New York, NY 10022

Manufactured in the United States of America
ISBN 0-8065-1341-1

10 9 8 7 6 5 4 3 2

Carol Publishing Group books are available at special discounts
for bulk purchases, for sales promotions, fund raising, or
educational purposes. Special editions can also be created to
specifications. For details contact: Special Sales Department,
Carol Publishing Group, 120 Enterprise Ave., Secaucus, NJ 07094

Library of Congress Cataloging-in-Publication Data

Hadleigh, Boze.
       The lavender screen: the gay and lesbian films: their
stars, makers, characters, and critics/ by Boze Hadleigh.
       p. cm.
       "A Citadel Press book."
       1. Homosexuality in motion pictures. I. Title.
PN1995.9.H55H34   1992
791.43'653—dc20   92-35975
                                   CIP

Dedicated to Ronald M. Boze

By the same author:

THE FILMS OF JANE FONDA
(*Citadel Press*)

HISPANIC HOLLYWOOD:
The Latins in Motion Pictures (*Citadel Press*)

CONVERSATIONS WITH MY ELDERS:
Gay Hollywood Interviews

THE VINYL CLOSET:
Gays in the Music World

ACKNOWLEDGMENTS

I extend my warmest thanks to Doug McClelland, film scholar *extraordinaire*, and to Sue Kutosh, artist *extraordinaire*. And to Manuel Cordova and Eduardo Moreno, extraordinary film enthusiasts and collectors.

Grateful thanks to my editor Allan J. Wilson and his associates at Citadel Press, including Gordon Allan, Jessica H. Black, Theodore W. Macri, Alvin H. Marill, and Gina Suarez.

Thanks also to: Nestor Almendros, Arthur Bressan, Stuart Byron, Simon Callow, Carlos Clarens, John Cluckie, Tom Connelly, Carl David, Samson DeBrier, Harold Fairbanks, John Gielgud, Mike Hippler, Christopher Isherwood, Jim Kepner, Ian McKellen, Robert Patrick, Jim Pinkston, Rex Reed, Dale Reynolds, Cesar Romero, Leonardo Rossi, John Schlesinger, Peter Sorel, Bob Thompson, Marc Allen Trujillo, Gore Vidal, Alec Wagner, and Kenneth Williams.

And, always, to Linda Fresia.

Photo Credits

Allied Artists, Allied Film Makers, American Film Theater, Arthur J. Bressan, Jr., Associated Film Distributors (AFD), Audubon Films, Avco Embassy, Cinecom, Cinema 5, Cineplex Odeon Films, Cinerama Distributing Co., Claridge Pictures, Columbia Pictures, Continental Distributing Inc., Hal Roach Films, International Spectrafilm Distribution, Island Alive, Lorimar Productions, Metro-Goldwyn-Mayer Pictures, National General Pictures, New Line Cinema, Orion Pictures, Paramount Pictures, Pathe-American Distributing Co., RKO Radio Pictures, Sigma Productions, Simon Film Productions, The Walt Disney Company, The M Company, The Samuel Goldwyn Company, Topar/Film 21, Touchstone Films, Tri-Star Pictures, 20th Century-Fox, United Artists, Universal Pictures, Walter Reade Organization, Warner Bros. Pictures, Z-Films, Zenith International.

And Granada Television, the British Film Institute, and the Billy Rose Theater Collection of the New York Public Library at Lincoln Center.

CONTENTS

THE LAVENDER SCREEN

Not a bad actor: Rock Hudson, who in over sixty films convincingly portrayed heterosexual heroes.

FOREWORD

IDENTITY

In *Giant,* rich-girl Liz Taylor tells poor-boy James Dean, "Money isn't everything." Popping his gay panda eyes, Dean replies, "Whew! Not when you got it, it ain't." All the gay kids in America "Whew'd" in recognition. "It" could have been that unappreciated hereto commodity, identity.

Identity is a concept of one's possibilities, which entirely controls one's life-choices, personal or social. It is not innate but acquired, most intensely through romantic, dramatic mythic images. In America, the dominant and commanding cultural images have been film stars.

Heterosexuals entered the world of film through clearly marked doors. There were inspiring heros or heroines for them to identify with, a rich array of dramatized examples, ideals, role models on how to live, to love. Even the unheroic could identify with bumbling, lovable, popular character players. But, as we sat in the dark among the straights, watching them take off into a celluloid stratosphere to come back with idols they could imitate right out in the open, at home, on the job, on dates, or in tanks and planes and trenches, homosexuals hit a yellow brick ceiling. Gazing into the wonderworld on the wall, we saw that we simply did not exist.

Other minorities had films from their native lands, however few, or Hollywood clichés, however artificial, providing images, however limiting, in stories, however hypocritical, which promised them advancement, however conformist. They longed to pass. Homosexuals had to.

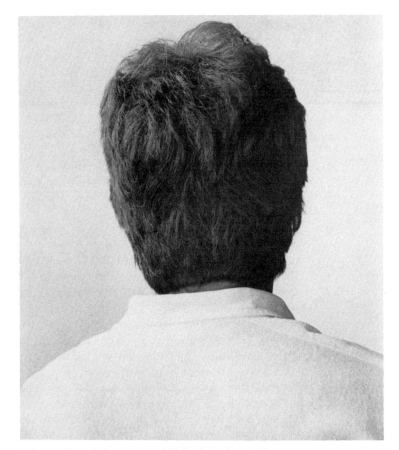

Hollywood's typical gay actor: Still faceless after all these years . . .

Hollywood's typical gay character: Not an individual, but a sex-defined, twenty-four hour "homosexual."

Outsiders trapped inside, we had our own ways of watching films. At worst, we viewed alien antics and became cynical or clinical observers like playwrights Joe Orton and William Inge. At best, we watched *Gone With the Wind* and identified with Scarlett because we loved men, with Rhett because we *were* men, with Melanie because we too had to be quietly wise, with Ashley because we too lived a lie, with the slaves because we too had masters, and with Belle Watling—well, just because. Such global empathy produced the finest sort of compassionate gays, like Thornton Wilder and Tennessee Williams.

Most of us fell in between, trying to cut an identity from chance frames of film. A few secret doors were ajar for us. Dean and Montgomery Clift let their gayness show, but they played straights, as we did; that was no gay identity. Some swung with Judy Garland's pregenderal anxiety or Bette's or Joan's struggles to have men's rights and women's hearts. We didn't swallow machismo, because we, of all people, knew how forced it was, but a Brando body and bike were good covers and attracted lovers. Judy, Bette, or Brando: a twitch, a bitch, or a butch; these were identities we could imagine for ninety minutes in the dark. If we tried to maintain them outside, we might soon find ourselves identifying and being identified with silly-ninny town aunties like Edward Everett Horton, Paul Lynde, Tony Randall. It was best simply to try to disappear, and to accept living only in the dark.

Then in 1961 in a British film called *Victim,* a character said the word "homosexual." We jumped! After a lifetime of hearing Mickey Rooney's problem in *Words and Music* defined as "being too short," John Kerr's problem in *Tea and Sympathy* as "being too sensitive," and Sebastian Venable's in *Suddenly, Last Summer* not defined at all, what a joy just to hear the word!

The word was spoken and the world didn't end, so more gay characters appeared. Almost all were villains and/or drags. That was better than being like Dracula, not reflected at all. But soon we got actual gay films, porn films. Our first star was Jack Wrangler. His plaid-lad image, all grin and groin, was cloned worldwide as the macho man, synonymous with gay pride. There was a catch. The old straight films had taught how to woo, but not how to screw, with neurotic consequences for the straight majority. Our porn films did the opposite, depicting a sleazy low-budget world where gay men met, auto-mated, and faded-out, without any life but love, with equally neurotic results for gay men and the gay movement. Broader images are obviously needed.

There have been non-porn gay films, most from Europe. U.S. examples (*The Boys in the Band, Making Love, Torch Song Trilogy,* and *Longtime Companion*) remain few, because they all failed financially. Foreign class acts like *Prick Up Your Ears, Querelle, Another Country,* and *Maurice* barely scrape by on international art-house revenues and create no wave.*

The gay population of America is large enough to make any film a Top-Tenner. Did the boys boycott the big-time gay films because of self-hatred, or because we have internalized surrogate straight images, or because they told us nothing we didn't already know? Was it from simple sensible fear of being mugged coming out? Or is it that, after centuries of being told that door is closed to us, we sit staring at it now that it is open like the Jews at the end of World War II who huddled in Auschwitz, staring in animal terror at the opened gates? We don't know. We won't know until fine romantic mythic image-making gay films regularly appear and give their natural audience the chance to acquire new habits. There are no signs that this wonder is imminent. Gay men in mainstream films today are defined by the compulsive anti-gay wisecracks in the unending "buddy movies," where gayness is the most demeaning insult. TV's frequent gay characters are not presented as people; they are brought on as challenges to the tolerance of sit-com stars or proof of the valor of middle-class mothers, but always, always problems: family-threateners, child-molesters, or vectors for disease.

Independent gay films like *My Own Private Idaho, Poison, The Living End,* and *Swoon* offer hope of greater things, but still draw nothing like the percentage of the audience that gays constitute, and present images that are unviable (that being apparently their point). Perhaps even independent film-makers cannot get backing for anything else.

Movies, and their TV spin-offs, remain at this moment in the hands of an increasingly narcissistic majority. Backers and sponsors are unlikely to support anything that does not flatter them. However, with the emergence of home video, it is now possible for films to show a profit through scattered individual rentals without ever being

*Exceptions like *La Cage Aux Folles* and *The Crying Game* only prove what theatre folk already knew: Americans fear gay men, but love a drag queen.

able to draw crowds. Just recently, a Hollywood porn star and producer, Kevin Glover, has begun marketing videos of gay plays from among the classics of the genre. Time will tell whether the new medium can sell a new message.

ROBERT PATRICK

Robert Patrick's latest books are Untold Decades, *from St. Martins Press, and* Temple Slave *from Starwolf Press.*

PREFACE
Lights, Camera . . .

The movies, they are a-changin'. Consider this: In 1983 Dustin Hoffman was nominated for an Academy Award as Dorothy and Michael in *Tootsie*. Julie Andrews was nominated as *Victor/Victoria*. Nominated for Supporting Actor were Robert Preston as Victoria's gay pal Toddy and John Lithgow as a transsexual in *The World According to Garp*. In 1984 Tom Courtenay was nominated as *The Dresser*, only the third nominee for Best Actor in a gay role. Nominated in the Supporting Actress category were Cher as a lesbian in *Silkwood*, Amy Irving as Barbra Streisand's wife in *Yentl*, and, the winner, Linda Hunt as male Billy Kwan in *The Year of Living Dangerously*.

In 1985 Vanessa Redgrave became the first actress nominated for playing a gay lead character, in *The Bostonians*. *The Times of Harvey Milk* won the first "gay" Oscar for Best Documentary. In front of an audience estimated at one billion, director Robert Epstein thanked "my partner in life, John Wright," and producer Richard Schmiechen affirmed Milk's "pride in being gay" and hoped that someday all people could dwell in "mutual respect."

In 1986 William Hurt became the first actor in a gay role to win the Best Actor Oscar, in the crossover hit *Kiss of the Spider Woman* (also nominated for Best Picture). The chance to act gay roles is now sought by a larger number of bisexual, heterosexual, and homosexual actors. Of course, most gay roles occur in straight-themed films, for Hollywood still makes few pictures focusing on gays.

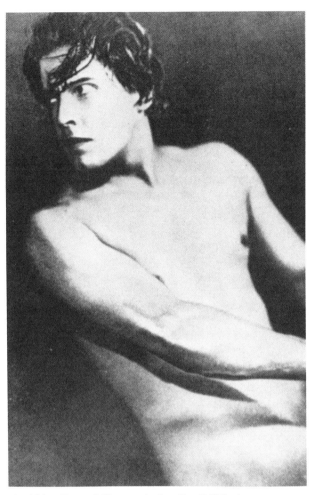

"Ravishing Ramon" Novarro in *Ben-Hur* (1926): A gay star whose career suffered because he refused to wed.

Casablanca (1942): Peter Lorre—"You despise me, don't you, Rick?" Humphrey Bogart—"I probably would if I gave any thought to it."

Anything goes: Bisexual Cary Grant as a heterosexual Cole Porter, who was gay, in the fictional film biography, *Night and Day* (1946).

Movies abound with *minor* gay characters, references, and plots. Robert Prescott, for instance, in the teen comedy *The Joy of Sex*, plays a heterosexual *and* his gay brother Richard, who has "the personality of a bobby pin." Richard Minchenberg was Shelley Long's swishy assistant in *Irreconcilable Differences*. His biggest "line"—prominently featured in the TV ads—was an orgasmic shriek. In the Catholic school comedy *Heaven Help Us*, Kevin Dillon spewed out "fag" dozens of times. (The actor defensively compared "fag" to "nerd," which does not, however, refer to sexual orientation.)

Individually and as a class, gays are still misrepresented and ridiculed in films—as sissies in *Purple Rain*, cowards in *Red Dawn*, white niggers in Eddie Murphy vehicles, villains in *JFK*, or vicious killers in *Silence of the Lambs* and *Basic Instinct*.

Barry Sandler, who wrote the epochal *Making Love*, declares that "the image of gay people on the screen has been one of perverts and killers or freaks or grotesques or screaming queens or interior decorators or *La Cage aux Folles*." Yet even that was progress, because prior to 1959 British and American movies relegated gay people to infamy and worthlessness via complete invisibility. By contrast, today few films lack some mention of homosexuality, even if it's often negative. The *Los Angeles Times*'s Sheila Benson made comment of the fact that *The Big Chill*, with its large cast, *didn't* include any gay characters.

Most movies pander to the lowest common denominator: sexists of all ages and adolescents whose

Lesbian tease: Vera Clouzot and Simone Signoret in *Diabolique* (1954), but one turns out to be heterosexual and kills the other.

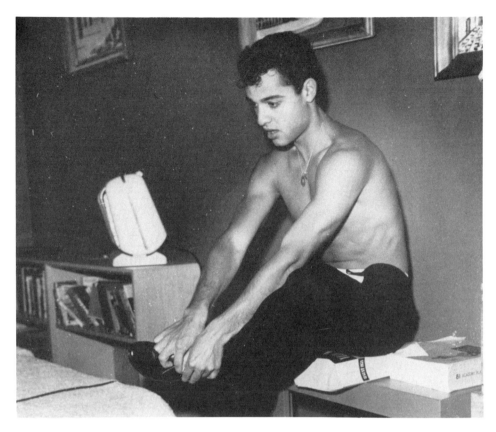

Switchblade Kid: Gay Sal Mineo played the screen's first gay teen, in love with James Dean in *Rebel Without a Cause* (1955).

Certain stars, like Barbara Stanwyck, have played lesbian on screen—and frequently off!—here as Jo in *Walk on the Wild Side* (1962).

Women without men—usually depicted as "bad girls": Merry Anders and Lisa Davis as Holly and Rose Dalton in *The Dalton Girls* (1957).

15

The color purple, but not lavender: Androgynous Whoopi Goldberg as a cop in female "drag" in *Fatal Beauty* (1987).

Openly gay directors like Paul Bartel (pictured here), John Waters, and John Schlesinger are helping bring a new honesty to film.

fears and biases are usually reinforced rather than alleviated and informed. But movies are propaganda as well as entertainment. Sandler notes, "The all-American boy who grows up pursuing and living the American dream, who turns out to be homosexual, exists. But people refuse to admit it. They can accept *La Cage* because it perpetuates a stereotype. But what happens when you show your brother, son, or husband, or the girl next door, as gay? It's

shattering, and that's what we have to do: shake people up to *see* what's around them."

Gay films depict not so much a homosexual world or lifestyle as straight society's assumptions. Pop star Boy George has said, "There's this illusion that homosexuals only have sex and heterosexuals fall in love." George feels that "People who aren't viewed as loving and whole are considered less than fully human, therefore more expendable." Indeed it's often been theorized that there is a direct relationship between treatment of gays in the media and growing anti-gay violence.

The late Peter Finch told this author, "Some of the most constructive and loving relationships I've seen are between men, or women. But because most gays hide their true nature, even from relatives, the world—made up of smaller worlds—doesn't realize this. Gay people need to be prouder, more defiant. . . . And I know that's easy for me to say!"

Gay-themed films may be taken on two levels: as entertainment and celluloid sociology. As a whole, the feature films included here—those with major gay characters or milieus—are the most fascinating and unusually revealing (of the pictures' makers, actors, and subjects; of cultural and religious bias; and of evolving social changes) of any group of movies. And despite many common traits and flaws, one of the most varied.

BOZE HADLEIGH

16

1

OLDEN DAYS:

Maedchen in Uniform

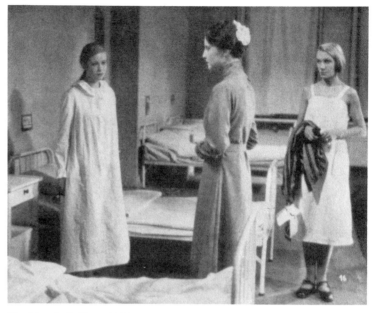

Maedchen in Uniform (1931): Manuela's (Hertha Thiele) crush on her teacher (Dorothea Wieck) becomes public knowledge at her Prussian boarding school.

Maedchen in Uniform. Deutschefilmgemeinschaft, 1931.
Director: Leontine Sagan; writers: Christa Winsloe and F.D. Andam.
Starring: Dorothea Wieck, Hertha Thiele, Emilia Unda, Erika Mann.

Until *The Killing of Sister George* in 1968, Germany's *Maedchen in Uniform* was the most famous lesbian film, and the first seen publicly in America. However, the first movie lesbian was Countess Geschwitz (Alice Roberts) in G. W. Pabst's *Die Buechse der Pandora* in 1929, starring Louise Brooks. British and American versions of *Pandora's Box* deleted the gay character, who wasn't restored until several decades later.

In 1919 Magnus Hirschfeld's Institute for Sexual Science sponsored *Anders als die Anderen* (*Different From the Rest*), the first gay film. (One of Hirschfeld's partners was Gavin Arthur, grandson of U.S. President Chester Alan Arthur.) This blackmail saga featured the first inevitable unhappy ending, offset by director Richard Oswald's epilogue: "Let us hope that we shall see the time when such tragedies will be impossible, when we shall no longer see intelligence become stupidity, truth become lies, and love become hate."

The Nazis attempted to burn all extant prints, and for decades *Anders* was believed lost, until two copies were located, one in East Germany's film archive. After years of negotiation, that print was screened at the 1983 San Francisco Lesbian and Gay

In a male role in a school play, Manuela passionately declares her love for Fräulein von Bernburg (Wieck).

Film Festival. (Also shown was *Mikael*, Carl Dreyer's 1924 love story about an artist and his male model.)

Germany's flow of pioneering movies ended with the advent of the Nazi regime in 1933. A year after

Hitler came to power, Hollywood formulated its Production Code, which effectively banned all gay themes, characters, even names, from the screen until 1959, when the Code was finally challenged. Pre-Code Hollywood hadn't served up fully developed homosexual characters or themes anyway. Germany was clearly in the forefront of film realism and compassion. And it was a German gay, writer-director-producer-actor Rainer Werner Fassbinder, whose tireless efforts through the 1970s single-handedly restored German cinema to its pre-Nazi international eminence as a portrayer of homosexual themes.

One of prewar Germany's last gay films was *Maedchen in Uniform*, based on an antifascist play by lesbian poet Christa Winsloe, the Baroness Hatvany, a colorful character in her own right. In 1931 Winsloe met political journalist and radio commentator Dorothy Thompson, then married to Sinclair Lewis. (Thompson, expelled from Germany by Hitler for her critical news reports, had been in love with Gertrude Franchot Tone, the activist-feminist and mother of actor Franchot Tone.) Lewis was aware of his wife's bisexuality and, at the time of her affair with Winsloe, wrote *Ann Vickers*, a turgid novel about a career woman "driven to suicide because of a lesbian relationship." This was his form of revenge and just another example of art not paralleling life!

Maedchen is set at a Potsdam boarding school, a symbol of totalitarianism, against which unhappy, motherless Manuela (Hertha Thiele) rebels. The student is miserable at the semimilitary academy; marching soldiers in the opening montage are mirrored by marching uniformed schoolgirls.

The day's highlight for most of the love-starved girls is the goodnight kiss bestowed by beautiful Fräulein von Bernburg (Dorothea Wieck). Manuela's crush on her teacher is reciprocated, and during a school assembly Manuela impetuously proclaims her love for all to hear. The scandalized headmistress banishes her to the infirmary. At the end of the film, the tormented, isolated Manuela tries to leap from the top of a stairwell but is rescued by her classmates, who defy the female führer's decree. By contrast, the play had ended with Manuela jumping from a second-story window. The movie ending was prompted by Hitler's rapid ascent in 1931. The first cooperatively made German film (it paid in shares rather than salaries), *Maedchen* was also one of the first made by women—politicized women.

Shortly after *Maedchen*'s release, its ending was retooled by Nazi censors, and the nonconformist Manuela fell to her death. When the weakened film became a hit and drew critical raves throughout Europe, Goebbels banned it for its "unhealthy" homosexual theme. Most of *Maedchen*'s filmmakers fled the country soon after. Winsloe, an anti-Axis activist, was murdered in Vichy France in 1944. The film's director, Leontine Sagan, an actress and theater director as well, escaped to England, where she made her second and last film in 1932, *Men of Tomorrow*, starring Merle Oberon, the wife of producer Alexander Korda. In his Oberon biography, Charles Higham draws a grim portrait of "mannish, strident, and aggressive" Sagan. Oberon reportedly "hated the formidable Sagan, who hated Merle. . . . Sagan constantly said to Merle, with snarling emphasis, 'Why do you spend so much time fiddling with your eyelashes? Try to spend more time studying your part. You're a lousy actress!' "

In 1934 the *Hollywood Reporter* announced that David O. Selznick had signed Sagan to direct for MGM, but Louis B. Mayer was wary of her and *Maedchen* with its all-female cast. (George Cukor later had to plead with Mayer to make *The Women*, a 1939 all-female hit.) Sagan eventually returned to South Africa, where she'd been married, and cofounded the National Theatre in Johannesburg. She died in 1974, at age eighty-five.

Maedchen costar Erika Mann—daughter of Thomas Mann and sister of gay author-activist Klaus Mann—escaped Germany by marrying British poet W. H. Auden; both husband and wife were homosexual.

Fräulein Professor is reprimanded by Frau Principal (Emilia Unda), a harsh pre-Nazi disciplinarian.

American distribution rights to *Maedchen* were sold quickly, but New York censors seized the print and delayed its exhibition—until 1932, when, despite additional editing, it was voted best film of the year by the New York press. The deletions included not only tender glances between student and teacher and the line expressing Manuela's love, but von Bernburg's vindication of "the great spirit of love, which has thousands of forms." The American version retained the exploitable "affair" but excised the love and romance between the women, thereby preventing their explaining or defending themselves.

Over the decades, American distributor John Krimsky insisted that *Maedchen* was not about lesbianism, and in the late 1970s he continued to withhold it from exhibition at any gay or women's film festivals.

In 1958 *Maedchen* inspired the first gay remake, starring Lilli Palmer, Romy Schneider, and Christine Kaufmann, and directed by Geza Radvanyi. The picture was a sensation at the Berlin Film Festival and a moderate hit in Europe, largely due to Palmer's and Schneider's popularity there. It was not exhibited in the U.S. until 1965, and then only fleetingly. Scarcely seen outside Europe, the 1958 *Maedchen* compares unfavorably with its predecessor. In 1978 Schneider told *Oggi* magazine, "The original was very moving—and very tame, despite the notoriety. But now *our* film seems tame and dated."

(Two other early thirties' German films were reincarnated as *Some Like It Hot* in 1959 and *Victor/Victoria* in 1982, both with cross-dressing and/or gay themes.)

German gay and lesbian screen characters went into hiding when the Nazis came into power. The few gay Hollywood film characters there were—usually more seminude than gay; i.e., a bare-bottomed galley slave in *Ben-Hur* (1926) and a scantily-clad slave boy at Nero's side in *Sign of the Cross* (1932)—disappeared because of pressure from religious groups.

Actually, Hollywood movies became more inhibited with the arrival of sound. Simultaneously, the Depression brought a return to more patriarchal values; as jobs grew scarce, women were routinely fired so as not to "deprive" a male breadwinner of work. With sound, female characters had voices, and their careers and aspirations seemed more threatening when given words. The social climate brought the Production Code, once the twenties

Olivia (1951): Directed by Jacqueline Audry, the French film set in a girls' boarding school starred Edwige Feuillère.

Probably the screen's first lesbian: the Countess Geschwitz (Alice Roberts, with Louise Brooks as Lulu) in *Pandora's Box* (1929).

19

Marlene Dietrich exemplified the "garçonne" (boy-girl) tradition popular in Europe in the twenties and thirties.

decades to come gay people were invisible on the silver screen. In the words of gay writer Christopher Isherwood, "The heterosexual dictatorship played out a sexual genocide against homosexual people on the screen. By making us invisible, they could pretend we didn't exist. By making us unmentionable, they made us appear more contemptible. . . . The love that dared not speak its name also didn't dare show its face."

ABOUT *MAEDCHEN IN UNIFORM*

Pauline Kael, the *New Yorker*: The teacher is not viewed as decadent or naughty; she [is] on the side

had ended and the times had stopped roaring forward.

The Code and its enforcer, the Hays Office, had been primarily aimed at curbing social change, and its chief victim had been the New Woman, particularly the *sexual* New Woman. But the new censorship guidelines drawn up in the mid-1930s also banned any hint of sexual diversity and sought to downplay sex in general. Homogeneity and conformity were the desired ends of the Code, and for

In *Morocco* (1930), Dietrich wore top hat and tails and kissed a female spectator on the lips.

Queen Christina (1933): An anti-factual bio of the lesbian Swedish monarch who, like Garbo, refused to marry.

Garbo wore men's clothing in much of *Christina*; here with Countess Ebba Sparre (Elizabeth Young).

The monarch kisses Ebba, her favorite subject.

of the liberal, humanitarian angels, yet unmistakably lesbian. This legendary film . . . is always described as sensitive, and it is; it's also a rather loaded piece of special pleading.

Nancy Scholar, *WomanFilm*: The fact that a *woman* enforces the militaristic values inherited from a patriarchal society warns against easy dichotomies between male and female values and indicates that corruption of power knows no sexual boundaries.

The erotic ambiance is explicit when Fräulein von Bernburg and Manuela passionately kiss, surrounded by a luminous halo; the photography is superlative. . . . The breakthrough comes with Manuela's open declaration of love and the girls' solidarity against the inhuman, emotionally sterile headmistress. . . . Once Manuela has been saved, she and von Bernburg are reunited; their faces merge, anticipating Bergman's *Persona* by thirty-five years.

21

Violet Venable (Katharine Hepburn) and an angel of death guard her late son Sebastian's "secret."

2

THIS HOMOSEXUALITY:

Suddenly, Last Summer

Cathy (Elizabeth Taylor) enrages Aunt Violet when she tells the truth about Sebastian's sexuality.

Suddenly, Last Summer. Columbia, 1959. Director: Joseph L. Mankiewicz; writers: Gore Vidal and Tennessee Williams; producer: Sam Spiegel.
Starring: Elizabeth Taylor, Montgomery Clift, Katharine Hepburn, Albert Dekker, Mercedes McCambridge, Gary Raymond.

Time critic Richard Schickel once queried, "Why do we have to have all of this homosexuality in our movies?" The answer, in part, is that the Catholic church is to blame for all of this homosexuality in movies. In 1959, in concert with the Motion Picture Production Code Administration, the church granted a special dispensation permitting *Suddenly, Last Summer* to include the first male homosexual in an American film. The *word* itself was never uttered, the gay character never spoke, and his face never appeared. The invisible man's name was Sebastian, after the saint whose multiple arrow-wounds were immortalized in the art of the Renaissance, when wealthy gay men—including church officials—often had their lovers painted as the nude, tormented martyr. The iconography made the figures, often displayed in public, tolerable and praiseworthy.

Gore Vidal's script for *Suddenly, Last Summer* was based on Tennessee Williams's one-act play, half of a 1958 Off-Broadway double bill titled *Garden District.* Though the controversial playwright received screen credit, Williams later claimed that he had nothing to do with the film. His explosive *Streetcar*

Vi enlists a doctor's (Montgomery Clift) help in trying to lobotomize the talkative Cathy.

Named Desire and *Cat on a Hot Tin Roof* had broadened tolerance of homosexuality onstage. But when the hit plays were translated to film, gay references—including Blanche's marriage to a gay man and Brick's sexuality—were dropped. *Suddenly, Last Summer*'s homosexuality was more crucial to the plot and the cause of its villain's gory demise. Its inclusion on-screen was therefore less objectionable to moralists.

The plot centers on Sebastian Venable's final summer and the effect his death has on his clinging mother, Violet, and his cousin, Catherine Holly. Elizabeth Taylor emerges as the movie's heroine, vindicated of insanity and transferred from Lion's View State Asylum to the care of Dr. "Sugar" (Montgomery Clift). As Mrs. Venable, Katharine Hepburn—second-billed to another actress for the first time—threatens to lobotomize her niece, whose "babbling" imperils the family's venerable name. But the truth is told: Sebastian used his mother, and then Cathy, to attract local youths for him.

Cathy screams as her cousin Sebastian is devoured by street urchins in a nameless Third World resort.

The cheesecake shot of Liz Taylor used to advertise the non-heterosexual-themed *Suddenly, Last Summer* (1959).

Monty Clift in his pre-*Summer* prime.

The movie reintroduced several stereotypes that its successors would repeat endlessly, most notably, the mad bully-mother in love with her son and trying unsuccessfully to keep his sexuality a secret. When she shows Dr. Cukrowicz ("sugar" in Polish) Sebastian's studio, she notes, "It was formerly the *garçonnière* where the young men of the family could go to be private." (The studio contains a painting of St. Sebastian, alongside male nudes.) Sebastian is a sickly pill-popper, moody and paranoid. His only friends are women, and he suffers from writer's block (his annual output is a single poem, published by his mother). Despite his lustfulness he seems asexual but prefers to gaze at boys.

Set in 1937 New Orleans, the play was inspired by a prefrontal lobotomy performed on Williams's sister, Rose, who was also the basis for Laura in *The Glass Menagerie* and Blanche DuBois in *Streetcar*. The character of Sebastian was inspired by Hart Crane, whom Williams admired; the poet died young, drowned in the Caribbean. Both writers idolized Herman Melville (the gay author of *Moby Dick* and *Billy Budd*) and became self-destructive when their talent diminished. Pursued by the children of Cabeza del Lobo, Sebastian throws coins to distract them. Williams copied this from Oscar Wilde, who did the same with North African street children. Dr. Cukrowicz was based on Rose's pioneering surgeon, Dr. Lawrence S. Kubie, while Violet, one of Williams's least believable female characters, was a pure product of his imagination and functions primarily as a psychological explanation for Sebastian.

In the late forties producer Sam Spiegel teamed with liberal, but antigay, director John Huston to form Horizon Pictures. In 1952, after Horizon produced *The African Queen*, Huston withdrew from the partnership. Spiegel was convinced there was a market for as-yet unexplored adult themes, so his British Horizon bought the screen rights to *Suddenly, Last Summer* in 1958. Elizabeth Taylor, fresh from her triumph in Williams's neutered *Cat*, signed on for her first project as a free-lancer. For her leading man she chose her friend and two-time costar Montgomery Clift. Hepburn accepted what her writer-producer friend Chester Erskine called a "character part" to justify second-billing to Taylor. He explained that Hepburn found the part "unsympathetic and wanted to play the woman as insane, to distance the role or remove herself from identification with it."

Though Hepburn's box office had slipped in recent years, Clift's career—three years after his injury in a car accident—had been pronounced dead. Clift's friend and agent Lew Wasserman told MGM that his client wasn't "fit to work and he was uninsurable." But Taylor insisted Clift was the only costar she would consider, and so production began at London's Shepperton Studios with Clift uninsured and uninsurable. It was an arduous shoot.

Albert Dekker, who played a doctor in *Suddenly, Last Summer*, was best known for his role as Dr. Cyclops in the 1940 film. His 1968 hanging suicide—handcuffed, wearing silk lingerie, limbs scrawled with lipstick—is chronicled in Kenneth Anger's *Hollywood Babylon*.

Joseph Mankiewicz's biographer, Kenneth Geist —producer-director of the documentary *Coming Out*—wrote that the director "suffered from a dermatological ailment that caused his fingertips to split open; it frequently afflicts him under situations of extreme pressure, like filming." Geist visited the set and watched "Mank," wearing white film-editor's gloves, massage Monty's neck and shoulders. "The result was astonishing. Clift's tremors subsided, and he maintained his composure through repeated takes."

Clift needed continual attention, but the director had little time to spare for him. A few weeks into filming, Mankiewicz demanded that Clift be fired. Taylor refused, as did Spiegel, who admitted, "We were frequently tempted, because it became increasingly difficult to work with him [but] I was very fond of him. I spent hours and hours practically nursing him—postponing shooting until I knew he was calm and we'd given him enough coffee and counter medicines to counteract whatever drugs he was taking." London had one of its hottest summers in years, and, making matters worse, the wordy script contained several long one-take scenes. One of Monty's lengthier scenes had to be broken into fourteen segments, each comprising just a single line. Taylor and Hepburn had more than usual patience in their scenes with him. In retake after retake Taylor bolstered Monty's confidence, and Hepburn ran lines with him, as she'd done with the alcoholic Spencer Tracy.

Ironically, Hepburn was known to be intolerant of male homosexuals, and, unlike most of Hollywood, she was unaware of Clift's homosexuality. She disliked Mrs. Venable because of the character's relationship with her gay son and felt that only an insane woman could have produced a Sebastian.

Hepburn took exception to much of her dialogue, complaining to Mankiewicz, "If you only *knew* what it means to me when I have to say those things!" She particularly objected to her pseudo-

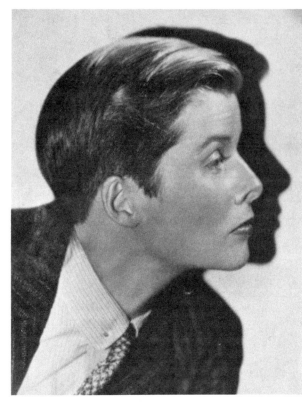

Portrait of the artist as a young man: Kate
Hepburn in *Sylvia Scarlett* (1935).

ship was altered to reprise the famous Taylor-Clift
embrace from *A Place in the Sun*, and a happy
ending was suggested. The film was granted the
Production Code Seal of Approval after two further
changes: the deletion of a scene in the Spanish town
with only *two* youngsters and a mention of the word
procuring.

Publicity stills were made of the unseen Sebastian,
showing him as a gauntly handsome man in a white

Hepburn in latter drag in *The Iron Petticoat* (1956).

incestuous memories of "that famous couple, Violet
and Sebastian, Sebastian and Violet." She couldn't
believe that a mother could harbor such feelings for
her son. In 1970 former friend Garson Kanin told
McCall's magazine that a year or so after *Suddenly,
Last Summer*, he and Tracy described various homosexual acts to Hepburn, who refused to believe
there were men who indulged in such "ridiculous
practices." In the early seventies Hepburn revealed
to the press her distaste for *Sunday, Bloody Sunday*
and other films with lovemaking men.

Though faithful to the play, the film relocated
considerable dialogue from the tropical Venable
garden to the asylum where Taylor is incarcerated.
Voyeuristic *Snake Pit*-like scenes were inserted. In
one, Cathy wanders into a crowded cell. From the
catwalk, she stares morbidly at male inmates staring
up her legs and skirt. When one of them seizes her
ankle, she panics and runs. Of course, utmost
discretion was reserved for the film's homosexual
facets. The script's biggest clue comes when Cathy
says, "Don't you understand? He used us for bait."
And Mrs. Holly drawls, "Oh, I used to love Sebastian. . . . His friends were always so well-dressed
and so arty." The platonic doctor-patient relation-

Most critics denounced the subject matter and focused on Taylor's beauty and performance. She and Hepburn were both nominated for Oscars but canceled each other out. (Simone Signoret won for *Room at the Top*.) Taylor won later for *Butterfield 8*, her least favorite film. She earned the award less in sympathy for the famous tracheotomy than for her work as Tennessee Williams's Cathy and Maggie the Cat. Williams rejected the film and in 1972 told the *Village Voice* that it "made me throw up" and that Hollywood had taken too many liberties with his play. In 1973 Mankiewicz described *Suddenly, Last Summer* as "a badly constructed play based on the most elementary Freudian psychology and one anecdote," the final revelation.

Today the film is of interest both for its subject matter—the treatment of which now seems Victorian—and the performances of its legendary stars.

Brick (Paul Newman) uses alcohol as a crutch in *Cat on a Hot Tin Roof*.

suit. Williams felt Sebastian was too stunning to be portrayed by an actor, that his presence would be felt more strongly via his absence. Likewise, the cannibalistic murder is left to the viewer's imagination; the camera turns away as the street urchins destroy Sebastian. Before he is devoured, his hand vainly grasps for help. The scene's horror is reflected on Cathy's face as she recalls it after having been administered a "truth serum."

Not surprisingly, the publicity stills of Sebastian were mostly unused. The ads pictured Liz/Cathy in a decolleté white swimsuit, on her knees in front of Sebastian (shown from behind, waist-down). The ad read, "Suddenly, last summer, Cathy knew she was being used for evil."

There were doubts that *Suddenly, Last Summer*, with themes of homosexuality, cannibalism, and psychosurgery could attract audiences. Perhaps because of such ingredients the movie was a huge hit and a portent of things to come. In 1961 an emendation to the Code made homosexuality a permissible theme, if handled "with care, discretion, and restraint."

One big unhappy family: *Cat on a Hot Tin Roof* (1958) omitted the homosexuality of Tennessee Williams's hit play.

Mankiewicz claims, "It was the best performance Elizabeth ever gave." He calls Hepburn "the most experienced amateur actress in the world" but judges her Mrs. Venable "brilliant." Gore Vidal believes, "Clift and Taylor were dreadful. Hepburn was miscast but interesting." Williams thought Hepburn and Clift were excellent and Taylor miscast: "It stretched credulity to believe that such a hip doll as Liz wouldn't know in the film that she was 'being used for evil.' I think Liz would have dragged Sebastian home by his ears and saved them both from considerable embarrassment that summer." George Cukor, Hepburn's confidant and frequent director, said, "I didn't know then that Kate's range extended to communicating such cruelty, but she proved that it did."

Suddenly, Last Summer was the first and last film based on Williams's work to feature a major homosexual character. "I have never found the subject of homosexuality a satisfactory theme for a full-length play," declared the gay author, who many call homophobic, in view of his plays' portrayals of sick, miserable, self-destructive gay men. In the seventies and eighties, television corrected two of Williams's movies: Ann-Margret's Blanche DuBois soliloquized about her suicide-husband, and Robert Wagner's Brick professed his love-hate for his dead buddy, Skipper. But much of the media was still stuck in the fifties. The *New York Times*'s obituary described the uncloseted Williams as "a lifelong bachelor," and a book reviewer wrote that Williams's 1975 memoirs had "shocked and disappointed readers with its luxuriation in the author's homosexuality."

ABOUT *SUDDENLY, LAST SUMMER*

Variety: Possibly the most bizarre film ever made by a major American company.

Time: In the play that Williams wrote, the action slithered about the spectator with the speed of a big snake, crushing in its clammy coils. . . . This story is nothing more than a psychiatric nursery drama, a homosexual fantasy of guilty pleasure and pleasurable punishment. The dead hero is really no more than a perverted Peter Pan, the cannibalism nothing more than aggravated nail-biting.

Sight and Sound: One may imagine Williams's hothouse fantasies of insanity, homosexuality, possessive mother domination, and cannibalism administering a short, sharp Grand Guignolish shock. . . . The film's hints are more wordily explicit than most statements. One episode—the flashback revelation of what really happened to Sebastian that summer afternoon—is surprisingly terse and carries its imaginative charge. The playing is dogged (Clift), arrestingly mannered (Hepburn), and courageously whole-hearted (Taylor). But the work itself remains a sickly fantasy.

3

SPECIAL FRIENDS:

A Taste of Honey and *A Special Day*

Jo (Rita Tushingham) and Helen (Dora Bryan) have a strained mother-daughter relationship in *A Taste of Honey* (1961).

A Taste of Honey. Woodfall/Continental, 1961. Director-producer: Tony Richardson; writers: Shelagh Delaney and Richardson.
Starring: Rita Tushingham, Dora Bryan, Murray Melvin, Robert Stephens, Paul Danquah, David Bolivar.

A Special Day (Una Giornata Particolare). Cinema 5/Columbia, 1977. Director: Ettore Scola; writers: Ruggero Maccari, Scola, and Maurizio Costanzo; producer: Carlo Ponti.
Starring: Sophia Loren, Marcello Mastroianni, John Vernon, Françoise Baird, Nicole Magny, Patrizia Basso.

Hollywood has found it nearly impossible not to tamper with the often friendly relationship between a gay man and a straight woman. The temptation to "save" the homosexual by initiating him into heterosexuality, thus effecting a quick character evolution, has been too great. So we turn to a pair of foreign films portraying this special friendship. Neither compromises the man's sexuality, and neither has a "happy" ending. Separated by sixteen years, the first film deals with a young stereotype, the second with a mature man.

The play *A Taste of Honey* opened in London in 1958, the same year as *Suddenly, Last Summer*. It was written by Shelagh Delaney, a working-class eighteen-year-old whose youth and material made her and the play overnight sensations. *A Taste of Honey* raised the tricky double issues of miscegenation and

When Helen abandons Jo for her latest beau, Jo meets Geoff (Murray Melvin), who works in a shoestore.

homosexuality. Jo, a working-class girl with a boozing, man-hungry mother, Helen, becomes pregnant by a "colored" navy nurse—unnamed, he is

29

Murray Melvin as the optimistic gay youth who befriends a pessimistic and pregnant Jo.

When Helen learns Jo is pregnant by a black sailor and living with a gay man, she moves back and shoos Geoff out!

referred to as "the boy." Jo is cranky and lonely until she meets sensitive Geoff. In keeping with the times, he is homo but not sexual—only Jo has a sexual history, only her past is explored. Against a diverse backdrop of carnivals and Lancashire tenements, the childlike young adults cavort and make plans, until grown-up reality intervenes. The prodigal Helen returns and chases Geoff onto the streets. When she finds out her daughter's child will be half-black, she leaves. Helen may or may not return; Geoff's return is implied.

The play, directed by Joan Littlewood, explored the interracial romance in its first act; Geoff (played by the unforgettable Murray Melvin) didn't appear until the second act. Because of its interracial theme and visible gay character, *A Taste of Honey* took longer to reach the screen than *Suddenly, Last Summer*. Hollywood expressed interest, but only if Jo were played by Audrey Hepburn (who chose *The Children's Hour* instead) and the nonwhite baby were born dead. Hollywood's unofficial code decreed that if the infant died, all would be squared—the suffering mother would be redeemed for her interracial affair.

Fortunately, the play was filmed by Tony Richardson, one of British cinema's brightest lights (in 1965 he directed the cult classic, *The Loved One*). Murray Melvin repeated his stage role, and Rita Tushingham made her movie debut as Jo. Dora Bryan was Helen, and Robert Stephens played Peter, Helen's latest beau. Paul Danquah's role as Jimmy, the sailor who loves Jo and leaves her, was abridged since the racial angle was downplayed to focus on Jo and Geoff.

One of the first gay antiheroes, Geoff is an outcast condemned for being different, rejected even by hard-up landladies. Moody Jo needles him about his failure with women; she's curious about what "people like you" *do*. When he makes romantic overtures—prompted by curiosity and his feelings for the unborn baby—Jo brutally shuts him off. Though he pays the rent, Geoff is not part of Jo's life, as she sometimes reminds him. He offers to marry her, for the sake of the child, but Jo is wary of marriage, motherhood, and mothers. She openly detests Helen and speaks of killing the baby at birth.

Nonetheless, the two friends share warmth, relative stability, and Jo's anxieties. Like Dustin Hoffman in *Tootsie*, Geoff is a better support for Jo's needs because of his feminine sensibilities. Jo won't find a nicer companion or a better father for her child, but when Helen throws Geoff out, it's for keeps. Helen's racist tirade is whitewashed, and she intends to stay with her daughter for the foreseeable future. Outside, Geoff is momentarily distracted by children playing before he moves on. Indoors, Jo is forlorn; Helen and motherhood are closing in. Her taste of honey is over.

ABOUT *A TASTE OF HONEY*

A. H. Weiler, the *New York Times*: Since Jo is a resilient sort, she gives understanding and sanctuary to an effeminate youth from whom, for the first time, she receives tender care and tacit affection. One has the feeling Miss Delaney chose abnormal characters to accent society's indifference to its disenfranchised. They are neither angry nor lachrymose and are, on occasion, a happy lot ready to laugh at themselves. Though involved in sordid circumstances, they tug at the heart without breaking it. Murray Melvin handles this difficult assignment in muted but effective fashion. Like Miss Tushingham, he is flesh and blood and not a caricature.

Pauline Kael, the *New Yorker*: A fairy tale set in modern industrial ugliness. Little, sad, shy, dignified Geoff is a combination Peter Pan, homemaking Wendy, and fairy godmother. Jo is stubborn, independent, whimsical, moved only by what interests her. The background music—children's songs—further aligns Jo and Geoff with the world of children. Their pleasures are innocent and carefree; by contrast, the grown-ups are horrible, sexual in a nasty, grotesque way.

The sad-eyed queen is the new hero . . . a new unfortunate [audiences] can clasp to their socialworker hearts: the pure-in-heart, nonthreatening male a girl can feel safe with. . . . They can feel tolerant and contemptuous at the same time: the man a girl can feel safe with is a joke; he's not a man at all.

In a 1977 *Blueboy* interview with this writer, Marcello Mastroianni discussed his role in *A Special Day*: "Sophia [Loren], who is very intelligent, reads the script and tells me I must accept. She tells me the role will change my image. I tell her, 'You want me to play a homosexual so I won't have to kiss you in the love scene.' She laughs and says every man has a homosexual side, and this is my chance to explore mine." It also brought Mastroianni's first nomination for an Oscar. Like Peter Finch in *Sunday, Bloody Sunday*, he didn't win but was consoled by Hollywood's regard for his performance and his nerve.

Unlike Geoff, Mastroianni's character, Gabriele, simply happens to be gay. Homosexuality isn't the

Marcello Mastroianni as a gay victim of Fascism and Sophia Loren as a downtrodden housewife in *A Special Day* (1977).

central fact of his life, and it only sets him apart after the fascist government so dictates. In Mussolini's words, "A man is not a man if he is not husband, father, soldier." In 1938 Italy known homosexuals weren't allowed to stay on the mainland, so thousands of men were interned on Sardinia. Gabriele is an ex-radio announcer, fired after his homosexuality is discovered. Like a cousin of his, from whom he hasn't heard since, Gabriele is to be shipped away and forgotten.

The film begins with the harried morning routine of Antonietta Tiberi (Loren). The Tiberi household also includes an unfaithful husband (John Vernon) and six demanding offspring, all living in a small apartment in a mammoth housing development. That morning all but Antonietta attend a giant rally honoring Hitler, who is visiting Rome to proclaim the Axis.

Alone in her kitchen, Antonietta savors the solitude briefly before commencing her daily chores. Rosamunda, the family mynah bird (who mispronounces Antonietta's name), escapes and flies to Gabriele's window across the way. Inside, Gabriele is addressing envelopes with his "pretty handwriting," the only work he's been able to get. Feeling despair over his imminent exile, he suddenly shoves the envelopes off his desk and contemplates using the gun inside the drawer.

At that moment Antonietta arrives to fetch Rosamunda. Lonely and curious, she initiates conversation. The two enjoy each other's company, and

Gabriele laughs at the ironic contrast between his recent death wish and Antonietta's desire for a seventh child that will earn the Tiberis a cash prize for large families. Gabriele reveals less about himself than Antonietta does. He conceals his job loss, but unlike Geoff, he doesn't feign heterosexuality to "impress" or conform.

Later in the day, Gabriele feels the need for companionship and visits Antonietta. They laugh and drink coffee. Gabriele rides a child's scooter from one room to another, and Antonietta lets down some of her defenses. Their special day is interrupted by a busybody neighbor who warns Antonietta about Gabriele; even worse than his love life is his anti-party attitude, she says. Unquestioningly profascist, Antonietta keeps a scrapbook on Mussolini. The new friends quarrel but call a truce. Gabriele follows her up to the roof, where she collects her laundry and, amid the windblown sheets, kisses him. When he does not respond, Antonietta (who hasn't understood the busybody's insinuations) asks for an explanation. She is furious at Gabriele's "deception" and returns to her flat.

Later, Antonietta comes to Gabriele's door to apologize. She likes him "just the way you are." They talk about his predicament, and Antonietta confesses that she's watched him every morning from her kitchen window. Her embrace turns into a gentle seduction that Gabriele doesn't resist, and they make love. Afterward, Antonietta tells him sex was never so good with her husband, who treats her crudely and disrespectfully. Like *Coming Home*'s Jane Fonda, who receives more loving pleasure from paraplegic Jon Voight than from her macho husband (Bruce Dern), Antonietta learns that a real man isn't a stereotype. She neither regrets nor is made to suffer for the infidelity.

Gabriele also doesn't regret the affair. He performed the motions but derived less pleasure than Antonietta, who, after all, is heterosexual. "Being the way I am," he explains, "it's not as if I can't make love to a woman. It's different . . . and it was beautiful. But I am still the same." Though he's had heterosexual affairs, Gabriele is basically homosexual. This surprises but doesn't faze Antonietta, who has made a true, if temporary, friend. When the jubilant masses return from the rally, the friends are forced apart. They go their separate ways, sharing a memory for the future.

Like many star-studded gay films, *A Special Day* was chiefly reviewed as a star vehicle. The *New York Times*'s Vincent Canby, for one, was mesmerized by Loren but dismissed Gabriele as "a suicidal homo-

sexual." He felt the affair would somehow "profoundly alter their view of life and themselves." Canby apparently missed Gabriele's postcoital declaration. *Any* one-day friendship is bound to have less impact on a man headed for a concentration camp. At film's and day's end, Gabriele leaves the apartment carrying a suitcase and his favorite painting. He is escorted by two government agents. Antonietta is watching, but Gabriele's thoughts are preoccupied with the future.

In both *A Taste of Honey* and *A Special Day* the men help the women primarily by relating to them as equals, helping them move closer to their potential. Jo might find that motherhood enhances her existence, but semiliterate Antonietta is determined to better herself. She begins to read her first book, *The Three Musketeers*, given to her by Gabriele, and she resists her husband's nighttime advances. In *A Taste of Honey* the male is the would-be sexual aggressor; in the other, the woman. The newer characters, though middle-aged, are more sexual. Also bolder.

Out of mutual curiosity, the "odd couple" have sex, then decide to be simply friends until he is deported.

The exasperated Gabriele defiantly yells from the rooftop, "I am queer!" using the vocabulary of the time.

Each film's biggest miscalculation is its failure to address the larger gay community. Geoff appears to be the only young gay in northern England; the only other gays he mentions are much older "johns." The possibility of Geoff pairing with another man isn't even raised. And since he's never "tried" women, he isn't positive he absolutely prefers men. Gay sexuality and a gay community are indirectly acknowledged in *A Special Day*. But Gabriele's past (friends and lovers) and future (internment) are little more than a minor backdrop. Unlike the housewife's world, the internment camp is unexplored—still a mystery.

ABOUT *A SPECIAL DAY*

Oggi: The mega-stars' best acting in years. . . . Gabriele's deportation is like bad fiction, until we re-

Usually cast as a Don Juan, Mastroianni (here in the 1960 *Where the Hot Wind Blows*) earned an Oscar nomination for his gay turn.

member some of the overheard forbidden stories our parents told. . . . More sad and shocking than the pair's deliberately provocative *The Priest's Wife*.

Pauline Kael, the *New Yorker*: This movie is perfectly calibrated for its teeny bit of courage: the big stars playing uncharacteristic roles. . . . Their humiliation draws them together for a few hours, and we see that society has wronged them, cruelly. . . . This strenuous exercise in sensitivity was directed in a style that might be called genteel shamelessness—the *Brief Encounter* turf so well tended by Noël Coward when he was being "real." There's one miscalculation: when Mastroianni is in bed with Loren, he lies there politely as she puts his hand on her magnificent melon breast. How can you have any feeling for a man who doesn't enjoy being in bed with Sophia Loren? You lose any interest in the radio announcer; he just fades away.

Murray Lyndon, *Lambda Times*: Two stories in recent months about gay men involved with women. *A Different Story* paired a gay and a lesbian. . . . In *A Special Day* a gay man befriends a married woman, and the sex grows from their desperation and the woman's released passion. The man doesn't become hetero, and the union symbolizes a brief marriage between two groups that until recently seldom found strength in unity, even under the oppression of a petty paterfamilias or a paternal political dictatorship.

The Loudest Whisper was the British title of *The Children's Hour* (1961): Karen Balkin tells grandmother Fay Bainter that her schoolteachers are lesbian.

4

SCHOOL DAYS:

The Children's Hour and *Thérèse and Isabelle*

The Children's Hour. United Artists, 1961. Director-producer: William Wyler; writer: John Michael Hayes. Starring: Audrey Hepburn, Shirley MacLaine, James Garner, Miriam Hopkins, Fay Bainter, Karen Balkin, Veronica Cartwright.

Thérèse and Isabelle. Audubon, 1968. Director-producer: Radley Metzger; writer: Jesse Vogel.
Starring: Essy Persson, Anna Gael, Barbara Laage, Anne Vernon.

In 1936 William Wyler directed a movie of Lillian Hellman's famous first play, *The Children's Hour.* The film was called *These Three,* for the same reason that Mae West's *Diamond Lil* came to the screen three years earlier as *She Done Him Wrong:* The public was less liable to be offended if the contents were *handled* and the title changed. *These Three* was about rumored adultery, involving Miriam Hopkins, Joel McCrea, and Merle Oberon, instead of suspected lesbianism as in the play. Bonita Granville (*Hitler's Children*) played the child-villain, and Hellman adapted her play (based on a true Scottish case—with a *happy* ending—detailed in the 1983 book, *Scotch Verdict*).

In 1961 Wyler paid $300,000 for rights to do a more faithful remake. With the huge hit *Ben-Hur* to his credit, he was allowed a freer hand by the Mirisch brothers, who released their often socially relevant films through United Artists. Wyler ini-

tially considered Katharine Hepburn and Doris Day as the schoolmistresses, but went with Audrey Hepburn (whom he had made a star with *Roman Holiday* in 1953) and Shirley MacLaine. Both actresses had been recently nominated for Oscars. For the male lead he called on James Garner of television's "Maverick." Miriam Hopkins was cast as MacLaine's Aunt Martha, who calls the women's relationship "unnatural," and whose failure to testify at their slander trial causes the women to lose their suit and their reputations, leading to Martha's hanging suicide.

Karen Balkin played the vengeful student and Fay Bainter her foolish grandmother who spreads the rumor after hearing it from the girl, a chronic liar. Pauline Kael wrote, "I developed a perverse sympathy for the old lady villainess—I thought the schoolteachers treated her abominably." Later, Martha (MacLaine) reveals to Karen (Hepburn) that the girl chose the one lie with a kernel of truth. Though there was never physical contact beyond the approved hugging and touching, Martha—because she's loved Karen over the years and wants her for herself—feels "dirty and ashamed."

Kael commented, "We're supposed to feel sorry for these girls because they're so hardworking and, after all, they don't do anything—the lesbianism is all in the mind (I always thought this was why lesbians needed sympathy—there isn't much they *can* do)." She concluded, "I'm not sure *The Children's Hour* would work even if you camped it up and played it for laughs; I don't know what else you could do with it."

The ads asked, "What made these women differ-

Shirley MacLaine as Martha, the schoolteacher who turns out to be a repressed lesbian.

ent? Did nature play an ugly trick and endow them with emotions contrary to those of normal young women? Or was it a child's vicious lie that caused them to live as objects of shame?" Today the cop-out suicide is indefensible; at least Karen calls off her engagement to Joe (Garner), mourns her friend, and refuses the townspeople's "sympathy." But the ease with which Karen and Martha's private girls' school and teaching careers are destroyed is less dated. In the late seventies, State Senator John Briggs initiated California's notorious Proposition 6, which, had it passed, would have barred gay or progay teachers from teaching. It was defeated by a narrow three-to-two margin.

Despite its obvious flaws, *The Children's Hour* (*The Loudest Whisper* in Britain) was the first major Hollywood movie about lesbianism, and the first with a major, visible gay character. It was also the first in which a star played a homosexual lead (though Barbara Stanwyck had a smaller part in 1961's *Walk on the Wild Side*). MacLaine told the press she'd researched her role by questioning psychiatrists. But by decade's end, she publically averred that everybody is inherently bisexual.

A year after the Wyler film, liberal Sidney Lumet's *A View From the Bridge* (by Arthur Miller) again illustrated the power of rumor. A heterosexual in love with his wife's niece jealously accuses the girl's boyfriend of being gay. To prove it, he kisses the youth on the lips, claiming that it's what the boy

Three into two won't go: Audrey Hepburn, James Garner, and Shirley MacLaine.

James Garner as Hepburn's fiancé, whose ardor cools when she is rumored to be lesbian.

wanted all along. In both films damaging accusations of homosexuality tend to stick, regardless of the accuser's reputation or motives.

The Children's Hour was not a critical or commercial success, but its female star-power rescued it from failure or anonymity. Wyler had promised, "It's going to be a clean picture with a highly moral story." Thus the "moral" ending. "The reason I chose Audrey is she's so clean and wholesome. I don't want bosoms in this." The stars made surprising and courageous career choices, though the word *lesbian* is never spoken. Both MacLaine (who specialized in playing hookers) and Hepburn (the elegant gamin) were mothers. It's interesting to speculate whether an unmarried or nonmaternal actress would have accepted either role.

For a time, Wyler considered changing the title to *Infamous*, "so people won't think it's a Walt Disney." Television insured that no one would be misled by always noting that *The Children's Hour* "is recommended for adult audiences"—guaranteeing that countless children would view it out of forbidden curiosity. Unfortunately, the powerfully propagandistic ending is still making its 1961 impression on today's televiewing girls and boys.

ABOUT *THE CHILDREN'S HOUR*

Picture Life (U.K.): *The Loudest Whisper* [U.K. title] redefines Hollywood's sexual boundaries. The

Karen comforts the guilt-ridden Martha.

These Three (1936): The first film of *The Children's Hour* changed the title *and* the lesbianism—into a triangle comprising Miriam Hopkins, Merle Oberon, and Joel McCrea.

"adult theme" is belied by the American title and the obligatory suicide. . . . The question is, does Martha's death help matters any? If all the Marthas did the same, would society come any closer to understanding, and possibly accepting, such impulses? Frankly, the spinster has long been with us, and while not perceived as the same social threat as the insistent bachelor, she isn't likely to go away just because of a whisper or an evolving production code.

Screen (Japan, 1979): Audrey Hepburn began to mature her pristine image in *The Children's Hour*. Though Hepburn is not the lesbian—Shirley MacLaine, who kills herself, is—she is posthumously devoted to her friend, and her engagement ends because of her own fears and the man's suspicions. . . . Shirley was one of the first Americans to play a lesbian normally and sympathetically. The plot is small, but the personalities and the conflicts with the wicked girl-child and local bigots keep the [black and white] picture rolling. . . . If there is a moral it is: where there's smoke there's fire. But true or false, no rumor should earn power to destroy a life or career.

Anne Revere and Katherine Emery in the 1934 Broadway production of Lillian Hellman's play.

Thérèse and Isabelle (1968): Schoolgirls Essy Persson and Anna Gael.

The German-made *Thérèse and Isabelle (Thérèse und Isabell)* was a "bird-watcher's" delight, distributed by Audubon and adapted by Jesse *Vogel* ("bird," in German). The then-shocking film derived from Violette Leduc's autobiographical novel, *Le bâtarde*. She noted, "I wrote with one hand, and with the other . . . I loved myself to love them [Thérèse and Isabelle]."

Director-producer Radley Metzger had hit paydirt a year or so earlier with his soft-core *I, a Woman*, starring Essy Persson. He then cast the brunette Scandinavian actress in this story of an unhappy adolescent who finds sex and companionship with a fair-haired classmate. Alas, the morning after the consummation, Thérèse's stern (and presumably psychic) mother withdraws her from the all-girl boarding school—echoes of *The Children's Hour*!

Years later, Thérèse returns to the empty school one summer accompanied by her fiancé (unlike Martha, she "outgrew" it). Memories come floating back, and the film shuttles through time. Voices and figures return to haunt Thérèse (and titillate the straight-male audience). The erotic scenes with their breathy offscreen whispers recall the grand tradition of Danish porn films.

Thérèse and Isabelle purports to deal with loneliness and self-discovery, but it trades in female nudity and lesbian love scenes performed by eventually heterosexual characters. It has little in common with *Maedchen in Uniform* or even *The Children's Hour*, despite their girls'-school settings. The films differ in tone and intent, even considering the different decades in which they were made. Of the three, *Maedchen in Uniform* was the most realistic, even though the most political—or possibly *because* it was the most political.

The Children's Hour casts a supposedly hip though jaundiced eye at lesbianism, while *Thérèse and Isabelle*'s focus is squarely on the bottom line. The majority of post-*Maedchen* lesbian films (nearly all directed by men) employ incidental plots as excuses to show women—gay or straight—as sex objects and fantasy (or nightmare) figures. *Maedchen*'s lesbian protagonists—individualistic women and catalysts of change—continue to be relevant though seldom emulated models for subsequent generations of filmmakers.

ABOUT *THÉRÈSE AND ISABELLE*

John Simon, the *New Leader*: The *Thérèse and Isabelle* soundtrack groans with the sex prose of the authoress (Violette Leduc), a cross between Jean Genet and Faith Baldwin. . . . Two naked females languidly loll about, reflected in a distorting vase or hidden by some interposed object. There are suggestions of cunnilingus, *soixante-neuf*, and the longest masturbation scene on film—[with] dutifully dreadful cunnilingus and masturbation music. The

Schoolmates . . .

whole thing tries desperately for art and pornography and flops as both. Essy Persson (Thérèse) has an ugly face, squat body, unsightly bosom, bad legs, and stubby fingers. . . . Anna Gael has a lovely face; but for her supposed age, overripe body. . . . The official brochure invokes comparison with *Maedchen in Uniform*, but in its vulgarity the film is more of a "Maedchen in Cunniform," and in its antiquity a "Maedchen in Cuneiform."

Renata Adler, the *New York Times*: A film about those failures of love on the part of adults that seem to create severe sexual problems in the young. . . . The affair is meant to convey loss of innocence. But both women are rather swaybacked and out of condition. . . . Long, frequent love scenes in the lavatory, open air, school chapel, and so on. It all has the not-quite-right air of people one finds late at night hanging about railroad stations and subway cars. The movie is, however, quite well photographed.

. . . and lovers: School daze!

5

WHITEMAIL:

Victim(s)

Victim (1961): The ad depicts a more anguished
Dirk Bogarde than ever appears in the film!

Victim. Rank/Allied Film Makers, 1961. Director: Basil
Dearden; writers: Janet Green and John McCormick;
producer: Michael Relph.
Starring: Dirk Bogarde, Sylvia Syms, Dennis Price, Peter
Copley, Anthony Nicholls, Norman Bird, Peter McEnery.

In 1961's Britain few could foresee that the propos-
als made in the Wolfenden Report of 1957 would
eventually become law. Male homosexuality was
illegal, but not lesbianism, thanks to Queen Victoria's lack of imagination. An estimated 90 percent of
blackmail victims were gay men. Director Basil
Dearden and producer Michael Relph wanted to
dramatize this problem and hired screenwriter
Janet Green, writer of *Sapphire*, a successful 1959
thriller about racism. The first actor approached
for the lead in *Victim* turned it down out of fear that
it would cost him an anticipated knighthood. Dearden encountered more bigotry than he'd expected:
"The distributor's solicitors found nothing libelous
in the script—just said they wanted to wash their
hands after reading it. . . . A cost accountant said he
felt like a gargle after he'd read it."

Dearden assured prospective leads that the script
didn't refer to its protagonist as a *poof, nancy, faggot*
or *homo*. (The more dignified term was *invert*.) The
watershed role of Melville Farr was eventually accepted by Dearden's friend Dirk Bogarde, who
called himself "the Loretta Young of England"
because he played young comedic roles well into
middle age. In his memoirs Bogarde called *Victim*

"the wisest decision I ever made in my cinematic
life." In one fell swoop "the fanatics who had been
sending me four thousand letters a week stopped
overnight," and Bogarde became a sought-after
dramatic actor in Britain and on the Continent.

Farr is a "respectably" married barrister with a
platonic gay friend named Barrett (Peter McEnery). The noble—because chaste—gay man is contrasted with less conformist gays like the working-
class Barrett and selfish upper-class "friends"
forever doomed to the closet. A blackmail ring
preying on homosexuals learns of the relationship
that existed between Barrett and Farr, who ended it
before sex could rear its tainted head. The ring
persuades Barrett to blackmail Farr, but when he's
arrested, Barrett repents and kills himself to save
Farr's career and marriage to Laura (Sylvia Syms).

Farr feels partly responsible and vows to avenge
Barrett's death. His quandary is that if he exposes
the blackmailers in court, he also exposes himself.
He seeks the advice of other gays. His self-pitying
barber tells him Barrett is "well out of it," *it* being
nature's "dirty trick." Professional friends advise
Farr to keep the silence, but he finally chooses the

Blackmailer: Peter McEnery.

Blackmailed: Married gay man (note wife's photo on the desk) Bogarde.

Bogarde confronts an unjust society in which blackmail was routinely used against closeted gay men.

lonely high road. By bringing the blackmailers to justice, Farr loses his wife, career, and friends, straight and gay.

Melville Farr was the first gay film character to be more hero than victim. By exposing the law as a virtual license to blackmail and engendering sympathy for its victims, *Victim* helped change attitudes in Britain, although it wasn't a hit. It did not fare well in the provinces, where "queer"—scrawled on Farr's garage door—still meant "ill" or "poorly." Many reviews didn't make the subject matter clear. London's venerable *Observer* titled its review "Ten-Letter-Word," coyly referring to *homosexual*, a term new to the silver screen. Much of the other media ignored *Victim* altogether. The film, which cost £154,000 and by 1971 had made a profit of £52,000, was soon forgotten in the ensuing wave of "permissive" British pictures.

In America, where it arrived in 1962—the same year as *A Taste of Honey*—*Victim* was viewed with alarm. *Time* labeled the imports "an epidemic." *Victim*, unlike *A Taste of Honey*, wasn't granted a Production Code Seal of Approval. *A Taste of Honey*'s gay character was a boy-buffoon, but *Victim*'s was a "normal queer," which made establishmentarians bristle with indignation. *Victim* had little impact on Hollywood; it was considered an only-in-England phenomenon. Pauline Kael explained, "English actors generally look so queer anyway that it's hard to be surprised at what we've always taken for granted."

The Production Code was instituted in 1930,

after talkies threatened to make "sin" vocal as well as visual. In 1934 it was toughened (partly because of Mae West's "monstrous lubricity") by Will H. Hays, former chair of the Republican National Commit-

41

Openly gay Sir Dirk Bogarde has played gay in *Victim, Death in Venice,* and other films.

homosexuality-in-disguise. *Darling,* directed by John Schlesinger in 1965 and starring Oscar-winner Julie Christie, features obvious gays on Capri. Bogarde played the straight role turned down by Gregory Peck.

In 1959 Bogarde starred in *Song Without End,* a conventional Liszt biography taken on by George Cukor (without credit) when director Charles Vidor died after a month of shooting. Capucine costarred. When Bogarde consulted her about playing Melville Farr, she said, "I don't see the problem. My God! You English—you think that nothing happens to you below your necks." Ten years later Bogarde and Cukor collaborated again on *Justine.* The cast included Michael York (*Something for Everyone, Cabaret*), Robert Forster (*Reflections in a Golden Eye*), Cliff Gorman (*The Boys in the Band*), John Vernon (*A Special Day*), and Anouk Aimée (*La Dolce Vita*).

Bogarde also worked with gay director Luchino Visconti on two of his best-known films, *The Damned* (1969) and *Death in Venice* (1970).

ABOUT *VICTIM*

Time: [*Victim's*] attack on extortion seems a coyly sensational exploitation of homosexuality as a theme—and, more offensively, implicit approval of homosexuality as a practice. The deviates in the film are fine fellows—well-dressed, sensitive, kind. . . . Nowhere does the film suggest that homosexuality is a serious (but often curable) neurosis that attacks the biological basis of life itself.

Pauline Kael, the *New Yorker*: I long for one of those old-fashioned movie stereotypes—the vicious, bitchy old queen who said mean, funny things—now that homosexuals are going to be treated seriously, like Jews and Negroes. . . . *Remembrance of Things Past* may soon be frowned upon like *Huckleberry Finn* and *The Merchant of Venice*.

There is a self-conscious, unconvincing attempt to distinguish between the "love" the barrister feels for his wife and the physical desire—presumably some lower order of emotion—that he felt for a boy who is more interesting in every way than the wife. . . . The irony is that Dirk Bogarde looks so pained from repressing his homosexuality that the film gives a black eye to heterosexual life.

Ivan Butler, *Cine-Britain* (1973): In its day this was considered the last word in adult filmmaking—perversion (or inversion) considered seriously rather than as an excuse for music-hall laughs. . . . It is demonstrated how the legal position of the time encouraged blackmail. . . . Though the times

tee and a member of Harding's cabinet. In 1956 the ban on drugs, prostitution, and "miscegenation" was lifted, and movies were finally free to explore those themes again. But the lifting of the gay ban in 1961 was the result of the success of *Suddenly, Last Summer* and big-budget movies like *The Children's Hour, Advise and Consent,* and *Walk on the Wild Side,* which had gay themes or subplots and were already completed. The Code revision was after-the-fact and economically motivated.

The Production Code Administration withheld its commercially requisite seal from *Victim* because it vocalized "homosexual" and "homosexuality" and treated its subject "clinically." Thus, *Victim* couldn't even be "suggested for mature audiences," the new PCA category for "questionable" films. Further Code revisions were made in 1966, forced by films like *The Pawnbroker* and *Who's Afraid of Virginia Woolf?* By then, *Victim* would finally have earned a seal from the group which held that "the basic dignity and value of human life shall be respected and upheld."

Bogarde's post-*Victim* films were often controversial and/or gay-themed. In Joseph Losey's *The Servant* (1963) he was a butler who takes control of his master's (James Fox) life. Both men are straight, but because of his blond good looks and indolence, the Fox character was called "effete" and "queerish." When the servant maneuvers his girlfriend (Sarah Miles) into his employer's bed, critics espied and fashions may have passed it by, in its day this was a brave venture, devoid of sensationalism.

• In 1919's *Anders als die Anderen*, Paul Korner (gay actor Conrad Veidt), a virtuoso violinist, falls in love with a male student. But Korner strays and seduces Bollek (Rheinhold Schünzel), a party-boy who is also a blackmailer. (Germany's infamous Paragraph 175.2 banned homosexuality.) The distraught Korner tries to change his nature, first with a hypnotist, then with a sex specialist. Like Farr, Korner bravely denounces Bollek to a tribunal. The blackmailer is convicted, but so is Korner, for homosexual acts. They receive identical prison terms, but Bollek leers triumphantly at Korner. . . . Fadeout. (*Anders*'s producer, Magnus Hirschfeld, was the gay founder of the science of sexology.)

• In *Pandora's Box* (1929) lesbian Countess Geschwitz (Alice Roberts) falls in love with high-class prostitute Lulu (Louise Brooks), who is having an affair with her newspaper editor-lover's son, Alwa (Franz Lederer). When the straight couple gambles away its fortune, Geschwitz raises funds for Lulu by allowing herself to be compromised by another of Lulu's male friends who she (Geschwitz) ends up strangling. (Lulu later returns to her old trade and is murdered by Jack the Ripper.)

• Otto Preminger's *Advise and Consent* (1961) includes the movies' first gay-bar scene, which so repels "ex"-homosexual Senator Brigham Anderson (Don Murray) that he ultimately cuts his own throat. Political enemies have tried to blackmail Anderson, using information from Anderson's Army buddy and ex-lover Ray (John Granger), now a prostitute. Ray blackmailed Anderson because "I was drunk. I needed money. You wouldn't see me." Henry Fonda costarred, and Charles Laughton played against type as a moralizing southern senator, Seabright Cooley. The ailing Laughton threw himself into his last role, patterning his accent after archconservative Senator John Stennis. Laughton avoided creating an evil caricature; his charm and even warmth made the homophobe's behavior and final outbursts more appalling.

It was hailed as Laughton's best performance, and the closeted but progay actor said it was his most strongly felt role. "The picture is also about blackmail," he stated. "Or rather, *white*mail, since it is perpetuated by white males against certain men, usually in white-collar positions." In her introduction to a posthumous Laughton biography, Elsa Lanchester revealed her husband's homosexuality, and in 1983 she wrote *Elsa Lanchester, Herself*. *Playgirl*'s reviewer inappropriately described how the actress "had to live with Laughton's neurotic homosexuality."

Victim of McCarthyism: In *My Son John* (1952), Helen Hayes suspects son Robert Walker of being red *and* lavender!

Victim of government homophobia: Michael McKean as secretly gay civil servant Mr. Green in *Clue* (1985).

Victim of the Depression: Robert Joy informs thirties spinster Dianne Wiest why he won't keep dating her in *Radio Days* (1987).

Victim of wealth: Evan Richards as the spoiled and aimless gay son in *Down and Out in Beverly Hills* (1986).

Victim of rape: In *Exodus* (1960), Sal Mineo confesses that the Nazis "used me like a woman!"

Preminger was the only major producer able to successfully release films without the Production Code's Seal of Approval. He defied the Code with movies like 1953's *The Moon is Blue* (use of the word *virgin*), 1954's *Carmen Jones* (a black cast for general audiences), 1955's *The Man With the Golden Arm* (depicting drug addiction), and 1957's *Bonjour, Tristesse* (unmarried lovers). *Advise and Consent* screenwriter Wendell Mayes said, "Look at the record—you'll discover that many of the changes in the Code were a result of Otto breaking the rules."

• Franklin Schaffner's *The Best Man* (1964) was based on a play by Gore Vidal about two contenders for the Democratic presidential nomination. Henry Fonda is Henry Russell, an Adlai Stevenson–type liberal with a mental crisis in his past. Cliff Robertson's Joe Cantwell is more conservative, although he had a homosexual experience in the Army. Each man learns the other's secret. The married Cantwell wants to make his information public; Russell doesn't. Eventually, Russell throws the nomination to an Eisenhowerian middle-of-the-roader.

The liberal Fonda had starred in the play, *The Caine Mutiny Court-Martial*, which was directed by Charles Laughton. In her autobiography Elsa Lanchester recalled, "During one rehearsal, Henry Fonda behaved miserably and insulted Charles in front of the whole company. From the stage, Fonda looked at Charles and said, 'What do you know about men, you fat, ugly homosexual.' It crushed Charles."

• Blake Edwards's 1974 Cold War love story, *The Tamarind Seed* (with Julie Andrews and Omar Sharif), has Fergus Stephenson (Dan O'Herlihy) married to Sylvia Syms (aka Mrs. Farr in *Victim*). Stephenson is a top British government official and a double-agent code-named Blue. The film hints that he became a spy after being blackmailed for his homosexuality. The man is pro-Communist but hates himself for being gay. His wife, Margaret, has two pastimes: affairs with "real" men and spewing contempt for her lavender-red husband.

• Spain's *El Deputado* (*The Deputy*) (1980) was directed by Eloy de la Iglesia and also has echoes of *Victim*. Robert Orbea (Jorge Sacristan) is a "happily married" influential member of the newly legal Socialist Party. He decides to run for office but has two strikes against him: He's a political idealist and he favors working-class youths. He falls in love with a hustler employed by members of the far-right, who want to regain the power it lost after Franco. Unlike Farr, Orbea isn't "destroyed" when his sexual orientation is revealed. He loses the election and may lose his job, but *El Deputado*'s gay community and genuinely liberal heterosexuals don't forsake him.

Victim of rape II: Ned Beatty (left) gets raped in *Deliverance* (1972), starring Jon Voight and Burt Reynolds.

45

6

UNIFORM:

Reflections in a Golden Eye and The Sergeant

Reflections in a Golden Eye. Warner Bros.-Seven Arts, 1967. Director: John Huston; writers: Chapman Mortimer and Gladys Hill; producer: Ray Stark.
Starring: Elizabeth Taylor, Marlon Brando, Brian Keith, Julie Harris, Zorro David, Robert Forster, Irvin Dugan.

The Sergeant. Warner Bros.-Seven Arts, 1968. Director: John Flynn; writer: Dennis Murphy; producer: Richard Goldstone.
Starring: Rod Steiger, John Phillip Law, Ludmila Mikael, Frank Latimer, Elliott Sullivan, Ronald Rubin, Memphis Slim.

Marlon Brando as the repressed gay Major Weldon Penderton in *Reflections in a Golden Eye* (1967).

"There is a fort in the South where a few years ago a murder was committed. The participants of this tragedy were: two officers, a soldier, two women, a Filipino and a horse." In 1941 Carson McCullers wrote a novella whose title refers to the all-seeing golden eye of a peacock painted by Anacleto (played by hairdresser Zorro David). The lesbian author (who married a gay man) wrote of the peacock's "immense golden eye . . . in it the reflection of something tiny and grotesque." The original prints of John Huston's film were processed in muted golden stock with a faded sepia tone. But after the public didn't flock to see Liz and Marlon, less expensive normally colored prints were circulated.

The strongest characters in *Reflections in a Golden Eye* are its apparent misfits, Anacleto and Alison

Langdon (Julie Harris). Like McCullers, Alison is frail and dies young. After her malformed baby's death, she tries to cut off her nipples with garden shears and becomes terminally depressed. But like Anacleto's peacock eye, Alison's aware of Leonora Penderton's (Elizabeth Taylor) relationship with her own husband (Brian Keith), and of the private's (Robert Forster) voyeuristic visits to Leonora's bedroom. The "something grotesque" doesn't necessarily refer to Major Weldon Penderton's (Marlon Brando) repressed sexuality, for when Private Williams glimpses the nude Leonora through her living-room window, her image is reflected in *his* burnished golden eye.

When Alison tries to reveal the truth, she is banished to a mental institution. She is followed by Anacleto, whom she had shielded from the disapproval of her spouse. Langdon believes that only the Army can "make a man" of Anacleto, who shares the cultural interests that separate Alison from her carnal husband. After her death, Morris twice wishes that Anacleto would return, even though it was "awful to see a grown man dancing on his toes" or "watercolor-painting funny pictures."

The focus is on the film's leads. Taylor's Leonora is an Army brat who—as in *Who's Afraid of Virginia Woolf?*—holds up the macho image of her father to her introspective husband. Horses are Leonora's love. When Major Penderton beats her favorite horse, for throwing him, she horsewhips him in front of her party guests. Leonora apologizes, saying that the whipping has cleared the air. Since the major seems to agree, it's possible he enjoys it on some psychosexual level.

Brando modeled Penderton's accent on his friend Tennessee Williams. The gay character was widely blasted and misrepresented by critics—Pauline Kael labeled the far-from-obese Penderton as "the fat, ugly major." Neither is Penderton a fetishist, although he keeps postcards of classical Greek nudes in a cigar box. He also saves a candy wrapper dropped by his favored private. But in the absence of a satisfactory sex life, looking at these mementos helps fill the empty hours. A captive of the regimentation in which he works and lives, Penderton forbids himself even a temporary partner of his choice.

The major's treasure collection also includes an antique silver spoon stolen from the home of Captain Murray Weincheck (Irvin Dugan), "the oldest captain in the Army." A friend of Alison's, the middle-aged bachelor plays the violin, reads Proust, and gives tea parties. Weincheck hasn't risen in rank because, in Penderton's words, he "lacks certain qualities of leadership." Eventually he quits the service—as Penderton had hoped.

Private Williams is introverted but *not* mentally retarded. After doing some garden chores for the major (but not to his *exact* specifications), he returns to the stables. Williams has a way with horses and secretly rides bareback after work. His naked body kindles Penderton's passion; he dabs on his wife's cold cream in order to look younger. But the primping major isn't remotely amusing, for he and the film take themselves very seriously.

Weldon often looks into mirrors and is by turns pleased—crisply saluting himself—and disappointed by what he sees. After becoming infatuated with the private, he uncharacteristically defends the departed Anacleto (and himself) to Langdon: "Is it better, because it is morally honorable, for the

Penderton suppresses his contempt for the exuberance and carnality of wife Leonora (Elizabeth Taylor).

square peg to keep scraping around the round hole, rather than to discover and use the unorthodox square that would fit it?"

Predictably, both Weldon and his love object are doomed. One night Williams returns to the Penderton house. The deluded major thinks he has a gentleman caller. But the private goes upstairs and crouches by the sleeping Leonora's bed. The major goes to his wife's room, discovers the adoring Williams (who is made to seem harmless and normal, compared to his would-be lover) and shoots him dead.

Reflections was to have starred Elizabeth Taylor and Montgomery Clift. But despite *Suddenly, Last Summer*, Clift's career was still stagnant. In 1962 he played *Freud* in John Huston's incomplete screen biography. His next and last picture was *The Defector*

The major's unrequited passion is for Pvt. Elgee Williams (Robert Forster), here with Leonora's horse, Firebird.

in 1966. It costarred Roddy McDowall, whom Monty credited with getting him through the shooting schedule. But Clift's best friend was Taylor, of whose myriad illnesses and operations he once said, "Bessie Mae is the only person I know who has more wrong with her than I have."

The number one star in the world at the time, Taylor had hoped to costar with Clift in *The Owl and the Pussycat*, then suggested they costar with her new husband Richard Burton in *The Macomber Affair*. After reading *Reflections*, Liz decided Burton should costar with her and Monty, as Morris Langdon, and direct the picture. But Burton wasn't interested in a supporting role (nor in the possibility of playing gay opposite his wife).

When producer Ray Stark told Taylor that Clift was uninsurable, she offered to pay his insurance herself. She also insisted Huston accept the casting of Clift. The men hadn't gotten along during *Freud*, for once Huston learned—to his utter amazement—that Clift was gay, he began to treat him like a pariah. In a syndicated 1983 interview Huston declared, "There's only one experience in life I'm aware of having rejected: homosexuality."

Bob LaGuardia's biography, *Monty*, describes Huston's reaction to Clift's sexuality: "John said to me [associate Wolfgang Reinhardt], 'Did you know this about Monty?' 'Yes, of course I knew,' I said. 'I think it's disgusting! Why didn't you tell me?' he asked. But why should I have told John? It wasn't his business. After all, Monty behaved like a normal

Climax: When the private sneaks into Leonora's, not Weldon's, bedroom, the major shoots him!

Brando as Mark Antony in *Julius Caesar* (1953): An actor for all seasons, and an icon for the fifties.

Last Tango in Paris (1972): In the early seventies, Marlon Brando came out as bisexual, in France.

man. If he had been swishy, obviously he wouldn't have been able to portray Freud. And Freud himself said that he detected homosexuality in himself and most men. So it was very out of place of John to have overreacted—especially on *this* film. I really think John would have fired Monty on the spot if Universal's backing hadn't depended so much on John's casting a major star like Monty, and who else could John have found at that late date?"

The book explains that Huston laid down the law to Clift, ordering him, during filming, "not to behave in a homosexual manner or have any kind of homosexual relationships," or drink, pop pills, or have "dependent friendships with older women." Clift agreed to the demands, but when his director practically refused to speak to him, he became defiant. The fact that Huston was editing homosexual references from the script further alienated the gay actor.

Pending Clift's participation, *Reflections* was continually postponed. Meanwhile, Monty's only other

Elizabeth Taylor took the bisexual plunge in *Secret Ceremony* (1968), sharing Mia Farrow's tub.

In *Zee & Co. (X, Y, & Zee* in the U.S., 1972),
Taylor ends up in bed with Susannah York, her
husband's mistress.

offers were Italian westerns. Sergio Leone, who
made a star of Clint Eastwood, wanted to sign Clift
for a quick, cheap production that would capitalize
on his past glory. Finally, Monty passed his physical
for *Reflections*, but he was still uninsurable and
considered unfit to complete the expensive production. Not until he signed to do *The Defector* was a
start-date for *Reflections in a Golden Eye* announced.
Shortly after completing the German-made *Defector*, Monty died of a heart attack, on July 22, 1966.

ABOUT *REFLECTIONS IN A GOLDEN EYE*

John Simon: In Carson McCullers's world, aberra-
tion is the norm and perversion is worn as a badge.
Her quaint style—schoolgirl baroque laced with
inversions—creates an atmosphere redolent with
morbid fascination. . . . A feebleminded sexpot (Liz
Taylor) is married to a sadomasochistic crypto-
homosexual afflicted also with impotence and fe-
tishism (Marlon Brando). He is obsessed by a mentally retarded soldier, another fetishist, who rides
about in the nude and suffers from advanced voyeurism and possible zooerastia (Robert Forster); she
is the mistress of her husband's fellow officer, a
crude ox (Brian Keith). The latter is married to a

refined psychopath (Julie Harris) who dotes on as
she is doted upon by a semi-demented, wholly
effete Filipino houseboy—a screaming queen
(Zorro David). Brando makes the husband not just
sick but disgusting, the perversions daubed on as
thickly as the accent. Julie Harris, for once, is
restrained, but having to lavish her affection on the
monstrous houseboy alienates her almost completely from us.

Andrew Sarris, the *Village Voice*: The covertly homosexual officer created by Mrs. McCullers has not
only been upgraded from Captain to Major, he is
boldly transformed into a course in cruising along
Third Avenue. . . . Brando is woefully miscast.
More crackers than cracker, he never suggests military discipline as part of his sublimated past. . . . It
may be that many, if not most, heterosexuals sup-
press their latent homosexuality, but it does not
follow that role-playing is necessarily ridiculous or
dishonest.

The two married couples form a crisscross of
sensitivity and stupidity. The sensitive-stupid
Pendertons, complemented by the stupid-sensitive
Langdons. The Langdon ménage is further embel-
lished by a Filipino fairy houseboy christened Anacleto. . . . Jolting them out of their dull routine is
Private Elgee Williams. . . . Anacleto is too broad
and Pvt. Williams too dim; the private remains a
boring mystery and the actor a hollow shell sharing
empty space with such mythic personalities as
Brando and Taylor.

If *Reflections in a Golden Eye* was muddled, *The
Sergeant* was worse, one of the least popular gay-
themed movies among gays, or anyone else. Over
two hours long, it's grimmer (in black-and-white
yet) than its Warners predecessor. Steiger's performance seems strangulated, and one critic felt he was
probably too ashamed to deliver a convincing portrayal—thus his twitchy embarrassment on screen.
Alternately bullying and flattering, sweating pro-
fusely, always tense, Master Sergeant Albert Callan
and his past are a blank. What is his personal
history? Has he ever pursued another soldier, or
anybody at all? What is it about Private First Class
Tom Swanson (John Phillip Law) in particular that
attracts him?

More self-loathing than the major in *Reflections in
a Golden Eye*, this sergeant displays no tenderness
toward his prey. He never looks at Swanson with
feeling. One critic remarked that Steiger looked at
Sidney Poitier in *In the Heat of the Night* with more
affection. When the prissy dipsomaniacal sergeant

The R-rated *The Sergeant* was advertised with the line "Just one weakness. Just one." The ad depicted Steiger with an anguished expression better suited to his "brother" Marlon Brando in *On the Waterfront*'s famous "contender" scene. Another prominent ad featured the film's unknown "leading lady" (Mikael) with Law sprawled atop her.

Progressive ironies: In the early seventies Brando informed the press, "Like many men, I too have had homosexual experiences, and I am not ashamed." In the early eighties Steiger appeared in Norman Lear's pro-liberty TV special, "I Love America," playing a homosexual citizen proudly advocating gay rights.

ABOUT *THE SERGEANT*

Rex Reed, *Women's Wear Daily*: Rod Steiger is so good as *The Sergeant* that he evokes sympathy. I was almost tempted to go along with the film's insistence that this kind of man might shoot himself through the head. But the G.I. (John Phillip Law) is too dense to be believable, and Dennis Murphy's screenplay (based on his novel) is so naive, so badly written, I was forced to remind myself that yes, Virginia, movies have changed since the days of the Hays Office, though the makers of *The Sergeant*

The Sergeant (1968): Rod Steiger as the monumentally repressed Master Sergeant Albert Callan.

finally does kiss Swanson, it is with a harshness bordering on malice. Even more unusual is the fact that, unlike German and French girls'-school movies, this Army-based picture never acknowledges that homophilia is endemic to such all-male institutions.

Callan is depicted as the sole aberrant individual on the entire base. The barracks denizens are boyishly innocent, and when Swanson is kissed, he's shocked to realize there actually are men-loving men in the world. Prior to the kiss, Swanson is shown courting and cavorting with his girlfriend Solange (Ludmila Mikael). Amidst so much "normalcy," the sergeant comes across like the Creature from the Lavender Lagoon.

Though a leader of men, the sergeant is lonely among men for whom he cannot express his love.

51

weren't watching while they grew up. Homosexuals can get away with it now. They don't commit suicide anymore, especially with Freudian symbols like guns. *The Sergeant* is about as courageous and interesting as sex in a granny gown.

Pauline Kael: There is something ludicrous and at the same time poignant about many stories involving homosexuals. . . . Crazier than Don Juan, homosexuals pursue an ideal man, but once they have made a sexual conquest the partner is a homosexual like them, and they go on their self-defeating way, endlessly walking and looking, dreaming the impossible dream. . . . Steiger chases after Law so long that when he grabs and kisses him it's the climax of the picture. Law slugs him and Steiger shoots himself and that's it. If Steiger had grabbed Law and been rebuffed an hour and a half earlier, he could have said, "All right, so I made a mistake," and maybe the picture could have gone on and been *about* something.

The hero's unrequited passion for Pfc. Tom Swanson (John Phillip Law) eventually yields to a kiss, then suicide.

7

COPING:

The Killing of Sister George and *The Fox*

The Killing of Sister George. ABC Films/Cinerama, 1968.
Director-producer: Robert Aldrich; writer: Lukas Heller.
Starring: Beryl Reid, Susannah York, Coral Browne,
Ronald Fraser, Patricia Medina, Hugh Paddick, Cyril
Delevanti.

The Fox. Warner Bros./Claridge, 1968. Director:
Mark Rydell; writers: Lewis John Carlino and Howard
Koch; producer: Raymond Stross.
Starring: Sandy Dennis, Keir Dullea, Anne Heywood.

In 1968 *The Killing of Sister George* became America's
first X-rated film with a legitimate cast. That year
also saw the release of Doris Day's three final movies. Ironically, the role of June Buckridge in the film
of Frank Marcus's hit play was offered to Day (who
also turned down Mrs. Robinson in *The Graduate*).
Bette Davis, another candidate, told Beryl Reid (the
stage June) that *she*—Reid—must play the part.

The role of Alice McNaught was offered to Julie
Christie, among others, but director Robert Aldrich
(*What Ever Happened to Baby Jane?*) settled for a cast
of unknowns (at least to Americans). The picture
revolves around the relationship between June/
"George" and Alice/"Childie." Alice (Susannah
York), thirty-two, has an adolescent daughter
"somewhere," but most critics overlooked the character's history and motivations to dwell on York's
bared bosom.

Beryl Reid's large-as-life portrayal of June was

Beryl Reid as June Buckridge as soap opera star Sister George.

June and her lover Alice (Susannah York) share a tempestuous, possessive relationship.

53

widely panned, while York, as the more conventional femme partner, was pitied or admired for her daring (she almost didn't go through with the breast-kissing scene). Coral Browne's Mrs. Mercy Croft—a discreet but manipulative BBC executive—is June's nemesis and serves to reinforce the pernicious older-dyke image. Similarly, Alice plays with dolls, wears a tutu-nightie, and eats George's cigar butt as a penance. George drinks excessively and hollers a lot. Like Charlie and Harry in *Staircase* (see chapter thirteen), George and Childie's mateship is an endurance test.

But for the most part the women are real. Both simply seek "love and affection." June resembles many jealous, domineering spouses—but with a strong dash of humor added. Alice is cowering, disloyal, and semiparasitic. Like many performers, June masks her homosexuality for professional reasons with an antiseptic character—the jolly country nurse on a hit television show. Alice, a "superior shopgirl," is much more closeted than June; she snaps at June, "Not all girls are raving bloody lesbians, you know!" (The word wasn't mentioned in the play.) June grandly ripostes, "That is a misfortune of which I'm well aware."

Mercy Croft seduces Alice after she condescendingly informs June of Sister George's impending "accidental" death and removal from the series. Mercy's vulnerability peeks through in the sex scene, and it's to the film's credit that Alice ends up with another woman, rather than with a man.

The Killing of Sister George underestimates motherhood. By polarizing the gay and straight worlds, both films imply that a woman can't be a loving mother and a loving lesbian at the same time. Asked about the unifying theme of his movies, Aldrich said, "It's the concept of a man struggling to redeem his self-esteem. That is thematically recurrent in all the pictures, whether it's *The Legend of Lylah Clare* or *The Killing of Sister George*."

Certain critics who complained that the film wasn't funny enough also felt the pathos was forced. They could sympathize with a straight man—Emil Jannings, crowing like a rooster in *The Blue Angel*, for one—who degrades himself over lost love, but not with a gay woman doing the same. After June loses her job and lover to Auntie Beeb (the BBC), she's offered the voiceover for Clarabelle Cow on a kiddie show. Lonely and insulted, she returns to the studio and vandalizes some of the equipment while "mooing" piteously. However, June is a survivor. Reid explained, "I thought of the word *indefatigable*, and I knew I could be a good Clarabelle and I'd find a hell of another girlfriend, too."

Sister George broke another barrier by shooting inside a real lesbian bar—Gateways, off King's Road. Unfortunately, that bar is peopled with the butchest, least sympathetic stereotypes imaginable. They make June—whose voice at one point is (inexplicably) dubbed by a man—seem matronly, despite her legs-apart posture. But in the final analysis the movie belongs to Beryl Reid. Whether she is dressed in tweeds or Oliver Hardy drag, Reid's performance is an unforgettable tour de force. Aldrich was certain she would receive an Oscar nomination, but she didn't. A comedic star in Britain, Reid has remained largely unknown in the U.S. and has had few offers of lead roles.

Advertised as "the shocking drama of a love triangle involving three women," *The Killing of Sister George* was pretty strong stuff in 1968, and the *Los Angeles Times* refused to run the original ad for it. Aldrich sued the paper for its "alteration of the drawing of a female figure and the deletion of a reference to deviate sexual conduct," which abridged the constitutional right-to-know. The petition was dismissed and affirmed on appeal, even though the *Times* had a "substantial monopoly, accounting for 80 percent of all morning daily circulation." The case set a precedent, allowing newspapers across the country to adapt film ads to their own tastes and "moral" standards.

Sister George was also certified "X" in Britain, and the British Board of Film Censors removed four minutes from "a lesbian love scene." But the Greater London Council only asked for a forty-second cut, and in the nearby county of Berkshire the film was exhibited without cuts. However, instead of boosting the movie as one might expect, the controversy on both sides of the Atlantic simply reflected public indignation or apathy, and *Sister George* was a flop. In 1978 Aldrich stated, "*The Killing of Sister George*, made in 1975 instead of 1968, would have been successful. It may break even in another five years. It will have taken fifteen years." By 1983, the year Aldrich died, it did break even, thanks partly to videocassette sales.

In addition to macho movies like *The Longest Yard*, *The Dirty Dozen*, and the antigay *The Choirboys* (from which author Joseph Wambaugh had his name legally removed), Aldrich directed 1968's *The Legend of Lylah Clare*. One critic called this film a combination of *Sunset Boulevard* and *What Ever Happened to Baby Jane?* In it Kim Novak starred as the replacement for a dead lesbian star whose personality she assumes. Bisexual actress Coral Browne played a bitchy columnist, and Rossella Falk (*Modesty Blaise*) portrayed a European lesbian on the

Alice and June dress up as Laurel and Hardy for a party.

Bette Davis was offered *Sister George*—instead, she went to England to play a one-eyed mother in *The Anniversary* (1968).

Mercy Croft (Coral Browne) comes between June and Alice, eventually steals Alice away.

prowl. The campy *Lylah* was an even costlier flop than *Sister George*.

Now, as then, *The Killing of Sister George* isn't warmly regarded by most gay women. Critic-film-maker Caroline Sheldon recalled, "I remember being depressed for days after seeing it, feeling: Sure, such a relationship may exist, but what a miserable one, and what's it doing on film to pervert young minds about lesbianism?" Female friends

55

had varying reactions, she said, "But the general impression was unease, despite the desire to have a film that was lesbian."

ABOUT *THE KILLING OF SISTER GEORGE*

Andrew Sarris, the *Village Voice*: *The Killing of Sister George* contains the most erotic sequence ever seen in an otherwise artistically respectable, responsible production. The baring of Susannah York's breast is less a demystification of lesbian tactics than a celebration of all sexual mysteries. Aldrich is merciful enough to interrupt the seduction at that point when shame engulfs curiosity. . . . It is silly to complain that the sex scene is gratuitous; the best things in movies often are. Also, air pollution is a more serious "problem" than lesbianism, but there have been few movies about it. . . . I'm afraid you can't create tragedy out of abnormal psychology. Somewhere, there should have been an intimation of virtue, of temptation overcome.

Harold Clurman, the *Nation*: The love affair is uninteresting because we don't give a hoot for any of the ladies in it: their "psychology" becomes falsely pathetic, a pretense of sympathy through frankness. The play's superficiality was one of its assets; the seriousness of the picture spoils the comedy.

Renata Adler, the *New York Times*: The only nice things in *The Killing of Sister George* are a few Anglo-Saxon epithets ending in "off" and meaning "go away" and a London nightclub where real-life young ladies with short hair and field hockey player walks give the only acceptable performances. . . . Susannah York seems, devoutly and understandably, to be wishing herself in some heterosexual part. . . . The simultaneously serious and mocking treatment of homosexuals inevitably turns

vicious and silly—as homosexuality itself inevitably has a degree of satire in it.

A scene involving Miss York's left breast sets a special low; Coral Browne approaches it like an ichthyologist finding something that has drifted up on the beach. The scene (Aldrich's attempt to gather refugees from *Thérèse and Isabelle*) is the longest, most unerotic, cash-conscious scene between a person and a breast ever.

Rex Reed: Beryl Reid's colossal performance as the dethroned BBC soap opera queen who in private life happens to be a lesbian is not only the best acting I've seen this year, but *The Killing of Sister George* is the best picture in quite sometime. It is also the *only* film I've ever seen that deals with homosexuality not as a problem or stigma but as part of the natural order—with humor, dignity, sincerity, and candor. . . . The story's power lies in its universality. Exchange any character with a member of the opposite sex and its truth is equally pungent. . . . One masturbation scene is likely to make a few old ladies uncomfortable, but the loss of a few Doris Day fans is a small price to pay for the liberation of the cinema from the archaic shackles that have restricted it from showing the passions of reality.

The Fox, from a 1923 novella by D. H. Lawrence, is about two women who cope—with more emotional and professional proficiency than their *Sister George* counterparts. They live and work together in a self-contained environment that is broken when a man proposes marriage to one of them. As in *The Killing of Sister George*, the lesbian relationship is torn asunder when the younger of the pair finds a new, domineering partner.

Although *The Fox* was released only seven years after *The Children's Hour*, the two had little in common—apart from the fact that, once again, the real lesbian dies gruesomely (though this time not by her own hand). *The Fox*'s stereotypes are much stronger, the relationship less matter of fact. Sandy Dennis is Jill—blond, frilly-feminine, and cloyingly dependent. British Anne Heywood (wife of producer Raymond Stross) is Ellen, the dark-haired self-reliant type, sporting boots and flannels. Jill is rich, Ellen isn't.

The setting is changed from Lawrence's English village to the Canadian wilderness where the women run a chicken farm. All's cozy until the symbolic fox raids the chicken coop. Paul (Keir Dullea), who'd worked on the farm before, returns to aid the distressed women. He shoots the furry predator, but he is himself a romantic predator. He

Sandy Dennis as Jill in the anti-lesbian drama, *The Fox* (1968).

comes between the women by unexpectedly proposing to Ellen, not Jill.

Paul and Ellen's vitality contrasts with housebound Jill, who tightens the emotional screws on Ellen. The new pair move in together nearby, but the proposal has aroused both women's suppressed lesbianism. Reticent Ellen belts out a bawdy song, "Roll Me Over," and masturbates in front of a mirror—this is meant to be symbolic of homosexuality, for in films self-pleasure is often equated with "perversion." John Simon felt the masturbation was "inconsistent with [Ellen's] generous character."

Needless to say, the screen characters are more explicit than Lawrence's. In the book the bisexual undercurrents stay below the surface. The movie also conveniently eliminates Jill's parents. Because Jill interferes with Paul and Ellen's bliss, Paul kills her by chopping down a tree that lands between her legs. In the book Jill's parents witness this scene. The book's male protagonist is a twenty-year-old hunter. In the film he's a farmer—thus, more domestic—and is no younger than the "spinsters."

The press kit from Claridge Pictures (a short-lived Warner Brothers subsidiary that released movies too adult for the studio's image) stressed the film's "phallic symbology": the shotgun, axe, carving knife, tree, and pitchfork. Directed by newcomer Mark Rydell, a former actor, The Fox made of Paul a sexual savior. But Paul's choice of the more independent, aggressive Ellen may betoken his own dormant homosexuality—by conquering the stronger woman, he can prove himself a total man. In the book he feels repressed by village life and wants to escape to Canada; Rydell's Paul wants to take Ellen to Vermont. Some critics resented the tampering with Lawrence, others the updating of the characters, still others the commercial sexualization.

Most critics praised Anne Heywood's performance as the bisexual Ellen. Years later, Rydell revealed, "When we started rehearsing, it became clear that Anne Heywood was not a very gifted actress. . . . I pulled away most of her dialogue and lit her in shadow—made her a mystery. . . . Photographed and edited properly, she could seem to give a very competent performance."

The Fox, like The Children's Hour, can be viewed as a contest between homo- and heterosexuality. But there is a difference. Martha's love is no passing fancy. Jill's love is neurotically manipulative, and Ellen's kiss seems merely impulsive. She doesn't grieve for Jill as Karen does for Martha. The film intimates that Ellen and Paul may not achieve permanence; in the book he's dismayed that she's still aggressive after marriage and wishes he'd left the women "to kill one another." After Jill's death, Paul insists Ellen will be happy with him. "Will I?" she asks. The movie ends on her uncertain expression.

Made for $1 million, The Fox was a hit with critics and the public and earned some $25 million. With The Killing of Sister George and Thérèse and Isabelle—all in 1968—The Fox went a long way toward sexualizing lesbian films, of which there had been few after The Children's Hour (which earned five Oscar nominations, including one for Fay Bainter as Best Supporting Actress—but won none of them). It was reasoned that generous doses of nudity would make sapphic films more attractive at the box office. But in pandering to the lowest common denominator, such movies began to rely on stereotypes and to lose name performers like Hepburn and MacLaine, who shied away from the nudity or from being half of a butch-femme couple.

Like The Children's Hour, the title of The Fox created some confusion. Lucille Ball screened it for her two teenagers. "I thought it was a Disney nature picture," she explained. "A few minutes into the picture my mouth dropped open, and I yelled, 'Stop the projector! Turn up the lights!'" (Years later, People magazine asked Lucy about gay rights. She stated, "It's perfectly all right with me. Some of the most gifted people I've ever met or read about are homosexual. How can you knock it?" A supportive letter to the editor noted, however, that "People don't have to be gifted or talented to earn or merit human rights.")

Jill and her mate Ellen (Anne Heywood) grow apart after Paul (Keir Dullea) enters their home and lives.

57

In 1981 Rydell's *On Golden Pond* was censured for not one or two but three lesbian jokes—e.g., Henry Fonda, asked if there are bears in the woods, replies, "Oh, yes, one came by last week and ate an old lesbian." Criticism was leveled at director Mark Rydell, but blame should fall to Oscar-winning writer Ernest Thompson, who wrote the jokes.

Stockard Channing (*Grease*) was starring opposite Burt Reynolds in Thompson's play *Answers* at Burt's dinner theater in Jupiter, Florida. When she had to miss a performance due to illness, she was replaced at the eleventh hour by Reynolds's friend, gay comedian Charles Nelson Reilly.

The men played the scenes "straight" and hugged rather than kissed. Next day, Thompson told *Daily Variety*, "I'm throwing up." Audiences, though, loved the team of Reynolds and Reilly, and Reilly continued for several days as Channing's replacement. This prompted producer Allan Carr to send the men a telegram. "If you're really happy in your work in *Answers*, are you ready to consider the long-awaited musical version of *La Cage Aux Folles*?"

ABOUT *THE FOX*

Pauline Kael: My guess is that *The Fox—The Children's Hour* in a woodsy setting—will meet with less critical opposition than *Reflections in a Golden Eye* because it is so explicit that it is "healthy," whereas the stifled homosexuality of Brando's duty-bound Major is grotesque and painful. . . . Both movies are about homosexual drives and how they lead to murder; neither would have been made even a few years ago.

John Simon: Much is made of masturbation and lesbianism, little of Lawrence. . . . Anne Heywood's Ellen, sensitively modeled and broodingly suggestive, is the most Lawrentian element. . . . Pauline Kael has observed that Sandy Dennis has "made an acting style out of postnasal drip." When [Dennis] is not a walking catarrh she is a blithering imbecile. She has carried that repugnant Method device—taking one or two trial runs on every sentence one utters—to the level of a tic: her every line issues in triplicate, ready to be notarized. Superimpose on this a sick smile befitting a calf's head in a butcher shop, an embryonic laugh that emerges as an aural stillbirth, and an epic case of fidgets, and you have not so much a performance as a field trip for students of clinical psychiatry.

Hollywood has gone to work on the characters' names. Nellie becomes Ellen (more like a starlet); Henry turns into Paul (only sissies are called Henry); and Nellie's favorite hen is elevated from Patty into Edwina.

Despite the removal of scenes containing nudity and self-pleasure, the Arts & Entertainment TV channel in 1990 felt it necessary to issue a warning against the lesbian-themed film: "Not suitable for younger viewers."

Paul, the symbolic fox, claims the hesitant Ellen for his own.

8

HUNKS:

Teorema; Entertaining Mr. Sloane; and *Something for Everyone*

Teorema. Continental, 1968. Director-writer: Pier Paolo Pasolini; producers: Franco Rossellini and Manolo Bolognini.
Starring: Terence Stamp, Silvana Mangano, Massimo Girotti, Anne Wiazemsky, Laura Betti, Andres José Cruz Soublette.

Entertaining Mr. Sloane. Continental, 1970. Director: Douglas Hickox; writer: Clive Exton; producer: Douglas Kentish.
Starring: Beryl Reid, Harry Andrews, Peter McEnery, Alan Webb.

Something for Everyone. National General, 1970. Director: Harold Prince; writer: Hugh Wheeler; producer: John P. Flaxman.
Starring: Angela Lansbury, Michael York, Anthony Corlan, Heidelinde Weiss, Eva-Maria Meineke, John Gill, Jane Carr, Despo.

These three films deal with the hunk as irresistible force—a stranger who charms and seduces his way into a family. The focus is on a pansexual angel for Pasolini and on a pair of devil-rogues for Joe Orton and Hal Prince. These fantasy-farces, usually created by gay writers, were anathema to general audiences and easily threatened critics, and are unlikely to be copied in the foreseeable future.

Teorema (*Theorem*) has the most surrealistic plot.

Angel of lust: Terence Stamp as the stranger who seduces an entire household in Pasolini's *Teorema* (1968).

Terence Stamp, the handsome Visitor, pops out of nowhere and into the household of a wealthy Milanese industrialist. Everyone falls in love with him, and he seduces all but the father. The looney-tunes daughter (Anne Wiazemsky) shows the Visitor her photo album, opens her blouse, and . . . *va bene!* The son (Andres José Cruz Soublette) peeks under the sleeping Visitor's blanket and coos at the perfect body. Stamp wakes and . . . *va bene!* The wife (Silvana Mangano) tosses her panties over the balcony, lies on the floor, and . . . *va bene!*

Suffering from an unnamed ailment, the husband (Massimo Girotti) has a brief spiritual love experience with the Visitor. Even the maid (Laura Betti) gets a turn. She's mowing the lawn and pauses to stare at the Visitor. Her lust overcomes her; she runs into the kitchen and tries to kill herself (never imagining that she, a mere servant, will also get lucky). But *he* saves her, takes her to bed, and . . . *va bene!*

All of this is moderately plausible so far. However, when the Visitor suddenly leaves, the family falls apart: The daughter goes into a coma, the wife becomes a streetwalker, the son leaves home to paint, and the husband becomes a flasher and a men's-room *habitué*. As for the maid, she moves into a vacant lot and exists by eating weeds. Her hair goes white, and she cures sick children while levitating them over a garbage dump. A cosmic joke? A Pasolini riddle?

Teorema is an unsolvable mystery, as is the 1975 murder of Pasolini, one of Europe's leading artists—poet, novelist, screenwriter, political essayist, painter, and director of *Medea* (with Maria Callas), *Salo, The Decameron, The Arabian Nights,* and *The Gospel According to St. Matthew.* Barth David Schwartz, author of a 1985 Pasolini biography, says, "He was born in the year Mussolini came to power and died the year the Communist Party had a role in government for the first time since World War II. In those fifty-three years, everything of interest and importance happened in Italy. Incredibly, he could be a household name there and almost unknown here [the U.S.]."

Like the late actor Sal Mineo, Pasolini's fame peaked with his murder, attributed to a "rough homosexual lifestyle." Pasolini's battered corpse was found in a deserted field near Rome. The fingers had been crushed, the head cracked open, the scrotum kicked in, and the body run over by the victim's own car. There was immediate pressure to find a murderer and solve the controversial case. The same night, a hustler nicknamed Pino the Frog was arrested. Under duress, he confessed he'd used self-defense against Pasolini's "sexual advances." Despite evidence indicating there was more than one murderer, the hustler was sentenced to nine years' imprisonment, and the Italian Supreme Court declared that the seventeen-year-old had acted alone; case closed.

Pasolini's friends and associates raised an outcry largely ignored by the press. Dutch filmmaker Philo Bregstein made a 1981 documentary, *Whoever Says the Truth Shall Die?,* in which he suggests conspiracy and asks, "Was Pino a pawn for a vendetta by the neo-Fascist Party, or was it a 'hit' by a group of underworld thugs?" Pasolini alienated many factions. The Catholic church considered him a "blasphemer," and the Communist Party had expelled him for "moral and political unworthiness." Critics of his films and writings took him to court thirty-three times on charges that included obscenity and religious defamation. He was acquitted each time. His friend Laura Betti stated, "There was a license to get rid of Pasolini. . . . He made big waves. The establishment didn't want to deal with him anymore. . . ."

Terence Stamp as the angelic *Billy Budd* (1962), who tempts Robert Ryan as Claggart, from Herman Melville's homoerotic novella.

ABOUT *TEOREMA*

Rex Reed: Pier Paolo Pasolini has a crotch fetish. His movies are always shot from the crotch, into the crotch, around the crotch. Which proves that Mr. Pasolini is [commercially] a very smart man. . . . *Teorema* is one of the silliest movies ever made; crotches aren't enough. People are walking out anyway. I stayed out of morbid curiosity. . . . Do not send me letters explaining how Terence Stamp is really God or an angel or devil, or that Pasolini's film is symbolic allegory. I've heard it all already. . . . Although it's a terrible movie in every conceivable way, I found it fascinating in its total absurdity. I laughed all the way through it—which kept me awake.

Joe Orton's entertaining Mr. Sloane isn't necessarily bisexual, but he uses his sexual charms to tempt and manipulate Ed (Harry Andrews), the kinky, macho businessman-brother of Kath (Beryl Reid). Kath discovers Mr. Sloane (Peter McEnery, dyed blond) sunning himself on a tombstone. Kath lives with her dithering Daddah (Alan Webb) in a house on the cemetery grounds. She rents the guest room to Mr. Sloane, whom Daddah recognizes as the murderer of his ex-boss, a photographer who'd asked hitchhiker Sloane to pose nude. (Sloane later murders Daddah, too.)

Middle-aged Kath acts like a teenage coquette (a riveting performance by the courageous Ms. Reid). She quickly seduces Mr. Sloane and becomes "pregnant." Brother Ed, once caught "committing a felony in his room," has been estranged from his puritanical father for twenty years. Ed reappears at the house and is bowled over by Mr. Sloane, whom he hires as his chauffeur and dresses in leather from head to toe. There is no sexual contact between the men, and Sloane—to Ed's disgust—is seeing young women.

When the siblings learn that their lodger has killed their Daddah, they agree to convince the police that the old man fell down the stairs—*if* Sloane will stay on as sexual partner to both of them. The lodger has no choice, and with Daddah's corpse in the background, Ed marries Kath to Mr. Sloane. Kath then reciprocates by marrying Ed to Mr. Sloane. Both kiss the stunned "bride," though Ed doesn't do it on the mouth, as Kath does.

Entertaining Mr. Sloane, like *Teorema*, employs its gayness as a lure, a tease, and (for hetero audiences) a dare. Both films include homosexual brothers. Gay sex occurs in *Teorema*, contrasting with *Entertaining Mr. Sloane*, which has no spiritual pretensions but is semi-Victorian in its coyness about homosexuality.

At thirty-four, playwright Joe Orton was murdered by his roommate-lover, who then killed himself. Orton's plays, reviled but always successful, caused a sensation in London and turned the staid theater upside-down. His first plays were produced through the influence of fellow gay playwright Terence Rattigan (*The Browning Version*), who admired the young man's rebelliousness. The stage version of *Entertaining Mr. Sloane* (1964) is better than the movie at spoofing English propriety, religiosity, closet queens, and familial relations. It remains Orton's most popular play and is often revived in the U.S. and in Britain. The movie received an even more limited American release than *Teorema*, though, like the other, it has since achieved cult film status.

ABOUT *ENTERTAINING MR. SLOANE*

Ins Kino (*In Cinema*, Germany): The late gay writer's black comedy ridicules English institutions. The

Turnabout: In *Victim*, Peter McEnery was the blackmailer; in *Entertaining Mr. Sloane* (1970), he is the blackmailed.

Marrying Mr. Sloane: Beryl Reid weds her brother, Harry Andrews, to leatherman Peter McEnery.

elder lady and her father are preposterous characters. Beryl Reid was last seen in *Star!* and starred in *The Killing of Sister George*. Here she's an altogether different character, in a see-through dress that reveals every matronly pound. . . . Her homosexual brother is a comment on society's forcing VIPs to hide their proclivities, and the handsome title character is an amoral symbol of England and modern society.

Advertised as a "contemporary fairy tale," *Something for Everyone* (titled *Black Flowers for the Bride* in Britain) marked the film directorial debut of Broadway's Hal Prince. The boldest of this trio of films, it too caused only a ripple at the box office. Based on Harry Kressing's novel *The Cook*, it was adapted by Hugh Wheeler (called "a flabby, floundering playwright" by John Simon). Wheeler, who wrote mystery novels under the pseudonyms Patrick Quentin and Q. Patrick, later won Tony Awards for *Candide* and *A Little Night Music*, and wrote the screenplays for George Cukor's *Travels With My Aunt*, Prince's *A Little Night Music*, and Herb Ross's *Nijinsky*.

The film's contemporary setting is a Bavarian never-never-land. Countess Herthe von Ornstein (Angela Lansbury), descended from Attila the Hun, has a castle, a title, and little money. She hires Conrad Ludwig (Michael York) as her butler (upgraded in the film from a cook). He murders his way up and then seduces the countess's handsome son Helmuth (Anthony Corlan). Conrad schemes to pump new money into titled blood by arranging for Helmuth to wed Annaliese (Heidelinde Weiss), the daughter of the kitschy nouveau-riche Pleschkes. Conrad then arranges a fatal accident for all three Pleschkes.

Finally, Conrad seduces the countess and prepares to become lord of the castle. But the countess's plump, bespectacled daughter Lotte (Jane Carr) blackmails him into marrying *her*, instead. Like Mr. Sloane, Conrad ends up with a partner not of his own choosing, thus paying for his crimes by pleasuring society's underdogs. That's part of the fun of these films: Sooner or later, the hunks play nondiscriminatory sexual providers in semiexotic locales. Pasolini once told *Der Spiegel*, "The young Greek god is everyone's secret goal and delight. But invariably he's either off-limits or a stinker."

ABOUT *SOMETHING FOR EVERYONE*

Rex Reed: Angela Lansbury is magnificent as a fading countess with a castle in need of repairs, and Michael York is all beautiful, silky, deadly charm and lean, hungry ambition as the young Machiavelli who seduces each member of her family to social-climb. There is a wonderful bit by Greek actress

Likes mother, likes son: Michael York seduces Angela Lansbury, her son, and sundry in *Something for Everyone* (1970).

Despo as Miss Lansbury's lesbian friend. . . . *Something for Everyone* is saturated with the howling humor of early Billy Wilder, bathed in the rich, intelligent décor of Ernst Lubitsch. . . . A monument to artistry and taste.

John Simon: Disguised homosexuality at its distorting worst. . . . For the first time in a major studio release male homosexuals kiss, however stagily and awkwardly. . . . Miss Lansbury looks like an aging female impersonator gone sloppy. God only knows where the notion that she has class originated. Her mugging and camping make her into that most degraded thing an *outré* actress can decline into: a fag hag.

Michael York is a supremely monotonous actor with the head of a blond rat. But he has good legs which, in mini-lederhosen, the camera keeps hugging. His sex with the young son (Anthony Corlan, a sullen dimensionless performer) is also lovingly dwelt on; heterosexual sex is shown as hasty and sordid. . . . The entire film exemplifies a kind of vengeance on the heterosexual world.

Family plot: Son (Anthony Corlan), seducing servant (York), mother (Lansbury), and daughter (Jane Carr).

Burt Reynolds is the center of attention in *Silent Movie* (1976), with Marty Feldman, Dom DeLuise, and Mel Brooks.

Knight in green leather: Timothy Dalton has played various bisexuals and gays, commencing with *The Lion in Winter* (1968).

Actor-director Paul Newman tried for years to launch a film of the bestselling gay love story, "The Front Runner."

63

9 _____

VILLAINS:

The Damned and *Cabaret*

Helmut Berger as Martin, the rich but ethically bankrupt protagonist of Visconti's *The Damned* (1969).

The Damned (*La Caduta Degli Dei*). Warner Bros., 1969. Director: Luchino Visconti; writers: Nicola Badalucco, Enrico Medioli and Visconti; producers: Alfredo Levy and Bauer Haggiag.
Starring: Dirk Bogarde, Ingrid Thulin, Helmut Griem, Helmut Berger, Charlotte Rampling, Florinda Bolkan, Umberto Orsini.

Cabaret. Allied Artists, 1972. Director: Bob Fosse; writer: Jay Presson Allen; producer: Cy Feuer.
Starring: Liza Minnelli, Michael York, Joel Grey, Helmut Griem, Marisa Berenson, Fritz Wepper.

After World War II, homophobes spread the myth that Nazism was somehow allied with homosexuality, that sexual "degeneracy" helped Nazism rise and flourish. Ernst Röhm and his SA (Storm Troopers) were held up as examples. And although Hitler was murderously antigay—as proved by the Night of the Long Knives, in which Röhm and the SA were butchered for political *and* "moral" purposes—it was hinted that even Hitler was *one of them*. Nazism in movies became frequently intertwined with homosexuality, especially in reviewers' minds. *The Damned* (*Götterdämmerung*) by gay director and closet aristocrat Luchino Visconti, is far less gay than most critics chose to believe. Only a few, including Rex Reed and Pauline Kael, noted that Martin (Helmut Berger) isn't gay at all. Martin is a sexual pervert, a prissy heterosexual who craves females, including his mother Sophie (Ingrid Thulin).

Martin is also not a transvestite. Confusion arose because he first appears—to spite his wealthy relatives—in Dietrich drag, his only drag in the film. (Critic John Simon mistakenly stated that Berger didn't do his own Dietrich vocals.) The detestable character's pouty, delicate mannerisms and squeaky monotone elicited automatic anti-gay responses from most critics. In the second half of the 150-minute epic, Martin hides in the family attic. Before his mother discovers him there, a servant is seen leaving the attic room. Several critics deduced that the departing man is a furtive lover. No such thing, as the openly bisexual Berger—who co-starred for a while in television's "Dynasty"—confirmed in Los Angeles in 1983. Likewise, Sophie von Essenbeck's "rape" is actually mutually desired by mother and son.

The film oozes with superficially attractive characters, from Dirk Bogarde and Charlotte Rampling to the SA youths, some of whom switch to black hose and garters after the beer-hall girls leave. Dramatically, the extended Long Knives scene—with men dancing or bedding down together—should have come at, or near, film's end. Placed in the middle, its bloody climax has less impact, followed as it is by the steely machinations of the von Essenbecks.

The garish, mesmerizing film, which begins and ends in an orange-hell blast furnace and plays green lights on its more reptilian characters, hasn't a single hero. The ad for it featured Berger dressed as Dietrich, with the legend "He was soon to become the second most powerful man in Nazi Germany." Small wonder that *The Damned* was an international hit. It's lurid, semifictional, and almost completely heterosexual, with female and male nudity. Like other Visconti films, it dissects a ravenous family organism while displaying handsome, sensualized males (recall *La Terra Trema* and *Rocco and His Brothers*).

Visconti originally planned a *Macbeth*-like story focusing on the female villain (Thulin) and her lover Friedrich (Bogarde). But the four-hour opus was edited down to 1933–34, when Hitler consolidated his power by winning over dynasties like the von Essenbecks (modeled on the Krupp Family) and eliminating all economic resistance. During editing, the emphasis shifted to "corrupted youth"—namely Martin, who is ideologically seduced by his cousin, the archvillain Aschenbach (Helmut Griem), a member of Himmler's SS (Elite Guard). (Visconti named the character after Thomas Mann's German protagonist in *Death in Venice*.)

The broadcasting of *The Damned* in the early seventies on American televison at 11:30 P.M. created a mini-furor. For a time, it looked as if its title would either be *The (bleeped)* or *The Darned*, and despite extensive cuts—including nearly all the Long Knives scene—some television critics felt the picture was "morally and sexually perverted."

"To work with Don Luchino was what every actor in Europe hoped for," said Visconti's discovery and protégé, Helmut Berger. In the early sixties Visconti starred Alain Delon in *Rocco and His Brothers* and *The Leopard*. For reasons unknown, they parted company. Berger made his debut in *The Damned*, and in 1972 Visconti starred him in *Ludwig*, a lengthy, colorful epic about the "mad" Bavarian monarch whose hobby was building baroque-fantasy castles. Pauline Kael opined, "Berger, who looks like a perverted mannequin during the first hour, is more fun when he loses his front teeth" to a passion for sweets.

Visconti suffered a stroke before completing *Ludwig*, but in 1975 he undertook *Conversation Piece*

Martin's mother, Sophie von Essenbeck (Ingrid Thulin), and her lover, Friederich (Dirk Bogarde).

Wealthy Friederich gives his support to the Nazi reign of terror, personified by Aschenbach (Helmut Griem).

(*Gruppo di Famiglia in un Interno*), directing from a wheelchair. It was, he said, his most autobiographical story; the Professor (Burt Lancaster) was based on Visconti. The role was first offered to Dirk Bogarde, who, in his autobiography, said he turned down the part because it was "too personal."

Konrad (Berger) is the professor's love interest in this more realistic version of *Death in Venice*. Here, the older man is invigorated, not destroyed, by the May-December relationship. But in spite of, or because of, its asexuality, *Conversation Piece* was a

Visconti admitted his crush on Nureyev.

critical and commercial hit in Europe. Critic Pauline Kael said, "One keeps waiting for the Professor to make a pass at Konrad. I was profoundly grateful that he didn't—the audience might split its sides if Burt Lancaster were to be shown coming out." Far removed from Hollywood rumor and reality, Kael never heard Lancaster tell Johnny Carson in the 1970s that he screened hetereoseuxal *and* homosexual educational films for his family.

The sexual credo of *Conversation Piece* is summed up in a poem by W.H. Auden and Chester Kallman, from *The Entertainment of the Senses*. A young woman recites it to the hesitant professor: "When you see a fair form, chase it/And if possible embrace it,/Be it a girl or boy./Don't be bashful: be brash, be fresh./ Life is short, so enjoy/Whatever contact your flesh/ May at the moment crave:/There's no sex life in the grave."

After *Death in Venice*, Visconti's greatest dream was to film Proust's *Remembrance of Things Past*, with Brando as the flamboyant Baron de Charlus. (In Volker Schlöndorff's 1984 *Swann in Love*, from a section of *Remembrance*, Charlus is enacted by Alain Delon.) The maestro's last film was *The Innocent* (1976), posthumously edited. After Visconti's death, John Simon—who served in the eighties as film critic for William F. Buckley's archconservative *National Review*—hurrahed, "I am glad to see the last of a director whom others may have considered as a major artist, but who, to me, was no more than a clever poseur exuding a certain type of homosexual sensibility—all gorgeous costuming, lush decor, melodramatic attitudinizing, and very little substance or depth." Simon went on to scatter ho-

mophobic terms and labels throughout his review, safe in the knowledge that—to date—there are no equivalent words for choice use against distasteful or embittered heterosexuals.

ABOUT *THE DAMNED*

Vincent Canby, the *New York Times*: Visconti's *The Damned* is a spectacle of such greedy passion, such uncompromising sensation, and such obscene shock that it makes you realize how small and safe most movies are. . . . Helmut Berger, a young Austrian actor, gives, I think, the performance of the year. . . . A movie of great perversity.

Richard Schickel, *Life*: One emerges from *The Damned* with the impression that the yeast causing the rise of the Third Reich was exotic depravity. . . . No one denies that the prewar German power elite was unhealthy. But to imply a cause-effect relationship between sexual and political perversion is historically inaccurate and socially irresponsible. It has an odd, insulating effect, making us feel that totalitarianism is a rare bloom that can flower only in very special soil. . . . Evil can happen here (or there or anywhere) at any time.

John Simon: In almost all his films, Visconti alludes to, suggests, toys with homosexuality. . . . Martin is conceived as a homosexual: we see Berger in drag, adoring and loathing his glamorous mother, spewing forth that ready, impudent wit that serves as the homosexual's offensive-defensive weapon. Yet Martin is suddenly revealed as a molester of girl children. . . . Later we see Martin's blowsy mistress, Olga. He now seems capable of a standard heterosexual relationship. Not for long; he does his dreadful thing to the landlady's small daughter, who proceeds to kill herself. Now you might think that Olga is a front, but he is still her lover at the end.

I submit that all this is nonsense. Martin detests his mother, yet feels dependent on, even chained to, her. This is a credible homosexual syndrome. What is not credible is Martin's seduction-rape of his mother. Sophie's makeup and costuming are such that this lovely woman emerges even sexually very nearly repellent. Particularly tendentious is an extreme close-up of just one of her breasts, the nipple roughly the size of the Matterhorn. It fills us with a Brobdingnagian horror, as Sophie becomes an anti-heterosexual nightmare. . . . The prize pratfall is the Night of the Long Knives, a long, flaccid revel with men in varying degrees of drag and disrobement lolling and loping around. The scene drags on and on.

Handsome Helmut Griem is the corrupting agent in both *The Damned* and *Cabaret*. In the latter he isn't a Nazi but a wealthy bisexual who seduces first Sally Bowles (Liza Minnelli), then Brian Roberts (Michael York). Based on gay Christopher Isherwood's autobiographical Berlin stories (*Mr. Norris Changes Trains* and *Goodbye to Berlin*), *Cabaret* is a popularized look at how various nationalities and individuals are affected by early-thirties Berlin. In the end everyone is alone, ashamed of relationships conducted in a city falling to wickedness. Again, Nazi villainy is partnered with the "villainy" of nonheterosexuality.

Although "divine decadence" doesn't extend to male bisexuality, the film abounds with sexual innuendo and disguise. Sally taunts Brian, "Maybe you just don't sleep with girls." He doesn't deny it when she suggests perhaps he sleeps with boys. Frau Schneider's rooming house has middle-aged lesbians dancing, while the Kit Kat Klub has men in drag as showgirls. When Baron Max arrives on the scene, he announces, "I think it's my duty to corrupt you [*both*]—agreed?" At Max's mansion, the trio dance together, and the two men become more than pals. They aren't shown in bed together (neither are Max and Sally), but when Brian shamefacedly rejects Max's gift of a gold cigarette lighter, it's clear what has passed between them.

During an argument over Max with Sally, Brian snaps, "Screw Max!" "I *do!*" she retorts, and he caps it with "*So do I.*" Somehow, Sally is shocked and calls both men "bastards." Sally becomes pregnant by Brian, but, without telling him, she has an abortion. She explains, "How soon would it be before you . . . ?" Brian's bisexuality is seen as a corruption of his heterosexuality, a recurring ailment. Brian doesn't remain long in Berlin, unlike Isherwood, who stayed several years and loved a young working-class German.

A subplot has Natalia (Marisa Berenson) and Fritz (Fritz Wepper) falling in love. She is Jewish, he isn't—or so it seems. But like many Jews (and gays) during the Nazi era, Fritz is "passing" for a member of the controlling, intolerant majority. Love forces his true identity, and the lovers marry and escape Germany.

In 1955 gay actor Laurence Harvey played the Isherwood character in the film version of the Broadway hit *I Am a Camera* (from which *Cabaret* was derived), with Julie Harris as an unlikely Sally

Oscar-winner Liza Minnelli as "divinely decadent" Sally Bowles does a musical takeoff on Dietrich in *Cabaret* (1972).

Bowles. Directed by Henry Cornelius, the film is less politically acute (and less sexually honest) than its 1972 successor. George Cukor had expressed interest in directing *I Am a Camera*. The film's most daring moment is Sally's invitation, "Shall we have a drink first, or shall we go right to bed?" "The balls were cut out of the script," said Cukor in the seventies. "It could have been a bang-up film. . . . Instead, it was soon forgotten." Cukor's last movie, *Rich and Famous* (1981), contains a Los Angeles party scene whose guests include Isherwood and his lifemate, painter Don Bachardy.

Cukor said of *Cabaret*, "I would have brought

Oscar-winner Joel Grey as the hetero but perverse emcee of Berlin's popular Kit Kat Club.

Ménage-à-trois, German-style: Michael York, Liza Minnelli, and Helmut Griem as a bisexual baron.

Julie Harris as Sally in the nonmusical precursor to *Cabaret,* the 1955 *I Am a Camera*—which had no bisexuality, even!

Michael York as "bisexual" Brian Roberts (based on gay author Christopher Isherwood) has an obligatory affair with Sally.

Brian out of the closet more. . . . But Nazi themes make me nervous. I've never done a gangster film, and Nazis are the ultimate gangsters and villains. It's hard to keep your fingers clean with them."

ABOUT *CABARET*

Silver Screen (Japan): *Cabaret* makes a star of Liza Minnelli. . . . Its music is evocative and tuneful, though it isn't a wholesome "Hollywood" musical. . . . It is also dominated by Joel Grey, with yellow teeth, red lips, and the malevolent victim's delight in being the only one inside a huge house on fire. Nazi or not, all the characters in Berlin are etched with ambivalence: the devilish emcee, Liza's superambitious American, Michael York as an Englishman who falls in love with the city and various inhabitants, and the seductive Baron (Helmut Griem), who misjudges the right-wing Nazis as "just hooligans" who will help rid Germany of left-wing radicals. . . . The movie's primary villains are unseen but not unfelt.

ABC Movie Express (U.K.): Bob Fosse's West German-made musical is restructured from the hit musical play. . . . The Briton becomes an American to accommodate Miss Minnelli's sizeable talent. The greatest loss is Lotte Lenya, who *is* Berlin. . . . Minnelli is overwhelming. York is a somewhat ineffectual leading man, overshadowed by tiny Joel Grey as the drag-Danteian guide to the rotting city's netherworld. . . . The film's bisexuality is bold but not belabored, and its German Jews are anything but caricatures.

PHOTO: JODY CARAVAGLIA

Michael York and Jeffrey De Munn played gay Holocaust victims in a Broadway production of Martin Sherman's powerful *Bent*.

69

10

AFTER FELLINI:

Fellini Satyricon

Martin Potter as Encolpius, the pleasure-loving antihero of Petronius's and Fellini's *Satyricon* (1969).

Fellini Satyricon. PEA/United Artists, 1969. Director: Federico Fellini; writers: Federico Fellini and Bernardino Zapponi; producer: Alberto Grimaldi.

Starring: Martin Potter, Hiram Keller, Max Born, Capucine, Alain Cuny, Fanfulla, Donyale Luna, Tanya Lopert, Lucia Bose.

The two-thousand-year-old *Satyricon* of Petronius Arbiter chronicles the picaresque adventures of two lusty Romans, the beautiful Encolpius and the priapic Ascyltus, and their lover Giton, an epicene Ganymede. Separately and together, they roam Nero's Italy, moving from one risqué episode to another. Federico Fellini's adaptation dispensed with the plot to make the screen a canvas for his own daydreams and nightmares, with Encolpius as the connecting thread. The director admitted that *Fellini Satyricon* (the official title, due to copyright exigencies) was 80 percent Fellini and 20 percent *Satyricon*. He said it was a "pre-Christian film for a post-Christian age. . . . Today we are finished with the Christian myth and await a new one." *Fellinicon*, as the media dubbed it, received more press coverage than any other Roman-made spectacular since *Cleopatra*.

Fellini first read the *Satyricon* in 1939, when he hoped to stage it as an antifascist parody. In 1969 he decided to do for imperial Rome what he'd done for modern Rome in *La Dolce Vita*, one of the first movies to offer a glimpse of transvestites and party-gays. Fellini's *I Vitelloni* (1953) features trans-

vestism, but the director was forced to delete a scene that implied one cross-dresser was gay. By 1960, homosexuals could exist on the Italian screen, and one *dolce* transvestite at the seashore proclaims that by the year 2000, "The whole world will be homosexual!"

Fellini told the press that he would cast major stars in *Fellini Satyricon*, "people who represent myths today to identify with the myths of the Roman era." The names ticked off included Taylor, Burton, Mae West, Brando, Bardot, and Charles de Gaulle. Fellini envisioned West as the emperor's mother (a part not in the script or film). "I liked her when I was very young. She is a myth of sex inserted in a fabulous pastiche. . . . Sometimes I say names to myself to make a picture like life." Fellini wanted Aristotle Onassis to play the munificent host Trimalchio. (Onassis's then-sister-in-law Lee Radziwill was eager to costar and sought a meeting with the director, but it never came off.)

Though he recently spoke of working with Boy George on a music video, Fellini seldom works with non-Italian stars, preferring his regulars like wife Giulietta Massina and Marcello Mastroianni, or a gallery of visually qualified neophytes. The three *Fellini Satyricon* leads were cinematic unknowns. Englishman Martin Potter, twenty-four, married and a father, dyed his hair blond for Encolpius. He recalled his audition at the Savoy in London: "For what seemed like an eternity, Fellini looked at me. Then he explained he was looking for a young man who was completely modern. But he didn't go into detail."

Potter found that details weren't Fellini's forte. During the gay marriage scene, Frenchman Alain Cuny (Lichas) kissed Potter on the mouth, then continued kissing him down to his stomach. Thus Fellini obtained Encolpius's dumbfounded look on the first and last take. This prompted Max Born (Giton) to tell a visiting journalist, "If Cuny gets to kiss Martin, I'm going to kiss him, too. I made love to him but didn't kiss him. It's ridiculous."

During a banquet scene, Fellini yelled at Potter, "Stop! Martin, you are eating like a British girl just out of school." He ordered, "Eat like a pig!" and shoved Potter's hands into the plate of food. Before filming, Potter enthused, "It's fantastic to start at the top!" But neither he nor any of the other newcomers achieved lasting fame.

Fresh out of *Hair*, Hiram Keller, twenty-four, was cast as Ascyltus. Keller's father was a Georgia state supreme court judge; Hiram gave up law school to study acting with Stella Adler and Lee Strasberg. Fellini advised Keller as Ascyltus, "You are evil and vulgar and cynical and you lay everything in sight."

Before meeting Fellini, Max Born "never worked for more than a week, except playing the guitar on the streets around [London's] Marble Arch or in the tube stations." The seventeen-year-old was hired when Fellini failed to find a suitable Giton in Italy and sought actors in London. "Fellini's scout went to a model agency in Chelsea," explained Born, "looking for boys and all kinds of freaks. A friend who had a hairdressing shop under the agency suggested I go upstairs...." When Fellini met Born, "He asked who I was and what I did. Martin Potter came to lunch, too, but they wouldn't let us in the hotel restaurant because we didn't have ties on, so we went to a Chinese restaurant.

"We talked about loads of things, including films. I'd seen [Fellini's] *Juliet of the Spirits* a number of times. It was one of my favorites because it wasn't straight." After Born got the part, "They did a

Beauty and the beast?: "Bride" Lichas (Alain Cuny) weds a reluctant Encolpius aboard ship.

Days gone bi: Polysexual Ascyltus (Hiram Keller) lends a hand, at least, to Tryphaena (Capucine).

makeup test and cut off my hair. It was halfway down my back and beautiful."

The images in *Fellini Satyricon* linger long after the "plot" is forgotten: doe-eyed Giton kissing Encolpius's arm. The outstretched arm of comic Vernacchio (Fanfulla) suddenly lopped off, to the noisy delight of an audience (whose members were taken from "the slaughterhouse and the insane asylum; they are more wise and obedient than normal people"). The Insula Felicles, a pyramid-like tenement, collapsing upon itself and many of its lovemaking inhabitants. Ascyltus in a gold lamé jockstrap, holding hands with Capucine (as Tryphaena, wife of Lichas). Feminine faces, lyrical or hideous, beneath intricate piles of hair and filigree ornaments. Dozens of jumping, chanting revelers in a Roman bath illumined by human-sized tapers; in front of the pool, lounging in a dry-ice mist, an impassive Nordic—facial cheeks studded with beads—is paddled on his bare ass.

The film begins with Encolpius losing Giton to Ascyltus. Encolpius decides to see the world. He visits a poet friend and they attend an orgy. Sated with food and sex, Encolpius is taken prisoner by Lichas, official pimp for Nero (played by Tanya Lopert, daughter of a United Artists executive). The men wrestle savagely, and after the macho Lichas wins, he turns into a simpering "bride" and weds Encolpius aboard his ship. Arriving at Nero's palace, the crew learns that the emperor has committed suicide before her/his bodyguards could beat him/her to it.

Reunited, Encolpius and Ascyltus make love with a slave girl in an empty temple, hire themselves to a nymphomaniac tied to a cart, and kidnap an albino hermaphrodite who dies in the broiling desert. On his own, Encolpius battles a minotaur who spares him after Encolpius humbly offers his friendship. The man removes his bull's head, announces, "I have made a friend this day," and embraces the startled blond. But by now the hero is impotent. He seeks out delicate handmaidens and a prehistoric black Venus to restore his virility. Revitalized, Encolpius takes matters into his own hands, while in the background Ascyltus becomes involved in a fight for his life. Encolpius doesn't lift a finger to help, and after his friend's death he sets sail for Africa and further adventures. The film ends in midsentence, the characters onboard frozen into a fresco.

Gay critic Parker Tyler called *Fellini Satyricon* "the most profoundly homosexual movie in all history." Yet his pioneering book, *Screening the Sexes*, provides little backing for the claim, beyond the fact that the protagonists are masculine and bisexual, and one is still alive at the end. The film doesn't remotely idealize gays or homosexuality, and the sex—mostly heterosexual—is frantic and mechanical. Only one male kiss is exchanged, between Lichas and Encolpius. Lichas then loses his head—as punishment?—to Nero's would-be assassins.

Even in his fickleness, Giton is passive and one-dimensional. The hermaphrodite, despite being an object of worship, is a pitiable freak, and Encolpius and Ascyltus's "friendship" is thin, as the latter's uninterrupted murder proves. Both men's relationships with Giton are less bonds of love or friendship than lusty possession. In Fellini's empire of violence, corruption, and constant surprise there's little room for tenderness or true eroticism of any stripe (most of the female "sex symbols" are grotesques). The director admitted that his primary aim was to shock. In so doing, he alienated most critics and the public—the latter was informed that *Fellini Satyricon* was brazenly homoerotic, though it's anything but. The leading men are pleasing to look at, but the implied acts are male-female; the true turnoffs in this otherwise riveting picture are the freak shows and the violence. Inevitably, *Fellini Satyricon* has become a cult film on campus, where Fellini's *Satyricon* overshadows Petronius's.

For all its gaudy splendor, the Fellini film cost only $4 million, a million less than budgeted. It had a cast of fifteen hundred and required five thousand wigs and eighty-nine sets in Rome's Cinecittà. Less than one-twentieth of the filmed footage was used. Numerous characters, including a dwarf with a permanent erection, were cut. The movie was a great success in Europe and heralded Fellini's return to prominence after a fallow period. He later made *Casanova* with Donald Sutherland, which largely overlooks its subject's bisexuality. *Fellini's Roma* features a multicolored fashion show of chic Vaticanites in haute confessionwear.

Fellini reportedly cast foreigners as the leads in *Fellini Satyricon* because "there are no homosexuals in Italy." But he also said, "My *Satyricon* is even more autobiographical than my *8½*." And:

"This is a science-fiction picture projected into the past instead of the future."

"They were much more open and free. There was no moral judgment. To be a homosexual was just part of sex. All our information comes to us from the Catholic church. The Latin texts were changed by the monks or censored, burned, condemned, or distorted."

"Who knows what the Romans were like? No-

Max Born as Giton, plaything of gods and grotesques, in this case Neronian comic Vernacchio (Fanfulla).

Maestro Fellini and an assistant put the finishing touches to a Roman statue.

Charles Laughton as a "daring" Nero in *The Sign of the Cross* (1932, precensorship Code), with a favorite by his side.

body. . . . I try to forget the myths and weaknesses of the Christian world, and try to love that pre-Christian world. . . . They have nothing of the Catholic desire and fear of sex which is considered impure. You are always taught sex is impure, but you know it is a lie."

"Pornography is in you, not in things. If we are not pornographic, then the film is not pornographic."

"If I made the picture with Catholic desire and

The bisexuality of Roman general Crassus (Laurence Olivier) in *Spartacus* was deleted until the 1991 film restoration.

education, it would be dirty and erotic. The picture will disappoint audiences who go to see it thinking it is erotic; it is not. The principal characters are asexual. They could be boys, girls, flowers even."

Like his unique film, Fellini's pronouncements were intended more for effect than meaning. The maestro uses words, as well as celluloid, to astonish and provoke, to create mosaics of future-memory.

ABOUT *FELLINI SATYRICON*

John Simon: Fellini has been faithful to the termites of time that have gnawed away large chunks of [Petronius's] work—not to the work itself. . . . Fellini always had a showman inside him dying to get out, but low budgets kept the showman from getting the upper hand. Now the showman avenges himself by keeping the artist locked in. . . . Sex takes quite a beating in *Fellini Satyricon*. It is always either ludicrous or horrible, and if at all passionate, it is pederastic.

The visual aphrodisiacs are meant to freeze the blood in our organs—without, however, proposing any alternative vision. The men in the film are all either asexual or homosexual—which would be all right if homosexual love were treated with sympathy as well as irony, as Petronius treated it; but Fellini makes it all just swishy-washy.

Robert Hatch, the *Nation*: Encolpius and Ascyltus are a bad lot, expending themselves on every vice save hypocrisy. But if their perverse appetites sink them below the beasts, their vitality raises them toward the gods—at least it has won them immortality. . . . The high wit and low merriment of the original are gone. The film cries "woe," "repent," like some Old Testament bluenose. The possibility of laughter does not arise, and Fellini makes wickedness seem leadenly repellent.

Martin Potter's Encolpius is a pretty young stud, but a blockhead. When he spoke for Petronius, this inexcusable rascal saw through everything, including himself; under Fellini, he couldn't see through a hole in the wall. Ascyltus (Hiram Keller) sneers—and sneers again. Giton (Max Born) is inanimate, as recessive as the leading lady in a Japanese costume movie. To do him justice, he must be played as the foremost male bitch in literature, until Genêt.

Stefan Kanfer, *Time*: There have been hundreds of Freudian films. *Fellini Satyricon* is the first Jungian one. In the course of two hours and seven minutes, images, totems, and archetypes rise and burst like hydrogen sulfide bubbles from the marsh of the collective unconscious.

Fellini seems anxious to have audiences compare his ancient Rome with the Twentieth Centurians. . . . Encolpius and his colleagues are obviously fashioned after contemporary faggots; the mourning widow is representative of Jackie Kennedy; wall friezes seem copied less from Roman basements than department store casements. The forced modernity denies complexity and weakens the work's polished irony. Still, no one else could have brought a tenth of the *Satyricon* to the screen without the customary lubricity and X-rated smirks.

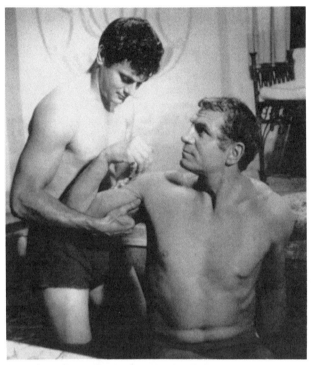

Antoninus (Tony Curtis) massages his flirtatious master Crassus in a scene cut from *Spartacus* but later restored.

Cleopatra (1963) features a heter-only Julius Caesar (Rex Harrison, with Elizabeth Taylor), though even Shakespeare described him as bisexual.

11

HIS STORY, HER STORY

The Loved One (1965): Robert Morley, who played Oscar Wilde on stage and screen, is bussed by costar Robert Morse.

The following being a chapter about historical men and women as portrayed—and often de-gayed—on screen. . . .

In Britain 1960 was the year of Oscar Wilde, with two film biographies released within one week. As recently as 1958 the British Film Censor had banned Wilde's life as a movie theme "until it becomes one that can be mentioned without offence." British television made the difference. While American motion pictures couldn't utter "homosexual" or "pansy," British television dealt with words and sexual topics like homosexuality, abortion, and venereal disease. The BBC felt that the public should be exposed to and educated about such issues.

Like *Victim*, both Wilde films revolve around legal cases and were interpreted by many as special pleading for reform of the 1885 anti-homosexual law. The first of the films was the superior *The Trials of Oscar Wilde* (*The Man With the Green Carnation* in the U.S., although the carnation is *lavender*, green being a "sickly" color . . .). The second was titled simply *Oscar Wilde*. The former, more costly ($350,000) color film was written and directed by Ken Hughes, who in 1978 helmed Mae West's last vehicle, *Sextette*.

Hughes felt that Peter Finch as Wilde in *Trials* "would level out any suggestion of the camp faggot because he's basically heterosexual. . . . Finchie surprised me. His performance was more thoughtful, delicate, and Wildean than I believed him capable of." The performance is the movie's highlight and

its sole redeeming feature. John Fraser's Lord Alfred "Bosie" Douglas looks and acts like a male Morgan Fairchild, and Yvonne Mitchell is the wife-martyr who later denies Oscar access to their sons, even by post. Lionel Jeffries's Marquis of Queensbury, Bosie's father, is a sputtering cross between Jerry Falwell and Daffy Duck.

Oscar Wilde is presented as a rather witty heterosexual who falls into an ill-fated gay relationship late in life. One British critic felt the film "omits the grotesque side of Wilde, so that he seems to be simply a decent family man who prefers stimulating small talk in the cafés to dull nights at home." Yet Wilde is too forthright to deny the nature and extent of the relationship. But where wife-love is pictured as sacred, and having no viable alternative, Bosie is merely a pouty, violent narcissist. Bosie isn't any kind of lover to Oscar, whom he uses as a bank and a means of revenge against his bully-dad.

One trial scene invokes "Christian charity and forgiveness," but as Wilde later asserts, "If this is the way Her Majesty treats her prisoners, she doesn't deserve to have any." When Wilde is released from jail, he sadly muses, "Each man kills the thing he loves. The coward with a kiss, the brave man with a sword." The film ends on this hopeless note. It implies that medicine or psychiatry, rather than an inhumane law, was homosexuality's "solution." Incredibly, the picture's advisors included Wilde's son Vyvyan Holland (whose gay twenty-first birthday party was attended by, among others, Henry James) and the then-current Marquis of Queensbury.

Finch won the British Academy Award for Best Actor in 1960 and Best Actor at the 1961 Moscow Film Festival. In the U.S. the print was detained by authorities; *Green Carnation* eventually got a limited release and did poor business (the black-and-white Morley *Oscar Wilde* was not released). Nonetheless, the National Catholic Office of Motion Pictures put both Wilde films on its condemned list. This body was the "new, more reasonable" successor to the Legion of Decency, which in 1956 requested that Deborah Kerr be killed off after her extramarital affair with suspected homosexual John Kerr in *Tea and Sympathy*.

Robert Morley made his movie debut as the sexless Dauphin in Norma Shearer's *Marie Antoi-*

Ben-Hur (1959): Charlton Heston admitted that Gore Vidal's screenplay was basically a man-to-man love story.

Love story: Gay star Ramon Novarro as *Ben-Hur* (1926) with mate-turned-enemy Messala (Francis X. Bushman, right).

nette (1938). (The film omits the queen's affair with Princess Marie Thérèse Louise, but depicts the Duke of Orléans as a raging, vengeful fag who almost single-handedly starts the French Revolution.) In 1953 Morley played half of *Gilbert and Sullivan*. Sir Arthur Sullivan was gay, and as historian Martin Greif noted, "He played by the rules that permitted the upper classes their 'vices' so long as there was no scandal. That Sullivan, unlike his straight partner, was knighted shows how prudently he played the game. . . . The Irish Oscar Wilde might not have died so young had he understood the English character as well as Sullivan." Morley played Wilde on stage during the fifties, as Vincent Price did in America in the late seventies.

Originally, only one Wilde film was to have been made, but a feud between the producers led to two. The second was directed by Gregory Ratoff, the man behind Mae West's disastrous *The Heat's On* (1943), her last film until 1970. Morley was closer to Wilde physically, and John Neville, another sharp-featured blond, played Bosie. But except for Ralph Richardson's portrayal of prosecutor-for-the-defense Sir Edward Carson (James Mason in *Trials*), *Oscar Wilde* was branded as slight and inferior to Hughes's picture.

Some felt *Oscar Wilde* should have been titled *The Wit and Folly of Oscar Wilde*, stuffed as it is with Wildean and Morleyesque epigrams. It was berated for being too free with the facts. A small but telling detail is the film using the correct spelling when portraying the unlettered marquis's note accusing Wilde of "posing as a somdomite [sic]." The Morley film is rarely seen today, but *Trials* occasionally shares a double bill with *Sunday, Bloody Sunday*, the latter seemingly made one hundred years after its predecessor.

• *The Importance of Being Earnest*, Wilde's most famous play, was filmed by gay director Anthony Asquith in 1952. However, it lacked John Gielgud's definitive stage Earnest. Sir John, who in the 1970s began speaking openly of his gayness, was long considered too "specialized" for films, until in later years he became *the* character actor. Kenneth Tynan had dubbed Gielgud "the finest actor on earth from the neck up," and in 1976 the stage and film director Peter Hall wrote of Gielgud's performance in *Providence*, "Not only is his acting subtle and rich but he suggests heterosexuality in a way I would never have believed possible for him."

Wilde's only novel, *The Picture of Dorian Gray*, was introduced as damaging evidence in his trial. It has been filmed several times. In 1915 a Russian version starred actress Varvara Yanova in male drag as Dorian. But the most famous *Dorian* is the 1945 film by Albert Lewin, who also directed 1942's *The Moon and Sixpence*. Hurd Hatfield (*The Left-Handed Gun*, *King David*) is the epicene, vaguely heterosexual Dorian. A 1970 German remake, *Dorian Gray*, starred the often topless Helmut Berger. The 1983 telefilm *The Sins of Dorian Gray* regendered Dorian into an ambitious model and costarred Anthony Perkins and Joseph Bottoms. (Garbo once told bisexual Katharine Cornell—married to bisexual producer Guthrie McClintic—that she wanted to do a remake with Marilyn Monroe.)

In 1922 Alla Nazimova (Nancy Reagan's godmother) financed and starred in an all-gay film of Wilde's play *Salomé*. An Aubrey Beardsley aficionado, Natacha Rambova (Valentino's second wife) designed the Beardsleyesque sets and costumes. Nominal director's credit went to Nazimova's contractual husband, and she wrote the screenplay as "Peter M. Winters." Ahead of its time, *Salomé* flopped completely, and Nazimova—who arranged both of Valentino's unconsummated marriages—is best remembered for the legendary hotel, the Garden of Allah. Her circle of lovers included director Dorothy Arzner and Oscar Wilde's Los Angeles-based niece, Dolly Wilde.

Friends. Noël Coward (played by Daniel Massey, Noël's real-life godson) was desexualized for 1968's superflop, *Star!* Julie Andrews played Gertrude Lawrence, a nonsaccharine real woman, and despite his fourth-place billing, Massey was her leading man. The real Coward was a conservative closet case (long denied a knighthood by Queen Elizabeth II nonetheless) whose posthumously published diaries expose his discomfort with and distaste for gay men in "crowds" of three or more. Sadly for him, Coward's homosexuality was far from a secret. And his mainstream stance was, in Wilde's words, "no guarantee of respectability of character."

In 1985 Rex Harrison—whose biggest comedy hit was Coward's *Blithe Spirit*—told *Vanity Fair*, "Noël was a terrible cunt, and I never liked doing his plays, because unless you were very careful you ended up sounding just like him." Harrison's ex-wife Rachel Roberts once averred, "Half of Hollywood thinks Rex is queer, just because of his voice!"

• Half a century before Coward's heyday, D. H. Lawrence alienated literary censors with his explicit heterosexuality. The bisexuality which he seems to have physically suppressed—but discreetly expressed in prose—wasn't admitted to by the literary establishment until long after his death. *Priest of Love* (1981) briefly and skimpily explores this aspect of Lawrence (played by openly gay Sir Ian McKellen), but ultimately swaps honesty for titillation—for example, the doubly uncircumcized nude but platonic seashore frolic of D. H. Lawrence and a young farmer (Graham Faulkner). The bisexuality of Mabel Dodge Luhan (Ava Gardner), patron of outcasts and the arts, is completely missing. (Gielgud is Herbert Muskett, the prototypical prude-censor.)

• Religious personalities invariably get the asexual treatment. Derek Jarman's *Sebastiane* (1976) recounts the martyrdom of the "gayest" saint. Franco Zeffirelli's *Brother Sun, Sister Moon* (1973) depicts the spiritual odyssey of St. Francis of Assisi. Francesco (Graham Faulkner), the son of wealthy merchants, renounces his privileged life in a touching scene which features rear nudity.

Zeffirelli's 1967 *The Taming of the Shrew* needlessly includes an effeminate (as opposed to feminine) milliner and designer. But in the eighties the director (*Romeo and Juliet, Endless Love*) disclosed his homosexuality to the *Advocate*. Zeffirelli's Shakespeare films are among the few financially successful ones that have been made. Elsewhere, the Bard is sometimes played for cheap laughs, e.g., Richard Dreyfuss's fey Richard III in Neil Simon's anti-feminist *The Goodbye Girl* (1977).

• Fictional detective Sherlock Holmes is debatably gay but wasn't depicted as such on screen until Billy Wilder's *The Private Life of Sherlock Holmes*, a costly 1970 flop. Robert Stephens's Holmes is a gloomy sort who attributes his sexuality to "a cruel caprice of Mother Nature." Colin Blakely's Dr. Watson is dim, cheerful, and straight. (More popular was *The Seven Percent Solution* [1976], which details Holmes's cocaine addiction.) The 1977 spoof remake of *The Hound of the Baskervilles* (released in the U.S. in 1981) features a fag-buffoon in the person of Kenneth Williams (of Britain's *Carry On* film series). As the Baskerville heir, Williams lisps and camps his "degenerate" way through an otherwise inventive Dudley Moore-Peter Cook vehicle.

• Charlton Heston was Hollywood's foremost player of historic heroes. His Michelangelo in *The Agony and the Ecstasy* (1965) and General Charles "Chinese" Gordon in *Khartoum* (1966) were predict-

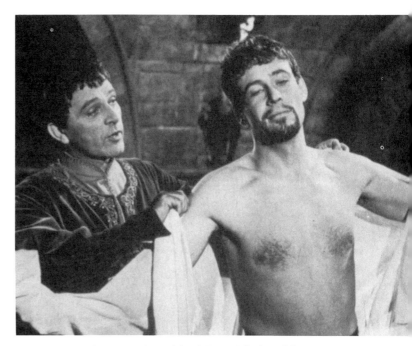

Becket (1963): Thomas Becket (Richard Burton) bathes, dries off, and dresses his friend, Henry II (Peter O'Toole).

The Private Lives of Elizabeth and Essex (1939): Elizabeth I as a heterosexual virgin (Bette Davis with Errol Flynn).

ably robbed of their homosexuality, although the latter was directed by *Victim*'s liberal Basil Dearden. Heston wanted to portray Sir Richard Burton, the bisexual African explorer and translator of *The Arabian Nights*. (Burton's life was recounted in the 1990 movie *Mountains of the Moon*.) Another titan Heston hasn't impersonated is Richard the Lion-

Hearted; George Sanders played him in the $3 million 1954 *King Richard and the Crusaders*, with gay Laurence Harvey and antigay Rex Harrison. *The Lion in Winter* (1968) offered a truer Richard (Anthony Hopkins) and his lover, King Philip of France (Timothy Dalton). Dalton also played Lord Darnley, husband of *Mary, Queen of Scots* (1971), and murderer of his ex-lover, Mary's advisor, David Rizzio (Ian Holm). Dalton, who in 1987 became the latest James Bond, has played various gay or ambiguous roles: *Permission to Kill* (1975), with Dirk Bogarde, and Mae West's *Sextette*.

• Peter O'Toole's *Lawrence of Arabia* (1962) isn't gay or bisexual but asexual, which—since a girlfriend is glaringly absent—audiences read as "queer." The subtle rape scene in the film has the anti-Eastern bias of 1978's *Midnight Express*; In 1965's *Lord Jim*, O'Toole is raped again, this time in the Far East. (After the premiere of *Lawrence of Arabia*, Noël Coward told O'Toole, "If Lawrence had looked like that, there would have been many more than twelve Turks queuing up for the buggering session.")

The prolific Coward himself treated homosexuality in a short story titled "Star Quality: Me and the Girls." It was filmed for British television in 1985, starring Tom Courtenay as song-and-dance man George Banks, and in 1987 was broadcast in the U.S. on *Masterpiece Theatre*.

• The Duke of Buckingham, a gay ancestor of British royals and various prime ministers, has yet to be treated on page or screen. Neither has a recent prime minister whom some call the British Jerry Brown, except for his conservatism. And television depictions of Edward VIII (Richard Chamberlain, et al.) have focused exclusively on "the love story of the century." But historian Martin Greif states, "Probably because of his arrest in a gay sex raid, and not because of the woman he loved (she later went on to an affair with homosexual Woolworth heir Jimmy Donahue), King Edward VIII abdicated the throne in 1936."

• Classical composers have either been "straightened" or else not depicted at all. The same for gay painters like Leonardo Da Vinci and Michelangelo. But 1986 saw the release of Derek Jarman's feature, *Caravaggio*, a bold, quirky, and homoerotic biography of the Renaissance's controversial master. British Jarman is himself steeped in controversy. He once told the press, "When I

meet heterosexual men, I know they have experienced only half of love." And Jarman's 1976 *Sebastiane* was a saintly gay love story spoken entirely in Latin.

• Not until the 1970s did the media begin to acknowledge that untold thousands of gay people were among Hitler's mass victims. (Several historians felt mention of gay victims would somehow demean the memory of slaughtered Jews, Catholics, Gypsies, and others—among whom the usual percentage was also gay.) Martin Sherman's play *Bent* dramatized Nazi homophobia and played in London (starring Ian McKellen) and New York (Richard Gere). There was even talk of a film version with Gere, who courageously told *Rolling Stone*, "Yes, I'm gay when I'm on that stage. If the role [*Max*] required me to suck off Horst, I'd do it. . . . This was the best play I'd read in years. It's about the nature of love, about accepting yourself and other people for what they are." Separated by barbed wire, Max and Horst (David Dukes) make verbal love. After Horst is killed, Max—who sought to improve his status in the camp by wearing a Jewish yellow star—exchanges his coat for Horst's, with the pink triangle, before being forced to throw himself on an electrocuting wire.

Marcel Proust, gay *and* Jewish, was referred to as such in George Cukor's *Rich and Famous*. But the line was cut from the 1984 network telecast—one example of the ongoing butchering of history.

Romans. Ancient Romans are luckier than others in their screen depictions. They've usually been portrayed as English gents in togas or as the empire-building, street-paving forebears of Americans, sharing the same benevolently patronizing relationship with Greece that the U.S. does with England.

The ancients' religious sympathies determined their depiction: From Egypt on, "pagans"—excepting "good" Romans—were always villains. Jews were okay, separated from "us" by the millennia, but Christians were "best." Burt Lancaster turned down the lead in 1959's *Ben-Hur* because of its spiritual one-sidedness. (Lancaster was to have played the gay window dresser Molina in 1985's *Kiss of the Spider Woman*, but a heart attack intervened, and William Hurt took over the ageless role.) Charlton Heston, originally offered the supporting role of Messala, played the Jew who eventually turns to the "true" faith. The all-time Oscar-champ movie was directed by Jewish William Wyler. *Ben-Hur* paints Emperor Tiberius (George Relph) as a pagan

Hitler, advocating a Roman master race (besides indulging in shady orgies on Capri).

Asked the gender of his first sex partner, Gore Vidal replied, "I don't know. I was too polite to ask." In Vidal's script for *Ben-Hur* (he didn't receive screen credit), Judah Ben-Hur and Messala (Stephen Boyd) are ex-lovers—the only explanation for their undefined enmity. Vidal let the bemused Boyd in on the secret, but Wyler feared "Chuck's" reaction if he knew. Yet, in 1977 Heston declared, "The story isn't really about Christ, and it's certainly not a story of Ben-Hur and Esther. It's a love story between Ben-Hur and Messala, and the destruction of that love, turning to hate and revenge—it's a vendetta story."

Starring in the 1926 *Ben-Hur* was gay sex symbol Ramon Novarro, Valentino's main Latin screen rival (and his sometime lover). The Mexican star's Hollywood murder—involving an Art Deco dildo given him by Valentino—is recounted in *Hollywood Babylon*.

• In 1956 Richard Burton played a too-busy-for-girls *Alexander the Great*. A late-seventies television series on Alexander, cofounded by the Greek government, also erased the Macedonian's homosexuality, as did Greece's touring museum exhibit, Treasures of Alexander. It was gay author Mary Renault who, in several bestsellers, detailed Alexander's life with his lifemate Hephaistion and sometime lover Bagoas, aka the "Persian Boy" (the planned film never got beyond a casting call).

• In the pre-restored (in 1991) 1960 film *Spartacus*, Roman General Crassus (Laurence Olivier) is "straightened out," as Julius Caesar invariably is—from Heston's 1970 *Julius Caesar* to Rex Harrison in *Cleopatra* (1963). (The latter's early villains are the eunuch Pothinos [Gregoire Aslan] and Ptolemy [Richard O'Sullivan], Cleopatra's half brother. Before the pair's execution, she tells Julius, "You've seen my brother—the way he talks—and that truly evil man to whom he belongs. . . .") Marc Antony was Caesar's favorite lover apart from his great-nephew Octavian, who became Rome's first emperor, Augustus—uncle and great-nephew are joined, however, in the months *July* and *August*. Antony was also essayed by Brando in the 1953 *Julius Caesar* and Heston in the 1971 *Antony and Cleopatra*.

• Most pre-Christian Roman emperors were villainized in varying shades of purple. Exceptions, like Marcus Aurelius (Alec Guinness) in the 1964 *The Fall of the Roman Empire* are rigid heterosexuals. In Cecil B. De Mille's 1932 *The Sign of the Cross*, Charles Laughton is Nero, with a nude slave boy at his side. The homophobic director didn't want the emperor played gay, but as a *straight* villain. Laughton won out, so to speak, playing Nero with a lisp. De Mille countered the Legion of Decency's objections by stating that the debauchery was biblical and made paganism (or polytheism) more heinous. Soon after, Laughton was cast as Claudius in *I, Claudius*, but leading lady Merle Oberon's car accident shelved that project.

According to historical accounts, Nero was an irredeemable villain. So was Caligula, overacted by Jay Robinson in two Christian spectacles: *The Robe* (1953) and its sequel *Demetrius and the Gladiators* (1954). Robinson's Caligula is a raving maniac who ogles women and feeds Christian after Christian to his lions. A more modern, vaguely bisexual Caligula is played by Malcolm McDowell in the 1980 Penthouse production, *Caligula*, the most expensive sex movie ever. *Caligula* begins with the identification "Pagan Rome" and a biblical quotation. Then comes the lust and the gore. Gore Vidal sued to remove his name from the title and credits of this would-be *Fellini Satyricon* successor. *Caligula* bears no writer's or director's credit. Maria Schneider (*Last Tango in Paris*) was to play Caligula's lover-sister Drusilla but quit when she found the production pornographic. (After she announced her own bisexuality, her name subsequently was removed from various biographical sources.) *Caligula*'s Claudius (Giancarlo Badessi) is a fat poof, unlike Derek Jacobi's upright straight version in television's "*I, Claudius.*"

McDowell also starred in the unfairly X-rated *If . . .* (1969) and in 1971's *A Clockwork Orange*, in which he's badgered by the lecherous Mr. Deltoid (Aubrey Morris) and questioned in prison, "Are you now, or have you ever been, a homosexual?"

Countrymen. From Cole Porter (*Night and Day*, 1946) to Clyde Barrow (*Bonnie and Clyde*, 1967) to John Reed (*Reds*, 1981) and Rudolf Valentino (*Valentino*, 1977), American gays and bi's have systematically been respooled. Cole Porter is Cary Grant. . . . Clyde Barrow is "impotent". . . . John Reed is Warren Beatty. . . . And Ken Russell's Valentino/Nureyev flaunts his buns but not his "preference." Franco Nero's television Valentino denies the "rumors" by shrugging, "They say that about everyone in Hollywood." They do—in *Hollywood*. The rest of the country gets the propaganda.

Hollywood used to churn out dubious biographical films of famous gays. Today history is left to the small screen. But possible biographies of heroes like tennis great Bill Tilden, or football's uncloseted Dave Kopay, among others, will likely secrete the subject's love life (as with Jack Kerouac), camouflage it with a long-standing marriage (Jack Benny), or simply bypass "troublesome" subjects. In the 1985 telefilm *My Wicked, Wicked Ways*, Errol Flynn (Duncan Regehr) is happily married to (fellow bisexual) Lily Damita (Barbara Hershey). From Stephen Foster or Kodak's George Eastman to Lorenz Hart and Edgar Allan Poe (in whose life Sylvester Stallone has shown interest), the untold

Holly-story: Lesbian *Marie Antoinette* (1938, Norma Shearer) and bisexual Court Fersen (Tyrone Power) as heter-only.

Bisexual nineteenth-century novelist George Sand (Merle Oberon) as just a cross-dresser in *A Song to Remember* (1945).

story will emerge only when audiences and film-makers demand the truth.

Women. The most widely depicted historical figure, Elizabeth I, is always portrayed as a freak-exception, a female torn between men, like Errol Flynn in *The Private Lives of Elizabeth and Essex* (1939), and her duty to England. Few have questioned whether the Virgin Queen was virginal only so far as men were concerned. Despite the formidable actresses who have played her (Bette Davis, Glenda Jackson, Flora Robson), she has usually been patronized by male moviemakers. The ad for Hal Wallis's *Mary, Queen of Scots* contrasted Mary,

Lawrence of Arabia (1962): Gay T.E. Lawrence (Peter O'Toole with Anthony Quinn) wasn't heterosexual on screen, but asexual.

"who ruled with the heart of a woman" (and thus lost her throne), with the more forceful Elizabeth, "who reigned with the power of a man." Elizabeth ruled not with the power of a man, but that of a monarch, in this case a queen.

• Like Elizabeth, Sweden's Queen Christina was a "bachelor" sovereign. But her love for women is fact, although posthumous examination found she was a virgin. Liv Ullmann played Christina in 1974's *The Abdication* (with Peter Finch as a Roman Catholic cardinal), in which the queen abdicates her throne and her faith. Garbo, whom Alice B. Toklas dubbed "Mademoiselle Hamlet," indulged her desire to cross-dress on screen in 1933's *Queen Christina*. In male attire she kisses her love, Countess Ebba Sparre (Elizabeth Young), on the lips before "falling in love" with a Spaniard played by John Gilbert, the only male with whom Garbo was romantically linked in real life.

• There were numerous homosexual popes, as opposed to nonsexual ones, but *Pope Joan* (1972) posits a female pope. Liv Ullmann is the posturing patriarch—until pregnancy intervenes. But the film about the legendary ninth-century pope won release in few countries and was "too feminist" to prosper at the box office.

Ballroom: Gay legends *Valentino* (1977) played by Rudolf Nureyev and Nijinsky (Anthony Dowell) tango—but that's all, folks.

83

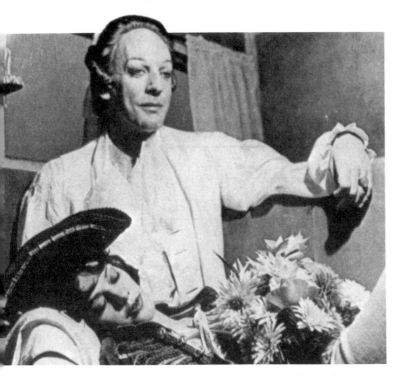

Holly-would: When a bisexual is the hero, he's made hetero, as in *Casanova* (1976, Donald Sutherland with Tina Aumont).

. . . and does: When epics require a villain, he's often made a gay stereotype, like nobleman Joseph Schildkraut in *Marie Antoinette*.

84

• More controversial still would be a factual biography of Eleanor Roosevelt. One of her sons blamed President Roosevelt's "need" for a mistress on Eleanor's attentions to "two masculinely dressed women." Jim Kepner, curator of the National Gay Archives in Los Angeles, says that "her intimacy with a secretary was much rumored in New York in the forties while she was serving with the United Nations and UNESCO." In the late seventies, over three thousand loving letters to journalist Lorena Hickok were discovered, and gay actress Pat Bond has toured in the play *Lorena Hickok and Eleanor Roosevelt: A Love Story.*

• In the early seventies Shirley MacLaine tried to launch a "herstorically" accurate film about Amelia Earhart. Television (and Susan Clark) beat her to the whitewashed punch. Almost none of the written or filmed Marilyn Monroe biographies have mentioned that she might have been bisexual. The first book on Monroe authored by a woman, Lena Pepitone, reveals Monroe's woman-to-woman sexual interlude. And Faye Dunaway's projected *Vicky,* a biofilm of Victoria Woodhull, the first female presidential candidate (in 1872), fell through partly because of Vicky's bisexuality.

Fashion designer Coco Chanel's life was sanitized for Broadway and Katharine Hepburn in *Coco.* The 1981 *Chanel Solitaire,* with Marie-France Pisier (*The Other Side of Midnight*) *blamed* Chanel's bisexuality on the lack of a man at certain times in her busy life—her business empire was the largest ever built by a woman. Chanel once declared, "Military history has shaped nations and economics, but sexual history (*les petites histoires*) has shaped peoples and culture."

The twentieth century's, and perhaps "herstory's," most famous lesbian relationship, Alice Toklas and Gertrude Stein, made it to the screen (via PBS's *American Playhouse*) in 1987 in *Waiting for the Moon,* financed by British, German, American, and French interests. Feminist director Jill Godmilow chose to do a fictionalized seriocomic version, starring the unlikely actors Linda Bassett as a much thinner Gertrude Stein and Linda Hunt as a much shorter Alice B. Toklas. The sexual and affectionate components of the women's lives were deliberately omitted—unlike the 1987 portrait of lifemates Joe Orton and Kenneth Halliwell, *Prick Up Your Ears.* On the other hand, the women's love story, unlike the men's, focuses on their joys and bond and eschews sensationalism.

12

BEING THERE:

Midnight Cowboy and *Cruising*

Midnight Cowboy. United Artists, 1969. Director: John Schlesinger; writer: Waldo Salt; producer: Jerome Hellman.
Starring: Dustin Hoffman, Jon Voight, Sylvia Miles, John McGiver, Brenda Vaccaro, Barnard Hughes, Ruth White, Viva.

Cruising. United Artists, 1980. Director-writer: William Friedkin; producer: Jerry Weintraub.
Starring: Al Pacino, Paul Sorvino, Karen Allen, Richard Cox, Don Scardino, Joe Spinell, Jay Acovone, Keith Prentice.

"In a way, I feel I have no right to be in the picture at all," said Jon Voight of *Midnight Cowboy*. "I don't know anything about homosexuality or transferring the feelings I've had for girls to what I might feel for a boy." He told the *New York Times*, "It's not whether I *am* Joe Buck that matters. It's whether I have compassion. . . . I don't want to say to an audience who doesn't know anything about hustlers, 'I'm right and you're wrong.' I just want to share something."

Hollywood in 1969 had no such objectivity and couldn't conceive of a totally heterosexual male prostitute. Yet the movie's hero couldn't be homo- or bisexual, so the trendy-but-establishment *Midnight Cowboy* was reworked to feature straight leads in a gay milieu. Ratso Rizzo (Dustin Hoffman) is a sometime pimp (for street girls), and Joe Buck is an infantile Texan who was once told he was "a helluva stud." He hopes to make it big in the Wild East where there's a lack of Real Men by dressing

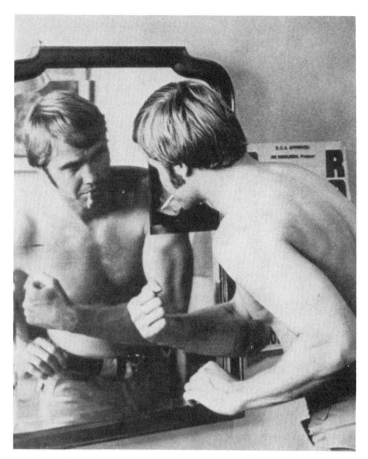

Joe Buck (Jon Voight) comes to Manhattan to earn money as a midnight cowboy.

Joe finds that New York women (like Brenda Vaccaro) aren't that responsive to his down-home charms

Ratso Rizzo (Dustin Hoffman) is upbraided for trying to steal food for himself and Joe.

in cowboy drag and catering to rich-bitch New Yorkers.

When Buck discovers that women don't have the economic muscle to support him, he turns reluctantly to male clients. The first is a setup by Rizzo, a self-abominating religious fanatic (John McGiver) with a chapel in his apartment. Later Buck deigns to be fellated by a penniless student in a Forty-second Street movie house (a missile launch on-screen drives the sexual point home).

Buck's final client becomes a victim of the two straights' need for money. Ratso's health requires a move to Florida, so Joe beats up an aged gay man (Barnard Hughes). Though there's no sex, Buck indulges in symbolic revenge, shoving a phone receiver into the bleeding victim's mouth. The 1965 novel by James Leo Herlihy plays the scene in terms of Joe's financial desperation, but the movie imbues the violence with voyeuristic sadism.

Voight and Hoffman delivered bravura performances but cancelled each other out for the Oscar, although the film won Best Picture. *Midnight Cowboy* reinforced stereotypes of gay men as predatory losers. Manhattan gays are simply obstacles on the path to Joe's redemption, and ultimately the movie is about idealized heterosexual friendship; it was one of the first buddy films.

Voight got a feel for his character by haunting the film's locations. "I came dressed in my cowboy stud clothes, and men would try to pick me up." He used small talk as a deterrent, and "they would get the message." He also frequented the Bowery, where "every bum has a buddy and they split everything fifty-fifty. It's beautiful, like the relationship between Dusty and me in the movie. It's really a love affair, though it never becomes sexual. But it's still love."

Hoffman's presence notwithstanding, *Midnight Cowboy* is virtually *The Perils of Joe Buck*. Once he's accustomed to heartless Manhattan—selectively uglified in garish color—Joe mistakes a veteran hooker (Sylvia Miles) for a potential client. He attends a Warholesque party (reviled by most New York critics) and is engaged for the night by Shirley (Brenda Vaccaro). Unsure whether he wants to service a woman, his indecision turns to determination after Shirley taunts him by rhyming words like *fey* and *gay*.

Flashbacks reveal Joe's past, including the traumatizing gang-rape of his girlfriend—apparently also of Joe, though the subliminal message eluded most reviewers. Rex Reed and John Simon were two exceptions. Reed interviewed Voight on location. The actor pointed to a drag queen. Reed uncharitably described the person as "something in purple stretch pants with an orange wig and a face full of

Ratso's premature death is foreshadowed in this cemetery visit.

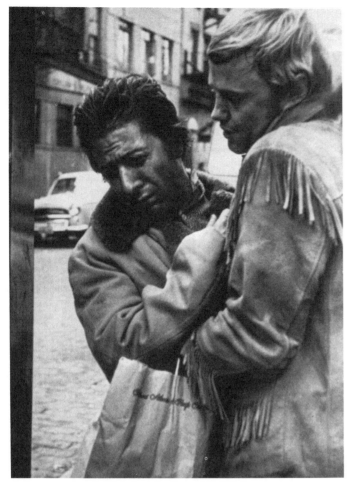

Joe comforts his ailing friend.

John Schlesinger, the openly gay Best Director of *Midnight Cowboy*, as well as *Sunday, Bloody Sunday; Marathon Man; Madame Sousatzka . . .*

PHOTO: SIMON MEIN

acne scars." "You wonder what a person like that does at night," said Voight, "where he goes. There's something to be said for being ready to admit to anything being possible.

"If you cared enough to stop and really talk to him, I'll bet you could understand him. That's what *Midnight Cowboy*'s about." The *book*, anyway.

Alone in New York, Joe is used and, at least in his own mind, abused. He isn't fulfilled until he befriends someone similarly needy whom he comes to trust and care for. The *New Republic*'s Stanley Kauffmann said that the film proves that "at any social level, the exchange of trust and devotion is the only sure spiritual oasis." However, that cinematic oasis excludes fellow-loving men, though Voight felt that "if we could break down some of our prejudices, we'd learn we're not too different from these people on Forty-second Street. We all hurt in the same places."

Were *Midnight Cowboy* remade in the 1990s, it would hopefully be more sexually honest. In the sixties and seventies, gigolos and hustlers were invariably portrayed as heterosexuals if they were protagonists—i.e., George Peppard's character, in Truman Capote's *Breakfast at Tiffany's*, who is kept not by a sugar daddy but by Patricia Neal. Also, before the 1980s there were few if any openly gay mainstream directors; no doubt John Schlesinger's approach to *Midnight Cowboy* would be significantly different today, probably truer to the novel and the realities of male prostitution.

The man who followed where Hollywood studios still fear to tread is openly gay director Gus Van Sant, who claimed *Midnight Cowboy*'s turf as his own, transplanting it to the Pacific Northwest. Van Sant debuted in 1985 with *Mala Noche*, about male hookers and the men who love them. It garnered numerous film-festival prizes, as did his *Drugstore Cowboy* (1989), starring Matt Dillon. Van Sant's biggest success to date has been his 1991 independent film *My Own Private Idaho*, romantically teaming teen idols River Phoenix and Keanu Reeves as hustlers, one gay and one heterosexual but flexible. *Idaho* offers a far more realistic look at midnight and round-the-clock cowboys than its shy yet spiteful predecessors. *Film Comment* deemed it "the best American movie of the nineties!"

ABOUT *MIDNIGHT COWBOY*

Andrew Sarris, the *Village Voice*: *Midnight Cowboy* might be a homosexual fantasy in which Joe and Ratso reflect *Camille*—Voight supplying the cowboyish coquettishness for the fate worse than death,

Hoffman the midnight cough for death it-self. . . . Truth in *Midnight Cowboy* is subverted by the devious sentimentality and dishonesty about real feelings that gave birth to the homosexual sensibility.

Richard Schickel, *Time*: A beautiful masculine relationship begins to take shape. . . . It doesn't work. One could accept mutually exploitive faggery; trained in human misuse, one could imagine the two using one another ill in their agony. . . . How are we to accept the delicate suggestion that if we only look closely at the top of the dung heap we will find a dear romantic pansy flowering there?

Howard Thompson, the *New York Times*: Joe is a funny, dim-witted variation on the lonely homosexual dream-hero who wandered disguised through so much drama and literature of the 1950s. . . . He comes to New York to make his fortune as a stud to all the rich ladies who have been deprived of their rights by faggot Eastern gentlemen.

John Simon: The "midnight cowboy" we see on-stage in *The Boys in the Band* is every bit as good-natured, stupid, and blond as Joe, but neither so pure nor heroic—and therefore believable. . . . This film, while ostensibly holding up heterosexual values, exudes a homosexual sensibility, increasing its dishonesty. Revealing . . . is the [casting] of the irritatingly unfeminine Brenda Vaccaro, a cube-shaped creature who comes across as a dykey Kewpie doll.

By 1980 and William Friedkin's *Cruising*, the term "midnight cowboy" had passed in and out of the language. John Schlesinger had long since directed *Sunday, Bloody Sunday*, and Stonewall's Gay Liberation had strengthened into the gay-rights movement. Friedkin, director of the "compassionate" film *The Boys in the Band*, optioned the 1970 novel *Cruising*—about "how we try to destroy in others what we hate and fear in ourselves," according to author Gerald Walker—and completely revamped it. The script did retain the psychotic gay-killer and two other characters. Friedkin changed the setting from Manhattan's baths to its leather bars and sex clubs—again the Big Apple is seen as a sexual symbol of rottenness to the core. *Cruising*, like *Midnight Cowboy*, has a lead character, Steve Burns (Al Pacino), who's apparently straight, though his past is also blurry.

Burns is a cop who goes undercover in Greenwich Village to capture the homophobic killer who may himself be gay. Is Burns gay or "latent?" Is *he* the

killer? The film implies that Burns is the murderer (another actor was used for silhouetted long-shots and the falsetto whisper announcing each sadistic murder). Pacino's bisexual bank robber in *Dog Day Afternoon* (1975) is far more familiar to straight and gay audiences than his crypto-sexual cop. Though open enough to appear seminude and bound in one motel scene, Pacino completely avoided the *Cruising* controversy. Whisked away after every take, he didn't talk with fellow actors or the press.

Cruising was the first gay-themed Hollywood project in some time, and script leaks during filming indicated homophobic elements. Gay activist leaders feared the picture would misrepresent gay lifestyles and encourage antigay violence. *Village Voice* columnist Arthur Bell led the attack. Twenty thousand pamphlets were distributed branding the movie "a rip-off"—*Cruising* used numerous gay locations and extras, including gay centerfolds as nude murder victims.

"This is not a film about how we live," said the literature. "It is a film about why we should be killed." At Bell's urging, committees formed and the production was widely picketed, causing expensive delays and debate over Hollywood's social responsibility. "The *Cruising* problem," wrote Bell, "has united all gay factions for the first time since the [Anita] Bryant campaign. What's different is that this time homosexuals are taking the aggressive role. Instead of 'poor us,' it's 'poor them.' " It was one of the first times a citizens' protest was mounted against a picture before its completion.

Many gays felt that if *Cruising* were really that bad, it would condemn itself. Others believed that the general public wouldn't be able to distinguish

Is he or isn't he?: Al Pacino as a cop who plays gay in Greenwich Village to catch a homophobic murderer in *Cruising* (1980).

Ted (Don Scardino) chats up Steve Burns (Pacino), who may be gay and may be the homophobic murderer.

truth from S&M fiction. Despite Mayor Ed Koch's pro-gay stand, his office refused to withdraw city participation, and Nancy Littlefield, New York City's movie liaison, reportedly hung up on a gay journalist after declaring that "anything that brings in seven million dollars is good for New York."

Ronald Gold of the National Gay Task Force stated, "We always find ourselves having to play civil libertarian to a bunch of bigots who want the right to express their hatred of us." He compared *Cruising* to *The Birth of a Nation*, which glorified Ku Klux Klan members. "Today nobody would dare. We're not asking for censorship. We're asking Hollywood to use the same system of self-censorship that it's used for other minority groups." Arthur Bell asserted, "If the First Amendment applied to me, I'd be willing to give it to others, but we don't have any civil rights in this country."

Friedkin felt that he'd been "smeared". "I told a story once at the New School about trying to have a gay experience and failing, and that story was distorted. My feeling about gay sex is that it's normal and a free choice. I support gay rights, I have gay people working for me, and I've never told anti-gay jokes."

In 1970 Friedkin told the press, *"The Boys in the Band* is not about gay life. It's about human problems. I hope there *are* happy homosexuals. They just don't happen to be in my film." In 1980 he said, "This isn't a film about gay life. It's a murder mystery with an aspect of the gay world as background." *Cruising* carried the disclaimer: "This film is not intended as an indictment of the homosexual world. It is set in one small segment of that world, which is not meant to be representative of the whole."

In the film Captain Edelson (Paul Sorvino) points out that the leather scene is "a world unto itself" and "not in the mainstream of gay life." However, it's likely that without the effective, well-organized anti-*Cruising* campaign, such qualifiers wouldn't have been included. Friedkin said his film was no more about all gays than "*Manhattan* was about all New Yorkers." The difference is that New Yorkers are portrayed as individuals, and there have been hundreds of films about them, very few of which start with self-hate and end in murder.

Whatever its makers' intentions, *Cruising* pleased almost no one. Despite Pacino's performance, straights weren't interested, and most gays who attended found that the "thrills"—jockstraps, rear nudity, simulated fisting, sweaty dancing—didn't compensate for the muddy plot, gratuitous violence, and mean-spiritedness. *Cruising* opened big but declined quickly. Notices were universally terrible, and much of the gay press didn't even review the boycotted film. A *Mandate* reporter asked, "Why give it undue importance? The straight press will do that." But they didn't, and *Cruising*'s only real impact was on Hollywood, which began to tread more carefully with its few gay projects, tending to greenlight only those with a comedic or asexual focus.

Cruising paints a grim portrait not only of its gay characters—who have few or no lines—but also of its sexist, sex-obsessed cops who all hate women and gay men. One officer, who forces a transsexual hooker to fellate him, says of women, "They're all scumbags." Steve Burns uses Nancy (Karen Allen) as little more than relief from his frustration. While working in a gay neighborhood, Steve returns to Nancy for a night of ferocious sex. Angry with himself and her, he warns, "Don't let me lose you."

Burns is seemingly impotent, or requires heavy stimulation. The murderer—whose semen contains no sperm—is likewise sexually frustrated. A sexually explicit film, *Cruising* is really about emotional repression and perversion. After the first stomach-turning mutilation-murder, the villain childishly murmurs, "You made me do it." In fact, he murders out of personally- and societally-nurtured hatred.

13

ROOMIES:

Staircase and Tell Me That You Love Me, Junie Moon

Barbershop duet: Rex Harrison and Richard Burton as longtime roommates Charlie and Harry in *Staircase* (1969).

Staircase. Twentieth Century-Fox, 1969. Director-producer: Stanley Donen. writer: Charles Dyer. Starring: Richard Burton, Rex Harrison, Cathleen Nesbitt, Pat Heywood, Avril Angers, Beatrix Lehmann, Gordon Heath, Shelagh Fraser.

Tell Me That You Love Me, Junie Moon. Paramount, 1970. Director-producer: Otto Preminger; writer: Marjorie Kellogg.
Starring: Liza Minnelli, Ken Howard, Robert Moore, James Coco, Kay Thompson, Fred Williamson, Emily Yancy, Leonard Frey.

It's hard to imagine what interested Stanley Donen (*Charade, Two for the Road*) in *Staircase*, Charles Dyer's self-flagellating play about two pathetic roommates who can't abide each other. (The West End production starred Paul Scofield and Patrick Magee; their Broadway counterparts were Eli Wallach and Milo O'Shea.) Donen decided to make a camp "comedy" of the drama, and to liven it up by casting two straight superstars. Elizabeth Taylor suggested that Burton—as the "wife," the stronger of the pair—move in with Harrison during filming, while she would take up residence with Rachel Roberts, Harrison's then-wife.

Unlike Harrison, Burton wasn't homophobic. When Donen joked that Burton might win Best Actress for his role, the Welsh actor replied, "You must establish your credentials as a man pretty thoroughly before you can afford to risk playing a poof." But he also told *People* magazine, "Perhaps most actors are latent homosexuals and we cover it with drink. I was once a homosexual, but it didn't work."

During shooting in Paris, Burton was asked how he planned to disguise his voice to "make it homosexual." Later he asked Liz Smith, "Are they [the press] even vaguely aware that some of the greatest voices in the theater belong to homosexuals? They frighten me, because they're supposed to be intellectuals. . . . I have never known anyone who took great exception to homosexuals that there wasn't something very wrong with that person."

Harry and Charlie are barbers. Charlie's been arrested for female impersonation in a bar, and as the date of his court hearing approaches, he grows increasingly fearful. Charlie feels superior to Harry because, unlike Harry, with whom he's lived for twenty years, Charlie isn't "poofey." Both men bemoan their sexual fates and curse their bad luck to be stuck together. The closer the hearing gets, the straighter Charlie tries to act, until his illusions finally crumble. Bitterly, the men resign themselves to each other. The pair make *Virginia Woolf*'s George and Martha look like honeymooners; in fact, *Staircase* was called a heterosexual revenge for Edward Albee's *Who's Afraid of Virginia Woolf*?

Dyer's play demonstrates some compassion for its victims by depicting the needless fear in which many gay men are made to live. The play included a *Golden Pond*-type scene in which Charlie has what looks like a heart attack, causing Harry's love to surface (though Charlie isn't aware of it). In the film Charlie brings home a hustler who resembles Edith Sitwell, prompting Harry to uncharacteristically attempt suicide. Rex Harrison said, "When I got the film script, I was totally sickened by what had been done with the story." Before shooting commenced, Harrison asked Burton, "Is it wise what we're doing?" Burton replied, "Listen, love. We're too old, too rich, and too famous to do it. So let's do it."

Donen hired Dudley Moore to compose the score and Ray Charles to sing "Forgive Them for They Know Not What They Do." Another song, "Staircase," is sung by two transvestites. But the symbolic staircase—steps on which the barbers hear life passing them by—was scrapped. The play was "opened up" to include the messy bedridden Mum upstairs, a picnic at the park (with two nude heterosexuals having sex), and visits to a cemetery and an old folks' home. The picture dwells on details like Harry's head-bandages (both a "remedy" and a disguise for his baldness) and the gratuitous gutting of a chicken.

In 1972 Parker Tyler wrote, "This sadomasochistic film, which insults all its viewers, is as securely interred as possible for so recent a film. Even TV won't likely retrieve it."

ABOUT *STAIRCASE*

Rex Reed: Rex Harrison is back and Richard Burton's got him. Rex is a depressing nit with lavender ties and varicose veins. Burton is a yellowing sow's ear with alopecia and a "face like a gibbon's bot-

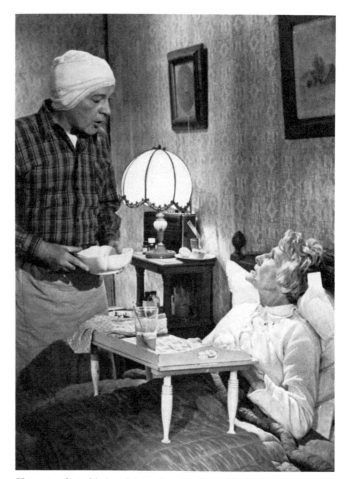

Harry tends to his invalid mother (Cathleen Nesbitt).

tom." The aging homosexuals from Charles Dyer's play have been stripped of their dignity and humanity in this reprehensible movie. Burton and Harrison—biting, bitching, slashing, and whacking away at each other like Mutt and Jeff in drag—are dreadful. When they aren't screaming at each other, there are closeups of urine and excrement in the bed of Cathleen Nesbitt, as Burton's toothless invalid hag of a mother. *Staircase* is a boring, humorless entertainment.

Stanley Kauffmann: *Staircase* is a flabby film that grabs frantically at bits of sordidness to prove it is serious. . . . It falls into the biggest trap for homosexual material: it pleads for pity. . . . The one validity in the film is Burton's Harry; there is no crack or crevice in the entire performance. Contrast it with Harrison's performance of the dapper Charlie. He seems unable to confront the man with honesty or sympathy. Watch Harrison's eyes, which remain dead—there is no emotional connection.

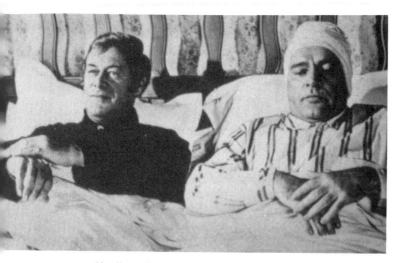

Charlie and Harry in bed.

Tell Me That You Love Me, Junie Moon is an instance of Something for No One. A career lowpoint for its stars, it's also a miasma of misinformation, stereotypes, and ignorance about Warren (Robert Moore), its gay third-wheel. Otto Preminger turned down the movie *M*A*S*H* (which has its share of homophobia) to direct possibly his biggest flop. "It fascinated me—the three characters' courage, the idea that they wouldn't depend on charity or pity." The depressing film was lambasted by the press. One critic asked, "Tell me why you do it, Otto Preminger?" *Junie Moon* sneaked through the Cannes Film Festival, completely overshadowed by his producer-brother Ingo Preminger's antiwar *M*A*S*H*, which won several honors.

Liza Minnelli is Junie Moon, whose arm and face were acid-scarred by a kinky, sadistic boyfriend (shades of Gloria Grahame in *The Big Heat*). Ken Howard is the stuttering, epileptic Arthur. Warren explains, "His diagnosis is as obscure as a crossword in Sanskrit." Redheaded, bearded, and quintessentially fruity, Warren was gay stage director Robert Moore's film debut. He asked Preminger to give him a small role so he could watch a film director at work. Preminger felt Moore was "just right" for Warren and signed him despite his lack of film acting experience. (In 1976 Moore directed Neil Simon's *Murder by Death*, with Truman Capote, James Coco, and Peter Falk in various shades of lavender.)

TV Guide describes *Junie Moon* as "Preminger's bizarre film about three handicapped people who join forces to conquer their disabilities." But what is Warren's major disability? Junie remains physically scarred at film's end; Arthur has died in her arms, after finally eliciting her "I love you." But Warren, the lucky one, has slept with a woman and, it's implied, is "cured," though he's still wheelchair-bound.

Junie rents a house for the outcast trio. As Warren puts it, "Between us, we have one good pair of hands, one good pair of legs, three good livers, three warm hearts, and one superior brain." Arthur gets a job with fishmonger Mario (James Coco), a lifelong bachelor. Though he may be gay, Mario is a bigot; he fires Arthur as soon as a neighbor complains that the employee—prone to epileptic fits on the street—is "a sex pervert."

Warren, who bakes brownies and casseroles, embodies every homosexual cliché in the book. He sprinkles the house with flowery decals, reads po-

Robert & Otto & James & Ken: Preminger directs Moore (left), Coco, and Howard in *Tell Me That You Love Me, Junie Moon* (1970).

Junie Moon (Liza Minnelli) strips in a cemetery at her boyfriend's request; then he disfigures her face with battery acid.

etry, and cheers his roommates by announcing "We represent at least *three* minority groups" and winking at Arthur. The blond snaps, "Don't wink at me—it makes me think you're queer." "So what if he is queer?" asks Junie. "You don't have to wink back!" Arthur—bighearted when it comes to dogs and fish—is intolerant of gays. From time to time, he sneers at Warren or yells, "You sit in your wheelchair like a little throne, giving orders like some queen!"

How did Warren get that way? He was raised by Guiles (Leonard Frey), a gay man who cooked "tuna

Three's company: Friends and roommates Robert Moore, Ken Howard, and Liza Minnelli.

Gay Robert Moore, in a wheelchair, helps heterosexual Howard cope with his coordination and epilepsy.

Gay actor James Coco (Oscar-nominated) as a gay actor comforting pal Marsha Mason in *Only When I Laugh* (1981).

fish flambeau" for his tolerant straight roommates. When one of them impregnates a girl, they toss a coin to determine paternity. But Guiles—pronounced *Giles*—assumes responsibility for the baby's upbringing. How was Warren crippled? During a rabbit-hunting trip when he was seventeen, he made a pass at a boy named Melvin and was "accidentally shot" in the legs.

The three deserve a vacation, so Mario gives them money to go to a swank resort where they impersonate rich people. (The money runs out, but their nerve doesn't.) One of the hotel's staff is Beachboy (Fred Williamson), who puts up with Warren's flirtations and carries him all over the hotel grounds. Meanwhile, Junie and Arthur go fishing, but they quickly toss back their catches, mangled but still alive.

Beachboy carries Warren into a black bar where he introduces him to two women, one a Shakespeare-spouting diva. Warren is entranced and drives with them to the beach, where Solano (Emily Yancy) seduces him. Warren stops calling Beachboy "a god," though he accidentally calls him Guiles.

When it's time to return home, the trio is presented with a bill. Beachboy saves the day, again; he tears it up. In the car Warren desperately tries to persuade Art that he did sleep with a woman. Back home, Arthur dies, and Junie and Warren attend the funeral before giving Arthur's stray dog to Mario—"You're gonna like me if it takes a lifetime," he tells it.

The movie purports to probe beneath the surface but is coy and disingenuous about the trio's sexuality. Until the magically transformed Warren breaks the spell, all three seem completely asexual, though Junie and Arthur feel obliged to stage the beginnings of a romance. *Tell Me That You Love Me, Junie Moon* shamefully patronizes its main characters. It wrings dry tears and hollow laughs out of their plight, and it emasculates Warren, particularly after his sexual conversion.

ABOUT *TELL ME THAT YOU LOVE ME, JUNIE MOON*

Rex Reed: *Tell Me That You Love Me, Junie Moon* is one of the most demented movies ever. It concerns a ménage à trois between an epileptic, a crippled homosexual with a yen for black bellhops, and a girl whose face has been burned with acid. . . . Instead of making it believable or at all palatable in the sensitive direction of, say, a Carson McCullers tale of survival among the misfits, Preminger accents all the bizarre aspects of Kellogg's novel and none of the poetic ones. The result is that *Junie Moon* is just plain repulsive.

Jeff Olson, *Lambda Times* (1981): Preminger, he of the trendsetting films of the fifties and sixties, conceived the 1970 clinker . . . which pairs two genuine misfits with a gay paraplegic. You get the feeling that Warren could walk if he really wanted to—men carry him around a lot. But maybe Preminger and Kellogg figured audiences might not think the character handicapped enough if he were only gay.

In another film dealing with a gay roomie situation, *Silkwood* (1983), Cher played a lesbian whose roommates don't try to hide or "reform" her. Her Dolly Pelliker is a natural, if unkempt, gay woman who rooms with Karen Silkwood (Meryl Streep) and Karen's boyfriend Drew (Kurt Russell). Director Mike Nichols told Cher, "This is a wonderful part. She's a lesbian, but she's a wonderful lesbian." She replied, "Okay, fine. I don't care." *People* magazine's cover read "Cher: She's gay and gritty in *Silkwood*, but off-screen she still loves glamour, glitz, and guys." Despite such inane coverage, Cher retained her dignity and integrity.

Cher told *Cosmopolitan*, "I didn't want to play Dolly with a pack of Marlboros rolled up in my T-shirt sleeve, but I was all set to cut my hair. . . . Mike said, 'Let's *not* make a statement about Dolly with a butch cut—let's have you *work* to get everything out without externals.' " The result is refreshingly unsensational. Cher noted, "I don't think Dolly's gayness is the thing you remember most about her." Cher's mom had reservations, but after viewing the film she said, "Cher, you were wonderful. I was so nervous—I thought you were going to be this dyke!" Cher told *Playgirl*, "I bought my son a doll once. He really loved it, but my daughter got a little angry with me. I said, 'Chas, he wants a doll, what difference does it make?' "

Unlike most gay film characters, Dolly was given a lover—a "femme" named Angela (Diana Scarwid). The women's relationship is casual, amusing (at no one's expense), *and* sexual. Angela, then Drew, depart, leaving Dolly and Karen alone together. At one point Karen blows up, saying nobody else would "put up" with Dolly, that others think she's crazy to do so. But the friendship remains strong. The *Advocate* said, "When Cher confesses her love for Streep, the rebuff is nervous but lacking in malice. When Cher collapses into Streep's lap on a porch swing, their pietà-like embrace resembles big sister and kid sister, weathering emotional storms in tandem."

Silkwood presented the year's best gay woman. It might have been an even richer portrait had Dolly been less the plain-jane lesbian we've become acquainted with from less well-intentioned movies.

One wears makeup, the other doesn't: Meryl Streep comforts her lesbian roommate Dolly (Oscar-nominated Cher) in *Silkwood* (1983).

14

MIX-MATCHED:

The Music Lovers and Sunday, Bloody Sunday

The Music Lovers (1970): Peter Tchaikovsky (Richard Chamberlain, left) and Count Chiluvsky (Christopher Gable, right).

The Music Lovers. United Artists, 1970.
Director-producer: Ken Russell; writer: Melvyn Bragg.
Starring: Richard Chamberlain, Glenda Jackson, Max Adrian, Christopher Gable, Izabelle Telezynska, Kenneth Colley, Sabina Maydelle.

Sunday, Bloody Sunday. United Artists, 1971. Director: John Schlesinger; writer: Penelope Gilliatt; producer: Joseph Janni.
Starring: Glenda Jackson, Peter Finch, Murray Head, Peggy Ashcroft, Tony Britton, Maurice Denham, Bessie Love, Vivian Pickles.

Ken Russell followed his critical and commercial hit *Women in Love* with the poorly received *The Music Lovers.* The Tchaikovsky biography is, as Glenda Jackson said, "about a homosexual married to a nymphomaniac." Costar Richard Chamberlain had moved from American television to the English stage and films; in *Lady Caroline Lamb* (1972) he played the bisexual Lord Byron. *The Music Lovers,* which refers to the parasites around the composer, was based on the 1937 book *Beloved Friend* by Catherine Drinker Bowen and Barbara von Meck. Russell, like his Hollywood counterparts, took historical liberties and was chastised for doing so. He was also criticized because he didn't disguise the composer's sexuality—neither, particularly, did Tchaikovsky, although he was guilt-ridden in later life, after taking to Russian Orthodoxy.

Pyotr Ilich Tchaikovsky died at fifty-three, apparently of cholera. But according to Jim Kepner of the National Gay Archives, "There is new evidence that his family convinced Tchaikovsky to take poison which would simulate the symptoms of cholera because of a high-level scandal that was about to break over his homosexuality, which would have had national repercussions."

One of Russell's and screenwriter Melvyn Bragg's strangest liberties was turning Pyotr's gay brother Modeste (Kenneth Colley) into a heterosexual. Modeste, like nearly all the nonmusical characters, is a grotesque leech, as is Count Chiluvsky (Christopher Gable), a flamboyant homosexual who lusts after Pyotr. All the composer's relationships are problematic. He loves his sister Sasha (Sabrina Maydelle) but also fears intimacy with her; some critics resurrected the Freudian theory of incest-fear as a "cause" for homosexuality (though critics never worry about or wonder what causes heterosexuality). Visits to Tchaikovsky's mother are less than pleasant, for she's often immersed in a scalding bath, her face and body festering with sores. Pyotr, whose mother died of cholera, is shown drinking unboiled water at the height of a cholera epidemic.

Kenneth Colley (left) as Peter's also gay brother
Modeste Tchaikovsky, and Christopher Gable as
Peter's lover Count Chiluvsky.

The film, originally titled *Tchaikovsky*, focuses on
Pyotr's relationship with his wife Nina (Jackson),
although the marriage lasted only eleven weeks.
Nina's rampant nymphomania is the illogical result
of early prostitution, and she dies in an insane
asylum. Nina enjoys stripping and flinging herself
at her horrified husband. In a rattling railway car,
under harsh blue light, she rolls on the floor naked
and cackles. (John Simon wrote, "Miss Jackson's
physical uglinesses from face to feet make for some
of the most hateful viewing in all my filmgoing
experience.")

Nina's mad scene in the asylum recalls Jackson's
earlier *Marat/Sade*. In front of her visiting mother
(Maureen Pryor), Nina allows herself to be groped
by madmen, in revenge for being forced into prostitution by the woman. Jackson's popularity with
most critics didn't save the macabre picture from
poor reviews, and the gay aspect didn't help either.
Simon, who bemoaned the fact that "although
Tchaikovsky's homosexuality is the center of the
movie, the problem is denied an iota of serious
examination," saved his damnation for the Oscar-
winning "actress of some talent whose persona,
however, is made up of contempt and even hatred

for the audience. . . . She allows the camera to pho-
tograph her from the most prying angles, including
one shot up her anus and vagina."

Pyotr's relationships with men are glossed over.
He's never shown in a romantic or loving affair,
although the real Tchaikovsky discussed his romances in his lengthy letters to Modeste (one of
Pyotr's longest love relationships was with poet
Alexi Apukhtin). The filmmakers also combined
two of the composer's associates into one character
named Rubinstein (Max Adrian), and inflated the
role of Mme. von Meck (Izabelle Telezynska), a
patron Tchaikovsky never actually met. She lascivi-
ously bites into a peach that Pyotr has left behind. In
another scene she sneaks into his room while he
sleeps, lies beside him, and has what appears to be a
static orgasm.

The most striking of numerous symbolic images
is the *1812 Overture* fantasy, wherein the audience
of "music lovers" is blown to smithereens by a
phallic cannon. It's the ultimate revenge by a
hounded, sensitive artist. *The Music Lovers* did little
for the film career of Richard Chamberlain, who
found small-screen stardom in varied heterosexual
parts. His best-remembered movie role is as Julie

Christie's wife-beater husband in *Petulia* (1968). The character was *read* as gay by many straight and gay viewers, on little more "evidence" than his wedding night impotence.

ABOUT *THE MUSIC LOVERS*

Jack Fisher, *Film Journal:* A film about sex, in which is reviewed every kind of sexuality except "normal" heterosexuality and perhaps zoophilia: several varieties of homosexuality, at least two varieties of inverted heterosexuality, incest, sadomasochism, voyeurism, and even displaced necrophilia. If all the sex were removed, what would remain would be a fifteen-minute entertainment starring Max Adrian. . . . The film's major statement is Tchaikovsky's homosexuality—the crippling malaise in the life of a talented man—and the vulnerability it creates in him to the people around him. . . . The inhibitions of homosexuality become a metaphor of [sic] the dark forces which strain relationships between men and women.

Gold (U.K.): Heaven help us past Ken Russell's queer intentions. The men have nice white teeth to the ladies' stained ones, but Russell suggests that Tchaikovsky (Dick and Glenda share *no* chemistry) may have hied his cast-off wife into bedlam. In fact, she wasn't confined until years after his death. . . . Many composers have been gay, but Russell's film bio yields neither insight nor information about this one. . . . Tchaikovsky's mother dies, in the film, when he's a child, not a teen, and the composer's life ends in suicide! So much for facts. Russell, who's gaga about death and lunacy . . . presents his nightmares and fetid visions as history. Bad show.

"Sometimes nothing has to be better than anything," says Alex Greville (Glenda Jackson) in *Sunday, Bloody Sunday.* She refers to the noncommitment of her bisexual lover Bob Elkin (Murray Head), whom she shares with Dr. Daniel Hirsch (Peter Finch). One of the best films of the seventies, *Sunday, Bloody Sunday* explores homosexual and heterosexual relationships via a complex but natural triangle. Ironically, it was made possible by John Schlesinger's *Midnight Cowboy.* The director explained *Sunday, Bloody Sunday* was a kind of present. "*Midnight Cowboy* was a huge success, and UA said, 'What do you want to do next?' and I said *Sunday, Bloody Sunday.* I was being offered a lot of big pictures, none of which attracted me as much. I thought, this is the moment. Cash in on the success

Dr. Kildare: In 1990, actor Richard Chamberlain reportedly "came out" in France.

to make something that we know may be a piece of uncommercial chamber music."

Early on, Finch and Head exchange one of the first gay kisses in a major movie. Predictably, the kiss offended many, and some walked out. But the kiss also attracted gay men who otherwise might not have seen the film and Finch's upstanding portrayal. His performance is doubly rich for the insights afforded into a warm, contemporary Jewish homosexual. Even more than Zack in *Making Love,* Daniel is a healer and a positive force in the lives he touches.

On the other hand, Bob is almost a *type,* a mechanism through which are examined two more interesting but disparate lives. Bob is a sculptor whose most notable trait, besides his bisexuality, is that he owns a toucan. In addition to kissing in greeting, Bob and Daniel exchange affection in and out of bed, although the screen nudity is exclusively female. John Simon wondered, "Is it in her contract that every film [Jackson] appears in must also feature that wretched bosom of hers? At least Schlesinger gives it short shrift."

The men ponder Bob's forthcoming visit to the United States. Bob says, "I don't know what to do. Should I go? What do you think?" Daniel says, "I told you, you've got to decide. I can see it might solve a lot of problems for you if you went." Emotionally immature, Bob quickly tires of things and people and minimizes responsibility. The film intimates that Bob will remain in America. An anonymous critic noted, "The pro-gay, pro-straight picture is nonetheless biased against its *bi* protagonist, whose sexual openness is considered indecisive and egotistic."

For the most part, the two older sides of the triangle are willing to share the third. Daniel is not only resigned to the situation but concerned that Bob treat Alex well. Alex protests against the situation and Bob's pending journey. When Daniel asks Bob if he's in love with Alex, he replies, "I don't think so, but I can't be sure." Bob also puzzles over Daniel's familial relationships: "You take a lot of trouble about your family, don't you?" In a notable scene Daniel attends a nephew's Bar Mitzvah and reception and recalls his own. The plot's cross-cuttings parallel the males' fears. The young man fears failure and embarrassment, and the doctor must confront—and verbally evade—solicitous female relatives who admonish his being "single." Both men fear their loved ones' disapproval.

As a member of two minorities, Daniel walks a tightrope, but successfully. Tolerant of others, he expects his differences to be accepted, and he lives and works in several different worlds. Unlike Bob or Alex, his interests extend beyond himself, and he derives pleasure from most of his family. Daniel Hirsch is a movie first. As Pauline Kael stated, he's not "fey or pathetic or grotesque. He is one of the most simply and completely created characters in recent films." Reviewing the film (written by fellow movie critic Penelope Gilliatt), Kael added, "Finch wears a *yarmulke* well, but he never overdoes being Jewish, and he doesn't overdo being homosexual."

Sunday, Bloody Sunday evoked the usual critical homophobia—though to a lesser extent than most gay-themed movies—as well as subtle and not-so-subtle anti-Semitism. Finch biographer Elaine Dundy said, "He munches chocolate cookies and *marrons glacés* like a Jew. He loses his temper with the answering service like a Jew . . . and he shrugs like a Jew; that racial, self-incriminating shrug that says, 'It's terrible—but it's funny, too.'" During preproduction, openly gay Jewish director Schlesinger was asked whether Daniel "need, on top of everything else, be Orthodox Jewish, too?" The

director felt dual-minority status would heighten Daniel's conflict and indicate the incompatibility of modern homosexuality and fundamentalist religiosity.

The film follows its protagonists through ten days, presenting slices of life that never pall. Some of Alex's familiars are a bit eccentric, but these nonglamorized intellectuals seem realistic, as does the two men's cozy relationship. Murray Head said of the kiss—shot several times, from different angles—"What really disturbed the crew about it was that it could happen with such *ease!*" He added, "The older generation, the *war* generation—and most crews are older—were very nervous, especially when neither Peter nor I made a big deal of it. They asked me, finally, if I hadn't been disgusted. I was glad to disappoint them." At one point a cameraman halted shooting and asked Schlesinger, "Is this really necessary?" The director snapped, "Yes, of course it is!"

Concurrent with *Sunday, Bloody Sunday*, Head, who performed the 1985 hit song "One Night in Bangkok," appeared on the stage in *Jesus Christ Superstar*. But for eighteen months after the film, Head didn't work. John Hurt, who was offered gay parts for a year after playing Quentin Crisp in *The Naked Civil Servant*, called the Finch-Head kiss "the kiss of death" and noted that Finch didn't do another film for eight months after *Sunday, Bloody Sunday*. However, Finch—overlooked by Hollywood until his posthumous *Network* Oscar in 1977— often took a year or more off between projects.

The London-born Finch (who was raised in Australia) was warned not to accept *Sunday, Bloody Sunday*, which starred Ian Bannen until he contracted viral pneumonia a month into shooting. Why did Finch replace him? He told this author in 1975, "I have a saying I live by: *Change!*" Finch, who entered a Buddhist monastery at age nine, remained a lifelong Buddhist. "I try not to be judgmental—Buddhism advocates tolerance and social progress." A "self-confessed heterosexual," Finch won another British Academy Award for his second gay role—he also received a Hollywood Academy Award nomination, a first for an actor in a gay part.

Finch said, "A man who's experienced only one sexuality is sexually incomplete. Yet most of us restrict ourselves, out of habit, fear, or dogma. *Why do we fear extending our horizons?* And I'm no exception. But I try, particularly in my work, to remedy that." Of *Sunday, Bloody Sunday*, he said, "Pictures about a minority are significant over the long run only if they're lovemaking—that is, if they

Bi ways: Gay Peter Finch loves bisexual Murray Head, and so does Glenda Jackson in *Sunday, Bloody Sunday* (1971).

Peter Finch as Dr. Daniel Hirsch, a Jewish gay man.

Head refuses to commit to either lover, and in the end leaves both for a career in America.

Peter Finch in *The Trials of Oscar Wilde* (1960).

help open an audience's heart, even if just for a few seconds."

The actor felt that Hirsch "is a strong man, with or without Bob. But he's a romantic. He wants that lasting, loving, perfect relationship." In the ending soliloquy, spoken to the camera, Hirsch was to have said, "All my life I've been looking for someone courageous and resourceful, not like myself, and he's not it." Finch spoke the lines but omitted "not like myself."

After listening to an Italian language-lesson

record, Hirsch states his feelings for the departed Bob (they were to have traveled in Italy). "They say he'd never have made me happy, and I say, I am happy, apart from missing him." The two met in Daniel's office when Bob had a cough. Daniel's previous relationships were briefer (he encounters one ex while driving through Piccadilly at night). Significantly, it's Alex, not Daniel, who has an outside affair during the relationship with Bob. Said Finch, "Daniel is a modern, moral man. He isn't delighted about his lover's other partnership, but he has standards which he sticks to. And he doesn't look down on others who can't keep to the same standards."

In 1985 Schlesinger recalled, "*Sunday, Bloody Sunday* was universally accepted in England, and people finally got behind it [in America] after the press caught on and gave it such a positive reception. . . . The film received four Academy Award nominations, and was a huge success at the Venice Film Festival, where Visconti dropped his mantle all over it. Even my mother admitted, 'It's your best film, dear.' The film was—is—very close to my heart."

ABOUT *SUNDAY, BLOODY SUNDAY*

Ivan Butler, *Cinema in Britain* (1973): It is difficult to work up feeling for or involvement with the three abnormal, egotistical people (a homosexual Jewish doctor, a divorced woman business consultant, both sharing the same young hetero-homo-lover) whose tortuous web is put before us. The young man escapes, and one can't blame him—though he did quite well while it lasted. The deep, unsentimental pity of *Midnight Cowboy* is missing, perhaps because of the worthlessness of two sides of the triangle. As the third side Peter Finch arouses, by his restrained and thoughtful playing, a certain sympathy.

CalArts: The theme is communication, sexual and otherwise, symbolized by a phone exchange: Finch and Jackson share the same stud—and answering—service. . . . The frailty, complexity, and sheer luck of relationships is symbolized by the phone wires linking the busy trio's lives. Finch is far the most sympathetic, though too mature for vacuum-headed Murray. He steals the show with an Oscarific performance, the worthiest screen homosexual to date—a credit to his, uh, race.

15

LITTLE MEN:

The Boys in the Band

The Boys in the Band (1970): This straightforward ad for the film was banned in most newspapers.

The Boys in the Band. National General, 1970. Director: William Friedkin; writer-producer: Mart Crowley. Starring: Kenneth Nelson, Leonard Frey, Laurence Luckinbill, Cliff Gorman, Peter White, Frederick Combs, Keith Prentice, Reuben Greene, Robert La Tourneaux.

In 1982 *American Film* stated, "Now that *The Boys in the Band*—the bugaboo of Gay Lib—has faded into the past, it's become the one film about which virtually everyone agrees; those who might have condemned it earlier for its demeaning picture of gay life now see it as an important historical piece."

George Cukor offered this author his own estimation: "It reminded me of Louisa May Alcott. You know, after the success of our *Little Women*, the studio contacted me about doing a masculine version, with similar settings and relationships. I told them Miss Alcott had already written *Little Men*. I doubt if their story department ever read it, for I heard nothing more about the matter. Then in the early seventies came *The Boys in the Band*. I saw it, and for some reason it reminded me of RKO's unusual proposition."

The Boys in the Band, the most widely discussed gay film until *Making Love*, has been praised and execrated. Its band of stereotypical characters has been used both as an argument for gay rights and a "confirmation" of homosexuality-as-affliction. Michael (Kenneth Nelson), the dominant character, is infinitely more butch than the flaming Emory (Cliff Gorman) but is the least happy being gay. After a self-pitying wallow, he rushes to midnight Mass. The *Catholic Film Newsletter* proclaimed Michael's variance from church morality the cause of his misery; the film was seen not as a reason to end bigotry but as an excuse to perpetuate it. The newsletter quoted *Boys*'s most famous line: "You show me a happy homosexual, and I'll show you a gay corpse." In 1974 *Blueboy* said, "You show me someone who's happy being traduced and discriminated against, and I'll show you a masochist."

As most over-thirty moviegoers know, *Boys* involves a birthday party for Harold (Leonard Frey) that turns into a miasma of gay doubts and anguish, stirred by "ex-homosexual" Alan (Peter White). But Michael's raving is somewhat offset by the attitude of his calmer pal Donald (Frederick Combs); Emory and Harold are balanced by happy-but-bickering Hank (Laurence Luckinbill) and Larry (Keith Prentice). The revel also includes Bernard (Reuben Greene as a "normal" gay black) and Cowboy (Robert La Tourneaux), a stud-for-hire.

The boys: (left to right) Laurence Luckinbill, Frederick Combs, Cliff Gorman, Robert LaTourneaux, Keith Prentice, Kenneth Nelson, Leonard Frey, Peter White, and Reuben Greene.

Best friends Frederick Combs and Kenneth Nelson.

Reviewers dwelt upon the stereotypes, warming to the queenish humor (which Pauline Kael felt there wasn't enough of) while condemning the queens. But for their time, Mart Crowley's play and film were revolutionary. They proffered an ounce of sympathy to their protagonists, none of whom die in the end. Rex Reed wrote, "The only way they 'pay' is to know who they are. Then they go to bed with a hangover and start over again the next day. Like life."

From Mae West's *The Drag* (1927) to Laurence Olivier in *The Green Bay Tree* (1933) and beyond, Broadway was not broad-minded about gays. Edward Bourdet's 1926 play *The Captive*, with Basil Rathbone, prompted Mayor Jimmy Walker to demand legislation banning onstage depiction of homosexuality in New York State (lasting until 1967). The law was sometimes just a scare tactic; *The Children's Hour* merely caused a scandal, as did *The Immoralist*, in which Louis Jourdan killed himself after falling in love with James Dean instead of Geraldine Page. But Mayor Fiorello LaGuardia (1934–45) personally shut down *Trio*, in which Richard Widmark tried to pry his girlfriend from a lesbian.

Boys made gay-themed plays more acceptable and proved they could be very profitable. Mart Crowley, a thirty-two-year-old Mississippian, "wrote it for my own fulfillment after years of failure. . . . There's a little of me in all the characters." *Boys* lent itself so well to the camera that, except for close-ups, a few updated lines, and the opening montage (the cele-brants heading for the party), the movie is virtually a filmed stage play (with the original cast).

Crowley worried that *Boys* wouldn't be funny. Director Robert Moore (*. . . Junie Moon*) said, "They've been laughing at faggots since Aristophanes—they're not gonna stop now." Initial audiences were mostly gay, and during the first months of its long run, *Boys* was the hottest ticket in town. Nureyev tried to get a ticket but couldn't, so he sat on a guest's lap. Kirk Douglas, who later bought the film rights to *One Flew Over the Cuckoo's Nest*, tried to buy the rights to *Boys*, and producer Ray Stark asked Crowley to write a film with gay characters for Barbra Streisand. Several studios showed interest, but Crowley declared, "If this is made as a movie, it will be made my way, written by me, with me as producer, and filmed in New York." So it was. He added, "If anybody's gonna screw it up, it's gonna be *me*."

In 1982 the following critics were asked about *Boys*:

Robin Wood said in British *Photoplay*: "I've only seen it once, when it came out. I was still married. I remember going to it with my wife and saying to her afterwards, 'Look what you saved me from.' [The British author-critic came out in the seventies.] That was how I think most people took it at the time, a film about how inherently miserable most homosexual lives are. But it was valuable to have *any* recognition of gay existence, even a negative one—anything is better than silence."

Doug Edwards wrote in *Silver Screen*: "Probably the most radical positive experience I had in film was *Boys*. There was a diversity of gay people shown, and although it had the trappings of semi-tragedy, it gave a sense of various kinds of homosexual identities—you could be flamboyant à la Emory or you could be a straight Ivy League jock or a suited businessman. That I found very reassuring."

Stuart Byron said in the *Village Voice*: "It was a transition piece. It's no accident that it became *the* hottest show six months or a year before Stonewall. Then when Gay Lib used it as this icon of stereotypical pre-Stonewall homosexuality, I was baffled. . . . I'm old enough to know that people in *Boys* existed. People who are twenty or twenty-five see it and say these people are a figment of an oppressed imagination! Media visibility of gays certainly had its effect on gay consciousness. If they're onstage for all the world to see, maybe it's less threatening."

Younger generations who view *Boys* today reject the melodrama while relishing lines such as "Give me librium or give me meth" and Emory's alliterative nicknames, e.g., Connie Casserole, Polly Paranoia, Gilda Guilt, and Harriet Hypocrite. Others pick up on camp references, as when Emory huffs, "What have you got against Maria [Montez]—she was a good woman." Some lines are less amusing—Emory dejectedly refers to his sexual nature as "my funny secret."

One of *Boys*'s major flaws is the contrived "truth game," an overwrought excuse for masochism and heterosexual flaunting. After Alan tells his wife (via a long-distance call) that he loves her, he seems the only happy nonmember of the group. The most "modern" characters are Hank and Larry, two "normal"-acting men who love each other and want to stay together. Their problem is Larry's polygamous nature, common to many straight and gay males. For the relationship's sake, Larry agrees to attempt fidelity. But in 1970 critics were especially cool toward Larry and Hank (who has a wife and offspring in his background). The media latched on to the "twisted" humor more than the movie's key line: "If we could just not hate ourselves so much," an all-in-the-family plea. *Boys* was one of the first pictures to exclude heterosexual characters and focus on a gay community.

One British film director said, "I liked *and* dis-liked *Boys* when I first saw it. I thought it very clever in parts, except for the generic public taking it as literal truth. . . . It's had more impact on gay audiences. Straights have forgotten it—it wasn't the first or last picture to misrepresent us. . . . I've seen it twice since, and it does have some points, however inept. It's fun entertainment, but I wouldn't care to see it with straights again."

Over the years the men behind *Boys* have fared better than the men in *Boys*. Friedkin went on to *The French Connection* and *The Exorcist*, while Crowley (who had a small role in *Nijinsky*) became television producer of his friend Robert Wagner's series "Hart to Hart." The actors' careers were allegedly stifled by "the curse of *The Boys in the Band*," although Laurence Luckinbill married Lucie Arnaz and has enjoyed continuing popularity on stage and screen, while Cliff Gorman followed his portrayal of Emory with a nellie murder victim in George Cukor's casbah flop *Justine*. Leonard Frey did fey cameos in *Junie Moon* and *The Magic Christian*; he also got an Oscar nomination as a straight in *Fiddler on the Roof* and later costarred in two short-lived television series (one starred an orangutan). Frey and Robert La Tourneaux have died of AIDS.

Frederick Combs, best remembered for the film's shower scene, recalled appearing in *Boys* on the London stage, in a 1981 *In Touch* interview. Princess Margaret attended the play with husband Lord Snowden. Combs said, "A week later we heard from this friend of the royal family that they loved the play. They were spending the weekend at a country estate, and laughed and joked and said [the line] 'Who do you have to fuck to get a drink around here?'

"The princess was serving tea, and everybody was uptight. Finally the princess says, 'You know, we saw this most amusing play about homosexuals. It's jolly good, but there was this most amusing line I don't quite understand. What is this rimming of a snowman?' Well, all you could hear was a dead silence and then teacups rattling. A week later, I was at a party with this terribly square, boring hostess. I mentioned that the princess asked, 'What is this rimming of a snowman?' There was no clue that this woman had any sense of humor, but she said, 'Oh, really, how extraordinary—after all, she *married* Lord Snowman!' I loved her from that moment on." (Combs died of AIDS in September 1992.)

ABOUT *THE BOYS IN THE BAND*

Pauline Kael: In the theatre, *Boys* was enlivened by actors carrying on onstage as actors often do backstage. . . . It was like *The Women*, with a bomber-

The Boys in the Sand (1971): The X-rated feature inspired by *Band* starred Cal Culver and Danny Di Ciocchio and had a 1984 sequel.

crew cast: a Catholic, a Jew, a Negro, one butch, one nellie, a hustler . . . and in place of the possible homosexual, a possible heterosexual, who acted like great-lady Norma Shearer herself. They didn't want to be the way they were, the characters kept telling us. The gist was "we homosexuals may talk like bitches and give you a laugh by degrading ourselves, but we have feelings, too."

On screen, *Boys* is full of exposition and such venerable devices as the host taking a swig of gin and turning from Jekyll to Hyde. . . .It's all so solemn—like Joan Crawford when she's thinking. . . . William Friedkin forces our attention to the pity-of-it-all with guilt-ridden pauses and long see-the-suffering-in-the-face close-ups.

Hollis Alpert, *Saturday Review*: Harold is "a thirty-two-year-old, ugly, pock-marked Jew fairy." It is rather a pity he doesn't arrive earlier in the film, because, when he does, his impersonator, Leonard Frey, takes malevolent charge of the proceedings. In his high, whining, vaguely fatigued voice he explains: "And if I smoke a little grass before I can get up the nerve to show this face to the world, it's nobody's business but my own." Mr. Frey is priceless. He all but carries the film on his sagging shoulders.

So much frankness, nudity, obscenity, and what was once known as pornography has engulfed us in the two years since the play was presented that the

Boom! (1968): Gay Noel Coward as the gay Witch of Capri visits his friend Elizabeth Taylor on her private island.

105

tears Michael sheds over the awfulness of his love and sex life have a crocodilian tinge. In fact, the attitude of the film toward its characters—that they are more to be pitied than censured—seems rather unnecessary during these ultra-liberated days.

The following films also treat gay men and boys":

• Written and directed by Mervyn Nelson, *Some of My Best Friends Are. . .* came out a year after *Boys*. Like *Boys*, it explores the ailing psyches of a group of gay men over the course of one evening—not in an apartment but a Mafia-owned gay club, the Blue Jay, operated by straights. Because of *Friends*'s bigger cast, the characters are less defined, and the feminine ones virtually steal the show. They include Lita, a spiteful fag hag (Rue McLanahan of "The Golden Girls"), Sadie, a jazz-singing Jewish earth mama (Sylvia Syms), and a wisecracking hatchecker named Mildred Pierce (Fanny Flagg). Also in the film are the late Candy Darling as a drag queen beaten up by a homophobic gay hustler (Gary Sandy of "WKRP") and Cheri/Phil (Nick DeNoia), hoisted above his cohorts with wings and a wand to the tune of "We Believe in Fairies!" (DeNoia was a cofounder of Chippendale's, the male-strip-club chain whose gay appeal—like *Playgirl*'s—is counterpointed by its anti-gay attitude.)

By placing its characters in a straight-run club, the gay ghettoization is emphasized. One patron is locked in the Blue Jay overnight. "He'll still be there in the morning," says the straight manager. "Where else has a faggot got to go?" *Friends* features every cliché, from the horrified mother of a gay son to the guy in makeup, the would-be heterosexual, the drag, the fashion photographer, and the one-line bitch—a crew of little men and oddfellows.

• "Audrey Hepburn—I always wanted to have a neck like Audrey Hepburn." The line is spoken by James Coco as Neil Simon's Jimmy Perino in 1981's *Only When I Laugh* (*It Hurts Only When I Laugh* in Britain). More fat than fem, Perino gets the evil eye from a Latino delivery boy (cut from television showings). He tells his best friends—both female— "Next to sex, dishing with the girls is the best thing I know." Of course, Jimmy has no sexual life or history, and no raison d'être. Asked what three people he'd rather have been, he readily confesses, "Audrey Hepburn, Laurence Olivier, and anybody else but me." He tells his friends, "The rest of the world can go to hell," so long as the threesome can still commiserate. Perino's aimlessness finally

prompts Georgia (Marsha Mason) to stop drinking and trade her unreal friends for her rather butch daughter Polly (Kristy McNichol).

• In Blake Edwards's *10* (1979), George Webber (Dudley Moore) tells his homophobic shrink that he'd undergo "a life of faggotry" if he could just be young and virile again. George and his gay musical collaborator are in the same boat, but George looks down on the tall, distinguished Hugh (Robert Webber). Both try to recapture their youth via younger lovers. Hugh loses his to infidelity, George is impotent or dissatisfied until he returns to Sam (Julie Andrews). Unlike George, Hugh doesn't get to discover anything about himself. He develops no stable relationship and is left in solitary limbo. Monogamy, held up as the ideal for straights and gays, is implied "for straights only." Still, Hugh gets in his licks: he tells the meddling hypocritical George that if *he* were George's shrink, George would be well-adjusted and gay!

Edwards's 1981 *S.O.B.* is less clear about sexual assignments. Dr. Irving Finegarten (Robert Preston) has "a wickedly witty tongue and a magic hypodermic"—apparently a gay quack. But Preston, who "jumped" at the chance to play the lavender-smocked doctor, denied that Finegarten is gay. *S.O.B.*'s other "nongay" character is Stuart Margolin's simpering, obnoxious personal assistant to Julie Andrews. Both men—one likable, one not— dress and behave stereotypically, so that despite the artists' intentions, the characters are read as gay by straight and gay audiences.

• The X-rated but not-quite-pornographic *Flesh* (not *Flash*, said the court-mandated ads) *Gordon* (1974) features a tolerant straight aided by a gay good-guy. Gordon returns the favor by letting the gay fellate him—it's seen indirectly, Gordon wearing nothing but an unecstatic smile. 1980's costlier *Flash Gordon* starred Sam J. Jones, who rose to fame in a 1975 *Playgirl* centerfold as "rich playboy" Andrew Cooper III. (Jones also played Bo Derek's bridegroom in *10*.)

• *Zorro the Gay Blade* (1982) is about a dull nongay blade (George Hamilton) who calls in his swishy brother (also Hamilton) for comic relief. Co-producer Hamilton considered dropping "gay" from the title, for fear it would alienate straights; it didn't. He explained, "Zorro's twin isn't gay. He's a fop—a dandy, a gentleman—like Leslie Howard in *The Scarlet Pimpernel*." The "nongay" Bunny Wigglesworth coos, "You do it with such manliness; I never

10 (1979): Robert Webber as Hugh, a gay composer who unlike his heterosexual associate remains romantically unfulfilled.

S.O.B. (1981): Robert Preston as lavender-smocked Dr. Irving Finegarten, a wit with a wicked needle.

Cats: Eric Idle and Michael Palin take paws during a break in filming *Monty Python's The Meaning of Life* (1983).

tire of watching"—the subject is walking "like a man."

Again, the subject is gender-bending-over-backwards in *Boom!* (1968), based on Tennessee Williams's play *The Milk Train Doesn't Stop Here Anymore.* Noël Coward played the Witch of Capri, written as a female role; some critics felt this was the closeted celebrity's personal "statement." The Witch provides exposition and temporary comic relief.

Boom! went bust and was the last Williams story on the big screen, except for Sidney Lumet's 1970 *Last of the Mobile Hot-Shots,* based on Williams's *The Seven Descents of Myrtle.*" Looking back, *Stallion* asked, "Who can blame Tennessee for his self-hatred? If he'd been happy, he wouldn't have felt the need to write every day, and the theater would have been much poorer." The magazine didn't note that more sophisticated theatergoers often discount stereotypes that moviegoers typically take to heart.

Zorro, the Gay Blade (1981): George Hamilton in the dual-ing roles of a hero and (here) his swishter brother Ramon.

107

16

TRANSSEXUALS:

Myra Breckinridge and Co.

Myra Breckinridge. Twentieth Century-Fox, 1970.
Director: Michael Sarne; writers: Sarne and David Giler; producers: Robert Fryer and Gore Vidal.
Starring: Mae West, John Huston, Raquel Welch, Rex Reed, Farrah Fawcett, Roger Herren, John Carradine, Andy Devine, Tom Selleck.

Myra Breckinridge's transsexual theme and its star-power ensured a glaring spotlight from the beginning. Its on-set feuds were the most publicized in ages: Welch versus West, Huston versus Reed, Reed versus Welch, Welch versus everyone, and everyone versus director Michael Sarne, who hasn't directed a major feature since. When the X-rated film finally opened, police were posted outside many theaters. The film was universally damned and made most critics' Ten Worst lists, including Reed's. The Medved brothers later cited Farrah Fawcett's as the Most Embarrassing Movie Debut of All Time, but the debuts of Reed and Tom Selleck—who played "Stud" to Mae West—also stymied *their* acting careers. West's big comeback pleased only her fans, who couldn't keep the picture from losing a fortune for Fox.

The movie stirred homophobic attacks against Reed and Vidal, as well as several what's-become-of-Fox-and-America? laments. Critics disparaged Welch's acting in a thankless role that Liz Taylor turned down (a real transsexual was briefly considered for the part). Although only nominally about a transsexual and not gay-themed at all, *Myra* was

Myra Breckinridge (1970): Left to right, John Huston, director Michael Sarne (on floor), Raquel Welch, Mae West, producer Robert Fryer, and Rex Reed.

treated as a gay movie, though it's dominated by sex symbol Welch. She even shares scenes with her male alter ego (Reed), and Myra's implied fellatio of Myron suggests that they're lovers, instead of before-and-after.

Transsexuals understandably avoided *Myra*, which is now an R-rated camp confection (with Farrah's breasts edited from her lesbian love scene with Raquel). In retrospect, it's hard to imagine what all the fuss was about. Indeed, most of *Myra*'s bad reputation was earned secondhand. Costume designer Edith Head stated, "Vidal's story was worse than pornographic. It was unpleasant, unreal, and contrived. I did Mae's clothes and saw her costume tests, but I did not view one foot of the film. I hear it was pretty horrendous—but it couldn't have been as bad as all the goings-on on the set."

The acrimony began with the enormous success of Vidal's novel, with its explicit *male* imagery and aggressive female antihero. But attacks on Vidal had started with his third novel, the gay-themed *The City and the Pillar* (1948), which the *New York Times,* among others, refused to advertise or review. The

Times boycotted his next several novels, and in the fifties he published mysteries under the pseudonym Edgar Box and wrote for television. Vidal, who began living with Howard Austen in 1951, also attempted screenplays. He wrote much of (but wasn't credited for) the subliminally gay *The Left-Handed Gun* (1958), starring Paul Newman, as well as *Ben-Hur*. He also adapted the filmed-for-TV murder mystery *Dress Gray* and his novel *Kalki*, an oft-postponed Mick Jagger project. In 1965 Vidal revised *The City and the Pillar*, making its ending more homosexually explicit.

Myra Breckinridge is about movie fan Myron, who transforms himself into the gorgeous Myra and heads for Hollywood to take over her share of an acting academy founded by uncle Buck Loner (John Huston), an ex-singing cowboy. Myra becomes an instructor and decides to tame her best-looking student, a chauvinistic hunk named Rusty (Roger Herren). After raping him with a dildo, she turns to his unliberated girlfriend Mary Ann Pringle (Farrah Fawcett). Rusty "turns gay" after his agonizing penetration, but first has a violent affair with talent agent Leticia van Allen (West), who makes Rusty a cowboy television star. Myra is hit by a car—probably driven by Buck—and changed back into a man (who in the book marries Mary Ann and moves to the suburbs).

The movie sheds no light on transsexuality and makes light of it in the opening scene, in which a surgeon (John Carradine) attends to Myron like a camp barber—silly scissors and all. The few "sex" scenes involve Welch: riding a torpedo and wearing an Old Glory bikini to symbolize her rape of all-American Rusty, and cuddling Farrah, who primly cuts it short. This "scandalous" film, not yet a cult item, is surprisingly asexual and about as corrupting (and quaintly dated) as Mae West's eleven other pictures.

ABOUT *MYRA BRECKINRIDGE*

Joseph Morgenstern, *Newsweek*: A horrifying movie, this sexless, joyless diary of a transsexual gives us *ill* humor.... Raquel, poor plastic dear, can't say the lines right, and they don't undress her to redress her wrongs. Reed, hapless wretch, plays with himself in a scene that will make strong men weep and weak women retch. Mae West, a ghastly travesty of the travesty of womanhood she once played, has a Mae West face painted on the front of her head and moves to and fro like the Imperial Hotel during the 1923 Tokyo earthquake. *Myra Breckinridge* is a nightmare—the perfect picture of

Sisters under the celluloid: Mae West (as Letitia Van Allen) and Raquel Welch (as Myra Breckinridge).

Myra goes west to acquire her legal half of her Uncle Buck's (John Huston) acting academy in Hollywood.

an industry that's down for the count, flat on its back, and playing with its sorry self.

John Simon: I have not read Gore Vidal's *Myra Breckinridge*, but having read some of his more ambitious efforts, I assume sophisticated pornography would be just about his speed. . . . What makes the picture pornographic is not the bisexuality Vidal so proudly advocates, but the eagerness of the film (and, I dare say, the book) to make us squirm.

Another dimension in horror is the casting and display of Mae West, perfectly mummified, as a nonstop sex talker. . . . Young men allegedly service and even desire her. Miss West, who is seventy-eight but according to the *Times* "looks years younger" (well, maybe two), is bedizened with a couple of feet of platinum wig and more solitaires than you would think it possible to fit on ten shrunken fingers. . . . I cannot, so shortly after struggling to analyze Miss Streisand's appeal, undertake the analysis of Miss West's. I suppose it has to do with the sweet notion that Americans might still enjoy a full sex life in Forest Lawn.

A minor though distinct horror is the presence of Rex Reed. I had hoped that this campy butterfly and self-styled critic—cast, I am told, so as to make certain things about Myron obvious without the script's having to spell them out—would portray himself on screen so that on the strength of his success, we would be rid of him as a writer. No such luck. His acting is on a par with his writing.

Transsexual-themed movies were a highly specialized lot, far from popular with critics or most audiences. *Myra Breckinridge* and the other films in this chapter span the early 1970s to the early 1980s—it's now a virtually extinct genre. . . .

• 1954's *Glen or Glenda?*—aka *I Led Two Lives*—is about a transvestite, though it was made to cash in on the publicity surrounding Christine Jorgensen's sex-change operation and includes a transsexual subplot, a "case history." Eventual-hero Glen (Daniel Davis) has a penchant for female clothing, especially angora sweaters. But the narrator vouches that Glen is "not a homosexual" and has a "normal sex life." After much soul-searching, Glen tells all to his fiancée (Dolores Fuller). Confused, she accompanies him to a psychiatrist but finally lets him wear her sweater. Of course, marriage "cures" Glen, and Glenda becomes just a dim memory. *Glen or Glenda?* was written by director Edward D. Wood, Jr., in one day, as was his subsequent *Plan 9 From Outer Space*, often acclaimed the Worst Film Ever Made.

Wood's own life was more intriguing than any of his no-budget films. A World War II marine, he landed on an enemy beach wearing bra and panties under his uniform. But his preferred articles were the angora sweaters he borrowed from his wife. Wood eventually became an alcoholic and a porno-novelist and went bankrupt. He died in 1978, at age fifty-three, wearing his favorite angora sweater.

• *The Christine Jorgensen Story* was made in 1970, directed by Irving Rapper, who made the unfortunate *Born Again* from Charles Colson's book. Based on Jorgensen's autobiography, the film starred blond John Hansen as both George—who feels "trapped in the wrong body"—and as Christine. The picture is truer to life than *Myra Breckenridge*, but to the real Ms. Jorgensen's regret, she was played by a youth with "a bull neck, Crawford shoulders, and ten or twenty extra pounds."

Though nearly all transsexuals are homosexual before their gender is changed clinically, George is shocked and repulsed when a man accosts him. Near suicidal, he decides he *must* have the operation. Afterward the press's mocking attitude to her story saddens her, but with the aid of friends and a kindly Danish aunt, Christine learns to adjust. The movie features a brief view of expanding breasts and an obligatory trying-to-become-a-man-with-a-whore scene. Both George and Christine appear to be asexual, since even the new woman evinces no interest in the "opposite" sex until film's end. But the individual's personality is at least consistent, in contrast to *Myra Breckinridge*, where the operation transforms milquetoast Myron into a *Gilda*-like hussy.

Writer/critic Parker Tyler said that *The Christine Jorgensen Story* "has the atmosphere of an operating room, a funeral parlor, and a society debut all in one: the butterfly solemnly unfolds her drying post-anesthetic wings. . . . The most uneventful science-fiction film of the year." Homer Dickens called it "dignified and low-keyed." He found *Myra Breckinridge* "tasteless" and was confused by a photo of Welch in Navy drag. He later wrote, "Raquel Welch played a Naval officer who has a sex-change operation and becomes the title character."

• Anne Heywood (*The Fox*) also played a male-to-female transsexual in 1972's *I Want What I Want*. Unlike John Hansen, she *ends up* playing her own gender. First she plays Roy—and more convinc-

The former Myron (Rex Reed/Raquel Welch) teaches acting while wearing Dietrich drag.

How high the moon: Myra prepares to deflower would-be actor and male chauvinist Rusty Godowski (Roger Herren).

Film clips used in *Myra Breckinridge* implied that the characters of Laurel and Hardy were gay!

What did I have that I don't have?: Myra's scar proves to a lawyer that she used to be Myron and is entitled to his estate.

ingly than Hansen as Christine—an intelligent, sensitive young man whose loneliness is deepened when his widower father leaves. Roy's "best friend" is Wendy, his female alter ego. Roy, who wears conservative suits and ties and close-cropped hair in the early seventies, is attacked—as Wendy—by a would-be rapist. This convinces him to have the operation. Like most movie transsexuals, Roy wants to avoid giving a partner a big surprise. Unlike gay men, Roy doesn't enjoy being male and can only abide sex with another man as a woman. Typical of transsexual-themed films, *I Want What I Want* smoothes and glamorizes the painful transition from male to female. These pictures also vigorously uphold traditional gender roles. Lauded by British critics as a "milestone film," it remains little-seen in the U.S.

• Rainer Werner Fassbinder's *In a Year of 13 Moons* was released in a few American cities in 1981. The gay German wunderkind served as director, producer, writer, editor, art director, and photographer of this 129-minute story of one Elvira Weishaupt, played by Fassbinder regular Volker Spengler. As a male, Elvira was beaten up for being feminine. Unfortunately, the beefy Spengler is anything but. Still, Fassbinder felt, "The story is the important thing, because most transsexuals resemble what they were—in the face, the skeleton. This story is about abuse, how society forces someone *not* usual to become the acceptable thing, psychologically and physically." He added, "This picture terrifies most people, including gays."

• Karen Black, who played a gay man in a student friend's short film, also played Joanne in Robert Altman's 1982 film *Come Back to the Five and Dime, Jimmy Dean, Jimmy Dean*. (Altman also directed the Off-Broadway play by Ed Graczyk.) On the twentieth anniversary of Dean's death, Joanne returns to McCarthy, Texas, to reunite with fellow Dean fans, Cher and Sandy Dennis—an extra in *Giant* who claims to have borne Dean's mentally retarded child. The panoramic mirror inside the rural diner reflects the *past*, too, including a neuter blond named Joe (Mark Patton). Halfway through the film Joanne reveals she used to be Joe and further confesses that Joe loved Mona (Dennis) and fathered her child. Cher is fascinated; the fundamentalist-Christian proprietor is disgusted. Aloof and viperish, Joanne is an interesting character but never remotely suggests male beginnings. In fact, Black seemed more "manly" as the flight-attendant-turned-pilot in *Airport 1975*.

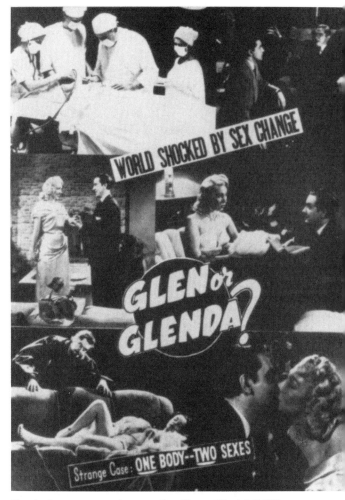

One body, two sexes: A poster for *Glen or Glenda?* (1953), made to cash in on Christine Jorgensen's famous sex-change operation.

• John Lithgow played transsexual Roberta Muldoon, a former tight end with the Philadelphia Eagles, in *The World According to Garp*, another 1982 film. The naturalistic performance was Oscar-nominated and put the six-foot-four Lithgow into the top rank of character actors. "Roberta is a beautiful, sensitive human being," he explained. "Her muscular build always hid a gentle nature, even when she was being clobbered by opposing linemen." Lithgow distanced himself from *Robert* by always referring to the character as "she," a woman without a past. He did allow that "no matter how strong our sexual identities, we all have something of the opposite sex in our makeup," and pointed out that females have only one chromosome-type, while males have both X and Y.

Lithgow didn't want to be "just another guy doing drag." He studied transsexual author Jan Morris's appearances on Dick Cavett's television show and

Tony Curtis points out to Debbie Reynolds that "he" has been reincarnated as a woman in *Goodbye, Charlie* (1964).

Roberta Muldoon (John Lithgow), a former tight end for the Philadelphia Eagles, hugs Robin Williams in *The World According to Garp* (1982).

Transsexual Ms. Muldoon receives a friendly welcome from three generations of Garps, including Glenn Close and Williams.

Ellen Barkin as Amanda, a male chauvinist reincarnated as a woman in *Switch* (1991).

read her book *Conundrum*. He also discussed women's feelings with his girlfriend, an economics professor whom he married after the filming. On the set—as Roberta—with his girlfriend, "we sat around, lounging like two affectionate lesbians."

Lithgow previously won a Tony Award as the helpless soccer player in *The Changing Room*, was nominated for another Tony for *M. Butterfly* as the lover of an Oriental transvestite, and in *Beyond Therapy* was a bisexual who exchanges his male lover for a female one. Such roles prompted the *San Francisco Chronicle*'s Judy Stone to wonder in print, "Is Lithgow a heterosexual, or is he not?" His response? "Oh, yes. My wife had a baby girl two days ago." Still, there was wry speculation in Hollywood that the actor might be nominated in the Best Supporting Actress category.

"I learned a lot about women by playing Roberta," said Lithgow. He also felt that Roberta retained some homosexual feelings—now expressed toward other women. That's not how it works, but most heterosexuals are still trying to figure out ordinary gay people.

113

17 _____

SOLITARY MANN:

Death in Venice

Tadzio, aimless on the beach in
Venice.

Death in Venice. Alfa/Warner Bros., 1970.
Director-producer: Luchino Visconti; writers: Visconti
and Nicola Badalucco.
Starring: Dirk Bogarde, Romolo Valli, Mark Burns, Nora
Ricci, Marisa Berenson, Carole André, Bjorn Andresen,
Silvana Mangano.

The time is before the Great War. The *Esmeralda*
sails majestically toward Venice. (Mahler's Third
and Fifth Symphonies are woven throughout this
largely silent film.) Before disembarking, Gustav
von Aschenbach (Dirk Bogarde) is accosted by an
old troll, a dandy in rouge and aspic (a harbinger).
Aschenbach arrives at the Grand Hotel des Bains
with its teeming, elegant lobby. As dinner is announced he glimpses the peerless Tadzio (Bjorn
Andresen), about fourteen. He lingers while
Tadzio and his Polish family wend their way into the
dining room, led by the ethereal mother (Silvana
Mangano). Tadzio turns, and the two men's eyes
lock. (Flashback to Aschenbach's colleague Alfred
[Mark Burns], arguing about Art with the middle-
aged composer.)

On the beach, Tadzio frolics with his boyfriend
Jaschiu (Sergio Garafanolo). Between mock fights,
the two are affectionate; the older boy kisses Tad-
zio's cheek. Later, in the elevator with Aschenbach,
Jaschiu whispers in Tadzio's ear, and they giggle.
Aschenbach is disconcerted: Are they talking about
him, laughing at him? (Another flashback to
Germany: Alfred yells at Aschenbach, "a man of

avoidance" with "rigid standards of morality."
Aschenbach is warned: "Mediocrity lies on the
mainstream.")

Aschenbach grows frustrated. After another mo-
mentary encounter with the youth, he whispers to
himself, "Farewell, Tadzio. It was all too brief. May
God bless you." He departs, but at the railroad
station his trunk has mistakenly been routed to
Como. He is secretly delighted and returns to the
hotel after *almost* aiding a dying man (another
harbinger). (More flashbacks: Aschenbach with his
wife [Marisa Berenson] and baby daughter; the
couple mourning their dead child; Aschenbach
apparently impotent after a session with a young
prostitute.)

In another encounter, Tadzio passes and Aschenbach whispers, "You must never smile like that
at anyone. I love you." Aschenbach enters a salon
and finds Tadzio playing "Für Elise" on the piano
(prompting a flashback to Esmeralda, the prostitute, playing the same piece). But Venice is being
overrun by a cholera epidemic even though Aschenbach's frantic inquiries are denied by officials.

114

In a fantasy scene Aschenbach warns the Polish lady to immediately take her family from Venice. He strokes Tadzio's hair but, even in fantasy, doesn't address a word to the youth.

The next morning, Aschenbach visits a barber shop and emerges a painted, brilliantined doll. Discreetly he pursues the Polish family on a walk through Venetian byways. Tadzio lingers temptingly, until summoned by the family governess. In frustration the feverish Gustav collapses onto the filthy pavement. He weeps, then laughs, at his hopeless predicament. (There is a flashback to a German audience jeering his music. Alfred yells that Aschenbach's music, like his emotions, is too repressed.)

In the final scene, on the nearly deserted beach, a woman sings a Polish lullaby (or dirge). Aschenbach installs himself in a beach chair with an attendant's help. This morning, he has heard that the Poles will depart in the afternoon. Tadzio and Jaschiu play nearby; but the older boy goes too far and wounds Tadzio's dignity. He shuns Jaschiu and wades into the still, shallow water, where, inadvertently, he poses—like a Greek statue. Aschenbach is mesmerized. Tadzio lifts his arm in attitude. To Aschenbach this is an invitation, a beckoning. He lifts his arm in response, struggles to rise, and slumps back into his beach chair. His heart has failed.

Despite its platonic love story, *Death in Venice* was originally rated R. Fifteen years and a video revolution later, it's PG. Today the endlessly unrequited love story seems strained, though romantic and gorgeously photographed. Gustav von Aschenbach —based on Mahler—is, like Mann and Visconti, very much a product of his times. In 1970, liberals praised the film's boldness, while many critics felt Visconti had gone too far. Some homophobes tried to ignore or deny the truth. Among these was Monica Stirling, Visconti's posthumous biographer, who wrote in 1979: "It's unfortunate that sexual permissiveness led some spectators to misinterpret the movie. For *Death in Venice* is in no sense a 'gay' story—and neither Mann nor Visconti would have understood people's giving their private sexual tastes a label suggesting mass hilarity."

Should one be grateful that Ms. Stirling even acknowledged the men's "tastes"? Thomas Mann admitted in an autobiographical essay, "Nothing in *Death in Venice* is invented. . . . All the facts were true and had only to be put in place."

When Visconti offered the role of Aschenbach to Dirk Bogarde, it was "like being asked by Laurence Olivier to play Hamlet, only better." Bogarde's portrayal is masterfully detailed, though one might wince at mannerisms like Aschenbach's slightly pursed smile in the presence of young males. However, they're in keeping with the character as originally written. For instance: "The vicissitudes of fate must have passed over this head, for he held it, plaintively, rather on one side." In his autobiography, the gay Bogarde reveals, "Aunt Teenie's dreadful twitch became the twitch on von Aschenbach's face at moments of stress. . . . My own shyness and diffidence and loneliness at those tennis or tea parties became his when he arrived, alone, at the Grand Hotel des Bains."

In search of the perfect Tadzio, Visconti placed ads in major Scandinavian newspapers. The first boy brought to his suite in Stockholm was Bjorn Andresen, accompanied by his grandmother. Visconti was seeking thirteen- to fourteen-year-olds, but Andresen, fifteen, was ideal. Because he felt an obligation to those answering the ads, Visconti continued his well-publicized search through Copenhagen, Oslo, and Helsinki. However, the hundreds of interviewees only confirmed the director's first choice.

Andresen's brooding beauty was compared to Garbo's. His carriage is measured yet boyish; in sailor suits and striped swimwear his gender is vague, a physical symbol who, presumably, couldn't threaten moviegoing heterosexual males. Parker Tyler felt that most men of a certain age could identify with Aschenbach: "Just as male heterosexuals, failing in virility, imagine that only some fresh young girl can renew their interest in sex, so men who have overlooked or automatically repressed past homosexual impulses become suddenly aware that some extraordinary young male has made them alive again to sex."

Visconti ordered all his actors, save Bogarde, not to read the book (published in 1912). He also instructed Bogarde to listen and relisten to all of Mahler's music, for therein lay the key to the story's characters and creator. Inevitably, Andresen read the proscribed book, confiding the fact to Bogarde. He exclaimed, "Hell, man, now I know who I *am*. I'm the Angel of Death, right?"

The film's small budget meant the natty Aschenbach had few suits for his Venetian sojourn. Bogarde was assigned only one white suit, so that the scene where he collapses on the garbage-strewn pavement couldn't be reshot. But pressure and Murphy's Law caused the actor to deliver the wrong laugh. "Too young, too aware," said Visconti. Much later in the day, the suit was cleaned, and a satisfactory second take made. Bogarde stated, "It was a *long* five-month shoot."

Tourists were avoided by shooting mostly between two and seven in the morning, six days a week. This was also done to create the overcast light of the sirocco, the climatic condition that spread the cholera. The exterior of the deluxe hotel was de-modernized until the start of the peak season, when it underwent extensive renovation.

Under Visconti's guidance, the company—most of whom took pay cuts to make the film—was briskly professional. Bogarde's quiet on-set relationship with his director was misread by some visiting journalists as disaffection. The actor recalled a female American photographer, "forced upon us by our American bosses." One morning she heard the men greeting each other. "They've stopped feuding," she remarked. When Bogarde reported this to Visconti, the older man patted his hand and smiled. *"Non capisce matrimonio, eh?"* ("She doesn't understand marriage, eh?")

After the success of *The Damned*, Visconti had imagined financing for *Death in Venice* would be readily forthcoming. But few American studio executives were interested in the "pederastic" story by "that kraut writer." One studio offered full financing if the lead were played by Sean Connery or Michael Caine. Visconti stood firm: "Bogarde is like pheasant—he is hanging in the game room, perfect and ready for the pot." The same studio also insisted that Tadzio be played by a girl. The idea was to make Gustav a Teutonic Humbert Humbert. Visconti was appalled by the idea. He was informed that no one in Wisconsin would want to see "a dirty old man chasing a kid's ass."

"But if I change Tadzio to a little girl and we call her Tadzia, you seriously believe that American audiences would be prepared to accept that?"

"We certainly do."

"You do not think that in America they mind child molestation?"

"Mr. Visconti, we do not envisage that kind of problem. We are not as degenerate here as you are in Europe."

Visconti finally went with Warner Bros., which was pleased enough by *The Damned*'s profits to let him make a prestigious, relatively inexpensive art film. Despite the low budget, the opening scenes in the hotel are lavishly peopled and costumed, with a Beatonesque look. And *Death in Venice* won the Grand Prix at the Twenty-Fifth Anniversary Cannes Film Festival and earned healthy profits in Europe.

Reporters of various nationalities trekked to Venice to observe—and sometimes prejudge—the much-heralded project. Bogarde described "the man from a big Chicago newspaper who eventually managed to corner Visconti in an alley while we were setting up a shot. Hot, sweating, furious at having been avoided, he attacked like an evangelist, his pencil and pad shaking with righteous anger. 'Look, I came all this way. I even passed up the really *big* picture they're doing in Padua with Loren and Mastroianni just to try and give you a *break*, and what is this? You say you don't care about publicity! You refuse to see me. We can do you a lot of good in our columns. You be careful. This is a very, very dangerous subject you're making. . . . Just who the hell are you making it for, Mr. Visconti?' He sat back in his canvas chair, fanning himself, a hot toad."

"Visconti raised his eyes slowly, looked at me with a little smile, deliberately patted my hand. 'For Bogarde and myself,' he said pleasantly."

Bogarde's only regret about the film was that "it marked the peak for me in work. Where do you go from the summit but down?" The actor later found that his definitive Gustav von Aschenbach "resulted in my being firmly established, at least in the filmmakers' minds, as an aging 'oddity,' apparently willing to play a wide range of schoolmasters with secret lusts for their pupils, either boys or girls (it didn't really matter)." After three demanding, "exotic" films in a row—*The Damned*, *Justine*, and *Death in Venice*—Bogarde took two years off from films and the press.

Both Bogarde and Andresen were surprised to find themselves overnight stars in Japan. Each received over one thousand letters from fans of the *bishonen* cult, which pairs young men with virile older males in unrequited relationships. *Bishonen*-themed plays, films, novels, and even comic books are enjoyed by millions, of all ages, particularly adolescent girls. *Death in Venice* was a major hit in Japan and continues to be very popular.

As for Visconti, he went directly into *Ludwig*, pausing just long enough to discuss his antagonists. "Ah, the press. You live by the press, you will die by the press. They say I am losing touch, that I shoot only the surface of the emotions, that I am degenerate. . . . They say so stupid things. They have only theory, not practice. They cannot construct, only criticize. And if they find something they do not comprehend, they get angry and destroy, like children! Pouf! You must think nothing of them. They do not *risk*, nothing, ever. How can they know, eh? Callas risks. Stravinsky, Seurat, Diaghilev all risked; even *we* risk. All true creators must."

Luchino Visconti directs his discovery, Swedish Bjorn Andresen as Tadzio—"the divine ephebe."

Venice, anyone?: Von Aschenbach (Dirk Bogarde) arrives in Venice and finds himself surrounded by youth.

Tadzio and a male playmate.

Mother and son: Silvana Mangano and Andresen in *Death in Venice* (1970).

Mother, son, and son's admirer: Mangano, Andresen, and Bogarde.

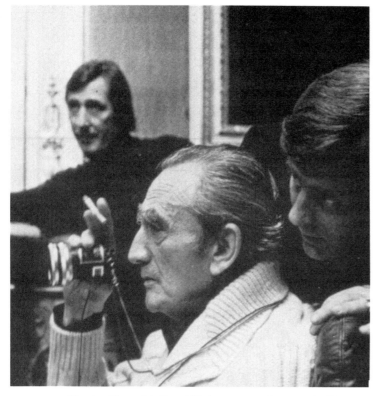

Maestro Visconti believed "in beauty—on the set and off . . ."

ABOUT *DEATH IN VENICE*

John Simon: Visconti is a liar when he says Mann wrote the story about Mahler, and a double liar in his representation of that composer's nature. Mahler was not a homosexual like this Aschenbach. . . . The novella is not homosexual, at least not overtly so. [Simon's 1982 postscript: "We now know from published diaries that Mann had repressed homosexual tendencies."] The little Pole—of the wrong sex and age . . . represents the Ineffable, the Unattainable, the Impossible. This desperate flirtation is a romance with death. In Mann, art and beauty are suspect and deadly; in Visconti, it is the protagonist who is dirty. Aschenbach/Mahler, a now simpering, now petulant fool, listens to Tadzio badly playing "Für Elise" only to be reminded of a favorite whore playing almost equally badly. The implication is that Aschenbach could not find fulfillment with his pretty wife, sought out whores, and failed as much with the profane love as with the

Visconti and actors during filming of *Conversation Piece* (1975).

Another Visconti discovery, Helmut Berger, starred as the gay Bavarian king *Ludwig* in the 1972 film biography.

118

Burt Lancaster and Helmut Berger in Visconti's penultimate
film, *Conversation Piece*.

sacredly conjugal. Homosexuality, clearly, was the
only possible answer!

Officiously ordering about the beach attendant
(one of numerous twentyish, corrupt-looking
youths with whom Visconti populates his movie),
ogling Tadzio with a sheepishness that keeps spill-
ing over into bovineness, Bogarde, in white togs and
funny hat, looks like *Monsieur Hulot's Holiday*. And
Tadzio? Instead of a fourteen-year-old ephebe,
Andresen is a sixteenish androgyne, a semi-de-
praved figure from Botticelli's *Primavera*. . . . Tadzio's playmate, rather than being in every way like
him only less attractive, is here about twenty, and as
darkly loutish as any male whore you can find on
the Via Veneto.

Gerald Peary, *American Film* (1984): Aschenbach
was the last man you'd expect to end his days
gulping overripe, unwashed strawberries, painting
his face with rouge, and chasing a young boy across

the beach sands at Venice. Yet that's just what
happens when an imbalanced all-Apollonian goes
suddenly all-Dionysian. Mann's pre-WWI novella
was a daring story about homosexuality told not
unsympathetically from the author's heterosexual
vantage. *Death in Venice* on-screen is a celebration of
homosexual passion by gay director Luchino Visconti, who employed his camera as an aphrodisiac—
spinning, panning, circling, zooming, approximat-
ing love's delirium.

Mann could only describe in words the beautiful
boy, Tadzio; Visconti, in a miracle of casting, actually found him. (Trivia: What's the kid's name?)
He's the perfect androgyne, romping in the surf,
being toweled dry by his indulgent mother, and
turning old Aschenbach on. An American remake?
Death in West Venice, with Jack Nicholson or Paul
Newman as Aschenbach, and—who else?—Michael
Jackson as a thriller of a Tadzio.

18

BENT:

Fortune and Men's Eyes and *Dog Day Afternoon*

Sal's blockbuster: Gay icon Sal Mineo starred in and directed the popular 1970 stage production.

Fortune and Men's Eyes. MGM, 1971. Director: Harvey Hart; writer: John Herbert; producers: Lester Persky and Lewis M. Allen.
Starring: Wendell Burton, Michael Greer, Zooey Hall, Danny Freedman, Larry Perkins, James Barron, Lazaro Perez, John Granik.

Dog Day Afternoon. Warner Bros., 1975. Director: Sidney Lumet; writer: Frank Pierson; producers: Martin Bregman and Martin Elfand.
Starring: Al Pacino, John Cazale, Sully Boyar, James Broderick, Charles Durning, Chris Sarandon, Carol Kane, Penny Allen.

In a nation where numerous states still deem consensual sex between adults of the same gender "criminal," homosexual men or women often have been considered quasi-criminal. Thus, straight film criminal characters frequently were changed to gays without a thought to gay sensibilities. Imagine turning the Boston Strangler black. And gay or bisexual criminals' sexuality is typically emphasized, the better to moralize or sensationalize. Lawbreakers may also be made comedic, as happened in MGM's abysmal *Fortune and Men's Eyes*. John Herbert's 1967 play was a chilling look at young men in a Canadian reformatory; Herbert drew on his own experiences "as a prisoner while very young." The cast of five men comprised a homophobic gay tough, a wicked queen, a reclusive "princess," an embittered guard awaiting his pension, and the so-called audience stand-in, a straight newcomer who becomes the meanest of all.

Grove Press's bias was apparent in the book's blurb about Smitty, "a naive and essentially noncriminal inmate who has been sentenced for a minor offense." The same is true for Mona, but being gay, he isn't "essentially noncriminal." Nobody in the *play* is gang-raped or murdered, and no one commits suicide. The movie took another tack. Television producer Lester Persky ("That Girl," "Poor Little Rich Girl") reportedly wanted a peepshow comedy and cast Wendell Burton (*The Sterile Cuckoo*) as Smitty and Michael Greer, a late recruit to the play, as Queenie, who performs a memorable drag number. (Greer also camped in 1969's *The Gay Deceivers*, about two straights who pass for gay to avoid the draft; Greer (in his film debut) plays Malcolm deJohn, a gay landlord who does Bette Davis impressions.)

The *film* includes gang-rape and suicides, plus characters named Screwdriver, Catso, Rabbit, Sailor, One-Eye, Drummer, and Cathy (a female). There's less characterization than in the play. Mona (Danny Freedman), for instance, is just another masochistic homosexual. In the play he's a sensitive, feminine youth, the perpetual scapegoat. He preserves his sanity by emotionally disengaging from his abused body. He therefore declines ("heterosexual") Smitty's offer of exclusive sexual partnership.

The play ends with Smitty staring down the audience—"I'm going to pay them back. I'll pay you all back." The play's villain is the institution and the society that allows it. Herbert was pleading for prison reform. But the movie tossed aside social concern and filled *Fortune and Men's Eyes* with fag and dyke jokes (the latter comparable to those in 1983's *Flashdance*) and sexual labels irrelevant inside a prison. In the movie passive homosexuality is the villain, and power is exclusively "masculine." Rocky (Zooey Hall) kills himself when Smitty seizes his power.

Vito Russo's trailblazing book *The Celluloid Closet* detailed the case of pro-gay director Jules Schwerin, who after thirty-one days of shooting was replaced with Harvey Hart, who, with John Herbert, followed the producers' dictates. Producer Lester Persky—a "close friend" of Truman Capote who bought movie rights to Capote's novella *Handcarved Coffins* for $500,000 in 1980—wanted extensive nudity and "that funny drag-queen quality." Mona's idealism and tenderness thus devolved into buffoonery, and the ad campaign declared "What goes on in prison is a crime," meaning homosexuality—which is forced on other inmates mostly by heterosexual prisoners. The *New York Times* noted that homosexuality was a "crime" in forty-five states, and critic Wyatt Cooper felt that "the film's spirit is offensive, for it tries to exploit every angle and pass judgment on the already condemned." One might add that noncaptive audiences stayed away in droves.

ABOUT *FORTUNE AND MEN'S EYES*

B.A.R. (1981): Some gay men enjoyed *Fortune and Men's Eyes*'s exhibitionism. But rape—gang- or any other kind—is never funny or erotic. . . . Today *Fortune and Men's Eyes* stands as a testament to Hollywood's knack for turning controversial, socially forwarding material into self-serving propaganda, for use against *us.* . . . A picture best not quite forgotten.

Fortune and Men's Eyes (1971): Rocky (Zooey Hall, left) and Queenie (Michael Greer) vie for prison supremacy.

Cellblock drag: Queenie performs for a captive audience.

In *Saturday Night Fever* in 1977, Tony Manero (John Travolta) hangs an Al Pacino poster in his bedroom and chants "Attica! Attica!"—a line from *Dog Day Afternoon*. The line, a reference to police harassment, is chanted by gays outside the bank that

Sonny (Al Pacino) is robbing to finance his lover Leon's (Chris Sarandon) sex-change operation. The extreme-looking gays contrast with conservatively dressed Sonny and set him apart. Yet the presence of a segment of the gay community was progress, as was Sonny, a married father also devoted to his hysterical, unhappy male lover.

The film was based on a true story that took place one ninety-seven-degree summer day in Brooklyn. John Wojtowicz, who received a twenty-year sentence for the crime, was a risky role for Pacino, who'd recently scored big in *The Godfather, Part II*. But when he first heard of the man, Pacino said he hoped to play him—"a real complex, fascinating character. Make a wonderful movie." Sidney Lumet directed from Frank Pierson's script, which was radical in that it didn't depict the robber as crooked. Andrew Sarris complained that Pacino and John Cazale (Sal) "are cuddly, and the honest citizens are boobs, bores, and bullies. Lumet has crossed the line between compassion and complicity." Some critics said the same about Sonny's sexuality.

Sonny is an ex-bank clerk and a Vietnam vet. His fumbling makes it clear he isn't cut out for crime—it also endears him to the audience. He treats his hostages and his dim-witted assistant Sal considerately. It's almost disappointing when Sonny finds the day's cash has already been picked up and there's little money to steal. The bank is surrounded by what seems to be the entire city police force. Hostages are taken so the men can escape to another country (Sal's choice is Wyoming). At the airport an FBI agent shoots Sal, Sonny is captured, and the hostages are released.

Sonny's private life is illustrated in scenes with his wife, kids, and lifemate. Sonny is a man dutifully trying to fulfill his numerous responsibilities. None of his dependents seems particularly worthy of him, and Pacino's charisma is such that it's believable that several tellers come over to his side. Sonny's bisexuality isn't revealed until well into the film. Newscasters covering the robbery refer to Sonny, his pre-transsexual lover, and his heterosexual accomplice as "homosexuals." Sal complains but Sonny says, "It doesn't matter, Sal. It's only a freak show to them."

Whether Sonny is bisexual, homosexual, or basically heterosexual is unclear. (Unlike his prototype, Sonny is Italian-American.) The thought-provoking film was a huge hit, and Pacino's lead encouraged other actors to accept less constricted roles. Pauline Kael commented, "New stars such as Pacino, Nicholson, Hackman, and De Niro go as far into their characters as they can; Redford could, but

he doesn't want you not to like the people he plays."

Lumet wanted to "examine Sonny's desperation in human, not legal, terms." Sonny is the screen's first sympathetic, fully rounded bisexual male. Lumet also expressed his social conscience in films like *The Pawnbroker, Fail-Safe*, and the documentary *King*. In 1982 he became a charter member of the Performing Arts Committee for Civil Liberties, founded by Woody Allen to fight threats to free expression. Writer Frank Pierson was hired by Barbra Streisand to direct *A Star is Born* (1976), and Al Pacino later sailed through *Cruising* on a tide of residual goodwill from *Dog Day Afternoon*.

ABOUT *DOG DAY AFTERNOON*

John Simon, *New York*: There is commendable striving for psychological and sociological accuracy in *Dog Day Afternoon*—note the mixed reactions of various policemen to Leon's outpourings. This homosexual "wife" is superbly played by Chris Sarandon, who must tread the delicate line between what might strike heterosexual viewers as maudlin or grotesque, but who with consummate histrionic restraint and human dignity neither over- nor underacts.

Pauline Kael: Sarandon gives one of the finest homosexual performances ever seen in a movie; he's true to Leon's anguish in a remarkably pure way—he makes no appeal for sympathy.

The following movies also explore the gay character as a rebel, a delinquent, or, more often, a criminal . . .

• Meyer Levin's 1957 play *Compulsion* was based on the 1924 Leopold and Loeb murder case. The title referred to the self-hate sometimes engendered in a minority by a bigoted majority. The two colleagues, who murder a fourteen-year-old for kicks, are secretly unhappy about being Jewish. In the 1959 movie they're secretly unhappy being gay. Alfred Hitchcock's 1948 *Rope* was also based on the Leopold and Loeb characters, but the director undertook the project simply as a moviemaking stunt (ten one-take reels). In *Rope* Farley Granger and John Dall played the arty idlers who conceal the corpse in a trunk in the very room where the victim's parents and fiancée attend a party. Another guest is their professor, James Stewart, to whom they drop boastful clues and thereby seal their fates.

The youths' "false love" was mentioned in *Rope*'s ads, next to a male-female pictorial. The unsuccessful film wasn't rereleased until 1984, by which time the men were brought out of the closet. Molly Haskell wrote in *Playgirl:* "[Hitchcock] treats homosexuals sympathetically but is more comfortable with *covert* neuroses" (italics mine). The *San Francisco Chronicle*'s John Stanley repeatedly referred to the murderers as "two homosexuals," "the homosexuals," etc.—drawing several letters to the editor.

Based on Patrick Hamilton's 1929 play, *Rope* was adapted by actor Hume Cronyn. The screenplay was by gay writer Arthur Laurents (*West Side Story*, *The Way We Were*). Nonetheless, *Rope* binds its Nietzschean would-be supermen to Nazism, as does *Compulsion*, which calls its elitist antagonists "powder puffs." *Compulsion* doesn't *need* to say "homosexual," either. Artie Strauss's (Dean Stockwell) and Judd Steiner's (Bradford Dillman) relationship is established as "strange"—the brilliant pair don't even like baseball! Artie is a "strange bird" rather than a girl-watcher, and "Juddsy" (the "husband") is a leering sadist.

Produced by twenty-four-year-old Richard Zanuck for his father's Fox studios, *Compulsion* sticks closer to the real-life facts than *Rope* does. Director Richard Fleischer (*Conan the Destroyer*) felt Hitchcock "skirted the issue" of homosexuality. But *Compulsion* is more anti-intellectual than anti-gay. It reiterates that "superior" intellects can warp morality—*TV Guide* refers to the "two wealthy intellectuals," and some reviewers called them "esthetes."

When Artie tries to rape a girl, he stops at the last moment, disgusted with her and himself. He has a pet teddy bear (like *Brideshead Revisited*'s Sebastian Flyte), an addled, coddling mother, and a partner he love-hates (they tell on each other, separately). The last third of the film has Orson Welles as a Clarence Darrow-type lawyer successfully arguing for a life sentence rather than death for "the dirty little degenerates" (as relatives and townspeople call them). Welles, Stockwell, and Dillman jointly won the Cannes Film Festival's Best Actor award.

• In her book *Running Time: The Films of the Cold War*, Nora Sayre discusses the fifties fascination with "latency": "Popular legend alleged that Dean and Brando and Clift and Cary Grant were bisexual; it was rumored that Sal Mineo was gay. . . . If those stars preferred their own sex, then sexual deception seemed necessary, and it was crucial to pretend that homosexuality did not exist." From a nineties perspective it's easy to see which characters should have been gay, e.g., Mineo's Plato in 1955's *Rebel Without a Cause*. In *Rebel* Mineo played the movies' first gay teenager, covertly in love with James Dean. Mineo's characterization of Plato

earned him an Oscar nomination, but the performance may have come easily; in real life Mineo was in love with Jimmy Dean. By inclination or typecasting, Mineo played several sexually ambiguous characters.

Among these was Dov Landau in *Exodus* (1961). A volunteer in the Israeli underground freedom forces, he confesses under duress that the Nazis "used me like a woman!" In 1969 Mineo directed a long-running Los Angeles production of *Fortune and Men's Eyes*, noted for its nude shower scenes. Mineo was murdered in 1976 by a robber unaware of his identity—not by a lover, seducer, or hustler, as the press widely speculated (little space was given to the murderer's true motive). (Mineo was killed during the run of James Kirkwood's *P.S. Your Cat Is Dead*, in which he played a bisexual cat burglar.)

• Implicitly gay crooks and villains became explicit by the late sixties. In Richard Fleischer's *The Boston Strangler* (1968), there were even gay suspects (including Hurd Hatfield, interrogated by Henry Fonda) for a series of heterosexual murders. The same year, Frank Sinatra starred as *The Detective*. Married to a "nympho" (Lee Remick), he's dragged into the gay underworld to solve several murders. Being a hero, he even socks a gay-basher. But it's no surprise when the murderer (William Windom) turns out to be gay himself. He declares, "I felt more guilty about being a homosexual than being a murderer."

In Roger Corman's *Bloody Mama* (1970), Shelley Winters plays Ma Barker as a maternal dyke. Two of her sons are Bruce Dern as a homicidal homosexual and Robert De Niro as a heroin addict—but a *nice* heroin addict. *The Anderson Tapes* (1971) includes Martin Balsam as Haskins, a thief-fop who provides his gang (and the audience) with "comic" relief. Writers Richard Maibaum and Tom Mankiewicz (son of Joseph) turned Ian Fleming's incidental gay villains into major characters in *Diamonds Are Forever* (1971). Mr. Wint (Bruce Glover) and Mr. Kidd (Putter Smith) are prime sadists. After blowing up a helicopter, they stride into the desert hand-in-hand, though one partner's fleeting admiration of a stewardess later comes between them. The two are symbolically dispatched aboard ship when 007 stabs each in the rectum with a flaming shish kebob skewer before tossing them overboard.

Deliverance (1972) features devils in gay disguise: Two neanderthals attack a male canoeing party and rape Ned Beatty. The offender is shot with an arrow by Burt Reynolds. Back home, Jon Voight sodomizes his wife while recalling the golden fleck

P.S. Your Cat Is Dead: Mineo played a bisexual cat burglar in the 1976 production of James Kirkwood's play.

in a fashion-model's iris, as in *Reflections in a Golden Eye*. Both Voight and Reynolds have issued progay statements while appearing in antigay films. Reynolds, who lived for twelve years with friend and director Hal Needham, told Barbara Walters that stars like Redford and Beatty are "so handsome I could be bisexual for them." And in 1975, in *W.W. and the Dixie Dancekings*, he says, in character, that the one man he could "go queer" for is Errol Flynn—also bisexual.

Gay Anthony Perkins and composer Stephen Sondheim made their screenwriting debuts with 1973's *The Last of Sheila*, in which several show-business types gather aboard the yacht *Sheila*. Each has committed a "crime" beginning with *S* or *H* or *E* and so on. One of the "crimes" is homosexuality—scriptwriter Richard Benjamin made love with producer James Coburn (who is killed, inferring the position he played) before marrying Joan Hackett. Richard Fleischer's 1975 *Mandingo* features slaveholders attracted to proud black bucks; the nudity includes that of Roger E. Mosley, later of "Magnum,

P.I." In *Drum*, the 1976 sequel, the sex object is boxer Ken Norton.

J. Edgar Hoover, who founded the FBI in 1924, lived for over forty years with Clyde Tolson. Neither married, and at his death Hoover left his entire estate to Tolson. *The Private Files of J. Edgar Hoover* (1978), with Broderick Crawford and the late gay actor-dancer Dan Dailey, offers a basic look at this right-wing figure who was uncomfortable with sex in general and certainly no friend to gay-rights activists. (In *Loving Couples* [1980] Dr. Shirley MacLaine tells Stephen Collins that, as a girl, she used to play doctor and made her boyfriend play nurse. "I wonder what happened to that boy?" asks Collins. "He works for the FBI." "That's reassuring.")

For centuries, popular fiction has obscured the fact that many sea pirates—who were often at sea for years at a time—were homosexual. Vanessa Redgrave, then Bo Derek, was to have starred as Anne Bonny, a cross-dressing female pirate whose lovers included co-pirate Mary Read. No doubt the film would have turned the relationship platonic, omitted it, or, in Derek's case, exploited it. But *The Pirate Movie* (1982), a teen musical with Kristy McNichol, includes a nonstereotypical male pirate couple befriended by the female hero. Christopher Atkins plays the film's usually-topless or frilly-shirted sex symbol.

Women's-prison films have always been an ex-

John Cazale and Pacino attempt to rob a bank, with seriocomic results.

124

Chris Sarandon as the would-be transsexual and lover for whom Pacino has turned bank robber.

Midnight Express (1978): Brad Davis as a real-life bisexual who in the *reel* version is heter-only, because he's the hero!

"Pipe the new fish:" Sapphic prison matron Hope Emerson casts an eye at new inmate Eleanor Parker (second right) in *Caged* (1950).

cuse for sensationalistic lesbianism on a low budget. *Fortune and Men's Eyes*'s leading female counterpart is the 1950 cult movie *Caged*, with Eleanor Parker as Virginia Kellogg, a nineteen-year-old jailed for a crime committed by her husband. She is corrupted by the prison system and *those* women (but not sexually). Agnes Moorehead is the brisk but motherly warden who advises Parker to find "a good man" to support her when she gets out. *Caged*'s most colorful character is matron Evelyn Harper (Hope Emerson), a massive, corrupt sadist with an eye for pretty prisoners (though a not-so-pretty one stabs her to death). Both actresses were Oscar-nominated, and Parker won Best Actress at the Venice Film Festival. In 1962, *Caged* was weakly remade as *House of Women*, with Shirley Knight and Constance Ford.

Parker's main claims to fame are *Caged* and *The Sound of Music*, but the fifties movie queen was tagged by producer Aaron Spelling to play Alexis, a new character on television's "Dynasty." She filmed one episode of the series, appearing in a heavy veil, but when contractual negotiations broke down she was replaced. When Alexis lifted her veil in the next episode, the face underneath belonged to Joan Collins, another fifties movie queen who'd never hit the top.

Lady Scarface (1941): The long arm of the law takes hold of murderess-in-disguise Judith Anderson.

19

OLDER MEN, YOUNGER MEN:

Butley and *Nijinsky*

British sex symbol Alan Bates, who in the seventies and eighties turned to more serious roles, several gay or bisexual.

Butley. American Film Theatre, 1974. Director: Harold Pinter; writer: Simon Gray; producer: Ely A. Landau. Starring: Alan Bates, Jessica Tandy, Richard O'Callaghan, Susan Engel, Michael Byrne, Georgina Hale, Simon Rouse.

Nijinsky. Paramount, 1980. Director: Herbert Ross; writer: Hugh Wheeler; producers: Nora Kaye and Stanley O'Toole.
Starring: Alan Bates, Leslie Browne, George de la Peña, Alan Badel, Carla Fracci, Colin Blakeley, Jeremy Irons, Anton Dolin.

Can an older man find happiness with a younger man? Not on-screen. Neither Hollywood nor Hollywood-on-Thames cares to treat older man/younger man relationships in a positive manner. Whether explored in-depth or superficially, the senior partner invariably comes off the villain or the fool. When the older man doesn't victimize his junior, he's either ruined by him (the Oscar Wilde films), entraps him (*Entertaining Mr. Sloane*), dies after wedding him (*Fellini Satyricon*), dies from not bedding him (*Death in Venice*), is betrayed by him (*Deathtrap*), loses him to a lesbian (*A Different Story*), loses him to a career move (*Sunday, Bloody Sunday*), is killed after brief happiness together (*Privates on Parade*), or actually *gets* the younger man, as *punishment* (*Querelle*).

In *Butley*, Alan Bates loses Joey (Richard O'Callaghan) to a man closer to Joey's age. In *Nijinsky*, Bates loses the dancer (George de la Peña) to a woman and insanity. Yet both films represent arguable advances over most previous films that treat the subject. Of course, Ben Butley and Sergei Diaghilev do have their unattractive sides. Butley loathes women: "I'm a one-woman man, and I've had mine, thank God." He's petty, jealous, and a snob—he ridicules Reg (Michael Byrne), his rival for Joey, for having a Northern accent and parents who work as a butcher and a traffic warden.

Diaghilev is a relentless taskmaster. He, too, dislikes women and is rude to them. He's an egotist who, when publicly defied by Nijinsky, slaps him. He is uncompromising—after Nijinsky marries, Diaghilev refuses to ever see him again. He is also callous and fickle, quickly replacing the ailing dancer with another handsome (and talented) youth.

Yet neither man is a villain. Diaghilev is portrayed as intelligent but not intellectual, artistically inclined but not effete, older but virile, charming, *and* well-adjusted. As master of his universe, he enjoys his work and his private life. Butley, on the other hand, is his own worst enemy, though his self-contempt doesn't stem from being gay. He is married, has a baby daughter whose name he forgets, and loses his neglected wife to "the most boring man in London." As an unpublished professor, he can barely abide his colleague Edna (Jessica Tandy), who's about to publish. All in one day, he learns of Edna's impending book, his wife's impending divorce, and, most importantly, of the impending loss of his live-in lover Joey, a former student, now an assistant lecturer who shares his office.

Through it all, due mostly to the winning performance by Alan Bates (who won numerous theater awards for the part), Butley is charming in a caddish sort of way. Underneath the vitriol and the nursery rhymes he incessantly recites (symbolic of arrested childhood?), Butley is suavely likable and boyishly vulnerable. Though bitchy, he's not a stereotype and represents his profession as much as his sexuality. Reg, a manly and appealing gay, is, however, still in the closet, seeking social conformity and the approval of his parents. Though a publisher, Reg is nonetheless provincial and represents a change of pace for the waspish but ineffectual Joey. Reg won't likely dominate Joey as thoroughly as Butley does. After losing Joey, Butley considers replacing him with Mr. Gardner (Simon Rouse), a hippie student. But Butley decides not to and in the middle of a tutorial asks Gardner to go. "I don't want to start again. . . . I'm too old to play with the likes of you."

ABOUT *BUTLEY*

Santa Barbara News-Press: Claustrophobic story of a man living in a nursery-rhyme world while all about him tumbles down. . . . Bates endows the sarcastic shell of a scholar with rumpled tolerability. But he gets his just desserts when he's abandoned and left in the sty of his university office. . . . The performances are literate and convincing, but the film drags. . . . For talk-loving Anglophiles only.

London Movie Express: Simon Gray's scathing play is brought to the screen by Harold Pinter, its three principals intact. . . . A tour de force for Bates as the appalling yet touching Ben Butley, with debonair Michael Byrne as the Northerner to whom he loses his young paramour, Joey Keyston. . . . The trenchant dialogue illuminates the academic scrap-

Butley's mate Joey (Richard O'Callaghan, right) finds a more stable partner in Reg (Michael Byrne), a book publisher.

ing bottom; however, the film never lapses into self-pity or deprecating humor. Over-long, but Bates's performance is worth the passing tedium.

In *Children of the Sun*, Martin Green wrote this of Diaghilev: "He made the dancer Nijinsky first his lover, then his choreographer, displacing Michel Fokine and inspiring Nijinsky to become the company's chief ballet-creator. Diaghilev's superb taste . . . was made manifest in this new Nijinsky, the choreographer, and in the ballets he created. These works of art were the children of Diaghilev's sexual passion. The same thing happened later with Léonide Massine and Serge Lifar. . . . These men created ballets under the spell of Diaghilev's passion, and he created through them."

Over the years, film biographies of Vaslav Nijinsky were attempted by several artists, but the projects never left the drawing boards. In the sixties, when Rudolf Nureyev became *the* dancer of his time, there was renewed interest, but ballet wasn't box office, and the gay theme was a deterrent. Only after the commercial success of *The Turning Point* (1977) was *Nijinsky* a real possibility. By then Nureyev was too old for the part, and so was *The Turning Point*'s Mikhail Baryshnikov.

The Turning Point's screenwriter Arthur Laurents had tried to give the film more ballet-world integrity by including a gay subplot, but he was opposed by director Herbert Ross and Shirley MacLaine. Said Laurents, "It was dishonest and lacking in texture to do a movie about the ballet world and not have homosexuals." The film's only gay reference is to MacLaine's dancer-husband who impregnated and married her partly to avoid being thought "queer." Although the parents encourage daughter Leslie Browne to become a professional dancer, they discourage their talented son.

Ross and his ex-ballerina wife Nora Kaye finally brought *Nijinsky* to the screen. One hindrance had been Nijinsky's widow Romola (née De Pulsky), who purged her husband's diaries and image of all gay references. Ross's film was based on *Nijinsky* by Romola Nijinsky and on the diary edited by Mme. Nijinsky, who finally died in 1978 (twenty-eight years after Vaslav). *Nijinsky* began filming in 1979, starring Russian-Argentine dancer Jorge (George) de la Peña, twenty-two—the same age Nijinsky was in the years covered by the film: 1912–13. But de la Peña's idol was Nureyev, whose career inspired him to become a dancer. Of his role, he said, "Nijinsky was very childlike. Diaghilev was his schooling and his strength, so that when Diaghilev was taken away from him, things fell apart."

The film points out that Nijinsky's family had a history of insanity, but it also suggests that the youth couldn't cope with success and never found his personal identity. A huge liberty taken by the filmmakers was the omission of the fact that although Diaghilev severed relations after Vaslav's marriage, it was his influence that got the dancer released from a Hungarian prison camp in 1916. Diaghilev also gave his ex-lover (who failed to succeed with his own company) a North American tour with his company and the chance to choreograph *Till Eulenspiegel*. A South American tour followed, but then madness struck.

Less knavish than pathetically naive, Romola develops a crush on Vaslav, insinuates herself into his needy nature, and turns him against his father-figure/lover, all the while thinking to make him heterosexual. The movie-Diaghilev pridefully informs the beseeching Romola that he will never see

George de la Peña as ballet genius Nijinsky.

Vaslav again or rehire him. At the last moment, he halfheartedly offers any necessary funds, which Romola pridefully declines, denouncing the heartless older man.

All three principals are fairly unlikable. Nijinsky is portrayed as a bratty, confused puppy—a fine dancer, but hardly an artist capable of creating ballets like *L'Après-midi d'un Faun* and *Le Spectre de la rose*. Many of the supporting characters are more diverting, particularly Jeremy Irons (*Brideshead Revisited, Swann in Love*) as Diaghilev's ex-lover Fokine, who jealously calls Nijinsky a "little pederast." Alan Badel plays the theatrically gay Baron De Gunzburg, a patron of the arts and a would-be rival for Vaslav's affections. It is De Gunzburg who arranges the overseas tour that inadvertently cleaves Vaslav from Sergei. (Diaghilev, who believed he would die on the water, wouldn't take sea voyages. He died in Venice and is buried there.)

Herbert Ross said, "I consider *Nijinsky* the first film of the 1980s. *Nijinsky* isn't just the story of the

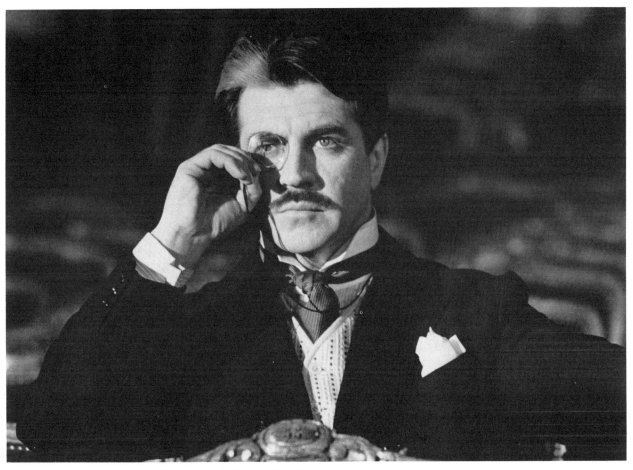

Nijinsky (1980): Alan Bates as ballet impresario Sergei Diaghilev, dancer Vaslav Nijinsky's discoverer and lover.

ballet. The epoch of Diaghilev's dazzling Ballets Russes provides the background, but the drama of this amazing dancer, his success, his tragedy, is that of the homosexual-heterosexual conflict involving Nijinsky, Diaghilev, and Romola. This engrossing relationship, common enough in psychiatric annals, has rarely been dealt with in major motion pictures."

But the public wasn't interested, and the picture should have been less a psychiatric case history and more a biography of the great male dancer of his age and the story of the great love of his life. *Nijinsky* is too focused on box office and the status quo; it features too little ballet (unlike *The Turning Point*), and the one male kiss is exchanged through a handkerchief, ostensibly because of Nijinsky's "inconvenient" head cold.

Adding insult and God-playing to injury was NBC's heavy-handed censorship when *Nijinsky* was telecast in early 1984. The film's opening—over five minutes—was scissored, including the hankie-kiss that lays the groundwork for the relationship. Also

Sergei and Vaslav share a private moment in their intense personal and professional relationship.

cut were Fokine's revealing line and a pastoral scene in which Diaghilev refers to some young men's sexual nature, which Nijinsky insists isn't his own. The network thereby cut the scanty homosexuality and turned *Nijinsky* into a heterosexual love story by neutering Diaghilev and resexualizing his younger lover.

ABOUT *NIJINSKY*

Samedi et Dimanche: The relationships are vague, although Bates is an admirably imperious Diaghilev, founder of the Ballets Russes de Monte Carlo and an aging lover afraid to risk his heart. . . . De la Peña makes the seventeen-years-younger Nijinsky too contemporary, and the famous relationship is here nonsexual. . . . Nijinsky's marriage seems motivated by puerile spitefulness. Mlle. Browne is a dull, flat Romola.

Out: Girl meets boy, girl marries boy, boy loses mind. *Nijinsky* hasn't a point of view to call its own. . . . Is marriage to blame for Nijinsky's balletic fall and decline into madness? Or is the culprit homosexuality? Is Diaghilev trying to convert the boychick to manlove, or is he Nijinsky's only true love? . . . A cautious, bland movie, notwithstanding sumptuous trappings and snippets from Nijinsky's best roles. . . . When the men "kiss," it's over with quickly, just to indicate their relationship. Both are vestal virginal, and Nijinsky reiterates that he isn't like the other fancy dancers. . . . The wife is a social-climbing fool, but he's all she has, so she devotes her life to his care and feeding. Are we to be happy that he found a good woman? . . . Ostensibly the story of two extraordinary men, *Nijinsky* should have been much, much more. . . .

Where the previous two films depict the gay relationships of younger with older men, the following ones rather fleetingly depict the relationships of young gay men with their parents and/or a patriarchally disapproving society. . . .

• Hollywood's message is: older or younger, hetero is better. The parents in *Summer Wishes, Winter Dreams* (1973) are aghast to hear that their ballet-dancing son (Ron Rickards) has taken up residence with another male in Amsterdam (Europe's gay capital). The film examines Joanne Woodward's relationships with her mother, husband, and daughter. But when she and husband Martin Balsam visit Europe, they bypass their son, who continues the separation until his parents can

somehow understand. . . . The script makes him seem defensive, yet he's such a minor character, one wonders why the filmmakers bothered.

The gay son takes center stage in *Norman . . . Is That You?* (1976), based on a play only a dinner-theater audience could love. Redd Foxx and Pearl Bailey are the parents of Norman (Michael Warren of "Hill Street Blues"). Norman's white lover is the flamboyant Garson (Dennis Dugan), and the supporting cast includes several television celebrities, from Jayne Meadows to Wayland Flowers and Madame. The film was directed by George Schlatter ("Laugh-In") and centers on the folks finding out about Junior. Needless to say, Foxx takes it less well (he hires a hooker to "convert" his manly son) than Bailey, who leaves Foxx for his brother.

A former UA executive recalls, "*Norman* was designed to attract blacks, whites, straights, gays, comedy-lovers, everyone—like 'The Jeffersons.' The studio thought it could hit big—it wasn't a downer like *Staircase*, and it wasn't foreign. . . . But so far, even the networks have been cold on it. . . . Somebody screwed up."

• Billy Joe McAllister (Robby Benson) is an uptight son of Dixie, an all-American Southern beau who has one (unseen) homosexual affair and kills himself by jumping off a bridge. His good name is preserved by a loving belle named Bobbie Lee (Glynnis O'Connor). She says, "He's on his way to becoming a legend around here. Cain't have people thinking he killed himself because of a man." The execrable *Ode to Billy Joe* (1976), a hit in Ruritania, was directed by Max Baer, Jr., Jethro on "The Beverly Hillbillies" series.

In *Fame* (1980) and *The Hotel New Hampshire* (1984), Paul McCrane played gay youths. *Fame*, directed by Englishman Alan Parker (*Midnight Express*), finds Montgomery the only gay student in the whole of the High School of Performing Arts. Like Jews of years past, he suffers in silence, as does *The Hotel New Hampshire*'s gay son Frank, whose loving family *accepts* him. The John Irving saga, directed by Tony Richardson (*A Taste of Honey*), pairs every character but the positive, emotionally supportive Frank. At film's end, each of his siblings romps with an "opposite"-sex-mate, while Frank frolics with the dog. He's the only gay person in his universe. (His bisexual sister, Jodie Foster, forsakes Nastassja Kinski for her own brother, Rob Lowe, and then another man.) The filmmakers—busy with straight characters—don't bother to match up their gay one. Whether the gay was included for "relevance" or "reality" or to earn some filmmaker a "with-it"

Alan Badel (left) as the Baron de Gunzberg offers funds and sympathy.

Star-to-be Jeremy Irons played Michel Fokine, Diaghilev's gay choreographer.

reputation doesn't matter. The result's the same: Young audiences figure that gay people are the loneliest people in the world.

Additionally, these films' scriptwriters avoid the word *gay* in favor of *queer*, a term then only somewhat more polite than *fag*. This treatment is reflected in reviews that demean the gay character, as in *The Hotel New Hampshire*, which is loaded with "murder, rape, incest, cruelty, inflicted blindness, homosexuality, suicide, illness, and accidental death." Characters like Frank and Montgomery aren't individuals, they're situations. (A letter protesting the above review, in *Hollywood Studio Magazine*, drew an apology and somewhat more thoughtful coverage.)

This backhanded treatment isn't limited to American or British filmmakers. In 1981's *Boléro* (*Les Uns et les autres*), written and directed by Claude Lelouche (*Un Homme et une femme*), James Caan plays dual roles: a father and his gay son Jason. But when an actor plays a straight, heroic parent, contrasting the two characterizations is not courage or chutzpah, but a safe acting trick. True, Jason doesn't have *mannerisms*, although he wears spectacles and has a higher hairline than his father. But, in this three-hour epic about four families, Jason suddenly tries to kill himself. Until then, he seemed well-adjusted and successful. The suicide attempt goes unexplained. Jason does have a relationship— with a selfish, argumentative type; their breakup *may* have prompted the suicide attempt, though they never seemed fond of each other.

Another of *Boléro*'s strange conceits is the ballet dancer (Jorge Donn), said to be based on Nureyev, but written as a heterosexual.

Younger man, older men: In *Rebel Without a Cause* (1955), Sal Mineo worries that Corey Allen (right) will come between him and James Dean.

Younger man, older man: Gay Sal Mineo had a crush on heterosexual Elvis Presley—who also had a crush on Elvis.

131

20

MUSIC LOVERS:

The Rocky Horror Picture Show

The Rocky Horror Picture Show. Twentieth Century-Fox, 1975. Director: Jim Sharman; writers: Sharman and Richard O'Brien; producer: Michael White.
Starring: Tim Curry, Susan Sarandon, Barry Bostwick, Richard O'Brien, Patricia Quinn, Little Nell, Peter Hinwood, Meatloaf.

The ultimate cult film, *The Rocky Horror Picture Show* has been called "the gayest film yet made by a major studio." It spawned a separate industry, including foreign-language albums of the film and play (Richard O'Brien's *The Rocky Horror Show*), books, T-shirts, makeup-and-accessory kits, dolls, newsletters, conventions, and even a flop sequel, the largely unrelated *Shock Treatment* (1981). Most recently, the entire soundtrack was recorded for *Rocky Horror* fans who want to throw *Rocky Horror* parties at home.

Provocative then and now, the movie's greatest asset is Dr. Frank-N-Furter, a "sweet transvestite from Transsexual, Transylvania." Tim Curry won immortality in black mesh stockings, rhinestoned heels, and garish makeup, courtesy of Mick Jagger's makeup man, Pierre LaRoche. Joyfully salacious, Frank-N-Furter is busy making himself a man, Rocky Horror (Peter Hinwood). Equal parts blondness and biceps, his creation is a far cry from Dr. Frankenstein's ugly monster. The outside world intrudes in the persons of Brad and Janet Weiss (Barry Bostwick and Susan Sarandon), uptight newlyweds whose car has stalled in front of the

Not Joan Collins Crawford, but Tim Curry as Dr. Frank-N-Furter, star-siren of *The Rocky Horror Picture Show* (1975).

spooky mansion. That night, the doctor visits Janet, then Brad, in separate guestrooms. Each thinks the amorous visitor is the other spouse, and Brad relishes his first homosexual affair.

The musical's dozen-plus songs are less than memorable. Not so the visuals: earth and/or outer-space oddballs of all shapes and sizes, and sets including a giant RKO Radio tower and an orgy-watertank. But although *Rocky Horror* smashes taboos and audiences cheer on the bisexual, transvestite hero, tradition is honored when the mad doctor's demise is brought about "for the good of society."

But he returns from the dead to revel and dance unapologetically. In front of the RKO backdrop, the male and female leads sing and kick up their heels, all dressed like their unsinkable host in garters and mascara. Likewise, the movie survived a brief and ineffective (for general audiences) ad campaign—scarlet Jagger lips: "a different set of jaws"—plus neglect by Fox, which didn't know what to do with the mere one-million-dollar production. It never achieved mainstream success, but *The Rocky Horror Picture Show* remains a solid-gold moneymaker. According to part-owner and record mogul Lou Adler, it plays Friday and Saturday midnight shows at 250 theaters nationwide, earning some $9 million annually.

Adler took over promotion where Fox left off, doing market research and opening *Rocky Horror* as a midnight movie, first in New York's Greenwich Village, then nationwide and overseas (many cinemas refuse to book it *before* the witching hour). The first audiences were mostly gays and transvestites and homophobic gangs. Eventually the gangs disappeared, and a wider spectrum of viewers joined the fun. However, there is still anti-gay violence outside some theaters from time to time.

Despite subsequent cult hits, *The Rocky Horror Picture Show* remains unique. Consider Frank-N-Furter's sexual credo, "Don't dream it, *be* it," sung mantra-style in flickering candlelight. His lusty paean, "In Seven Days I Can Make You a Man," is warbled to a muscled surfer in gold lamé bikini and boxing shoes. And when Janet, the fallen bride, sees her husband in close quarters with their host, she croons to Rocky Horror, "Touch-a, touch-a, touch-me, I want to be dirty," urging him to pleasure her monstrously.

Sexual symbolism and references to other famous films and artworks abound, from phallic workhorses and a giant plaster David to Michelangelo's *Creation* painted on a pool's bottom. Columbia (Little Nell) wears *Wizard of Oz* ruby shoes, and her sometime lover Magenta (Patricia Quinn) sports a hairdo borrowed from *The Bride of Frankenstein* (which was directed by gay James Whale, who also helmed *The Old Dark House*, which inspired the *Rocky Horror* manse). The drowned doctor, floating face-down in the pool, recalls *Sunset Boulevard*, while *King Kong* is invoked when Rocky Horror carries his master's body up the RKO tower.

ABOUT *THE ROCKY HORROR PICTURE SHOW*

Screen Play (Australia, 1977): Susan Sarandon finds herself surrounded by homosexuals and bisexuals, among whom she can count her once-straight-and-narrow groom, played by winsome Barry Bostwick (check out those thighs, Sheila). . . . No nudity and scarce profanity, but lots and lots of radical sexuality and gender-bending. Not for tots.

Out (1980): On its fifth anniversary, *The Rocky Horror Picture Show* is still the champ of live-and-let-love entertainments. . . . Embraced to the padded bosoms of hordes of late-night thrill-seekers, it holds up well. . . . Tim Curry is the last word in sexy high-camp. He's the darker side of Marilyn, and his performance ranks with Margo Channing and Mildred Pierce in the Over-Rouged-Bitch Hall of Fame.

• Gay author-columnist Ethan Mordden apparently hadn't seen *The Rocky Horror Picture Show* when he labeled *Can't Stop the Music* (1980) "the first gay musical." The Allan Carr extravaganza does have a gay subtext—subtle enough for most audiences to miss. The mere presence in the movie of the music group Village People raised many eyebrows, and their biggest hit, "YMCA," is prominently featured, with a poolside bikinied chorus line, locker-room nudity, sweaty male camaraderie and—to stay on the safe side—bouncing Valerie Perrine.

Can't Stop the Music is considerably more progressive than Carr's homophobic *Grease* (1978). But when trade publications dubbed it "gay-themed," Carr demanded retractions. The Village People story is loosely interspersed with the white-bread affair of Perrine and athlete Bruce Jenner; Carr attempted to cram his film with something for everyone: The Village People; Perrine, who as Carr put it, "saved Superman's life and fondled *Lenny*'s private parts;" Jenner for sports lovers; Steve Guttenberg, "the Jewish John Travolta," for quiche-eaters and teenyboppers; the Ritchie Family for blacks; Tammy Grimes for the Broadway bunch; June Havoc and Barbara Rush for seniors; and for feminists, Nancy Walker in her movie directorial debut.

Producer Carr even tossed in some good intentions. The Village People sing "Liberation," a gay pride anthem written by group founder Jacques Morali. One line says, "When will you learn, my friend, that your right is mine?" The song is partly used as background for a miming scene in a record studio (but is available in its entirety on the soundtrack album). An EMI executive noted, "A million or two million gay men can make an album a hit, but we have to enlist the 'hets' to make a hit of a major picture." Within the film, Ron White (Jenner) goes from three-piece suits ("Corporate thinking sucks,"

I can make you a man: Frank-N-Furter creates himself
a new lover, Rocky Horror.

Peter Hinwood as Rocky Horror!

says mother Hayoc) to bare thighs and stomach. Sam (Perrine) helps him become "nonjudgmental" toward her offbeat friends, to "accept people as they are."

Can't Stop the Music was shunned by the gay and straight press. Arthur Bell called it "a stupid gay movie for stupid straight people." But straight critics savaged it. *Film Comment* said, "Watching it is akin to witnessing a disco interpretation of the Dance of the Seven Veils in which Salomé turns out to be a male chorine who Couldn't Resist the Chiffon." Stephen Harvey mistakenly described, and derided, the film's target audience as "those eight-year-old boys whose favorite movies, when they grow up, will be *Auntie Mame* and *All About Eve*. . . . By the year 2100 it's probably going to be hailed as *The Gang's All Here* of the eighties."

Aside from Australia, the film was a major flop, not even a likely candidate for culthood. Ethan Mordden noted, "What you have here, folks, is camp that doesn't even bother to *be* before it *turns*. *Can't Stop the Music* and *Xanadu* are the fast-food trays of the Hollywood musical: little lies in bags."

Before *Can't Stop the Music*, the Village People went from a novelty act—with some openly gay members—to the big time. And the straight time. San Francisco's *B.A.R.* said, "They entered their 'Liberace' phase, flaunting their homosexuality without labeling it." A propos of the film's costly failure, Glenn Hughes (Leatherman) told *B.A.R.* in 1983, "Our fans knew our music and wanted to get

to know us as individuals, but by the time Allan got through adding the twelve books of the apostles to the cast, we were only in it for thirty-five minutes." During preproduction, filming, and postproduction, individual Village People had to agree not to be gay. "Movie money is very conservative. We had to keep a low profile . . . stay home and watch the late show." The group began disintegrating after *Can't Stop the Music*; a few members were allegedly fired when their private lives came uncloseted.

Felipe Rose (Indian) was the original Village Person, discovered by Morali in Manhattan's Anvil bar. He told *B.A.R.*, "I'm gay. I can't hide it. But I wouldn't say it on national television. . . . I'll tell the gay press I'm gay. If the straight press asks, we tell them it's none of their business. Or none of their *fucking* business, depending on how they ask."

Queried about the Village People's official posture, Rose said, "It didn't matter whether the group was gay or not. The statement was there—more or less." Interviewer Steve Warren wondered, "What statement? When an obviously gay person denies his gayness, it suggests there's something wrong with being gay. It gives our oppressors a hold on us and keeps other closeted gays from developing a sense of self-worth. We don't lack role models

Bi-bi babies: Riff Raff (*Rocky Horror* co-creator Richard O'Brien) and Magenta (Patricia Quinn) prepare for blast-off.

Pants tighter than the bark on a tree: Barry Bostwick, who played the initially very straight Brad in *Rocky Horror*.

anymore, but everyone who stays in the closet is keeping countless others in there, too."

Men in musicals have always been "suspect," from Nelson Eddy to Chevalier, Dan Dailey, and Prince. The three deceased stars were, in fact, gay or bisexual. According to one of Judy Garland's biographers, Garland suspected costar Gene Kelly of having an affair with her husband, director Vincente Minnelli, during the shooting of *The Pirate* (1948). In reality many male musical stars are gay. But typically, offbeat musical stars who make the transition to movies are homogenized, or *heterogenized*—from Liberace in *Sincerely Yours* (1955) to Prince in *Purple Rain* (1984).

Nonconformist musical stars have a harder time in films, musicals or otherwise. David Bowie, the first major rock star to publicly admit to bisexuality, now denies he was ever not straight. Even so, his movie career has been mixed. In his maiden feature, *The Man Who Fell to Earth* (1976), he played an intergalactic husband and father. Yet Pauline Kael described his "lesbian-Christ leering, his forlorn, limp manner, and chalky pallor." "Lighted like the

The bride of Charles Laughton: *Rocky Horror* borrowed from the campy *Bride of Frankenstein* (1935, Elsa Lanchester and Boris Karloff).

135

woman of mystery in thirties movies," he looks "like Katharine Hepburn in her transvestite role in *Sylvia Scarlett*." He then played the title role in *Just a Gigolo* (1979), Marlene Dietrich's last film, and a straight vampire in the lesbian-themed *The Hunger* (1983).

Merry Christmas, Mr. Lawrence (1983) found Bowie androgynously heterosexual, the love object of Japanese rock star Ryuichi Sakamoto. In this stark World War II drama, homosexuality between Japanese and Europeans is punished (by the Japanese) only because bonding between enemies is strictly forbidden. Mick Jagger postured similarly in 1970 in *Performance*, then considered the latest in outrageous "unisex." Wearing a girlish hairdo and makeup, Jagger makes love with boyish-looking girls. James Fox costarred as a gangster who shoots the rock singer in the head—after he himself tries on drag and is bound, bottomless, with ropes. Unlike Bowie, Jagger is pro-gay. He told *High Society*, "If we're going to worry about any form of sexuality, it should be the prissy, repressed people who never enjoy any form of sex.

"I have as many gay friends as straight. I don't worry about being seen with either. And let's not be unfair to the bis. Bisexuals are probably the fastest growing population in the world."Asked if he's bi, Jagger responded that he doesn't fellate and has never had active anal sex. In another interview he revealed that his cultural hero is Diaghilev and that he feels Americans are "too sex-oriented."

The third of rock's big boys was Elton John. At the height of his fame, in the mid-seventies, John was the number-one pop-rock star. His admission of "bisexuality" in *Rolling Stone* created shock waves but didn't kill his career. Years later, *Creem* asked

Invitation to the dance: Terpsichorean icon Gene Kelly in *An American in Paris* (1951).

Gym dandy: *Can't Stop the Music* (1980) marked the Village People's screen debut *and* decline (here doing the song "YMCA").

Purple Rain (1984): Prince's film bow found him rejecting his previously sexually ambiguous image.

Staying Alive (1983): John Travolta, body by Nautilus, as a heterosexual dancer who replaces a gay one in a Broadway show!

what prompted him to reveal "such a personal thing?" "I felt I'd rather be honest than try to cover it up or get married for the sake of appearances." In 1984, for reasons best known to him, Elton did marry. In 1979 he allowed, "Tom Robinson has been the only one who has come out and admitted to being 100 percent homosexual, which is a very brave step." (Robinson was joined by Johnny Mathis in 1982.)

Asked if the revelation changed his life, John noted, "I don't think people care, especially in Britain. In America I've had more people insult me in the streets." He was also stung by Bowie, who called him a "token queen." Elton responded, "I try not to be bitchy, even though he's had a couple of go's since. But Bowie [once] admitted to me over dinner that he always wanted to be Judy Garland, and that's the God's honest truth."

Michael Jackson had been sought to play the title role in *Peter Pan* (written by the gay Sir James M. Barrie). Despite his public homophobia, Jackson may have trouble making the transition to the big screen; critics found him unbelievable as a would-be

macho man in the music video "Thriller." But the most offbeat potential leading man is Culture Club's Boy George, who discussed his bisexuality with interviewers Joan Rivers and Barbara Walters. In an *Advisor* interview with this author, he explained, "It's a business where numbers count, so you don't want to offend the 90 percent any more than you have to. But if you have courage, you don't deny the 10 percent, either."

"Would you agree to play a conventional leading man?"

"How conventional?"

"Hollywood style."

"Oh, please. . . ."

21

BEING THERE II:

The Ritz

Heterosexual Jack Weston hides out in a gay bath, so naturally Rita Moreno (as Googie Gomez) thinks he is—gay, that is!

The Ritz. Warner Bros., 1976. Director: Richard Lester; writer: Terrence McNally; producer: Denis O'Dell. Starring: Jack Weston, Rita Moreno, Jerry Stiller, Kaye Ballard, Treat Williams, F. Murray Abraham, Paul B. Price.

The Ritz exposes a lighter side of New York City than that of the cruising midnight cowboy. Set in the pre-AIDS era, it was the first film to take place in a gay bathhouse, and probably the last, for a while. Terrence McNally's play won Tony Awards for him and Rita Moreno, whose career it revived. McNally reportedly wrote *The Ritz* after seeing Moreno's "Googie Gomez" act at a party (the loopy Puerto Rican singer believes that Streisand became a bigger star only because she got better breaks).

The play introduced thousands of theatergoers to a gay bathhouse. None of the main characters is gay, and the situational joke involves straight Gaetano Proclo, a Cleveland garbageman who is hiding from his Mafia brother-in-law in the gay baths. Proclo asked a cabdriver to take him "to the last place in the world anybody would think of looking for me." Gay humor is augmented by Italian-Catholic humor, and the schizophrenic play drew large, varied audiences.

Director Richard Lester (*A Hard Day's Night, The Three Musketeers*) offered the role of Michael Brick, a dumb, handsome, straight detective with a soprano speaking voice, to John Travolta. The actor chose instead to play a dumb, handsome, straight

"sweathog" in television's "Welcome Back, Kotter." Treat Williams got the part. The movie retained most of the original stage cast, including Moreno, Jack Weston, and Jerry Stiller.

The main characters are: Proclo (Weston); Carmine Vespucci (Stiller), his would-be assassin, who believes his sister married a "sissy"; Brick, hired by Vespucci to find Proclo; Googie Gomez, entertainer at the Ritz à la Bette Midler at New York's Continental Baths (minus the talent); Vivian Proclo (Kaye Ballard), dismayed at finding her husband—"the man in the mink coat"—in a gay bathhouse. "I just hope you're not going to insist on mentioning this in confession," she cries.

Art doesn't mirror life in this farce; the bath's patrons aren't attractive, but the straight detective is. Its gays are an outlandish bunch, except for Tiger (John Everson) and Duff (Christopher J. Brown), the young bathhouse managers. Their principal customers include Claude Perkins (Paul B. Price), a bald, mustachioed, bespectacled chubby-chaser who falls in love with portly Proclo, and Chris (F. Murray Abraham), curly-haired and middle-aged, a party-type desperate for action. In fact, sex does not occur in *this* bathhouse.

The happy ending finds Vivian twisting her brother's hairy arm when it turns out that the Vespucci clan owns both the baths and Aida Cab, one of whose drivers steered Proclo to the Ritz in the first place. True to farce, mistaken identities, not sexually transmitted diseases, proliferate—the straight men think Googie is a transvestite, the gays think the straights are gay, Brick thinks Proclo is Vespucci, and the heterosexuals come close to un-witting defloration. When the naive Proclo first spies an apparent homosexual, he asides, "People like that really shouldn't be allowed in a place like this." Tiger doubtfully asks whether Proclo's ever been in a similar establishment. "Oh, sure. We got a Jack LaLanne's in Cleveland."

Proclo's first social encounter is with Chris, who explains, "The thing that no one understands about me is that sex is just my way of saying hello." When Proclo realizes where he is, he asks Chris, "You mean *everybody* here is . . .?"

"Gay. It's not such a tough word. You might try using it sometime."

"Nobody is . . . the opposite?

"I sure as hell hope not. I didn't pay ten bucks to walk around in a towel with a bunch of Shriners."

"What about Tiger and Duff? I thought they were normal."

"They are normal. They've also been lovers for three years."

Most of *The Ritz*'s points are made with humor, ribbing straight institutions, gay culture, and het-erosexual assumptions. But homosexuality-as-af-fliction rears its problematic head. La Gomez prom-ises Brick, whom she assumes is gay, "Googie's gonna straighten you out between shows." Vivian, thinking her husband is at the Ritz for pleasure, cries, "You're going through a stage. Last year it was miniature golf." She sobs, "I'll get over this. I get over everything. It's my greatest strength."

Chris provides most of the gay viewpoint. He tries every ploy to get a man into his room, announcing, "Telephone call for Joe Namath in Room 240!" He puts on a scarf and yells through a closed door, "You've got my son in there! Tell him his mother wants to see him." Scouting the rooms, Chris discov-ers Brick and Proclo under a bed, hiding from Vespucci. "I always wondered what you straight guys did together. Now that I know, I'm glad I'm gay." Finally he accepts that the baths are asexual: "It's like some strange heterosexual gypsy curse has been put on this place."

In a rare somber moment Chris says, "I'll tell you something about straight people, and sometimes I

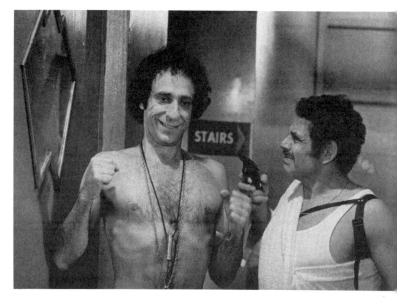

Heterosexual mobster Jerry Stiller encounters gay baths patron F. Murray Abraham.

Stiller, on a vendetta against brother-in-law Weston, lands in the pool of the gay bathhouse *The Ritz* (1976).

The man in the mink coat: Kaye Ballard is chagrined to find her husband at The Ritz.

Happy ending: Would-be murderer
Jerry Stiller is dragged off to jail.

set bears little resemblance to the Turk Street or any
other baths. . . . Treat Williams *is*, once you get past
the squeaky voice, and Rita Moreno nearly steals the
show with cracks about Broadway revivals she's
starred in. However, Googie seems strangely homophobic for someone who dreams and works in a
gay bathhouse.

London Movie Express: Filmed in Britain, the New
York comedy is a showcase for Miss Moreno and
Jack Weston, the underrated comic actor. . . . Included are dubious characters from the criminal
and "gay" subcultures. . . . The film tries to appeal
to both preferences with odd heterosexual protagonists and the homosexual setting and jesters. The
implication is, once you get to know your hosts
you'll love them. In the interest of verisimilitude, a
bewildered "gay" who'd never been to a bathhouse
should have been included, to compare notes with
his "straight" counterparts. . . . Hold on to your
disbelief, but go to enjoy the gay repartee.

think it's the only thing worth knowing about them.
They don't like gays. They never have. They never
will. Anything else they say is just talk."

Proclo says, "For twelve years I was the butt of
every sissy joke played at Our Lady of Perpetual
Sorrow." After marriage, he was bullied by mobster
Vespucci. But in the end the underdogs, gay and
straight, have the last laugh: Proclo, the mistaken
homosexual, shakes hands with Chris, the real homosexual, and says if he's ever in Cleveland to stop
by—his wife makes great lasagna. Like Charrier in
La Cage aux Folles, Vespucci winds up in drag,
humiliated. His delighted brother-in-law delivers
him to the bullying cops. Proclo is less forgiving
than Albin and Renato, but then, revenge is a
heterosexual film prerogative.

ABOUT *THE RITZ*

Coming Out: The straights are all fools. The gays are
crazy or kinky—like the blubber-lover—or both.
Everyone gets put down, but somehow it's clever,
and certain lines persist in memory. The story is
chopped liver, and the movie's saving grace is its
characterizations—everyone but Jerry Stiller is to
laugh. . . . Don't expect nudity or passion-in-the-
tubs; *The Ritz* is family-style sanitized, and the gaudy

Post-*Ritz*, Treat Williams reverted to his own hair color and
natural voice in films like *Prince of the City* (1981).

140

22

MEN'S WOMEN:

Bilitis and Personal Best

Patti D'Arbanville discovers that young love begins at home in the soft-focus, erotic *Bilitis* (1977).

Bilitis. Topar/Film 21, 1977. Director: David Hamilton; writers: Roger Boussinot, Catherine Breillat, Jacques Nahum, and Jean-Louis Roncoroni; producers: Sylvio Tabet and Nahum.
Starring: Patricià D'Arbanville, Mona Kristensen, Bernard Giraudeau, Gilles Kohler, Mathieu Carrière, Catherine LePrince.

Personal Best. Warner Bros., 1982.
Director-writer-producer: Robert Towne.
Starring: Mariel Hemingway, Scott Glenn, Patrice Donnelly, Kenny Moore.

Naked young women frolic at a swimming hole. Nude females bask in the stinging showers of a gym. Writhing feminine forms kiss and join in lingering caresses, their intertwined limbs lovingly photographed. Casual but passionate affairs . . . and then the *real* women switch to men for less esthetic but *meaningful* coupling. The women's women are alone, until the next few minutes of feminine pleasure—and all for the masculine eye.

Bilitis and *Personal Best* are lovingly crafted male fantasies. They celebrate female nudity and are open to charges of exploitation, but both avoid the extreme stereotypes of their 1968 predecessors, *The Killing of Sister George* and *Thérèse and Isabelle*. Nobody dies, and lesbianism isn't an overt issue. However, to directors David Hamilton and Robert Towne, most women-loving women aren't gay—they simply have wider erotic horizons than the average woman. Each picture includes a lesbian who serves as a sexy foil for the woman who opts exclusively for men.

The title character in *Bilitis* is a lesbian whose difference from her classmates is symbolized by her dislike of horses. *Personal Best*'s lead is more ambiguous. Both characters are in their teens, in keeping with screen portrayals of lesbians as either sapphic rosebuds or wilted neurotics who prey on youth. *Bilitis*, a French film with an American star, and *Personal Best*, an American film with an athletic star, were both R-rated, highly erotic, and—as films about women—nonpolitical. Their distributors didn't see them as statements or consider them threatening. Yet few viewers labeled either one a "woman's picture," for they weren't made with women in mind.

An anonymous actress in *Bilitis* told *Paris Match*, "We functioned as extensions of our sex lives and desirability. They could have given us, or made some of us, male partners. But they would have had to *deal* with the men . . . and men's nudity would have distracted male viewers from our bodies." The American film does include male nudity, and its women strenuously pursue their goals—goals that are physical, not cerebral. Another cultural difference is that the French film glamorizes its (slightly) older woman while the American film masculinizes her. *Bilitis* is more realistic insofar as the restless younger woman is the aggressor, but none of the characters exhibits stereotypical "dykey" traits.

Bilitis begins and ends with the titular character (Patricia D'Arbanville) sitting on a bed, musing over her summer spent with her guardian Pierre (Gilles Kohler) and friend Melissa (Mona Kristensen) at their country villa. Idyllic days at a nude swimming hole are also recalled. At the dorm, Bilitis's girlfriend Hélène (Catherine LePrince) joins her in bed. Girlish, aggressive Hélène sports the requisite cropped brown hair. Bilitis mildly protests when Hélène makes love to her.

Continuing in flashback, Bilitis goes to stay for the summer with her sexually brutal guardian, Pierre, who loves horses and affairs, and there she becomes infatuated with lovely, stern Melissa. She sees Pierre rape Melissa, which increases her mistrust of men, but she conducts a flirtatious friendship with Lucas (Bernard Giraudeau), a handsome photographer. Bilitis receives her first male kiss from him—but it's as far as she'll go. Meanwhile, she seduces Melissa, who enjoys it, but then vows "Never again." Hurt and confused, Bilitis is still determined to find Melissa a man more gentle than Pierre, who's away in Monte Carlo.

Bilitis photographs every handsome male in sight and takes the pictures home to Melissa, who's only vaguely interested in one, Nikias (Mathieu Carrière). When Nikias met Bilitis, he mistook her for a prostitute because she said she was searching for a man. Nikias states that he isn't available to *anyone*. (Gay? Impossible. Films with lesbians almost never have gay men.) Eventually, Melissa goes to Monte Carlo with Bilitis. There's a party and Nikias is there. When he and Melissa dance, she tells him he isn't the man for her and he leaves with two chums. Lucas is also there, and he and Melissa dance. Bilitis realizes she's giving up the woman she loves to the man she (platonically) loves. "I told you it could only be someone I loved," she tells Melissa. Before leaving, Bilitis joins Melissa's hand with Lucas's. The couple dances the night away, and the next time we see Bilitis she's sitting on her bed, her suitcases packed to leave.

The story takes second place to the actresses' display. Tellingly, the film's focus shifts in the second half from Bilitis to Melissa. By virtue of her virtues (heterosexuality and passivity), Melissa takes center stage. A stubborn little lesbian, Bilitis is, so to speak, odd man out.

"It's natural for a girl and a boy," Lucas tells Bilitis, but her love for Melissa is more natural for her—"Her every word is a womb to me," she says. Unfortunately, cold and condescending Melissa doesn't merit adulation, so Bilitis's grand passion is

wasted. No doubt Bilitis will love again, but it's too soon to know whether she'll keep choosing women exclusively. But the implication is that if she does she'll remain outside the ungentle but charmed circle of "ordained" love.

No cheap softcore effort, *Bilitis* features elegant photography by Bernard Daillencourt and the plaintive music of Francis Lai (*Love Story, Un Homme et une femme*).

ABOUT *BILITIS*

Out: Newcomer Patricia D'Arbanville resembles a young Shirley MacLaine, especially the eyes and speech pattern. She shifts from petulance to childish worry to passion. Though she's no Monroe or Mansfield upstairs, she has sex-symbol looks, and her pensive unpredictableness is endearing. She dresses in simple summer clothes or, for school recitals, Grecian garb. But girl-watchers of both genders get several chances to view Ms. D'Arbanville and others in the buff. . . . Bilitis doesn't renege on her feelings toward men, marriage, and sexual politics, but this is set forth as immaturity, not integrity.

Samedi et Dimanche: Based on *Les Chansons de Bilitis* by Pierre Louÿs, *Bilitis* is a pastoral tale of innocent desire. . . . The beauties of the French countryside and young womanhood sustain interest for an hour and a half. . . . The lesbianism, like the gauzy cinematography, is soft-focused for viewing facility.

Personal Best examines four years in the lives of two female athletes who meet at the 1976 Olympic trials and become lovers. Their relationship grows strained as they compete; the macho observers keep saying it won't last, even after three years have passed. Predictably, Chris (Mariel Hemingway) swaps Tory (Patrice Donnelly, a former hurdling champ) for a male athlete (Kenny Moore). Rounding out the starring quartet is Scott Glenn as Chris's coach.

At two-hours-plus, the film devotes enough footage to running, hurdling, pole-vaulting, and swimming to fill a documentary. In between the athletics there's leisurely lovemaking, eating, talking, and showering. *Personal Best*'s widely discussed depiction of feminine homosexuality created little controversy in the straight-male-oriented media but stirred up a hornet's nest in the gay press. Chris is completely defined by the men around her, dependent for guidance and inspiration on her father, then her coach, then her boyfriend. In competition with Tory, Chris is bound to lose, for she doesn't have the lesbian's (or a man's) "killer instinct." Accident-prone and vulnerable to crying jags, she's berated by her coach: "I could have been a *men's* coach! Do you really think Chuck Noll has to worry that Terry Bradshaw is going to cry if Franco Harris won't talk to him?"

Personal Best made a star of Mariel Hemingway, who stole the anti-rape movie *Lipstick* from older sister Margaux. But her publicity comments alienated many people. On the *Today* show she said, "To me the [love] scenes never seemed homosexual . . . and the scene is not explicit. You don't see anything!" *The Advocate* questioned her: "You said on TV that you don't see anything. . . . Two women naked in bed, caressing each other, legs wrapped around each other. Not explicit?"

D'Arbanville comes of age in *Bilitis* when she realizes her appeal to both genders.

"No, no. What I'm saying is . . . well, you don't see them going down on each other. I mean, being naked is not being explicit. You never see them making out . . . or tongues down the throat or anything." Though *Personal Best* dwells on the women's three years together, Hemingway felt, "It's not a statement about lesbians at all! Oh, it *is* in the sense that you can come away from seeing the film and say, 'If that's lesbianism . . . it's not so bad.' "

Soon after playing Chris, the actress had her

Girls' boarding schools often serve as settings for sapphic crushes and affairs, as in *Bilitis*.

breasts cosmetically enlarged and portrayed fatally exploited *Playboy* centerfold Dorothy Stratten in *Star 80*. She explained that the surgery wasn't for the movie but for her own sense of femininity.

As a brunette newcomer—without a famous surname—Patrice Donnelly's press appeal couldn't compete with Hemingway's or Towne's, and she purposely avoided controversy. Scott Glenn, who played Off-Broadway in *Fortune and Men's Eyes*, spoke to *B.A.R.* His female manager courted the gay press and predicted stardom for her ruggedly handsome client. She informed *B.A.R.* that in his next picture, *The Keep*, "Scott has lavender eyes, wears lots of leather or nothing at all, and saves the world."

But *Personal Best* was Robert Towne's baby, a five-year project and his directorial debut. The top-paid screenwriter (*Bonnie and Clyde, Shampoo*) explained, "There was a great movie many years ago, *The Trials of Oscar Wilde*, which stays with me because of the pain of that relationship. I could identify with that pain . . . that hopelessness. When I saw *Wilde*, I was struck with the idea that only in a so-called deviant relationship would it be possible to express anything romantic between two people anymore. There's so little danger in anything heterosexual that it's not terribly dramatic anymore."

Because of his reputation and the film's subject, Towne had no trouble getting generous studio backing for *Personal Best*, which was marketed for general audiences. It also tried to lure sports lovers, straight romantics (with its triumphant heterosexu-

143

Mariel Hemingway as Chris Cahill, a casually bisexual pentathlete in *Personal Best* (1982).

Mano a mano: Donnelly and Hemingway portray competitors who become friends, lovers, then "just friends" again.

Patrice Donnelly as Tory Skinner, a lesbian pentathlete and the lover of rival Cahill.

ality), and voyeurs of male and female nudity. Covering all bases, the Warners press kit likened Chris and Tory's relationship to "any romance, whether between Elizabeth Barrett and Robert Browning, Clark Gable and Vivien Leigh, or Paul Newman and Robert Redford."

Usually reclusive, Towne did extensive publicity for his picture. He told the *Los Angeles Times*, "I don't think in any way this is a lesbian or homosexual movie. I'm interested in how you deal with a society that encourages competition, and still care about others." *Newsweek*'s Jack Kroll dubbed the film *Chariots of Desire* and lauded Towne because "he dares, with delicacy and insight, to show a loving sexual relationship between two young women, not as a statement about homosexuality but as a paradigm of human intimacy."

Questioned by *The Advocate* about Chris and Tory's lesbianism, Towne offered, "It's an extension of their being children, discovering what they are through their bodies—in competition, in love. Whether or not these girls had prior sexual contact with other women, clearly this is the first significant contact for both."

Towne's screenplays emphasize macho values, yet he declared, "I'm a man who really likes women, whatever shape, size, or sexual preference. I can identify with them. The screenwriter is in a position not terribly different from women; he gives birth to a film but then isn't given the political power to take charge of it." About homosexuality he said, "A gay relationship is almost a metaphor for losing yourself in someone because you *are* of the same sex. It's like, I'm not going to be able to tell where I end and someone else begins."

Towne felt his film's "affection, love, and romance" were universal, "crossing *all* sexes," and would attract mass audiences. But one reviewer felt that the very lack of affection in *Personal Best* was alienating: "*The Fox*, many years back, had far more tenderness, love, and compassion, even though it was ruined by a Hays Code ending." A few gay and straight critics felt that Hemingway's misguided quotes—not *Personal Best*'s ads or length—hurt what the public perceived as a Hemingway vehicle. Hemingway delivered the coup de grâce when she revealed that neither Chris nor Tory is definitely gay. They come together, she felt, only "out of need." Hemingway wanted or needed to believe that Tory's homosexuality "doesn't necessarily mean that Tory couldn't fall in love with another guy and love him as much as she loves Chris."

ABOUT *PERSONAL BEST*

Norma McLain Stoop, *After Dark*: *Personal Best*, to paraphrase Groucho Marx, is about women's bodies and competition and women's bodies and winning and women's bodies and growing up and women's bodies. . . . No filmmaker ever went broke showing two beautiful women making love—just ask Russ Meyer—and Towne plays it safe by having

Chris and her chauvinistic coach (Scott Glenn) don't always see eye to eye; he admits he'd rather coach males!

Hemingway dump her female lover for a male one. In the world according to *Personal Best*, homosexuality is like acne—an inconvenient adolescent affliction one prayerfully will grow out of. Yeah. Sure.

Donald McLean, the *Village Voice: Personal Best* is about foul-mouthed, burping, farting dykes who live in a man's world by men's standards, told through a man's eyes. . . . Towne's fixation on crotches is all that separates them from being men. . . . Integrity goes down the drain when the coach makes a pass at the girl after a few slighting remarks about "female love." Hemingway is wimpy and weepy as the "little boy Daddy always wanted," who blossoms into womanhood thanks to a good man's love in a "tasteful" scene where she demands to hold his penis as he urinates. . . . Hemingway wins the Mush-Mouth of the Year award; half her dialogue is unintelligible—buried in her crotch no doubt.

Your Paper: The best movie yet on female jocks glorifies women's bodies by demonstrating strength, flexibility, and *choice*. These young athletes select their goals as they select their lovers: deliberately and unsentimentally. Their strong bodies and useful lives aren't male-defined, and the lesbian relationship is the most natural yet filmed. The lesbian-sex scenes are so graphic I'm amazed they didn't draw an X-rating. When the couple break up, it's disappointing. But competing with a lover—or a spouse—is tiresome. The ambiguous ending leaves room for doubt. Chris says, "He's cute . . . for a guy." Tory laughs, "Are you kidding?"

At the Olympic trials, Chris Cahill gives her all—however, her personal goals are less clear.

23

LESBIANS YOU
LOVE TO/OR HATE

*This chapter focuses on secondary lesbian
characters who run the gamut from stereotypical
villains designed to be hated by mass audiences to
career women, antiheroines, and role models
beloved by lesbian and gay movie buffs.*

• In 1963 Lotte Lenya played *the* archetypical
screen lesbian-villain: *From Russia With Love*'s "killer
dyke," Colonel Rosa Klebb. Her lust for Garboesque Daniela Bianchi is ludicrous to behold—
beauty and the Commie beast who carries brass
knuckles in her handbag. When Klebb meets and
attacks James Bond, she sports sensible shoes with
retractable switchblades. The butch Marxist is too
easy a character, in the cheap-shot tradition of
smearing Russian womanhood as homely and virile,
ergo villainous.

In *The Roman Spring of Mrs. Stone* (1961), Lenya is
a slightly less venal variation of she-devil: the corrupting European aristocrat. She plays the Contessa Magda Terribili-Gonzalez in the film from a
story by Tennessee Williams. A leering, avaricious
madam, she hires out Warren Beatty to repressed
"nymphomaniac" Vivien Leigh. When Beatty casts
an eye at Jill St. John, the contessa is jealous—of
Beatty. Directed by José Quintero, the film contains
cameos by Coral Browne (*The Killing of Sister George*)
and Ernest Thesiger (*Bride of Frankenstein, The Old
Dark House*), the ancient gay eccentric who died
soon after making this one. One of Lenya's last roles
was a butch masseuse in Burt Reynolds's 1978
suicide comedy *The End*.

PHOTO: LORRAINE DAY

Bi, baby!: In 1991 Madonna came out as bisexual and
admitted that she's fantasized about Marlene Dietrich!

• Candice Bergen's movie debut was in Sidney
Lumet's 1966 *The Group*, as the lesbian Lakey, who
wears severely tailored clothes and hangs out with a
countess. Judith Crist wrote that by the 1960s "the
'neuter dedicated-career-type' had been turned
into a lesbian; 'a *Sapphic*, a *lesbo*,' says the script, with
a vulgarity that even Miss [Mary] McCarthy eschewed." In George Cukor's *Rich and Famous*
(1981), Bergen rejects Jacqueline Bisset's invitation
to a New Year's kiss, despite a relationship some
critics adjudged "latent," a term usually reserved
for the male of the species.

• When gay director John Waters (*Polyester*) interviewed Pia Zadora for *American Film*, she confessed she's always gotten along with gay friends.
Her childhood idol was Liberace. "I'm Polish, too,
and I played the piano as a child." When Waters
suggested a cinematic teaming, she exclaimed, "Oh,
God, what kind of audience would that have? Jeez!
Talk about diverse." In *The Lonely Lady* (1983), Pia
has a lesbian affair and immediately showers fully

146

clothed because she feels *dirty*. "That was pretty funny," gushed Waters. "It was intended to be serious," said Pia, who revealed that "*Lonely Lady* wasn't meant to be trash—it was just so badly done that it looked campy, and people thought it was meant to *be* campy."

• Helena Kallaniotes portrayed two memorably sullen lesbians. In *Five Easy Pieces* (1970) she's a hostile, whining hitchhiker who is picked up with her straggly girlfriend by Jack Nicholson and Karen Black. In 1972's *Kansas City Bomber*, based on an original story by Barry Sandler (*Making Love*), Kallaniotes is a super-tough roller-derby queen threatened by newcomer Raquel Welch. In Sandler's version the lesbian athlete falls in love with Welch, but MGM honchos mandated a more sexually neutral dark-haired, dark-spirited villainess.

• Anne Baxter's obsessed, underhanded (*All About . . .*) Eve has gained a new perspective over the years. In her book *Running Time*, Nora Sayre wrote, "Baxter's ardent infatuation with [Bette] Davis seems thoroughly lesbian. If the sexes were reversed, imagine a film of 1950 that dared to portray such a relationship between a famous male actor and a worshipful young man—which would have been unthinkable."

Eve has two particularly suggestive moments: when she tenders a smile to a female neighbor from whom she has nothing to gain, and when (at film's end) she's approached by Phoebe (Barbara Bates), a young actress who uses the same tactics Eve used on Margo Channing. The star permits the young intruder to stay and basks in her calculated adulation. The famous multiple-mirror image—an army of Phoebes—symbolizes the women who use and need other women.

• Jane Fonda had her crypto-bisexual moments in an orgy scene in 1969's *Spirits of the Dead*. The scene was less controversial, though, than one with a "shocking" kiss with brother Peter. In *Barbarella* (1968) Jane is pursued by Anita Pallenberg's slinky Black Queen.

The central relationship in *Julia* (1977) is sisterly but nonsexual—both in the film and as originally written by Lillian Hellman (played by Fonda). When an associate suggests that Julia (Vanessa Redgrave) is more than a friend to Lillian, Fonda knocks him flat with a manly punch. The scene is needlessly homophobic, a puzzler to fans of the activist superstar.

Arthur Bell asked whether Fonda's pro-gay stance drew flak from coworkers. "Yes, from cowboys. When I was doing *Comes a Horseman*, a few of them would say, 'So you're out there with the gays, eh?' It's difficult to answer . . . but it doesn't go unnoticed by me that *they* like to spend time with the boys. And these same men can't understand that I have three black people working for me. You can only hope that they'll like you and listen to you and one day question their own beliefs."

• Meryl Streep, who had a small part in *Julia*, played Woody Allen's ex-wife Jill in the homophobic, misogynistic *Manhattan* (1979). She leaves Isaac (Allen) for Connie (Karen Ludwig), whom "Ike" tried to run over with a car. The two chilly women rear Willie (Damion Sheller), listed in the credits as "Ike's son." Though Isaac is the more loving parent, the mother is awarded custody—seldom the case with real-life Jills. Isaac asks Jill, "Does he play baseball? Does he wear dresses?" Jill writes a vindictive best-seller about life with her ex-husband.

• Barbara Stanwyck, who starred in 1942's *The Gay Sisters* and was studio-wed to Robert Taylor, played one of Hollywood's first lesbians in *Walk on the Wild Side* (1962). Jo is a hard-hearted madam in thirties New Orleans. Hallie (Capucine) is her true love and best girl, until Laurence Harvey comes between them. When Jo's ineffectual husband questions the relationship, Jo rips into him, demanding what a mere man could *possibly* know about a wom-

Henry & June (1990) depicted the real-life affair of Anais Nin (Maria de Medeiros) and Henry Miller's wife, June (Uma Thurman).

an's true feelings. Hallie is killed accidentally during a shoot-out. The "vice queen" simply goes to jail until her money and connections can get her out. (Moral: If you must be butch, be crooked.) The "adult" novel on which the film was based didn't include lesbianism. Producer Charles K. Feldman explained, "We're updating the story for sixties audiences, who want more spice in stories about girls who go bad."

• Miss Fellowes (Oscar-nominated Grayson Hall) in John Huston's *The Night of the Iguana* (1964) is a classic screen lesbian. Wildly jealous of Charlotte's (Sue Lyon) attraction to men, the spinster is taunted by fading sexpot Maxine (Ava Gardner) about the "dykes of Texas." Defrocked Reverend Shannon (Richard Burton) rebukes Maxine, informing her that "Miss Fellowes is a highly moral person. If she ever realized the truth about herself it would destroy her." The script by Huston and Anthony Veiller added homophobia not in the Tennessee Williams play, which starred Bette Davis.

• *Rachel, Rachel* (1968) features a spinster who sublimates her lust into old-time Protestant religion. Calla (Estelle Parsons) invites her friend and colleague Rachel (Joanne Woodward) to a religious revival. Later, as they eat ice cream, Calla suddenly kisses Rachel on the lips. *Both* women are stunned and embarrassed, and their friendship becomes strained. Rachel tries to find a man, but, as Rex Reed—who should have known better—put it, "They're all married or queer." In *The Effect of Gamma Rays on Man-in-the-Moon Marigolds* (1972)—another Paul Newman-directed film—frumpy, embittered Betty (Woodward) yells "faggot" at a man who isn't attracted to her.

• A candidate for most-twisted-gay-villain is Elizabeth Ashley in 1980's *Windows*. Andrea has a fixation on heterosexual Emily (Talia Shire). She intends to win her love by turning her off men. To accomplish this she hires a sleazy taxi driver to rape Emily. But Emily is rescued by rugged detective Bob Luffrono (Joseph Cortese). The Gordon Willis film was justifiably condemned by critics. *New York* magazine's David Denby called the flop one of "the perverted fantasies of men who hate lesbians so much they will concoct any idiocy in order to slander them."

• One of the meanest lesbians of all time is Kate Murtagh's hulk-madam, Frances Amthor, in Ray-mond Chandler's *Farewell, My Lovely* (1975). Robert Mitchum's Philip Marlowe is dainty by comparison. After asking him not to smoke, Amthor slugs him to emphasize her point. When Marlowe doesn't deliver required information, she puts him through a narcotically induced nightmare. And when Sylvester Stallone paws her favorite girl, Amthor stampedes him but is quickly shot down. Author Chandler once confessed, "In the artistic society of London about one man in three is homosexual, which is very bad on the ladies but not at all hard on me."

• Susannah York finds herself in bed with Elizabeth Taylor in *X, Y and Zee* (British title: *Zee and Co.*) (1972). Liz/Zee is a shrew whose husband Bob (Michael Caine) is cheating with Stella (York). Zee attends parties with her fruity friend Gordon (John Standing) and "befriends" Stella to discover her Achilles heel: She was expelled from school for falling in love with a nun. To get back at Bob, Zee lures Stella into bed but arranges it so he "catches" them. One English critic called the X-certified [in Britain] film *Who's Afraid of Bloody Sunday?*, and Edna O'Brien charged "mass mayhem" on her script—she sought to appear on British television to discuss it but was prevented by Columbia Pictures. "Had I appeared, I intended to say only one thing: That if I ever meet [director] Brian Hutton, I will kill him."

The *TV Guide* synopsis draws an irrelevant parallel between parenting and fidelity: "Elizabeth Taylor and Michael Caine depict the love-hate relationship of a London couple whose childless union is disrupted by an attractive widow."

• One of Elizabeth Taylor's oddest films was 1968's *Secret Ceremony*, costarring Mia Farrow as the child-woman Cenci. Leonora is a London hooker who befriends Cenci because she reminds her of her dead daughter. Leonora moves in with the girl, and the pair soak in a large tub and exchange nonfilial endearments. NBC's butchered version is the one exclusively seen. In the television version Leonora is a wig model, and the bathing and massage scenes are missing. Cenci kills herself, and at the funeral Leonora stabs the girl's stepfather (Robert Mitchum). Apparently with Universal Pictures' okay, NBC scissored the violence, had Leonora arrested, and had new footage shot with a pontificating psychiatrist-narrator. A priest was also added, by request of a censor for the National Bishop Company.

• Henri-Georges Clouzot's 1955 *Diabolique* (*Les*

Diaboliques) was based on the novel *La Femme qui était* (*The Woman Who Was*), about a murdering lesbian couple. The film turned them heterosexual, although first-time viewers get the impression that Simone Signoret is Vera Clouzot's butch lover. (Need one mention that an American television remake with Joan Hackett and Tuesday Weld was even more hetero than its predecessor?)

• Mercedes McCambridge is Emma Small, the lesbian vigilante, in the anti-McCarthy *Johnny Guitar*. Nicholas Ray's 1954 western was considered "unbelievable." A liberal film in a conservative genre, it was hotly condemned by John Wayne and others. Today it's a high-camp cult classic, on- and off-campus. Joan Crawford is Vienna, the cool, cultured saloon-owner whose land will soon be bought to build a railroad. Emma, who wears only black with her men's cowboy boots, wants Vienna's land. She contrives to lynch Vienna, charging guilt by association (a bank robber frequents the saloon). Inevitably the two women shoot it out, and reason triumphs over darkness.

Critic Michael Wilmington wrote, "In light of Emma's sexual hangups, we can see why the Kid's robbery of her bank enrages her: Not only does he have the gall to penetrate her vault, but he kisses her rival, Vienna, at the very entrance." One of the screen's first terrorists, Emma bears Vienna a sexually motivated love-hate that stays beneath the fifties surface. (The film's title—the name of an ex-lover of Vienna's—was a "required" selling point in that male-ruled decade.)

In her homophobic autobiography, *The Quality of Mercy*, McCambridge describes her dog, who possesses "the normal appetites of any self-respecting male—of whom there seem to be very few left, of any species!" She ridicules "the most mincing member of our wardrobe crew" on *Johnny Guitar*. "Being gay, he shouted gaily, 'I've saved the day, dear hearts. Fear not, the problem is solved. I mean it's actually solved!' " McCambridge tells the anecdote about the crewman with amazing recall; though the actresses loathed each other, McCambridge is much too "lady-like" to rat on Crawford.

• *Jacqueline Susann's Once Is Not Enough* (1975), features two rich and famous lesbians in the movie's warmest relationship. Alexis Smith is the world's fifth richest woman. Her lover Karla (Melina Mercouri, later a Greek Cabinet Minister) is a legendary Garboesque recluse. Smith marries Kirk Douglas only for appearances, though "the divine Karla" ("a German peasant" before stardom) relishes an occa-

Teutonic Sappho: Rachel Roberts as Hildegarde Schmidt, lady's maid, in *Murder on the Orient Express* (1974).

Alexis Smith is the fifth richest woman in the world, with a for-show husband (Kirk Douglas), in *Once Is Not Enough* (1974).

sional hunk, to her lover's dismay. But fireplace aglow, the women snuggle and kiss on the mouth, swathed in a fur bedspread. Loving well is the best revenge.

• *Goldfinger*'s Pussy Galore (Honor Blackman) isn't really a villain, just a capable woman. Like the

When Captain Lewis (Eileen Brennan) is transferred to Europe, she switches to women, in *Private Benjamin* (1979).

Smith's true love is Garbo-esque film legend Karla (Melina Mercouri) in the film of Jacqueline Susann's novel.

Melina Mercouri is "unhappily married" in *10:30 P.M. Summer* (1966), while Romy Schneider's in love with Melina's husband!

novel by the late Ian Fleming, the 1964 movie sketches a cold beauty who probably had an early bad experience with a man. After James Bond knocks her about a bit, she's ready for men—ideally, just one. In the book Pussy's admirer Jill Masterson sets out to avenge her dead sister; in the film she's just a passing, expendable blonde.

• The Canadian *By Design* (1980), stars Patty Duke Astin and Sara Botsford as successful dress designers and lifemates, happy except for their childlessness. Helen and Angie try to adopt, then consider artificial insemination. Finally, Helen (Duke) recruits a male employee to impregnate her. The *Advocate* noted, "A woman's distaste at coupling with an attractive man presents an unfamiliar, unsettling screen image." Also unsettling was the fact that the women never kiss. According to director Claude Jutra, "We wanted to avoid the problem of pornography, even the possibility. . . . Their homosexuality is taken for granted—*that's* positive." Avoiding lesbian affection (and the word itself) didn't help, for *By Design*—which ridicules feminists

Viveca Lindfors as the lesbian, with Rita Gam (note the stereotypical outfits) in Sartre's *No Exit* (1962).

Viveca Lindfors as a lesbian librarian telling private eye George Maharis of her love for *Sylvia* (1965).

and gay men—was virtually unseen in the U.S., prior to its video-cassette release. The happy ending finds Helen and Angie happily parenting Angie's baby, the result of a one-night stand. (Helen's baby was stillborn.)

• 1951's *Olivia* was released in the U.S. three years later as *The Pit of Loneliness*, a variation on *The Well of Loneliness*, the most famous lesbian novel until *Rubyfruit Jungle*. Julie (Edwige Feuillère) and Cara (Simone Simon) run a French finishing school, one of whose students, Olivia (Marie-Claire Olivia), has a love affair with the elegant Julie. The tale is slight, the romance is breathless, and the teacher tearfully gives up Olivia to the straight status quo. (The mid-fifties U.S. version deleted a kiss-on-the-lips that *was* acceptable in 1930's *Morocco*; but then, Marlene Dietrich was engaged in the film to Adolphe Menjou *and* in love with Gary Cooper.) Colette wrote the script, and the film was directed by Jacqueline Audry (born 1908), whose career spanned the forties to the seventies and included the nonmusical *Gigi* (1949) and *La Garçonne* (*Bachelor Girl*) in 1957.

Jacques Tourneur's *The Cat People* (1942) starred Ms. Simon as a fashion designer who refuses to consummate her marriage. Subsequent events—real or imagined—indicate she may be turning into a cat. Or, offered one critic, she may be "a lonely, neurotic, possibly lesbian woman driven to brute violence by her obsessive fears."

Candice Bergen and Jacqueline Bisset, lovingly competitive writers in George Cukor's *Rich and Famous* (1981).

151

Fonda *Julia* (1977): Hollywood wags nicknamed the film, starring Jane Fonda and Vanessa Redgrave, "Reds in Bed."

Fonda *Barbarella* (1968): Queen Anita Pallenberg (right) covets Jane Fonda, who covets the Blind Angel, who doesn't covet anyone!

Candice Bergen (in sleeveless leather, center) made her film bow as Lakey, the chic lesbian, in *The Group* (1966).

• Swedish Viveca Lindfors has played several lesbians. The most "popular" one, in *The Way We Were* (1973), is chummy with Barbra Streisand, who defends her to Robert Redford by informing him that she's a grandmother. Lindfors loves Faye Dunaway in *Puzzle of a Downfall Child* (1970), set in the world of high fashion. In *No Exit* (1962) Lindfors is more restrained with Rita Gam, and in 1965's *Sylvia* she's a prim librarian. (Lindfors's handsome son Kristoffer Tabori starred with Alan Alda in one of the first [partly] gay telefilms, *The Glass House* [1972], by Truman Capote. Tabori was the prison newcomer who gets raped and jumps to his death.)

• Real-life psychiatrist Penelope Russianoff was stripped of her gayness in the final cut of *An Unmarried Woman* (1978). Perhaps giving Jill Clayburgh a female shrink was deemed progressive enough. However, when the doctor bumps into Jill in a party scene, she has a younger female "friend" at her side; party scenes are harder to edit.

152

• *My Brilliant Career* (1979), directed by Gillian Armstrong, was hailed as a feminist breakthrough. Yes and no. Sybilla (Judy Davis of *A Woman Called Golda* and *An Unsuitable Job for a Woman*) chooses a career over marriage, which is not surprising. In the book she's a lesbian. In the movie—which at A$900,000 had the biggest budget of any previous Australian film with a first-time director—Sybilla isn't gay. Armstrong declared that the ending was the backers' choice and that "no one in the press took me to task for it." A hit Down Under, *My Brilliant Career* won the Catholic Church's Christopher award for "most moral film of the year." Armstrong noted, "They completely missed the sexual tension in it . . . or perhaps not." Her second film, the musical *Starstruck*, features a gay television host and a chorus line of musclemen-lifeguards. Then Hollywood beckoned with *Mrs. Soffel*, starring Diane Keaton and Mel Gibson.

• One of Holland's biggest hits in 1979 was the sexplicit *A Woman Like Eve*, starring Monique van de Ven (*Turkish Delight*) and Maria Schneider and directed by Nouchka van Brakel. At a feminist conference, Eve (van de Ven) falls in love with Liliane (Schneider), a gay commune worker. Eve's enraged husband divorces her and gets custody of their children, but Eve finds fulfillment in her new life. *Eve* played only a few U.S. cities, and van de Ven said, "We are fortunate in Holland to have audiences who can handle a lot. Here you have to deal with studio heads and Midwestern taste. . . . This film is for housewives, a film that *had* to be made."

A San Francisco engagement for *Eve* was arranged only after Shirley MacLaine viewed the film, "loved it," and used her influence. Monique van de Ven, married to a male cinematographer and with "more gay friends than straight ones," tried to publicize *Eve* but couldn't get booked on television. The Dutch star later moved to Los Angeles and compared it with "Amsterdam, where people are very advanced. There is no problem with homosexuality, and never since I was a child has it been considered strange. But outside the city it's the Middle Ages. . . . "

• Another rarely seen foreign film is *Richard's Things* (1980), directed by Anthony Harvey (*The Lion in Winter*) and written by Frederic Raphael (*Two for the Road*). Richard's widow Kate (Liv Ullmann) spitefully arranges meetings with Richard's girlfriend Josie (Amanda Redman). "I wanted to kill you," says Kate, but "Jojo" seduces her, and they become lovers and roommates. Jojo encourages the affair "to keep Richard alive a little longer. . . . After all, what would we be on our own?" But the possessive Kate is jealous of Jojo's young friends and outside life. She is confused about her feelings and regretfully ends the affair to find a life of her own. The pair split amicably, and both women's futures are open doors.

• The myth of lesbianism as an immature or vengeful *choice* is presented in *Private Benjamin* (1980). Captain Doreen Lewis (Eileen Brennan) is heterosexual until she catches her man two-timing her with a female private. Doreen transfers to Europe and goes gay—revenge in a foreign climate. In the later television series Captain Lewis stayed on U.S. soil and kept her head screwed on "straight."

24

FAIRY TALE:

A Different Story

A Different Story. Avco Embassy, 1978. Director: Paul Aaron; writer: Henry Olek; producer: Alan Belkin. Starring: Perry King, Meg Foster, Valerie Curtin, Peter Donat, Guerin Barry, Lisa James, Doug Higgins.

As the opening credits roll for *A Different Story*, Albert (Perry King) is at the airport to meet an older man, Douglas, his lover and employer (Peter Donat). Albert is Douglas's chauffeur, and they are on their way to a gay party in Beverly Hills. But Douglas has a wandering eye and picks up a young hunk. The next day, he fires Albert and puts his new friend in the driver's seat.

Al's homeless, so he showers in a vacant house-for-sale that he and Doug had seen. A chic young real estate agent, Stella Cook (Meg Foster) is showing the house to clients. She hears noise in the bathroom and investigates. The doorknob sticks, but Stella's strong; the door flies open and out tumbles Al. He falls on top of Stella, but, being gay, he quickly gets off.

Stella takes pity on the homeless Belgian (who doesn't have an accent because "I didn't want one") and lets him stay at her house. Stella is a slob—her house is a mess, and she eats directly from the cooking pot. This makes Al nervous. "Don't worry," she reassures him, "I'm not gonna touch you. I'm just a nice person." At the dinner table, "Al-bear" (the way Stella pronounces it) suddenly blurts out, "Yes, I *have*. Several, and not particularly." These are the answers to the usual unasked questions,

"Have you ever slept with a woman, and did you like it?"

They go to bed, separately. Al starts to remove his undershirt—we see half a perfect chest. Then he glances toward Stella's room and decides to wear the undershirt.

Albert might not be much use to Stella in the bedroom, but he proves to be handy, first in the kitchen, and then in the dressing room. Though Stella seemed chicly dressed, she knows little of fashion. Al accessorizes her and lets down her hair. The next day, when Stella announces that her date Chris is coming, Al is surprised to find that Chris is a woman (Lisa James). The two women kiss, and Stella teases Al: "Yes, I have. Several, and not particularly." She means *men*.

Al moves to the gay baths, where he is cruised by Roger (Doug Higgins). Al gives him the cold shoulder. Staring at the pool full of steaming men, Al says, "I *hate* hot water. I don't even know why I'm here." We do.

Al returns to Stella's, where she and Chris are making out. Phyllis (Valerie Curtin) barges in. She's Stella's hysterically insecure lover; they have an open relationship—but only on Stella's side. Phyllis makes a scene and Chris sneaks out.

Al proves to be a perfect housekeeper. But when Stella's late for dinner, he is hurt. "You could've let me know you'd be late," he says. "There is such a thing as a phone." "I can't plan my life around your meals," says the working woman. "My Swedish meatballs are all dried up," he wails. "My beans are shriveled!"

Al gets revenge on Stella by dating Roger, who picks him up at Stella's (but the men don't kiss—that's lesbian stuff). Stella looks in Al's room; it's decorated with his own fashion sketches and designs for album covers. She is feeling lonely and rings Roger, but Al had left almost as soon as they arrived. She is relieved.

Stella's parents invite themselves to dinner. She insists Al *has* to help her. Apparently the folks have never been to dinner and don't know that Stella can't cook. Like some male Dolly Levi by Tom of Finland (in his bell-bottoms and hiking boots), Al plans the evening.

Although Stella's father is an old stick, the evening is a smash. When her parents leave, Al and Stella giggle on the couch, somewhat smashed. Doug calls and is rebuffed by Al. Doug calls again to threaten him, and Al hangs up. The evening ends with Al and Stella making love.

Al is an illegal alien. Doug turns him in to immi-

Close: Perry King as a gay man and Meg Foster as a lesbian. Just friends.

Closer: When the men break up, King—he works in the fashion business, of course—gets to know Foster better.

gration agents, who threaten to deport him. But the solution is simple: Al marries Stella, a U.S. citizen and now ex-lesbian. As a married man Al has two goals: To have sex with Stella and to look for man's work. A musical montage shows Al and Stella falling deeper in love—on his motorcycle—to the tune of "Let Tomorrow Be Until Tomorrow."

Al becomes a parking-lot attendant and runs into Phyllis, who hasn't been told her lover is now married and heterosexual. Phyllis worries about how distant Stella has become, but she's working it out with her therapist, Dr. Sonderheim. At home, Al makes Stella a dress while they discuss the problem of Phyllis. Stella's afraid to tell her: "She'll start popping pills." But when Stella becomes pregnant, she *must* tell her. She calls Phyllis, who becomes suicidal.

Al and Stella rush to Phyllis's apartment but find the ungrateful, psychotic Phyllis has a gun. She aims it at the couple but finds she forgot to load the gun. So much for her.

And so much for homosexuality. Al finds work at a pattern factory, where he advances quickly, even though his boss Ned (Guerin Barry) is queer. Stella gives birth to a blond baby boy whom they name Albert, and the couple's happiness seems complete.

In short time Al grows a mustache, buys a Mercedes 300D, and starts wearing suits. He and homemaker Stella buy a mansion. Al is away a lot, and Stella is getting suspicious. Al has less sex with her, works nights, and is driving her to junk food. Could he be backsliding with Ned? She confronts him; he storms out. Next day, Stella goes to the pattern factory and catches Al in the shower. He's not alone. Stella opens the door and sees him—with another woman. Somehow, she's not relieved, and she moves in with her parents.

Closest: More than friends!—only in Hollywood could a gay and a lesbian add up to a heterosexual pair.

155

Al hopes to win Stella back. He tries a number of schemes but decides there's only one way: Use force. While Stella's showing a house Al drives up, pulls her aside, and apologizes: "We can't throw away what we are to each other." Is she made of stone? Think of the *baby*, he implores. But, she lets him go. Al gets on his cycle to ride away, forever. It veers to the side and he's thrown. Horrified, Stella runs to her husband.

But Al was just *pretending* to be hurt. The couple kiss and make up. Yes, Stella will return to Al's home and bed. Once again, they'll be the perfect nuclear unit. Fadeout. It really wasn't a different story, after all.

Meg Foster and Valerie Curtin almost found fame on television in "Cagney and Lacey" and "Nine to Five," respectively. Both were fired because of sexism. According to *TV Guide*, network executives felt Foster was "mannish" and her relationship with Tyne Daly on "Cagney and Lacey" "dykey." She was replaced by blond Sharon Gless, and "Cagney and Lacey" became a hit, even though feminist and high quality. Curtin played the Jane Fonda film role in "Nine to Five" but was ousted (like executive producer Fonda) when it was decided to defeminize the story and increase its T&A quotient. The revamped series jiggled into early syndication. Primarily a screenwriter, Curtin (with husband Barry Levinson) wrote *Best Friends* and *. . . and Justice for All*, in which "Dynasty"'s homophobic patriarch, John Forsythe, is a despicable judge in drag.

Stardom eluded Perry King through several films until he found his niche on television's "Riptide." Today he says he's "tired" of questions about *A Different Story*. In 1983 he told the *Chicago Tribune*, "People sometimes think I'm gay because I once played a gay in a movie. It's funny. Audiences don't think you're a murderer if you play a murderer. . . ." When he was offered the film, he ignored friend Sly Stallone's reported advice: "Don't play no faggots." (Yet, in *Staying Alive*, Stallone and Travolta took pains not to put down the gay dancer character whom Tony Manero replaces. Unlike *Saturday Night Fever*, the sequel wasn't anti-gay.)

In a 1977 *Blueboy* interview King discussed *A Different Story*: "It was the best experience I ever had. I love the result; for the first time, I want to [promote] the film; I'm going to do a lot for it." As for its double dishonesty, he felt, "The film is not exploitative. . . . Nor is it, and it really isn't, about homosexuality." True, though it's ceaselessly homophobic. "It's about being true to yourself, not

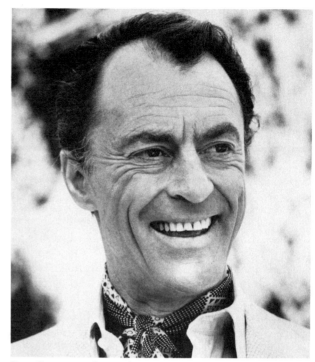

Peter Donat as a Bernstein-esque conductor, the demanding lover to Perry King.

allowing your life to be dictated by society's policies." Society's policies are precisely what *A Different Story* upholds and confirms.

With his well-turned foot in his mouth, King continued, "It's a love story, and that's more important than a movie about gays." He then talked about Anita Bryant. "She's helped the gay cause more than anyone. . . . For the movement of freedom of the right to choose, it's the best thing that could happen. . . . These people are discriminated against for something that has no connection at all with the rest of their lives."

The "right to choose" is irrelevant, since sexuality isn't chosen. And the statement implies that if gays' sexuality is connected with the rest of their lives—whose isn't?—then discrimination may be excusable. Good intentions (if such they were) can't excuse the participants in an effort like *A Different Story*, which panders to and perpetuates *ignotry* (to use Arthur Bell's term). Passing itself off as liberated and pleasing to straights and gays—in that order—it dupes straights and denies gay men and women.

But there is a happy ending: Avco Embassy, which financed and distributed *A Different Story*, became Embassy Pictures, co-owned for a time by pro-gay feminist Norman Lear, who did more than anybody to combat gay stereotypes on television.

ABOUT *A DIFFERENT STORY*

ABC Film Guide (U.K.): A schizoid picture which heterosexual audiences may find reassuringly old-fashioned and homosexual audiences unintentionally hilarious. . . . The actors are comely but stiff. Supporting characters are better delineated, including Peter Donat [as] Perry King's conductor-employer.

Jeff Olson (1982): Gay-lesbian roommates fall in love, marry, and live reproductively ever after. Except there's more statistical chance of an affair between two same-gender "straights." Five to ten percent of the population may be gay, but in *A Different Story* there's hope for everybody. . . . If the Moral Majority were in the movie business, this is probably what they'd produce—only with more crucifixes, and a few crucifixions. *A Different Story* is itself a crucifiction.

By design: Gay MGM designer Adrian (who wed lesbian star Janet Gaynor) and single sapphic legend Greta Garbo.

Vaselino was his nickname: Rudy married twice—both times to lesbians.

Perry King was advised by Sylvester Stallone (here directing John Travolta in *Staying Alive*, 1983), "Don't play no fags."

Making hay?: Studio-engineered marriage between gay (later bisexual) Robert Taylor and lesbian Barbara Stanwyck.

25

DRESS REVERSAL:

Outrageous!, Too Outrageous!, and Victor/Victoria

Writer-director Dick Benner and star Craig Russell of *Outrageous!* (1977) and *Too Outrageous!* (1987). Both died of AIDS in 1990.

Outrageous! Cinema 5, 1977. Director-writer: Richard Benner; producers: William Marshall and Hendrick J. Van der Kolk.
Starring: Craig Russell, Hollis McLaren, David McIlwraith, Jerry Salzberg, Andree Pelletier, Helen Hughes.

Too Outrageous! Spectrafilm, 1987. Director-writer: Richard Benner; producer: Roy Krost.
Starring: Craig Russell, Hollis McLaren, David McIlwraith, Ron White, Lynne Cormack, Frank Pellegrino.

Victor/Victoria. MGM, 1982. Director-writer: Blake Edwards; producers: Edwards and Tony Adams.
Starring: Julie Andrews, James Garner, Robert Preston, Lesley Ann Warren, Alex Karras, John Rhys-Davies.

During his "Rockford File" years, James Garner told *Photoplay* he preferred "the old-fashioned way of making films." He recalled *The Americanization of Emily* (1964) with Julie Andrews. "Oh, we had a nude scene, but that was done with good taste. And that was a girl with a guy, which is the way it should be. . . . I prefer clean rather than dirty."

Outrageous! and its sequel and *Victor/Victoria* are progressive gay-peopled pictures bearing the imprimaturs of their makers. They feature musical comedy and show-business plots, but all refuse to deal with long-term male-male relationships. As in *A Taste of Honey* and *A Special Day*, their focus is male-female friendships.

Outrageous! and *Too Outrageous!* center on Robin (Craig Russell), a feminine hairdresser whose penchant for performing in drag gets him fired. Eventually Robin goes from drag to riches. The beauty-shop owner in *Outrageous!* is a gay man who looks down on "fems" and demands a "straight" image from his employees to attract female customers, who like being touched by *men*. The film also includes a homophobic psychiatrist, a feminist who deprecates gay men, and a mother who drives her unstable daughter "crazier."

Liza Connors (Hollis McLaren) is Robin's best friend and roommate. When Liza becomes pregnant by her boyfriend, he leaves. The baby is born dead, and Liza's hopes of normalcy are crushed. Mrs. Connors (Helen Hughes) blames the death on *Robin.* "It's *somebody's* fault!" she snaps. Why not the gay's?

Unemployed Robin becomes a female impressionist, talented enough to move from a small Toronto club to Manhattan's Jack Rabbit, then to an uptown straight club for which he tones down the act. But Robin keeps a foot, and his heart, in the gay ghetto. He rents an apartment for himself and Liza in a "freaky" neighborhood. His agent, ex-cab driver Bob (David McIlwraith), scores with men he meets at the club, but he helps push Robin to the top of his field.

The movie ends with Robin's success. He tells depressed Liza: "You're not dead inside, honey. You're alive and sick and living in New York, like eight million other people. You're never gonna be normal, but you're *special*, and you can have a hell of a lot of fun in this world."

In *Too Outrageous!*, Robin finds that the fun things in this world have little to do with professional success. Liza is still disturbed, loves are found

Robin Turner (Russell) as Judy
Garland, entertaining friends Manuel
(Frank Pellegrino), Liza (Hollis
McLaren), and Tony (Paul Eves).

. . . as Tina Turner . . .

. . . and as Peggy Lee.

Robin hits the big time as Eartha Kitt . . .

and soon lost, and in keeping with the times and
setting, one character has AIDS. (Tragically, both
Russell and writer-director Richard Benner succumbed to AIDS in 1990.) In his act Robin plays
black singers, including Eartha Kitt and Tina
Turner (although the ads featured him as Mae
West, with the tag line, "When the going gets tough,
the tough get gorgeous!").

159

In both pictures Robin finds little fun or friendship apart from Liza and his wigs and costumes. His sex life gets shortchanged. Plain, plump, and feminine, he must pay a gay model for sex, to his surprise and disillusionment. He sublimates his sexual energy—in both the original and the sequel—into his work and the strenuous platonic relationship with Liza, his virtual ward.

Admirers dubbed the original "Courageous!" and compared it to *Rocky*. It premiered at Manhattan's Cinema II, where *Rocky* had done excellent business. The ticket lines grew to equal those for *Rocky*, as people of all backgrounds flocked to see the little-man-conquers-adversity tale. *Outrageous!* eventually earned many times its $160,000 cost and became a cult classic. Its publicity stressed the integrity of Benner and Russell, who was named Best Actor at the Berlin Film Festival.

United Artists hired Benner to adapt and direct its 1980 *Happy Birthday, Gemini*, based on Albert Innaurato's play *Gemini*. The unsuccessful film starred Madeline Kahn and Rita Moreno, with a subplot about a gay son. In *Gemini* gay Francis Geminiani has a girlfriend. The film, however, makes it clear that they're friends and she's not a "cure." Benner also added a scene in which the father accepts his son's gayness, just so long as he's happy—unlike many heterosexuals—he says.

Benner declared that gays in the film industry have a responsibility to create positive gay characters and themes. "If it's real and honest, people will go for it. People who underestimate the intelligence of the audience are always in trouble, as *Cruising* proves."

The sequel to *Outrageous!* wasn't lacking in honesty or integrity. It just didn't seem to have much more to say. The message had been well and fully expounded in the original, and ten years later drag was further from the mainstream of gay life. *Too Outrageous!* was too much of a rehash and a filmed concert of Russell's act. The original had been on the cutting edge; the sequel glittered but had little gold. Next to other concurrent independent features like *Prick Up Your Ears*, *Desert Hearts*, and *My Beautiful Laundrette*, it appeared merely quaint.

ABOUT *OUTRAGEOUS!* and *TOO OUTRAGEOUS!*

Gay Vancouver: Gay filmmaker Richard Benner's iconoclastic movie challenges stereotypes among *gays*. The message is that gays who impersonate females—professionally or not—don't have to adopt traditional sex roles like most gay men. . . . Almost in the mainstream, *Outrageous!* is boy-loves-girl that doesn't undermine anyone's sex preference. . . . Craig Russell is a crack impersonator whose repertoire includes Judy, Barbra, Mae, and Peggy Lee. Partly funded by the Canadian Film Consortium, *Outrageous!* is finding acceptance in the U.S. as a the-*boy*-in-the-band.

Lavender Age: The one-man drag show is a clever, amusing though paltry home movie. Cheerfully tacky, it's an updated *A Taste of Honey*, with the fairy-guy turning disadvantage to profit. . . . *Outrageous!* wags a finger at intolerant macho gays and feminists who see MCPs [Male Chauvinist Pigs] in every corner. The characters are stock, with Hollis McLaren as a demented Blanche DuBois, but the ending is touchingly real.

Helen Knode, *Los Angeles Weekly*: Too maudlin! Ten years later, Robin Turner (Russell) picks up the frayed hem of his life. Still an undiscovered diva of gay dives, he lives with Liza (Hollis McLaren), his costumer and a functioning schizophrenic who writes to purge her head of "voices." He's discovered by a big-time New York agent (Lynne Cormack) and sent back to Toronto to polish his act in preparation for a one-man/woman show on Broadway. The purpose of all this is to teach Robin "the price of success," which he discovers is too high. . . . On top of everything else, female impersonation is an art form that only tourists tolerate in 105-minute doses.

The surprise hit of 1982 was based on Rheinhold Schünzel's 1933 *Viktor und Viktoria*, remade in Britain in 1935 as *First a Girl*, with Jessie Matthews. In *Victor/Victoria* the story was updated to include club entertainer Toddy (Robert Preston) and Squash (ex-football star Alex Karras), a beefy bodyguard who confesses his homosexuality to his gangster boss, King Marchand (James Garner), after the latter falls in love with Polish Count Victor Grazinski (Julie Andrews). Squash's gruff, blustery exterior, he explains, was developed in boyhood to conceal a sensitive nature. The confession doesn't alter the men's relationship.

Blake Edwards wrote Toddy so that his laughs aren't at his own expense. The film's humor is situational, and Toddy doesn't don drag until the anticlimactic finale. *Victor/Victoria*'s potential female impersonator is Norma (Lesley Ann Warren), with Harlow curls, Betty Boop voice, and Mae West libido.

On the minus side, a major flaw in the film is Victoria's male impersonation, which is less than believable, though Andrews makes a stunning

Bowie-like count. Quentin Crisp told this author, "There should have been a scene where Mr. Preston shows Miss Andrews how to camp." It was suggested that Liza Minnelli or Lily Tomlin could have pulled it off better; Tomlin's "Tommy Velour" character is sometimes mistaken for a real man. Victoria also falls in love too quickly with the older Marchand (the part was first offered to Tom Selleck). And later Victoria gives up Victor too eagerly and conventionally (in a flowing feminine gown). Victoria has found she enjoys drag and, more importantly, working, which she doesn't intend to give up for a man, though she says, "[Someday] I may be lucky enough to celebrate my womanhood as Mrs. King Marchand."

Another flaw—though perhaps a necessity for a film that Edwards called "a bridge between films on homosexuality and ordinary movies"—is the shower-scene revelation of Victoria's gender to the so-relieved Marchand. However, problems arise when others think Marchand is romancing a man. But the problem is cleverly solved: The tuxedoed couple go out dancing. The camera pans back from the two and reveals a gay ballroom, a sea of like-attired men dancing together. The scene is unprecedented in scope and impact.

Toddy's personal life is somewhat more detailed than *Outrageous!*'s Robin Turner's, but both men's abiding relationships are with women. Though Toddy is a supporting character—the heroine's mentor—Edwards gave him depth and background. (He also has the unfortunate appellation Carol Todd; Carol is not a man's name in America.) Initially Todd is involved with a gigolo; the movie opens with the men in bed. When Victoria asks Toddy, "At what age did you become *a* homosexual?" (italics mine), Toddy replies, "At what age did you become a soprano?" instead of "At what age did you become a heterosexual?" Explaining "his" background, Victor matter of factly notes that his family disinherited him when they found out he was gay.

When Toddy teams up with Squash, they are seen in bed together—sitting up, with teacups and pajamas. Unfortunately, that relationship isn't expanded. Earlier, Squash allows that the mob "doesn't consider homosexuality an acceptable lifestyle." In response Toddy ruefully comments, "Kill him, but don't kiss him." Toddy winds up a professional success, literally filling Victor/Victoria's shoes. Toddy ends up without a lover; Robin (in *Outrageous!*) at least has a roommate and gay friends and associates.

The men in these films are a girl's best friend and are therefore—perhaps only for that reason—ac- ceptable to general audiences. In the musical number "You and Me," Preston and Andrews sing, "We're the kind of people other people would like to be." They're dressed as gents, but, essentially, an actor and an actress musically confirm male-female friendships and tolerance—rather than gayness. Toddy's gay outlook is better expressed in "Gay Paree"; where straights see straight, Toddy sees gay. For him, the Champs-Elysées is "perhaps the one thing that's straight as can be." *Chaqu'un à son goût.*

Even more than Robin, Toddy functions as efficiently as any heterosexual character. He is as happy and more helpful. Like women who must work twice as hard as men to compete, movie homosexuals must be twice as nice as straights to rate equal approval. But approval is a first step toward understanding and acceptance, and *Victor/Victoria* and *Outrageous!*—with their gay or pro-gay makers and stars—mark significant progress in the depiction of homosexuals.

ABOUT *VICTOR/VICTORIA*

Clifton Montgomery, the *Advocate*: As funny as it is pro-gay, *Victor/Victoria* offers delicious moments of role reversal and sexual abandon, especially as Garner's attraction to Andrews's woman-pretending-to-be-a-man reaches fever pitch, and he admits he doesn't really care *what* she/he is. . . . Robert Preston is a marvel; romantic *and* a realist, he paints perhaps the richest, most humanely rewarding picture of an aging gay man yet. Witty, entertaining, generous, self-accepting, sexually active, he defies cliches.

Sheila Benson, *Los Angeles Times*: Blake Edwards's homosexual characters have charm, wit, warmth, and humanity; they are firm about their sexuality and at peace right where they are. . . . Toddy (Preston) and Victoria have enormous rapport and a chemistry missing from Andrews and Garner. . . . When Norma makes a play for Toddy, he turns her down with the truth. "I think the right woman could reform you" is her arch retort, which homosexuals have been batting back for centuries. "I think the right girl could do the same for you," Toddy replies.

Judy Stone, *San Francisco Chronicle*: When Edwards tries to illustrate how deceptive appearances and sexual labels can be, his choices are frequently unclear. There's no reason for "Victor" to weep during *Madama Butterfly* or wooden-faced Garner to assert his masculinity in a tough Parisian bar

Toddy and Victor perform the double-entendre song, "Gay Paree."

Isosceles: Heterosexual man (James Garner), heterosexual woman posing as gay man (Julie Andrews), gay man (Robert Preston).

Julie Andrews in her Oscar-nominated roles as *Victor/Victoria* (1982).

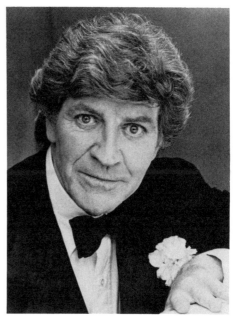

Robert Preston in his Academy Award nominated role as Toddy, Victoria's friend who persuades her to become a male impersonator.

. . . . Preston can even add a touch of class to a silly, meaningless line like: "There's nothing more inconvenient than an old queen with a head cold." His unpretentious humor and un-self-consciousness is more authentic than anything yet seen in American films that have dealt more directly with homosexual themes; Edwards's live-and-let-live attitude has a refreshing sweetness and generosity.

James Garner falls in love with Victor who's really Victoria, then discovers his bodyguard (Alex Karras) is gay!

26

MESSIEURDAMES:

La Cage aux Folles I, II, and III

Longtime companions: Albin (Michel Serrault, left) and Renato (Ugo Tognazzi) of *La Cage Aux Folles I, II, and III*.

La Cage aux Folles (Birds of a Feather). PAA/United Artists, 1978. Director: Edouard Molinaro; writers: Francis Veber, Molinaro, Marcello Danon, and Jean Poiret; producer: Danon.
Starring: Ugo Tognazzi, Michel Serrault, Michel Galabru, Claire Maurier, Remy Laurent, Benny Luke, Carmen Scarpitta.

La Cage aux Folles II. PAA/United Artists, 1980. Director: Molinaro; writers: Veber, Poiret and Danon; producer: Danon.
Starring: Ugo Tognazzi, Michel Serrault, Benny Luke, Marcel Bozzuffi, Paola Borboni, Giovanni Vettorazzo, Gianrico Tondinelli.

La Cage aux Folles 3: The Wedding. DaMa/Tri-Star, 1986. Director: Georges Lautner; writers: Michel and Jacques Audiard; Danon, Lautner, and Gerard Lamballe; producer: Danon.
Starring: Michel Serrault, Ugo Tognazzi, Michel Galabru, Antonella Interlenghi, Benny Luke, Stephane Audran.

La Cage aux Folles, America's most successful foreign-language film, was the first unquestionable gay hit. It was also the first gay movie to spawn not one but two sequels. Like *Auntie Mame*, *Cage* began as a "straight" play, became a nonmusical film, then recaptured Broadway with music and lyrics by Jerry Herman.

What helped make all *The Cages* hits are the characters—they are undeniably funny, grow on the audience, and don't threaten heterosexuals. They function as clowns, particularly the movies' Albin-Zaza (Michel Serrault), the aging, high-strung, and egotistical but tenderhearted wife-cabaret star of Renato Baldi (Ugo Tognazzi). Serrault, who did over seventeen-hundred performances in Jean Poiret's play, is also the films' heart. Only the language barrier kept him from Broadway; George Hearn admirably filled his wedgies, earning a Tony Award and turning in a more "manful" performance.

Even apart from the stereotypical drag, there is much to deplore in the films. Albin and Renato (renamed Georges in the musical) bicker constantly —Albin is given to shrieking fits—and they dwell in a jokey gay-movie ghetto. The more masculine Renato derives his status from the son he fathered during a one-night stand. The gay couple scrupulously observe gender roles but never exchange a kiss or a hug. The musical was also criticized for omitting a kiss, but Georges and Albin's love and affection are made touchingly clear.

Renato's son, Laurent (Remy Laurent), is comfortable with his gay parents but fears outsiders' disapprobation. Engaged to the daughter of a homophobic politician, he seeks to reunite his biological parents while the prospective in-laws come to inspect his (the men's) home. Laurent, who wants to banish Albin for "just" a night, would rather sacrifice the men's integrity than the others' bigotry. In the film he neither repents nor apologizes. The fun in *Cage I* is watching Albin perform in the St. Tropez nightclub (literally "The Cage of Crazies"), walk like John Wayne, and impersonate a mother for the benefit of Charrier (Michel Galabru), the villain. Gays and straights enjoy Albin's gentle revenge when he puts Charrier into drag. Ironically, this saves the man's gay-baiting career, while Albin and Renato's only gain is a set of in-laws who will try to shield the grandchildren from the "crazies."

It's not clear what keeps the gay couple together. The hyper Albin is occasionally suicidal, and Renato is adulterous (or bisexual) enough for Simone (Claire Maurier) to possibly re-seduce him when he visits her office to ask her to meet Laurent's fiancée. Simone was dropped from the musical, but all *The Cages* feature the racially stereotypical servant Jacob (Benny Luke in the films). That Jacob is strictly Third World is apparent from the Broadway and touring companies' exclusively black or Oriental actors and understudies in that role. More positively, *Cage I* makes the point that some female impersonators are heterosexual; one such asks club owner Renato for a raise because he has an *eighth* child on the way. But after Laurent's announcement, Renato croons, "I always hoped you would fall in love with a girl. . . . It's right as could be." By contrast, the musical's parents wonder, "Where did we go wrong?"

When Charrier's superior, the head of a "morality" party, dies in bed with a prostitute, she is not only a minor but "colored." And although town straights treat the foolish gay couple graciously, it's their considerable purchasing power that they're courting. Even though this rings true, and *Cage* was one of the first films to depict a longtime male couple, the humor is mostly sour and the pathos forced. The villain is also a caricature, and his ranting religiosity is omitted, so as not to offend any fanatic who might chance to see this gay French movie.

Cage II's forgettable plot is mere formula. Albin, angered at Renato's suggestion that he's too old to play Dietrich (in blackface), dresses up and huffs out, to catch a supposedly straight hunk's eye and prove that he can still *pass*. At a corner café, Albin becomes embroiled in a spy mix-up that forces the gay couple to escape to Italy, where Albin develops a mutual infatuation with a big earthy peasant.

Before the moment of truth, identities are unscrambled, and Albin and Renato return to St. Tropez and their home-front follies.

The play and films were intended for straight audiences. The play, which debuted in Paris in 1973, ran seven years and had several foreign productions. *Cage I* earned over $50 million in North America, even in limited release (it ran over a year in some theaters). After Dustin Hoffman saw the play and film, he expressed interest in cross-dressing on-screen. He inquired about the sequel, which was already underway. Michel Serrault told *Paris Match* he'd love to work with Hoffman in the third *Cage*, (which was released in 1986). *Match* asked Serrault whether playing Albin so long had affected his mannerisms: "Haven't you become effeminate?" "I don't think so. Nita, my wife, is the one who could say whether anything in my behavior has changed." Nita Serrault: "I haven't noticed anything . . . at any rate, not in my presence."

Ugo Tognazzi offered "I don't make academic preparations; I didn't study homosexuals for *La Cage*. I enter the psychology of my characters physically and instinctively. . . . I'd have preferred to be French rather than Italian; in Italy the public is the husband, and the actor is the wife. But I try to be a modern, feminist wife who'd say, 'No, you can't force me to do only what *you* want!' "

The *Cage* films' success convinced many in Hollywood that general audiences prefer laughable, condescending stereotypes. Scriptwriter Francis Veber was asked to write his first American movie; he returned to France immediately after one picture, *Partners*. Several of his French films were remade in Hollywood, including *Le Jouet*, as *The Toy*, and *L'Emmerdeur* (*The Farter*), as *Buddy Buddy*, the latter by Billy Wilder. (The ad graphics for the Wilder film were banned in Utah because the screw-shaped "y" of the first *Buddy* extended into the "u" of the second *Buddy* underneath; the title words were re-placed side by side, so that Mormon minds wouldn't mistake the mechanical screw for a sexual one.)

Incredibly enough, director Edouard Molinaro was nominated for an Academy Award, and Home Box Office—catering to and reinforcing majority preferences—broadcast both *Cages* during prime time (but held *Making Love* until later hours).

However, good gays sometimes finish first. The musical, largely the work of uncloseted artists, is an eye-opening, politically correct extravaganza. The musicalization began as *The Queen of Basin Street*, set in New Orleans, but producer Allan Carr decided to keep the film's title, setting, and basic plot. After the project attracted the talents of Harvey Fierstein, Jerry Herman, and director Arthur Laurents, its quality and integrity soared. *La Cage aux Folles*, which won nine Tonys in 1984 and earned back its $5 million cost (more than either film) in less than a year, attracted many people who saw *Cage I* and its mildly popular sequel.

On a liberating historical note, Fierstein became the second man to thank his male lover during an acceptance speech on a nationally telecast awards show. In 1983 John Glines thanked his lover Lawrence, after acknowledging his gay "brothers and sisters." Glines later produced Harvey Fierstein's *Torch Song Trilogy*, which won its author his first Tony and became the first gay-themed Best Play. In 1984 *La Cage* became the first gay-themed Best Musical.

ABOUT LA CAGE AUX FOLLES I and II

Out: *Birds of a Feather*—contrived, shrill, hysterical—is funny like a car crash. . . . It mocks women and boasts racism and cowardice. . . . An Anita Bryant-style politician is already terrorizing homosexuals, but this "couple" (who parody heterosexuality) is blessed with a son who wants to temporarily convert his father and stepdad. . . . Big progress, from *The Boys in the Band* to this.

Wilde News (U.K.): The most amusing transvestite romp since *Some Like It Hot* and far more frank. Many will find *Cage* offensive, but no one will keep a straight face. . . . There is tenderness in the relationship, as when the protective butch tries to teach the fem how to walk and talk like a chap—a Pygmalion turnabout. We laugh *with* Serrault, a fabulously inventive actor last seen in a homophile bit in Alan Bates's *King of Hearts*. Tognazzi is bland but serviceable. Benny Luke as a skinny manservant tries to resurrect Hattie McDaniel. . . . A specialised cup of tea for gentlemen who prefer Messrs. Danny LaRue and Quentin Crisp.

Pauline Kael: *Cage II* isn't as original as the first picture but gives the actors more range. . . . The middle-aged homosexuals [get] out of their apartment and into the straight world. The movie is most inventive when they're in Italy, and Albin, dressed as a peasant woman, is toiling in the fields among the women; he looks youthful and radiantly fulfilled—he really believes he is one of them. . . . Maybe it's only in this exaggerated form that a movie about the ridiculousness and tenderness of married love can be accepted now.

Monde Arcadie: Renato and Albin's return is less than believable, but Zaza fans won't be disappointed. The pair travel to Italy and find their love tested by the 007-type plot tricks; Zaza is almost unfaithful but returns to "her" true love. The chases are tiresome, the handsome toughs stiff as cardboard. If there's a third time, one hopes Zaza will return to the more intriguing domestic front. . . . Last time, the offense was gays trying to act like their opposites. This time it's heterosexual cops acting like supposed homosexuals after "instruction" from their two new recruits—could they really be secret agents for the CIA?

The English-language title (*Birds of a Feather*) is the less offensive and makes the point that, contrary to popular assumption, opposites usually do not attract.

The American release of the second *Cage* film sequel came in 1986. *The Wedding* was the latest in—as Tri-Star put it—"the continuing saga of filmdom's favorite married couple." This time, the top-billed actor was Serrault, who'd won the French César and the Italian David di Donatello (Oscar equivalents).

Albin/Zaza's (Serrault) aunt in Scotland dies and leaves him a fortune, providing that he marry and father an heir within eighteen months. The proviso serves to contrast Zaza's nightclub act and feminine behavior with his nervous attempts to turn stud. After fainting at the prospect of heterosex, Albin—again with coaching from the financially strapped Renato—tries to force himself. But, even with the lure of a prospective fortune, Albin can't bring himself to go through with it.

In the end Renato and Albin decide their partnership is more important than money. They marry in a traditional ceremony, with Zaza in "her" traditional wedding gown. The pair expect to forfeit the inheritance to a curmudgeonly straight cousin, who turns out to be not such a bad guy when a financial compromise is reached.

This second *Cage* sequel was subject to the law of diminishing box-office returns. It was less successful in the U.S. than in Europe, perhaps because gay rights and the AIDS crisis made the *Cage* syndrome seem more archaic and less responsible than ever. Will *Cage 3* mark the end of the cycle? Don't count on it. Renato and Albin were instant classics and may prove unsinkable. Their madcap adventures, though predictable, are lived with verve and sincerity. As *New York* magazine said: "Albin and Renato send sexual roles spinning so wildly, one comes out

Albin is served newsprint in bed by his saucy French maid Jacob (Benny Luke).

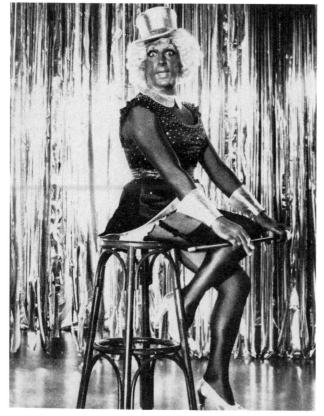

Renato Baldi is co-owner of the French Riviera's successful tranvestite nightclub La Cage Aux Folles.

Black and Blue Angel: Albin, the undisputed diva of La Cage, here in dark Dietrich drag.

Show business partners as well as lifemates, Renato and the temperamental Albin have their ups and downs.

dazed, no longer sure what is meant by straight or gay or why any of it matters. What remains plain enough is what the two men feel for each other. . . . They are obsessed with trivial things—yet they are absolved in the end of triviality. . . . Time has increased their dignity. They have become the most improbable of male screen heroes—the last faithful married couple on earth."

ABOUT *LA CAGES AUX FOLLES 3*

The *Advocate*: In *Cage 3* Tognazzi and Serrault have the dispirited look of party guests who should have departed long ago but haven't yet thought up a good excuse to enable them to do so. . . . A nice chunk of the budget has gone into Serrault's wardrobe: matronly street drag; a Queen Bee stage get-up featuring wings and black-and-gold lamé in which she sails through the nightclub on wires; and a bridal gown with a pearl-encrusted headdress which makes her look like a Renaissance handmaiden in mortician's makeup.

Predictable, derivative, and listlessly directed. Skip this boner and rent the video of the original instead.

Edward Guthmann, *San Francisco Chronicle*: At its best, *Cage 3* is lightly diverting and enjoyable for Serrault's ever-broadening performance. At its worst, it's marred by slack pacing, predictable plotting, and poor post-dubbing of the dialogue track.

Perhaps because the first *Cage* didn't challenge gay stereotypes—but merrily and shamelessly exploited them—it was easy for straights and gays alike to love Zaza, the squealing drag-revue diva with the fluttering fingers, and Renato, his/her easily flustered, all-suffering mate. But enough is enough!

Suite: Albin checks into a hotel with an unsuspecting young man (Gianrico Tondinelli).

Queen bee: Albin rehearses a new number for his act.

Obelisk: Albin pleads with a secret agent (Giovanni Vettorazzo).

27

MLLE. HAMLET,
M. OPHELIA

*Women playing men, and vice versa, men in
women's clothing, women in uniform . . . a
gender-bending chapter . . . .*

I. BE IT

• "I was scared to death at the idea of playing a
man," said Linda Hunt, the four-foot-nine actress
who won an Oscar as Billy Kwan in *The Year of Living
Dangerously* (1983). Hunt "worried that no one
would believe it," yet many filmgoers were unaware
that Kwan was played by a woman until they read
the credits. One reason Hunt took the role—for
which director Peter Weir couldn't find a satisfactory male actor—was political. "It was an opportunity to make a statement. We judge people so much
from what they appear to be physically. To open
people's eyes is a political action. . . . To be able to
reveal the way in which we're all connected—our
mutuality—is exciting."

San Francisco magazine's Naomi Wise wrote that
Kwan "is a wholly *other* sort of man—delicate, cultured, fearless, compassionate, a Eurasian wise guy
and a heterosexual outsider to Western models of
masculinity." The *Advocate* called Hunt's portrayal
"the first bit of cross-sex casting that doesn't have
stunt written across it." Like the Hindu shadow
puppets on which he dotes, Billy is an instrument,
illuminating for others their motives and truest
selves.

• *Liquid Sky* (1983) could have been called "Last
Orgasm in Manhattan." It's about Margaret (Anne

WACs face off: "Florence" (Cary Grant) and
Ann Sheridan in *I Was a Male War Bride* (1949).

Carlisle), a punk-model whose roof becomes home
to a small flying saucer. Margaret, who "prefer[s]
women to men," has a sadistic, drug-dealing lesbian
roommate (Paula E. Sheppard). Margaret has sex
with a succession of men, but because of the UFO,
each lover dies during orgasm and evaporates.
Margaret is safe because—until the finale—she
does not have an orgasm. Carlisle also plays Jimmy,
"the most beautiful boy in the world." Jimmy, a
model, is surly, gay, and a drug addict. He evaporates after Margaret fellates him in front of a
fashion-photography crew.

The New Wave film—a "Hoffmannesque fairy
tale"—was directed by Russian emigré Slava
Tsukerman and coproduced and cowritten by his
wife, Nina Kerova. It ran almost a year at the
Waverly, making it Greenwich Village's biggest cult
hit since *The Rocky Horror Picture Show*. *Liquid Sky*,
which refers to heroin, boosted Carlisle (one of the
cowriters) to neuter stardom. "I'm no less androgynous than David Bowie," she told this author, "and I
want to turn gender roles upside-down." The *East
Village Eye* felt her double performance "has such
perception and authority that Dustin Hoffman [in

Tootsie], with whom she has been vulgarly compared, ought to be inspired to go back and try again."

• One of the funniest and least self-conscious crossover roles is Alastair Sim's Miss Millicent Fitton in 1954's *The Belles of St. Trinian's*. Based on Ronald Searle's cartoons about an unruly British girls' school, where students make gin in chemistry class, bet on horses, and generally wreak havoc, the comedy hit spawned three sequels between 1957 and 1966 (*Blue Murder ât. . . , Pure Hell of . . .*, and *. . . Train Robbery*). Sim also played Clarence, the ne'er-do-well twin of the harried headmistress. "I didn't feel I was doing a drag character," he said, "just a lovable lady whose primness belies her sense of fun. I felt more at home with Millicent than with her brother the bookie."

Sim reprised Miss Fitton in *Blue Murder at St. Trianian's* (1957). Joining him in (less convincing) dress reversal was Lionel Jeffries, a jewel thief posing as the captain of a girls' polo team.

• Debbie Reynolds played a man reincarnated in a woman's body in *Goodbye Charlie* (1964). Charlie Sorel is a playboy-screenwriter who, after getting shot by a jealous husband, returns as a shapely blonde (portrayed in George Axelrod's Broadway play by Lauren Bacall). Friend Tony Curtis eventually falls for the reincarnated "him," as does Pat Boone (author of a homophobic "guidebook").

• "Divine," said critic Wyatt Cooper, "is a tight-fitting sex symbol for a nation that thrives on obesity and surface impressions." The three-hundred-pound star of *Pink Flamingos* (1972)—"the most tasteless movie ever made"—and *Female Trouble* (1975) was a camp cult fixture of the seventies and eighties. *Lust in the Dust* (1985), with gay idol Tab Hunter (who coproduced), was the most widely distributed Divine opus yet. However, la Divine (né Harris Glenn Milstead) and his longtime lifemate were notoriously quiet, private people.

• "Has any woman on-screen had such jittery authority?" asked *Film Comment*'s David Thomson about Mercedes McCambridge. "This is the spirit of looks too raw or plain to make a star but burning with anger . . . always biting her lip with the dream of taking over the picture." The actress played a male motorcycle-gang member in Orson Welles's *Touch of Evil* (1958). In the scene McCambridge is part of the gang that watches as Janet Leigh is raped in a motel room. She was unbilled in the Welles film (and in William Friedkin's *The Exorcist*, in which she dubbed the voice of the devil).

The actress won a supporting Oscar as Sadie Burke in *All the King's Men* (1949). To explain why Sadie never married, the character was written as being secretly in love with her boss, Broderick Crawford.

• The 1932 horror classic *The Old Dark House* was directed by James Whale, a Briton whose Hollywood career was cut short because he refused to stay in the closet. George Sanders, who acted in Whale's *Green Hell* (1940), stated, "He was a brilliant director and very honest. In our business the two don't mix. Jimmy was civilized in an uncivilized time and place." Whale's last film was *They Dare Not Love* (1941). Suffering from ill health and a stymied career, Whale died a broken man in 1957. (His relationship with producer David Lewis lasted several years.) His brilliant career included *Frankenstein* (1931), *Bride of Frankenstein* (1935), and *Show Boat* (1936). In *The Old Dark House* he cast friend Elspeth Dudgeon as the ancient, bedridden man upstairs. *She* was billed as John Dudgeon.

II. DRAG-TIME

• Pauline Kael wrote, "Why did Lucille Ball do *Mame*? Did she discover in herself an unfulfilled ambition to be a flaming drag queen? Mame is a female-impersonator's dream woman: constantly changing her wigs, gowns, and décor. Mame has to be played by a smashing, crisp actress who makes it clear why homosexuals find her a turn-on. . . . *Mame* doesn't rise to camp except when Beatrice Arthur is on. She's monstrously marvelous. If she had played Mame, the material could have gone beyond camp into a satire of the whole crazy female-impersonator tradition of modern musical comedy."

The 1958 film *Auntie Mame* costarred Coral Browne as bitchy Vera Charles, Mame's "*oldest* and dearest friend." Mame (Rosalind Russell) is a hostess ahead of her time. But when her nephew Patrick reads aloud a list of "new words" overheard at his first party, Mame—unfazed by *lesbian*—stops him at the mention of *heterosexual*. The seldom-used adjective implies its black-sheep counterpart.

The 1974 movie musical brought out the gay subtext. Bea Arthur's heavily madeup Vera is both bitchy and butch. "The man in the moon is a lady," she croons. In another number she tells Mame, "I'll always be Alice Toklas, if you'll be Gertrude Stein."

Surprisingly, neither the play's nor the musical's Vera has a beau, even for appearances, and the love-hate between Mame and Vera is one of the most durable relationships in both their lives.

• Dame Cicely Courtneidge played a motherly lesbian in Bryan Forbes's *The L-Shaped Room* (1962), starring Leslie Caron as a girl who decides against an abortion and moves into a run-down Notting Hill boardinghouse. Courtneidge, an ex-music-hall star, tries to cheer Caron by performing her old routines, which include the drag "Burlington Bertie From Bow." Forbes created a "sympathetic portrait" of an older gay woman who has lost her lifemate but remains fulfilled in her final years. He based the character (which is not in Lynne Reid Banks's book) on a woman he met while touring as an actor with Gertrude Lawrence. Coincidentally, Julie Andrews did "Burlington Bertie" in *Star!*, the 1968 Lawrence film biography. (Another *L-Shaped* resident was Brock Peters as a gay jazz musician. In *The Pawnbroker* in 1965 he played another character with a stereotypically black profession, a gay pimp.)

• *The* classic drag farce is *Charley's Aunt*, which has been filmed five times, most recently in 1952. The best-loved version starred Jack Benny in 1941. It was reportedly his favorite role. As in *Tootsie*, Charley's aunt—Doña Lucia from Brazil—finds "herself" pursued by an older gent. But Benny enjoys Edmund Gwenn's attentions more than Dustin Hoffman likes those of Charles Durning. . . . By many accounts, Benny was gay or bisexual. He once told Johnny Carson on the "Tonight Show," "I do everything like a girl." Carson corrected, "*Almost* everything." Benny insisted, "No, *everything—that, too.*"

• The next film after *Charley's Aunt* to sustain drag throughout the plot was Billy Wilder's *Some Like It Hot* (1959). Again, drag is a hetero's last resort. (In 1941's *Blondie Goes Latin*, a desperate Dagwood [Arthur Lake] masquerades as a female drummer in a ship's orchestra.) In *Some Like It Hot* Joe (Tony Curtis) and Jerry (Jack Lemmon) become Josephine and Geraldine, members of an all-girl orchestra, to save their necks. When the "women" meet bandleader Sweet Sue, Curtis introduces himself as Josephine, but Lemmon skips a beat, then—out of the blue—announces that his name is *Daphne*. Like *Tootsie*'s Dorothy, Daphne is a separate entity. On the other hand, Curtis quickly sloughs off female drag for a Cary Grant impersonation.

Osgood (Joe E. Brown) falls in love with Daphne, who girlishly frolics on the beach with Sugar (Marilyn Monroe). When Daphne dances with Osgood, "she" unself-consciously enjoys herself. But the ambisexuality is made humorously explicit when Osgood, who has proposed to Daphne, lets the offer stand after Daphne confesses she is a man. "Nobody's perfect," says Osgood with a twinkle in his eye. It was Hollywood's most positive gay statement to that time, and for years to come.

The *San Francisco Chronicle*'s John Stark felt that *Some Like It Hot* was more pro-gay than *Victor/Victoria*. "How can *Victor/Victoria* be considered a daring comedy about homosexuality when the leading man knows all along that the object of his desires is a woman? . . . Wilder was saying, 'Live and let live.' Edwards says, 'Some of my best friends are. . . .' "

On the "Tonight Show," Curtis claimed that he learned how to "use" his wrists by studying male homosexuals. Later, on the "Mike Douglas" television show, he denied Joyce Haber's allegation that he was gay or bisexual. The less chatty Lemmon reprised Daphne in Cantinflas's 1960 vehicle *Pepe*.

• Like *Tootsie*, *Yentl* (1983) used a "gay" theme in a profitable movie designed for straights—although its audience was primarily young females and gay males. Yentl (Barbra Streisand), dressed as the male Anshel, weds Hadass (Amy Irving), but homosexuality is not apparent. Yentl tells Avigdor (Mandy Patinkin) that in God's eyes a marriage between two women is void, not a marriage at all. When Avigdor questions his feelings for Anshel, Yentl—who earlier asked, "Who can say what's natural?"—assures him that he's "normal." It was *her* fault he felt *strange* when he looked at or touched Anshel.

In view of the fact that she has many homosexual fans, Streisand's films have been oddly anti-gay. In *The Owl and the Pussycat* (1970) Doris calls George Segal the whole litany of homophobic names. In *The Way We Were* (1973) Katie insists a left-wing friend (Viveca Lindfors) isn't gay. In *For Pete's Sake* (1974) Henrietta mocks a bespectacled supermarket cashier, leaving him with a box of Fruit Loops: "*You* might *enjoy* them!" *Funny Lady* (1975) features a peripheral aging chorus-boy-fruit (Roddy McDowall), and the "feminist" *Up the Sandbox* (1972) uses lesbian stereotyping as a joke, when Fidel Castro turns out to be a *macha* dyke (deleted from the television showings).

Rub-a-dub-dub?: Henry Fonda doesn't realize the chap's really a woman—Annabella—in *Wings of the Morning* (1937).

Birds of a feather: Alec Guinness as Lady Agatha d'Ascoyne, suffragist, in *Kind Hearts and Coronets* (1949).

The way they were: Phil Silvers, Buster Keaton, Jack Gilford, and Zero Mostel in *A Funny Thing Happened on the Way to the Forum* (1966).

• In *Bringing Up Baby* (1938) Cary Grant has the distinction of being the first star to use *gay* as a homosexual adjective. When May Robson asks why he is wearing one of Kate Hepburn's frilly dressing

Avoirdupois!: Divine (né Glenn Milstead) in *Pink Flamingos* (1973).

Girls just wanna have fun: Tony Curtis and Jack Lemmon cavort in *Some Like It Hot* (1959).

The man from "Hollywood Squares" (Paul Lynde) meets "The Man From U.N.C.L.E." (Robert Vaughn) in *The Glass Bottom Boat* (1966).

Venomous fishwife?: George Sanders as The Warlock in *The Kremlin Letter* (1970).

Anne Carlisle as Jimmy in the 1982 cult film, *Liquid Sky*.

Linda Hunt won an Academy Award as male Billy Kwan in *The Year of Living Dangerously* (1982).

gowns, he jumps up and exclaims, "I've suddenly gone gay!" Critic Carlos Clarens wrote, "Grant usually plays a passive role and is often pursued by an aggressive woman." In the 1949 *I Was a Male War Bride* (*You Can't Sleep Here* in Britain), Grant dons drag to marry aggressive WAC lieutenant Ann Sheridan. In modified drag, Grant is no lady, but he's strangely erotic in black stockings, his skirt hiked up to reveal a garter.

The bisexual Grant—who once roomed with handsome Randolph Scott—was the subject of a biography by Richard Schickel, who averred that only Grant's enemies or enviers would think to call him gay!

• Before it was acceptable, let alone fashionable, lesbian sharpshooter Martha Canary, alias Calamity Jane, routinely wore men's clothes. The performer was allowed idiosyncratic garb on-screen, but her true sexuality was avoided. In 1931 the substantial Louise Dresser played a mannish Jane in *Caught*. Doris Day played her as a tomboy tamed by Howard Keel's Wild Bill Hickok in *Calamity Jane* (1953). The film includes the song "Secret Love" but never hints that both Westerners were gay. Like many gay people at the time, they probably fled the repressive cities for the freer wide-open spaces. . . . The most recent Jane-loves-Bill saga was a 1983 telefilm with Jane Alexander. She stated, "Jane drank too much, swore like a sailor, and occasionally had sex for money"—presumably with men. Hollywood has yet to acknowledge that a large percentage of prostitutes are lesbian or bisexual. Alexander also noted that Hickok "always had his hands manicured, his curls washed and set, and was a crack shot."

• In the dismal *Sahara* (1984) Brooke Shields joined the bandwagon and sported drag for a few minutes. She *looked* the part but made no effort to sound or seem male. The publicity gimmick didn't aid the anemic story of a twenties jazz baby who enters an all-male desert car race. Shields (whose mother was executive producer) was outfitted in a five-thousand-dollar wig and Brooks Brothers' finest. "On the set," said producer Menahem Golan, "people were coming up and asking, 'Who *is* that handsome guy?' "

• In 1983's *To Be or Not to Be* (a remake of the 1942 Jack Benny classic), James "Gypsy" Haake played Sasha, Anna Bronski's (Anne Bancroft) hairdresser—a mincing, eye-rolling caricature. Haake, emcee of the La Cage aux Folles nightclub in Los Angeles, appeared on "A.M. San Francisco" to make it clear that many female impersonators aren't homosexual—an unintended service to the gay community. In the film Sasha is arrested by the Nazis and is to be sent to a concentration camp. Mel Brooks's picture may have been the first to indicate the fate of gays in Nazi Germany, but it did use the gay man as a joke. Also, Brooks/Bronski notes in the script that without "Jews, Gypsies, and gays" (the Nazis' chief targets), theater would cease to exist. For some reason, this was changed in the film to

"Jews, Gypsies, and fags," nullifying most of the picture's liberal intent.

• Marlene Dietrich was the woman who made male dress fashionable for women on-screen and off-. Several of her memorable films feature her in a tuxedo or Navy uniform. In *Morocco* (1930) she not only sings in top hat and tails but kisses a female spectator on the lips, then savors her bemused astonishment. Dietrich was still at it in 1940, crooning "The Man's in the Navy" in *Seven Sinners*. Lesbian writer Mercedes de Acosta's book *Here Lies the Heart* recounts her own affairs with Dietrich and Garbo. Kenneth Anger's *Hollywood Babylon* tells about bisexual Dietrich's "sewing circle" of girlfriends and her alleged affair with Claudette Colbert.

• In *A Song to Remember* (1945), about (gay) composer Frédéric Chopin, Merle Oberon played bisexual, cross-dressing novelist George Sand, née Amandine Dupin. Turgenev wrote to Flaubert after Sand's death, "What a good man she was, and what a kind woman." Questioned about Sand's sexuality, Oberon offered, "She never wrote about that, if you read her novels." True. Sand had enough trouble establishing herself as an independent woman and author.

In 1943 Oberon starred in *First Comes Courage*, the last film directed by Dorothy Arzner (1900–1979). Hollywood's top female director, Arzner guided stars like Anna Sten (*Nana*, 1934), Katharine Hepburn (*Christopher Strong*, 1933), and Joan Crawford (*The Bride Wore Red*, 1937) through several features. In 1929 she directed Paramount's first talkie, *The Wild Party*, with Clara Bow, and she made several films in 1930, including Paramount's biggest hit of the year, *Sarah and Son*. Alone among leading directors of the thirties, Arzner's work has not been reassessed, and she has yet to be the subject of a biography.

• One of Katharine Hepburn's and George Cukor's biggest flops was *Sylvia Scarlett* (1935), in which the actress spends most of her time dressed as a handsome youth, Sylvester. Cukor explained, "Originally Sylvia was to start out in boys' clothing for the fun of it, then make her way in a man's world. But RKO insisted on a prologue which explains that her mother has died and she must disguise herself to travel to England with her father, Edmund Gwenn." In London Sylvester is a professional success, assisting "his" con-man dad and pal Cary Grant. Brian Aherne is drawn to Sylvester and

frets, "There's something very queer going on here." A maid also finds the lad attractive, in a brief sequence. However, the conventional ending finds Sylvia in a skirt and Brian's arms.

When the picture failed at the box office, producer Pandro S. Berman told Cukor and Hepburn, "I never want to see either of you again." Cukor took the rejection to heart and stated, "The picture did something to me. It slowed me up. I wasn't going to be so goddamned daring after that." Yet he felt "it wasn't the daring part of *Sylvia Scarlett* that failed, I see that now. It was when we tried to play it safe!"

• *The Kremlin Letter* (1970) was billed as "John Huston's cinematic exercise in amorality." Accordingly, it included a lesbian and a gay male. Pauline Kael said, "The film demonstrates that the methods of American spies are as disgusting as those of Russian spies." A black lesbian seduces a Russian diplomat's daughter (homosexuality in the service of heterosexuality). And George Sanders is a transvestite spy in San Francisco. The character was "fagged up" by Huston and his cowriter Gladys Hill, who felt a plain gay wouldn't do. Surrounded by limp-wristed young things, Sanders wears basic black—slit from ankle to thigh—pearls, and a boa. His scenes were filmed at Rome's *in* club, the Kinky, but his baritone number was later dubbed by a woman. "I was appalled," he said, "because I have a marvelous voice."

• *Tootsie* (1982) eclipsed *Some Like It Hot* as the most popular drag-themed movie ever, though *drag* isn't the word for Dustin Hoffman's Dorothy Michaels. But once the euphoria passed, gays perceived that, though feminist, *Tootsie* is far from pro-gay. The charming but not-overly-feminine Dorothy could conceivably be taken for a lesbian, but Michael Dorsey, her alter ego, recoils at the thought. He insists she's a "nice" lady who deserves the best, from a bigger bust to a spotless reputation. Michael is also upset when his girlfriend Teri Garr and his longtime roommate Bill Murray think *he's* gay.

Julie (Jessica Lange) "mistakenly" thinks Dorothy is gay and terminates their friendship. Lange's father (Charles Durning) courts Dorothy, then, after the revelation, meets Michael in a straight bar. "The only reason you're still alive," he growls, "is we never kissed." He demands, "Do you like 'em—girls?"; Michael meekly says "yes."

The American ad campaign for *Tootsie* ran "What do you get when you cross a hopelessly straight,

Mandy Patinkin doesn't understand his feelings for Barbra Streisand in *Yentl* (1983) until she discloses "he's" a she.

Dustin Hoffman as Dorothy (but usually Michael) in *Tootsie* (1982).

Honorary drags: Gloria Swanson (notice her first-billing in the Polish poster) in the 1950 *Sunset Boulevard* and Cruella De Vil in Disney's *101 Dalmations* (1961).

starving actor with a dynamite red sequined dress? America's hottest new actress." The British ad read "He's Tootsie. She's Dustin Hoffman. Desperate, he took a female role and became a star. If only he could tell the woman he loves." Cable television's ad was predictably nonfeminist: "This week, invite a very special girl home for dinner." And several critics referred to Dorothy as Tootsie, despite the point "she" makes in the film about names and labels.

"Dorothy makes me cry," Hoffman told the *Chicago Tribune*. "She doesn't have a man. She never got married. She never had kids. And it hurts me 'cause she's not pretty." He said that before playing Dorothy he consulted Glenn Close (*The World According to Garp, The Big Chill*), who was starring in *The Singular Life of Albert Nobbs*, a play about a woman who spent her adult life impersonating an Irish waiter. Hoffman's stage debut was in a Sarah Lawrence production of Gertrude Stein's *Yes Is for a Very Young Man*. In 1964 he played Immanuel, "a hunchbacked homosexual," in *Harry, Noon and Night*.

When Arthur Bell asked whether *Michael* might be gay, Hoffman replied, "I don't think Michael has had homosexual experiences—the character is basically me." Years before, he'd wanted to play a gay role, as a challenge. "That related to *Midnight Cowboy*. Jon and I wanted to take the characters further. I thought they should be sleeping together. But in those days they didn't do that."

28

HUSBANDS:

California Suite and *Deathtrap*

California Suite. Columbia, 1978. Director: Herbert Ross;
writer: Neil Simon; producer: Ray Stark.
Starring: Alan Alda, Michael Caine, Bill Cosby, Jane
Fonda, Walter Matthau, Elaine May, Richard Pryor,
Maggie Smith.

Deathtrap. Warner Bros., 1982. Director: Sidney Lumet;
writer: Jay Presson Allen; producer: Burtt Harris.
Starring: Michael Caine, Christopher Reeve, Dyan
Cannon, Irene Worth, Henry Jones.

In 1970 Michael Caine said, "I respect Ken Russell:
and I'd love to have done *Women in Love*. He offered
it to me, but I told him I couldn't do the nude
wrestling scenes. There's no way in my nature. It's
nothing to do with art or pornography. It's purely
emotional. Either you can appear nude in front of a
camera or you can't, and I can't. Besides which, I'd
have been cuddling a nude man, which I'd have
found a bit distasteful.

"Also, I'm very aware that however good your
performance, the audience would be looking at one
thing only: To see how large it is!"

Caine achieved fame as the woman-crazed *Alfie* in
1966. By the late seventies his star had faded, and
he began to accept the character roles at which he's
proven adept. The actor, who once called Rex Reed
"a snowflake" on the "Tonight Show," essayed his
first gay part in Neil Simon's *California Suite*, four
stellar, unconnected playlets set in the Beverly Hills
Hotel.

Caine and Maggie Smith are Cowardesque so-

Hollywood matrimony: Robert Redford playing a gay star
weds Natalie Wood playing a screen newcomer in a
studio-engineered match in *Inside Daisy Clover* (1966).

phisticates named Sidney Nichols and Diana Barrie,
in Hollywood for the Academy Awards, where she's
been nominated for an Oscar—as Glenda Jackson is
every other year, Diana disdainfully notes. Sidney
would rather be back in his London antique shop,
amid friends and lovers, but he enjoys the occa-
sional glamour and is a considerate husband. He
good-naturedly tolerates Diana's name-calling. Because he's a model gay and is played by a star,
Sidney doesn't respond in kind.

The mutually convenient arrangement gives Sidney the image he's been taught to value—supposedly good for business—and affords Diana an es-
cort and shoulder to cry on. The two have grown to
love each other with time, to share companionship
and comfortable familiarity, but they lack the sexual
component Diana desires. With Sidney, Neil Simon
and Hollywood rose above cheap laughs and stereotypes. The movies have seldom portrayed one of
Hollywood's commonplace gay/straight (or gay/gay
or bisexual/straight or bisexual/bisexual) marriages,
a subject worthy of more extended treatment.

Diana doesn't win the Oscar, and when she and
Sidney return to their suite she's disappointed and
sexually excited. "Tonight, Sidney, let it be me," she
entreats. Sidney is apologetic, though one would
think Diana would by now be resigned to the arrangement. But, the audience is spared a vain or

Blanche DuBois (Vivien Leigh) cracks up in *A Streecar Named Desire* after discovering her husband is gay—but he was omitted from the 1951 film.

halfhearted sex scene, the homosexual's remorse, or, in the not-so-old days, suicide. Diana vainly reproaches and belittles Sidney. Tears come, and he embraces her tenderly, assuring her of his love and commitment—they love each other without being in love.

Maggie Smith won a Best Supporting Actress Oscar, while Caine, breaking new ground, didn't even get nominated. Nonetheless, he was pleased with the role: "The timing was everything. Doing that character was like walking on a razor blade. Very difficult and enervating—but afterwards, uplifting." In interviews he discussed coming to terms with his "masculine and feminine sides, which every man has."

Two years later, Caine played Dr. Robert Elliott, the psychopath-transvestite in *Dressed to Kill*. He said afterward, "I didn't worry what people would think. As an actor you have to do things you've never done. I'd already played a homosexual in *California Suite*, besides which I don't have that romantic image. I couldn't imagine Robert Redford doing it, because it would hurt him.

"It was very awkward, because Elliott had to be normal and straight to the point of boredom—you couldn't give an inch. . . . The film was well-researched. It wasn't even about a transsexual; we showed a real transsexual to demonstrate this, on the television. It wasn't some cheap exploitation film. The picture it's been compared with is *Psycho*—so if any film is responsible, it's *Psycho*."

ABOUT *CALIFORNIA SUITE*

Pauline Kael: The entire point of the anguish exhibited by Maggie Smith and Michael Caine is that, though he is homosexual, they really love each other. . . . Caine performs like a professional used to doing the dramatist's job for him. He creates a decent, wary character: The sagging and thickening of the muscles in his face suggest the husband's defensiveness and pain. Maggie Smith and Caine waltz through ridiculous WASP glitz dialogue with heads held high. . . . She is obliged to play one of the most degrading of all scenes: a woman pleading with a man—who does not desire her—to make love to her. This is Simon's idea of the moment of truth, and Herbert Ross brings the camera in for a close-up of her desperation.

Murray Lyndon: Caine sheds his cockney macho to play a sensitive antiques dealer married to a tart-tongued actress. The happy picture they offer the world is tinged with private bickering. Maggie wants sex, but Michael gets his back at the shop.

Maggie taunts Michael, and he says "biological discrepancies" are involved. Is gay more *biological* than straight? Especially as we're all raised to be hetero-or-else! . . . A pat on the back to Caine, who has more guts than stars who only take regulation parts. . . . Now, how about Sean Connery as Seblon in Genêt's *Querelle de Brest*? Or Roger Moore and Parker Stevenson in *The Front Runner*, transplanted to a preppy English school?

Caine's well-received gay and transvestite roles were followed by Sidney Bruhl, the bisexual husband in the movie of Ira Levin's play *Deathtrap* (Alan Bates had the role on the London stage). As with Sydney in *California Suite*, Bruhl's sexuality is just one aspect of his life. In *Deathtrap* it isn't even an arguable point; the intricate plot and Machiavellian characters are the focus. Though marketed as a comic thriller, *Deathtrap*'s unofficial publicity included Caine's kiss-on-the-mouth with Christopher Reeve. The kiss was reportedly the brainchild of female scenarist (and executive producer) Jay Presson Allen (*The Prime of Miss Jean Brodie, Funny Lady*). It gave the film "relevance" and shock value and attracted bigger urban gay audiences. It was the first male kissing scene with two top stars.

The 1971 *Sunday, Bloody Sunday* kiss drew some strong negative reaction, while the kiss in *Making Love* evoked no outward negative response, at least at three showings attended by this author. The shorter kiss in *Deathtrap* (also 1982) brought reactions: Female cries of "Oh, my *God!*", "Ooh, gross!" and nervous seat-shifting. Why the contrast? The age discrepancy between Finch and Head and Caine and Reeve may have been a factor. The *Making Love* kiss was exchanged by two young men; the kiss was a prelude to sex. The other couples exchanged more "domestic" kisses. Finch and Head were fully dressed, as was Caine, but Reeve's bare torso pointed up Caine's chubbiness. Perhaps "classical" art has conditioned us to be more accepting of youthful kissing.

Superman I and *II* had made a sex symbol of Reeve, and many girls couldn't distinguish between Clifford Anderson (his character in *Deathtrap*) kissing Sidney Bruhl and Superman (or even Clark Kent) kissing another man. Some hero-worshipping straight men were also shocked. Disappointed viewers (when this author saw the film) included a preteen moaning, "Superman—how *could* you!" An older man remarked how seldom Superman got physical with Lois Lane: "He didn't even *kiss* her." (He did, though.) The role of Clifford put Reeve's Kryptonian identity into perspec-

Michael Caine played Sidney Nichols, a gay man
with a heterosexual wife in *California Suite*
(1978).

Maggie Smith won her second Oscar as Diana
Barrie, an actress married to a gay antiques
dealer in *California Suite*.

Triangle: Gay husband (Michael Caine as Sidney Bruhl), his
wife (Dyan Cannon), his lover (Christopher Reeve) in
Deathtrap (1982).

tive; after *Deathtrap*, a viewer couldn't watch *Superman*, or Reeve, with the same taken-for-granted attitude.

One gay critic concluded, "People going to *Making Love* knew what to expect. *Deathtrap*'s a thriller; the ads and most reviews didn't mention the gayness, which is part of the plot twist. So it came as a real surprise to most."

Michael Caine pronounced *Deathtrap* his best work to date and added, "Not too many American actors would have taken the role of a transvestite in *Dressed to Kill*. And there weren't too many rushing to play the bisexual [sic] in *California Suite*." He later corrected himself and described Sidney Nichols as homosexual.

Reeve's role in *Deathtrap* was described by Warners' publicity department as "a man of blurred moral and sexual edges." The actor said, "There's a certain 'gee whiz' quality about Clifford when you first meet him. But once you get to know him better, an experience about as comfortable as dining with the Borgias, he's a very peculiar fellow."

Ironically described by *American Film* as "*Diabolique* with the sexual preferences switched around," *Deathtrap* is one of the few films that simply happens to include gay characters. Both are murderers, but the same story could have been told with heterosexual characters—say, Caine and a girlfriend murdering his wife. Whether Sidney's and Clifford's gayness was intended to make them more despicable is open to argument. The fact remains that these gay roles were filled by stars usually seen in sympathetic or heroic parts, and neither actor—particularly Caine—wallowed in stereotypical characterization. Finally, despite the kiss, *Deathtrap* earned the universal PG-rating, a sign of slow, sure progress.

ABOUT *DEATHTRAP*

Variety: Amorous relationship between Caine and Reeve, physicalized by a quick kiss between the two stars, adds this to the list of current gay-themed pics. . . . Caine and Reeve are attractive, highly sympathetic screen presences; they undoubtedly relished the opportunity to play more sinister types here. Actors turn in pro jobs, with Reeve skillfully walking the fine gay-straight line of his pretty-boy part. But the characters are so constantly shifting morally and ethically that it becomes frustrating never to grasp their true personalities. Actors' charm doesn't balance out the characters' distastefulness.

Donald McLean, *The Voice*: Caine is forced to deliver an overwrought performance with little of the sly comic delivery he does so well. Reeve is matinee-idol gorgeous and dandy in the cartoonish psycho role. To make sure we know these two are *homosexual*—neon lights will twinkle "faggot" for ten minutes—Lumet never misses a chance to shove it down our throats. What was referred to in the play with a couple of lines is now cheap and graphic, with Caine and Reeve kissing, fondling, calling each other "love" and "dear," and Reeve doing a totally unnecessary semi-swish turn. Let's make sure those farm folks out in the Bible Belt don't miss the fact that these guys are queer as three-dollar bills. Thank you, Mr. Macho Lumet.

Sarah Craig, *GayLife*: Two people stand in the way of still suave Michael Caine's triumph: His dizzy wife (played by a not gracefully aging Dyan Cannon) and a psychic neighbor (portrayed with crazy style by Irene Worth). . . . Hunky Christopher Reeve is an absolute charmer—especially when he's playing a gay man.

In 1983 the contractually married Caine noted, "I can't play essentially American characters, so I usually wind up playing homosexual killers, transvestite lunatics—strange characters Newman or Redford or Reynolds wouldn't play. When they want someone to be rotten and dastardly, they say 'We've got to get a foreigner.'

"I know that there is a place called the Midwest, where the minute I open my mouth on-screen everybody's gonna yell 'goddamn liberal commie fag!' I talk different than they do."

In 1984 the non-contractually married Reeve alienated some fans by defending his antifeminist character Basil Ransom in the subtly homophobic *The Bostonians*. Ransom woos and wins a young woman out of the arms and influence of repressed lesbian suffragist Olive Chancellor (Vanessa Redgrave). Reeve's comments resurrected the myth of feminist-as-man-hater and did nothing to make Ransom seem more ethically attractive.

The following films touch upon gay or bisexual men contractually married to women—usually a marriage in name only, the only legal kind a non-heterosexual is allowed.

• Munson (George Macready) is married but not happily. His young wife fears rather than loves him. Then Munson saves Johnny Farrell (Glenn Ford)

Hunk: Christopher Reeve (as Clifford
Anderson) kisses Michael Caine on the lips in
Deathtrap.

Reeve's earlier incarnation as the Man of
Steel—holding a rod in *Superman II* (1980).

A man named Jacky: Raul Julia as hairdresser Jacky Manero
tries to kill ex-wife Jane Fonda, then wed a millionairess in
The Morning After (1986).

from a mugger and decides to employ him. Johnny
gratefully refers to the night he met Munson as "the
night I was born." Although he owns a thriving
Buenos Aires casino, Munson advises Johnny that
"women and gambling don't mix." The older man
forbids Johnny to get involved with women while in
his employ—"Statistics show that there are more
women in the world than anything except insects."
The obedient Johnny lights Munson's cigarettes
and becomes furious when Munson's beautiful wife
does a mock-strip at the casino. Of course the movie
is *Gilda* (1946), and Glenn Ford ends up with Rita
Hayworth, who was pretending to be "bad" just to
get some attention.

Munson's phallic substitute is his walking stick,
fitted with a stiletto; after meeting Johnny, Munson
proposes a toast to "the three of us." Munson's sense
of masculinity is derived from the stick, the unsexed
sexpot, and power, supplied by Nazi connections.
Johnny is saved from a similar cardboard fate by a
redeemed, newly pliable woman. The title, ads, and
glory may belong to Gilda/Rita, but the movie is
about Johnny.

• Why would an ambitious, possibly gay man

181

Two men and a beard: Alfred Lunt, Noel Coward, and Lynn Fontanne in Coward's play *Design for Living*, considerably bolder than the 1933 film version.

marry a plain-jane "tramp?" The question goes unanswered in Alfred Hitchcock's *Strangers on a Train*, with Farley Granger as Guy, the married tennis pro, and Robert Walker as Bruno, Guy's fan and tempter. Bruno knows everything about the tennis champ, including his wish to marry his mistress, a senator's daughter. During a fateful meeting on a train, Bruno proposes swapping murders. He murders Guy's wife, who wouldn't give him a divorce. But Guy doesn't honor the bargain he never really struck—to murder Bruno's disciplinarian father. The film ends with Guy, remarried and redeemed, moving away from a clergyman who has no doubt given the couple his blessings.

The script was written by Raymond Chandler, who didn't get along with Hitchcock, who in turn hired Czenzi Ormonde for a rewrite. Although virile and attractive, Walker's Bruno is essentially stereotypical. The "demented playboy" (according to *TV Guide*) believes "you should do everything before you die." But like Hitchcock's Norman Bates, Bruno is mama-bound, to Marion Lorne, who is dottily devoted to her devilish son. Bruno wears the sort of robe, tie, and tiepin that in 1951 labeled him *bizarre*. He even gets manicures. In the end Bruno is destroyed by a runaway merry-go-round.

Hitchcock, who wanted a more commanding presence to play Guy, was obliged to cast Granger

(*Rope*). The dominant Walker, who died at thirty-six, played another gay man in 1952's *My Son John*, a hysterical parable about an all-American couple with a commie son.

• Star-on-the-rise Wade Lewis (Robert Redford) is pressured by his studio into marrying real star Daisy Clover (Natalie Wood) to aid both their careers in *Inside Daisy Clover*. Gavin Lambert's script included Lewis's homosexuality, but Warner Bros. and director Robert Mulligan altered him into a kind of bisexual. 1966 Hollywood was not ready to explore this 1930s-set gay/straight marriage, even superficially—or to touch on Wade's relationship with apparently gay studio aide Roddy McDowall. Also, Redford—who later termed Paul Newman's offer to costar in *The Front Runner* "ridiculous"—declined to play gay.

The screen Wade, a charming cad with spotless patent-leather shoes, is portrayed by Redford as "a narcissist," someone who "bats ten different ways: children, women, dogs, cats, and men." To Redford's continuing chagrin, the filmmakers added a phone conversation which reveals Wade's bisexuality—a case of an editor phoning in a role.

• *Women in Love* (1969) is famous as the first mainstream movie with full male nudity. The candlelit scene overshadows the whole, and Rupert

Birkin remains Alan Bates's most notable role. He recently said, "It was the first time you got to see the *actual* stars' *actual* organs. Big deal!" The film established the careers of actress Glenda Jackson and director Ken Russell and was written and produced by Larry Kramer, who later wrote the novel *Faggots* and the screenplay to the 1973 film *Lost Horizon* for producer-partners Ross Hunter and Jacques Mapes. Kramer cofounded the Gay Men's Health Crisis and ACT-UP and authored the AIDS-themed play *The Normal Heart*.

Some critics felt *Women in Love* should have been titled "Men in Love," especially as far as Birkin, the D. H. Lawrence stand-in, was concerned. Lawrence's suppressed bisexuality has since been widely noted, and Richard Gere has expanded the horizons of male screen nudity, but *Women in Love*'s wrestling scene is still stunning. It might have been more so had Gerald Crich been a blond—as Lawrence intended—instead of dark-haired Oliver Reed. (Lawrence conceived Crich as Birkin's complete opposite and complement.) Panting on the floor afterward, Gerald asks, "It wasn't too much for you, was it?" Rupert answers, "No. We are mentally close, so it's right that we should be physically close, too." The *New York Times* demanded, "*Is* Birkin or *isn't* he? You never really find out." Today it's obvious that Rupert is a closeted bisexual.

Birkin marries Ursula (Jennie Linden), the more conventional of the titular sisters; the fiery Gudrun (Jackson) has a long affair with Gerald. She asks him, "How are your thighs? Are they strong? Because I want to drown in hot, physical, naked flesh." Gudrun finally taunts Gerald by having an affair with Loerke (Vladek Sheybal), a sinister bisexual artist. After she runs off to Berlin with Loerke, Gerald walks to his icy death in the Tyrolean Alps.

Early on, Rupert finds that marriage isn't enough. He tries to explain this to Ursula. She asks, "Aren't I enough for you?" He responds, "No. You are enough for me as far as a woman is concerned." While Rupert attempts to express his wide-ranging feelings, Gerald is confined by his work and carnal urges. Gudrun tells him, "Try to love me a little more and want me a little less." Gerald's inflexibility and inarticulateness may have masked loneliness and insecurity; Rupert lives on to contemplate the limitlessness of love.

• Laurence Olivier is Loren Hardeman, a Ford-like auto tycoon who seduces his daughter-in-law (Katharine Ross) in 1978's super-trashy *The Betsy*, based on Harold Robbins's novel. The seduction is viewed as acceptable because Hardeman's son is a homosexual and a weakling (redundant, in Hollywood). Junior (Paul Rudd) takes poison afterward. The marriage is neither explained nor meant to be taken seriously. The marital victim is Ross, not the dead man whom society pressured into a "marriage" that suited no one but his monster-dad. Harold Robbins's subsequent novel, *Dreams Die First*, delved deeper into bisexuality, and the author told *People* magazine that he "experimented" to find out what it was like.

Longtime lawless companions: The real Clyde Barrow was gay or bisexual, but Warren Beatty and Faye Dunaway in *Bonnie & Clyde* (1967) were both hetero.

In Hitchcock's *Strangers on a Train* (1951), Robert Walker exchanges murder plots with Farley Granger, who has a wife he wishes to be rid of.

29

LOVEMAKING:

Making Love

Making Love. Twentieth Century-Fox, 1982. Director: Arthur Hiller; writer: Barry Sandler, from a story by A. Scott Berg; producers: Daniel Melnick and Allen Adler.
Starring: Michael Ontkean, Kate Jackson, Harry Hamlin, Wendy Hiller, Arthur Hill, Nancy Olson, John Dukakis, Asher Brauner.

Thirty-three-year-old A. Scott Berg conceived *Making Love* after six of his friends came out after marriage. "This is the next big social movement," he said, after the men left their wives for other men. "What the black movement was in the sixties, and the feminist movement in the seventies, the gay movement will be in the eighties." Berg, a writer, had never written a screenplay and contacted his friend Barry Sandler, who'd written the films *Gable and Lombard, The Duchess and the Dirtwater Fox,* and *The Mirror Crack'd.*

Sandler hesitated, because the story "touched certain buttons I'd never allowed to be touched in my work." Sandler later became the only out-of-the-closet member of the *Making Love* production team. He told the *Advocate,* "I went through a period of telling myself that my homosexual tendencies were just a phase and I was only experimenting." This is reflected in Zack Elliot (Michael Ontkean), who marries, both despite and because of his homosexuality. Marriage to Claire (Kate Jackson) is happy and sexually fulfilling, but. . . .

"I've been involved with men in the past," said Sandler of his prior relationships, "but I was always

the one to break if off." This is the case with Bart McGuire (Harry Hamlin), who—though long uncloseted—is unwilling to commit to relationships beyond a physical level.

Sandler's script was backed by Daniel Melnick, a former Columbia Pictures chief who was one of the biggest single contributors to 1978's Anti-Proposition-6 political campaign in California. Melnick decided *Making Love* would be the first project from his new company IndieProd. His partner was *Cosmo* Bachelor of the Month and ex-Columbia vice president Allen Adler. Melnick, producer of *All That Jazz,* with its straight and gay dance couples, said, "All the great romances are when two lovers can't be together. *Making Love* and *Love Story* are in a direct line from *Romeo and Juliet.*" It was Melnick—after Arthur Hiller was hired to direct—who described *Making Love* as "the *Love Story* of the eighties." The ads relied heavily on "From the director who brought you *Love Story.*"

Condescending reviewers failed to mention Hiller's other credits, including *Hospital, Popi, The Americanization of Emily,* and *The Man in the Glass Booth.* Another *Making Love* backer was Fox executive Claire Townsend (after whom the Jackson charac-

184

Love triangle: Zack (Michael Ontkean), Claire (Kate Jackson), and Bart (Harry Hamlin)—bisexual, heterosexual, and homosexual.

The woman between: Claire is contractually married to Zack, who unlocks his homosexuality via Bart.

Doctor and novelist meet, and their attraction is instantaneous.

ter was named). She predicted, "There's too little romance in today's movies, and we may get criticized for bringing it back."

After the male leads were turned down by actors like Harrison Ford and Michael Douglas, the filmmakers agreed to go with "unknowns." Melnick referred to *Staircase*: "We decided *Making Love* would not be best served by having a star who was identified as heterosexual. . . . It would be like carrying a sign: 'Hey, I'm only playacting.' " Melnick signed "Rookies" star Michael Ontkean, a Canadian who came to the U.S. on a hockey scholarship and starred in *Slap Shot* and *Willie & Phil*.

Ontkean said, "Zack is a character in transition, trapped by the expectations of those closest to him. He's allowed others to shape him and tends to live

185

by their rules. He doesn't fully know himself. It isn't until he meets Bart that he begins to break through, to come to terms with his sexual identity. Zack is determined to avoid a double life. He knows the only shame is in lying."

Zack is the sole bond between Claire and Bart, who never meet. Both speak directly to the camera about him, and Bart also reveals his feelings and his past, which includes a relationship with a "coed." Claire discusses her insecurity and need for a father figure. It is Claire with whom straight audiences identify, and she was the ads' centerpiece, posing with both men. "I felt you needed Claire to give the audience a grounding," said Sandler. "Most people find two men together alien or threatening. . . . Even after Zack comes out, Claire says she wants her baby to have somebody like him to look up to. The audience discovers the situation isn't as threatening as they may have thought."

Best known for television's, "The Rookies" and "Charlie's Angels," Jackson lost the lead in *Kramer Vs. Kramer* (overseen by Melnick) to Meryl Streep because of her heavy television schedule. Alabama-born and -bred, Jackson "used to believe all homosexuals lived in New York." When she told her mother about *Making Love*, Mrs. Jackson noted that a local couple had had the same experience as Zack and Claire. "If it could happen in Birmingham," figured Kate, "it could happen anywhere."

Harry Hamlin starred first in the title role of the television version of *Studs Lonigan* and then as Perseus in *Clash of the Titans*. A graduate of San Francisco's American Conservatory Theater, he did more research for his role than Ontkean. Both viewed *Women in Love*, and Hamlin said, "It helped me in relation to working with Michael. Without being blatantly sexual, it's the best male-male relationship on film—about the need men have for another man in their lives, be it sexual or not. We came out of the film with a succinct idea of what we wanted to do."

Hamlin, who later gained fame on television's "L.A. Law," also hung out at Mother Lode, a Los Angeles gay bar and *Making Love* location. "A guy almost picked me up. When I told him I was doing research for a film, he said, 'I've heard that before.'" The actor, who screened *Cruising* and "didn't like it at all," determined "not to play Bart stereotypically. I wanted to depict him as an individual who happens to be gay, whose wariness of commitment is characteristic of a lot of people, regardless."

Hamlin's personal publicity during this period focused on his relationship with over-forty Ursula Andress, with whom he had a child. Initially he had qualms about *Making Love*: "I thought, I can't do this. But it was what I wanted to do, and I finally thought, If people don't accept it, screw 'em." He told *Us* magazine, "Perhaps *Making Love* will help break down negative attitudes. It's absurd to accept murderers and psychotics and not someone in search of their own romanticism—with men or women."

As for the Kiss, he explained to *After Dark* magazine, "I wasn't apprehensive. Michael and I never really discussed or rehearsed it. We wanted the element of surprise, as it would have been in the real moment." There were two takes; the first was printed. Later, Hamlin told the press that he'd thought of his "girlfriend" during the scene. Eleven years earlier, Peter Finch answered the same stupid question (one never asked of gay performers doing straight love scenes). He said, "I just closed my eyes and thought of England."

Making Love's gay sexuality is presented gradually. Driving through Los Angeles, Zack spots a handsome, rugged male couple on motorcycle. At night, he parks in a gay backstreet, lets a man into his car, then suddenly changes his mind. He visits a gay bar but retreats the first time a man makes advances. But that same bar is Bart's home away from home, where he picks up Tim, a handsome young trick played by John Dukakis. Dukakis—whose father was running for reelection as governor of Massachusetts at the time—asked his agent, "Would you play a homosexual if your father was running for office?" Answer: "Sure. But if I were *really* gay, I wouldn't." Similarly, some extras in the gay-bar scene declined to be included in the still photographs. They may have recalled that at least one lesbian spotted in newspaper photos taken during the filming of *Sister George*'s bar scene lost her day job.

When Zack and Bart meet, they go back to Bart's house. They kiss in a long-shot, after Bart admits he's gay and Zack allows that he's "curious." The men move into the bedroom. In a medium-shot, they remove each other's shirts and kiss passionately on the lips. Next they appear in bed together, and Bart permits Zack to spend the night. One gay critic, more attuned to the more blunt *Taxi zum Klo*, called the kiss "as tasteful as a Harlequin romance." But for straight audiences it was heady stuff.

Zack's basic decency is established by his active sympathy for a female mastectomy patient, and he's shown to genuinely love Claire. A brief scene proves that he's also a dutiful son to his parents Arthur Hill and Nancy Olson. Somewhat stereotypically, Zack and Bart reminisce about youthful failures at sports and their unrequited affection for stern fathers. But the diversity and general contentedness of gay men is made apparent. When Claire visits Ted (Asher Brauner), a trick of Zack's whose address she finds in a matchbook, she asks if Ted is "happy." He answers that if pricked, he bleeds. Ted explains that he dislikes having to pay a disproportionate amount of his salary to buy hamburger, etc., but, yes, he's really happy.

Associate producer Sandler noted that the idealized Zack is "balanced out by Bart, who isn't necessarily a negative view of gay life but certainly an honest one. . . . Say what you will, but I don't believe any gay person will walk out of this movie feeling any degree of shame. This is what I intended," he told the *Los Angeles Times*.

Sandler fully expected irrelevant criticism from the straight press. "What I'd like, and what's important, is for a gay man to be able to take his parents to *Making Love* and see solid, human, decent gay men. I'd like a seventeen-year-old boy sitting in the back of a theater in Oklahoma City, terrified of the feelings he's experiencing about other men, to see the models and conflicts and say, 'This is what I am; I'm going to go for it and ultimately be happy.'" *Making Love* was a turning point for Sandler. "I can't go back. None of us can. The negative stereotype is out. Straight and gay people want positive images."

The "positive stereotypes" were decried by straight critics as well as by some gay ones. Dr. Newton Dieter, head of the Gay Media Task Force, said, "There have been so many projects, such as *Cruising*, which have portrayed gays as psychotics, suicides, murderers. There are gays who are those things, and there are also a great many more gays who are warm, giving, and well-adjusted. If the script over-romanticizes in that direction, my reaction is, 'So what?'"

ABOUT *MAKING LOVE*

Clifton Montgomery, the *Advocate*: *Making Love* is a bittersweet romance from the same time-honored tradition as *The Way We Were* . . . . Herein lies its importance, because for the first time, attractive, intelligent characters *who are gay* have been plugged into the formula. . . . The men grow and benefit *because* of their acceptance of their sexuality.

Jeff Barber, *Lambda News*: The gay breakthrough movie. For the first time in a production by a major

Bart and Zack begin courting, but once the relationship is underway, Bart fears committing himself.

Zack and Claire must face the fact that their marriage was never right for Zack and would now be unfair to Claire.

American studio, two men are allowed to kiss romantically, appear in bed together, and whisper "I love you." Unlike all the Hollywood films we grew up with, being gay is no sin in *Making Love*; no one is "punished."

Not only is *Making Love* politically correct, it is tender, funny, and warm. Zack's coming out is portrayed as difficult and painful; it takes enormous courage to risk the rejection of family and friends. . . . You can recommend *Making Love* without reservation to straight family and friends as an honest, positive portrayal of gay life.

Michael Lasky, *B.A.R.*: *Making Love* is a great title: something we all do, with a societally accepted partner or not. . . . The first film from Hollywood to broach the untouchable theme of Gay sex, it is also the first to treat Gay people maturely and really no different—a socially and historically significant film.

Making Love treats Gay lovemaking with kid gloves, which is okay. It guides easily upset straights at their own pace. The filmmakers are eyeing the middle-American audience first. Gays already know what this picture has to say. Middle-Americans don't. *Making Love* puts Fox into the twentieth century; gays should be overjoyed that it actually got made, not cynical and demanding that it isn't blatant. Hollywood has packaged homosexuality attractively enough to break down some hard-edged preconceptions. This picture is the first step. If it goes over at the box office, more pictures will explore farther. Amen.

Howard Weiss, *Bicoastal*: I saw *Making Love* in a suburb north of New York City. Though the town has a gay bar or two and plenty of closet space, the hetero audience's reaction was shocking. I heard catcalls every time Zack and Bart touched. One woman screamed, "Oh, my God, he's a doctor!" People actually walked out in the middle. Why did they come to see it in the first place? Upon leaving the theater, I noticed many gay singles and couples present; they appeared to be thinking what I was—however, to speak it would probably have led to a lynching.

David Castell, *Photoplay* (U.K.): *Making Love* is candied when it should be candid. Hiller phrases his film in the clichés of old movies—Hamlin is a video buff who watches weepies like *An Affair to Remember* and emasculated films of homosexually-oriented plays like *Cat on a Hot Tin Roof*. Hiller demonstrates that those movies had more style. . . . Wendy Hiller represents the spirit of romantic love that the gay world, shown here, rejects. . . . Hiller's film trails light-years behind the movie from which the idea is taken—*Sunday, Bloody Sunday*.

Buddhist Eye (Japan): The ideologically advanced movie treats its gay characters honestly and realistically. Both care about women and friends, the doctor more so. . . . The two marrieds find more suitable partners but remain loving to each other, while the novelist stays alone by choice . . . . The personalities' appeal is exceeded only by the revolutionary intentions of the open-hearted creators.

Making Love (1982): (left to right) director Arthur Hiller, producers Daniel Melnick and Allen Adler, and screenwriter Barry Sandler.

30

FRIENDSHIP:

Partners and *The Dresser*

Associates: Gay cop Kerwin (John Hurt),
heterosexual cop Benson (Ryan O'Neal); Benson
looks down on Kerwin.

Partners. Paramount, 1982. Director: James Burrows;
writer: Francis Veber; producer: Aaron Russo.
Starring: Ryan O'Neal, John Hurt, Kenneth McMillan,
Robyn Douglass, Jay Robinson, Denise Galik, Rick Jason.

The Dresser. Goldcrest/Columbia, 1983.
Director-producer: Peter Yates; writer: Ronald Harwood.
Starring: Albert Finney, Tom Courtenay, Edward Fox,
Zena Walker, Eileen Atkins, Michael Gough, Lockwood
West, Cathryn Harrison.

Can a straight man and a (by implication) *bent* man
find friendship and happiness? Can they even stand
each other? According to these two films, a macho,
womanizing American can barely tolerate his fey
partner, while a culturally domineering Englishman depends on *and* deprecates *his* fey partner.
Being an American comedy, *Partners* takes the cute
route and makes its men play married. It's a gayer,
racier *Odd Couple*, with Ryan O'Neal's bare buns and
Robyn Douglass's tits—the filmmakers weren't taking any chances. John Hurt is the rather asexual,
gay cop, and O'Neal is the antigay one.

Against their wills, Benson (O'Neal) and Kerwin
(Hurt) are teamed by police chief Kenneth Mc-
Millan, who jokes about Kerwin's "time of month."
They go undercover in West Hollywood to track
down a murderer of gay centerfold models. The
gay community is presented as a caftan- or leather-
clad bunch of cliches, and the "happy couple" are
flamboyantly welcomed to their cute new abode by
their landlord, played by Jay (*Caligula*) Robinson.

Associated: Kerwin and Benson are assigned to pose as a gay
couple in order to trap a homophobic murderer.

Kerwin becomes lovesick over Benson, who periodically leaves for one-day-stands with Jill (Robyn Douglass, of television's *Her Life as a Man*). As part of the operation, Benson poses as a nude centerfold in an uninspiring layout photographed by Jill who turns out to be a secondary killer. The main killer is Douglas (Rick Jason), who kills two of the three victims before strangling Jill. In the line of duty Kerwin is seriously wounded, and Benson comforts him and urges him to think of the life they can share (as friends) if he survives. The movie ends with the chief informing Benson that Kerwin is recuperating—only one thing is giving him the will to live: "He said you two are setting up housekeeping together."

Partners was rated R—for "rancid incompetence," said *Newsweek*. The film's ad featured an exasperated O'Neal with a gun to his head and Hurt with a hair dryer to his. Typical of *Partners'* mind-set are Hurt's pastel outfits, expertise in the kitchen, mothering fixation, and the couple's pink convertible that honks "Mary Had a Little Lamb."

The film was produced by Aaron Russo, Bette Midler's ex-manager, and directed by James Burrows, of "The Mary Tyler Moore Show," "Taxi," and "Cheers." Frenchman Francis Veber, who scored with the first two *Cage* films, wrote the script and was executive producer. He "explained" the comedy to the *San Francisco Chronicle*: "At the beginning you have a cat and a dog. At the end they are friends. I love stories of friendship." He should have written one. "Comedy is better for men than women; I don't believe in female clowns. Maybe I love women too much to have them make faces." Veber also announced that he had no intention of writing the third *Cage aux Folles*. After *Partners* he returned to straight French themes.

John Hurt played gay in "The Naked Civil Servant" and swishy in "I, Claudius." But *Us* magazine revealed him to be heterosexual, and Hurt disclosed, "This film doesn't delve into the miserable problems of homosexuality. It has nothing to do with sexuality. It's not a *Cruising*, nor does it take up the gay cause. It's a thriller, a farce."

ABOUT *PARTNERS*

Variety: There's a big difference between characters living in and around a female-impersonator's club in the south of France and gays residing in an American, middle-class urban environment; nobody thought that was worth explaining to Veber. . . . The unlikelihood of someone as scared and inexperienced as Hurt being put on such a dangerous caper doesn't matter to the filmmakers, who believe it's a given fact that there is no other gay officer on the squad.

People: Nobody would dare make a film today in which all the blacks were dumb shufflers or all the women helpless darlings. . . . This film is as insulting to straight people's intelligence as to gays' sexuality. . . . *Partners* makes *Cruising* seem a model of intelligence by comparison. Almost every gay character is a raving queen. . . . Even Hurt is ghastly, and the murder plot feebly inept. Burrows and partners ought to get back in the closet.

Dean Tomich, *Lambda News*: I enjoyed most of it but was uncomfortable watching scenes in which most gay men were portrayed as lisping, limp-wristed, screaming faggots. I'm tired of being categorized as only one particular element of the gay lifestyle. . . . There were good statements about how degraded women must feel when being mauled and molested by straight men, how some police treat gays in a demeaning, humiliating way, and how a gay man relates to another man the same as a straight man relates to a straight woman.

Clifton Montgomery, the *Advocate*: This smirking, ignorant film does serve a purpose, reminding us how fragile the hard-won victories of more than a decade of gay liberation are, how tempting it is to become complacent. . . . The thoughtful analysis, discussion, and controversy engendered by *Partners* may partly offset its reinforcing fear and hatred in some viewers. . . . It's instructive for uncloseted, self-accepting gays to see this movie. (If you are closeted and don't like the fact that you are gay, stick to television's "Love, Sidney.") One can learn from *Partners*, but don't expect to like it.

The Dresser features a master-servant relationship, but the two men are not partners; each knows his "place." Sir (Albert Finney) is a grand old wreck of an actor-manager, touring 1942 England doing Shakespeare repertory. Sir depends entirely upon his gay dresser Norman (Tom Courtenay). The company also includes Sir's wife (Zena Walker); Madge (Eileen Atkins), the cold, efficient stage manager who looks down her nose at Norman; and an icy homophobic thespian, Oxenby (Edward Fox). The other players are, in Sir's words, "old men and nancy boys"—all the *men* are at war.

Based on Ronald Harwood's 1980 play, which has been translated into twenty-three languages, *The Dresser* draws its insight from the fact that Harwood

The gay cop and the antigay cop come to like each other once they set up house in West Hollywood and start shopping together in *Partners* (1982).

relationship with the egocentric, senile Sir is the heart of the movie. Norman keeps Sir, and therefore the company, alive. Like Caesar, he is both wife and husband to the doddering "great man."

The film concentrates on Norman's struggle to prepare Sir for his 227th performance of *King Lear*. Afterward, Sir, sensing his own death is near, presents his embittered and once-lovelorn stage manager with his special ring. To Norman he leaves nothing, and Sir's prerecorded final words thank everybody, down to the carpenters and electricians—except Norman. With a sudden jolt the dresser realizes that he and Sir, whom he considered much more than an employer, never shared a single meal or drink together.

Earlier in the film, Norman demonstrated his strength in a pep speech about the nation's struggle for survival and his own need not to give in to despair. But now he breaks down and raves against the dead Sir. His spent fury turns to worry about his future—no one else in the company will have him—and Norman feels sadness and loss. He realizes, "I had a friend. . . . I loved him." Sir's widow and Madge arrive shortly to take possession of the body and charge of the future.

Harwood has provided Norman no sexual history and no gay relationships. When he dutifully

Oscar nominee Tom Courtenay as *The Dresser* (1983).

was himself a dresser. Courtenay created the title role on stage, and in 1984 he and Finney were each nominated for an Oscar as Best Actor. Courtenay won a Golden Globe as Best Actor, but *Film Comment* quoted a critic who felt he shouldn't have been in that category: "Tom Courtenay playing Roddy Mc-Dowall should be Supporting." Because *The Dresser* is primarily a drama (albeit with many light moments), several straight critics were uncomfortable with Norman. *Vanity Fair* called the performance "all lavender-tinted prissiness—*The Boys in the Band*-style gay-face." Pauline Kael typically praised Finney but found Courtenay's act "all dried up."

Courtenay's mincing mannerisms offended many gays. "He speaks through his teeth, arches his back, walks with tiny, hurried steps, and holds his hands before him like a begging Pekinese dog," said Quentin Crisp. However, Norman's twenty-year

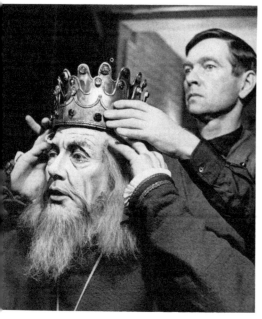

With Norman's assistance, Sir prepares for a final performance as King Lear in wartime England.

Norman (Courtenay) is the loving, dedicated dresser to Sir (Albert Finney), an aging stage star.

Sir gets the royal treatment from his dresser but usually treats him like a lackey in return.

No people like show people: Norman, Sir and
the assembled touring stage company.

attends to Sir, Oxenby insults him: "Your nose is browner than usual." Sir himself refers to "the pansy fraternity" and notes, "I don't hold a brief for buggerers." Although he wields influence, Norman never talks back, yet producer-director Peter Yates declared that there were no complaints from the gay community about any aspect of Courtenay's performance. "Norman is camp, but he's *theater* camp. He's not necessarily homosexual camp—we never really *say* he's homosexual." But it is impossible not to see that Norman is, uh, different. "We made a strong point that there should be no cheap laughs got at Norman's expense." The titters, instead of laughs, result from Norman's persona, rather than a specific line or situation.

Hollywood and British films seem incapable of depicting friendship between a homosexual and heterosexual of the same gender (it's seldom attempted with women). The filmmaking establishment perceives no basis for equality and is usually tempted to introduce romance into a friendship, with either or both characters (typically the straight) trying to force his or her particular sexuality on the other.

Yet much of America is ready to deal with gay-straight friendships and bisexuality. Response to one Phil Donahue television show about interracial lesbians, who had a child by having the brother of one impregnate the other, indicated that viewers were far more upset about the black and white aspect than the gayness. On another "Donahue," Ann Landers quoted a survey of male and female Ivy League students that found that more of them would choose "a bisexual affair than group sex"—a principal reason was the stronger possibility of friendship between a pair than in a group.

However, on the screen, male friendship is competitive, and sex is evangelical. Even an asexual gay can't be a heterosexual's pal. The straight Hollywood male needs something to conquer, be it a woman, a situation, or a gay man. Until homosexuals of both genders are viewed as human first and sexual second, gay-straight friendships will never be partnerships, on or off the screen.

ABOUT *THE DRESSER*

Quentin Crisp, *Christopher Street*: The dresser is part bossy nanny, part abject slave. In his own eyes and everybody else's, the only justification for his existence is that, with the passage of time, he has come so completely to understand his master. . . . There are many homosexuals who will be annoyed by this performance; I would say that no gay man who wears a mustache should see this film.

Judy Stone, *San Francisco*: Finney's monument of enfeebled power is so persuasive it's difficult to credit Sir's dependence upon Norman. The performance springs out of conviction; Courtenay is all studied frills and furbelows, his little finger always delicately crooked—not an uninteresting piece of acting, but increasingly irritating until Courtenay erupts with rage at Sir's betrayal.

Advocate letter to the editor: The tyranny committed by Sir upon his colleagues is a kind of fascism generated by its victims' submission, mirroring the conflagration outside the auditorium. For Sir, keeping Shakespeare alive means subjugating others: His repertoire favors the powermongers of Lear, Richard III, and Othello. Norman realizes this after Sir's death. His "what's to become of me?" wail is a challenge to all the world's Normans to recognize their plight and break free from those bonds.

31
CLASS OF '82

It was a Hollywood first: Five gay-themed films were released in the first months of 1982: *Personal Best, Making Love, Victor/Victoria, Deathtrap,* and *Partners. Us* magazine ran a series asking "Does a Secret Gay Mafia Run Hollywood?" The press ran features on gays in films. Some cited *Cruising,* the last previous major outing, as a nadir from which the gay celluloid image had nowhere to go but up. Hollywood gambled $70 million on the five pictures, betting that general audiences were ready to accept gays as film characters.

Studios worried about the Moral Majority and the kind of publicity and boycotts that had made bombs of *Myra Breckenridge* and *Cruising.* But perhaps the majority concentrated too much on television programming, or perhaps they realized that movie audiences had become younger and irreversibly sexualized, for the mass protests never came, not even against the watershed *Making Love.*

Personal Best won mostly favorable reviews and considerable publicity in sports publications as well as in *Playboy.* The R-rated movie was eventually advertised as "Featured in April issue of *Playboy.*" It opened small but built interest, aided by real-life publicity about lesbian athletes (especially in tennis) and glowing notices from heterosexual critics like Roger Ebert, who "had trouble" with *Making Love.* The *San Jose Mercury-News* critic described *Making Love*'s "sex play," and the "love play" of the far more explicit *Personal Best.* These men didn't so much review as affirm their sexual persuasions.

With a $16-million production budget—partly financed by "bachelor tycoon" David Geffen (who came out in 1991)—*Personal Best* was the twelfth-biggest money-loser of 1982 (number one: Rever-

All the good ones are gay or married—and sometimes both: Harry Hamlin, Michael Ontkean, and Kate Jackson in *Making Love.*

end Moon's *Inchon,* which lost over $44 million). *Personal Best* earned only $3 million in domestic rentals. Several factors kept audiences at bay. Gay and straight women were alienated by the misjudged ads, with their quotes about erotic female nudity. Gays took offense at star Mariel Hemingway's and writer-director Robert Towne's press statements. Towne, who hadn't intended spearheading an unprecedented gay wave, told *Time,* "The movie is not *Personal Fruit.* There are two minutes of lovemaking and an hour of competition in it, and, as far as I know, sex between any genders has not yet qualified as an Olympic event."

The ads, featuring a plain-jane Hemingway, didn't grab straight males, who were sidelined by the "woman's film" and "gay film" publicity. Female nudity could be had elsewhere, minus the sweating and relevance. After Towne sued Warners for $150 million, *Personal Best* plummeted, overtaken by the other gay films and the traditionalist hits *On Golden Pond* and *Chariots of Fire.*

Advertising for *Making Love* was more extensive

and better targeted. The movie cost $8 million and had a $5 million ad budget. Fox studio chief Sherry Lansing felt, "If the film is reasonably successful, it will do an enormous amount to erase some of the negative clichés." (One cliché being that gay themes are box-office anathema.)

Besides distributing twenty-five million *Making Love* matchbooks in supermarkets and gay bars, Fox placed different ads in gay and general publications—Hollywood's biggest specialized-marketing effort in years. The publicity didn't attempt to minimize the gay aspect. The announcement story called the film "the bold and compassionate love story of a young couple who after eight years of marriage must come to terms with the husband's attraction to another man." Other publicity called it "the story of three young people who emerge from a crossfire of love with a new understanding of themselves." Television ads emphasized the marriage while highlighting the third party—Kate Jackson smashing a dinner plate to get her husband's attention.

Daniel Melnick, afraid that exhibitors would shun the film, refused to sneak preview *Making Love*. It opened, on a holiday weekend, much stronger than anyone expected: It was the number-two film that week, after *On Golden Pond*, and it took in over $3.5 million. On the strength of its first week, *Making Love* opened in more movie houses (five hundred total), but its decline thereafter was steady. Nonetheless, it earned over $5.5 million in ten days and eventually $16–18 million domestically. Overseas, it earned some $7 million, although in Britain it was X-rated and off-limits to under-eighteens. At year's end, several magazines (among them *Time* and *California*) prejudicially and erroneously called ·*Making Love* a "flop." In fact, with the addition of cable television and video rentals and sales (it sells consistently to gay audiences), the film's profit is still growing.

Fox was pleased that it didn't lose money on *Making Love*, a project that was certainly a calculated risk. Studio spokesman Joe DiSabato noted that the audience demographics were what Fox had expected: mostly women under thirty-five, gay men, and lesbians. In a letter sent to members of the gay press, he wrote, "Consider urging your readers to respond if they strongly disagree with views of local critics. It's an opportunity to open people's eyes with letters to the editor, which have great educational value."

Making Love's positivism and measured reality made an imprint on many gay and straight viewers. Film historian Vito Russo felt, "You can't toss away the psychological impact for a fourteen-year-old gay person seeing his first gay man on the screen and he's Michael Ontkean. My first gay man on the screen was Don Murray in *Advise and Consent*. He slit his throat." *Making Love* was rated R—semi-restricted for under-seventeens—because of its gayness. It had no nudity and some graphic language, which today would probably have earned it a PG rating.

Making Love elicited an outpouring of letters to gay publications, many along this line: "Maybe it is like a soap, but to actually *view* such men, who contribute to society, is nothing short of revolutionary. Maybe straight people in New York or California are aware of gay men in this light; in Texas they are not. I sat in a crowded theater with about a 60 percent-straight audience who were *shocked* by the lovemaking and actually, I feel, learned to look at gays in a new light."

Other letters asserted that straight critics' accusations of over-idealization and blandness were one-sided—that Zack's heroism is offset by Bart's promiscuous narcissism, that the bittersweet ending is non-pat, and so on. "Why didn't straights put down the white-bread characters in *Ordinary People*? Both films are about middle-class WASPs, full of control, afraid of their own emotions. I also recall that most of the Tracy-Hepburn films we all loved were filled with affluent, successful people in immaculate clothes. . . . At any rate, it's better to be looked over than overlooked!"

The biggest hit of these five was the rather mainstream *Victor/Victoria*, which functioned partly as an old-fashioned star vehicle for Julie Andrews. Of the five, only it received any Oscar nominations—mostly for acting, including Andrews, Robert Preston, and Lesley Ann Warren.

Prior to casting James Garner and rescripting, *Victor/Victoria* promised to be even more provocative than it turned out to be. The male lead was to have been a continental baron, not a Chicago gangster. Blake Edwards described the plot in 1980: "The baron takes Victoria to a whorehouse as a man, after finding out 'he' is a woman. She says, 'I don't want to get laid.' 'Why not?' 'Because I'm homosexual.' He takes her back to his apartment and says, 'By the way, so am I.' It gets complicated because the baron is married and his wife won't give him a divorce. Victoria decides to compromise his wife, as a woman. She goes on the make and that gets screwed up because it really happens. She finally says, 'I'm a woman.' The wife says, 'Terrific, I love ladies.' "

Victor/Victoria was a major hit in Paris, and it won

the César (French Oscar) as Best Foreign Film. But the film that introduced many Americans to their first positive gay character wasn't as popular domestically. MGM/UA failed to follow up excellent reviews and word-of-mouth with stepped-up advertising. The studio's prestige push was behind the less successful *Shoot the Moon*, and the big push went to *The Beast Within* and *Diner*. Marketing consultant Michael Mahern felt the studio "played off both *Victor/Victoria* and *My Favorite Year* too quickly, either through ignorance or a desperate need to service a $600 million debt. These comedies had broad, long-term potential, but they needed to be nursed."

Credit for the chic lips-and-mustache ad campaign went to auteur Edwards, who, with Preston, had decided Toddy shouldn't be shown in drag until the finale. *Victor/Victoria* earned $10 million domestically and is still popular on video and cable.

Andrews and Preston participated in the most publicity of any of the five films' stars. *People* magazine called Preston "as masculine as five o'clock shadow" and called his Toddy "a slightly dangerous Liberace." The sixty-four-year-old actor told the press, "I've been free all my life. In the old days there were even rumors about me! I have friends who have not come out of the closet and aren't happy with their lifestyle." As for "learning" Toddy, he stated, "I knew how to walk; I didn't have to mince. For Toddy, being gay means he and Victoria can have their warm, wonderful relationship without sex rearing its beautiful head." After seeing "The Naked Civil Servant," he said, "It's unfortunate it's on public television—it should be on CBS. But CBS thinks even 'Life on Earth' [a British nature series] is too sexy."

Asked if he was *ashamed* during his drag scene, he said, "No, and I read a review that said the only true drag scene was played by Lesley Ann Warren."

Queried about the other gay films, Warren replied, "I was disappointed in *Making Love*. I didn't believe the relationship. It didn't reach me emotionally, though I appreciate that the film was made. . . . I liked *Personal Best* a lot—it had a reality, a simplicity, honesty." Meanwhile, Stephen Schaefer wrote in *Us*: "Warren, bursting with energy and talent to fuel three comedies, is delightful, shaking her hips and moving her lips while a drag star grabs her honey. What she would have done to (and for) *Making Love*!"

Deathtrap was the least publicized of the five, and its gay theme the least noted, due to the murder-mystery plot. It was also the only picture with gay villains, and though this drew some criticism, the

Letting go: Contractual couple Ontkean and Jackson realize they can't go on pretending.

Victor/Victoria's stars Robert Preston and Julie Andrews, producer Tony Adams, and writer-director-producer Blake Edwards.

Le jazz hot: Julie Andrews sizzles as a woman pretending to be a singing female impersonator.

homosexuality wasn't played up—the characters were neither representative gays nor Gay Villains. *Deathtrap* opened fairly strong, but business plummeted. Like Christopher Reeve's other non-*Superman* films, it failed to attract his fans. A Warners spokesman said, "Some media analysts felt the Reeve-Caine relationship hurt attendance by heterosexuals. Bull. The relationship and the kiss were a *surprise* to most. . . . The play was a great hit here and in London; it wasn't a potential hit movie. If Lumet, Caine, and Reeve hadn't fronted it, it probably wouldn't have gotten made."

Partners was an all-around discredit to Paramount. It opened big, but its lack of starpower, goodwill, and humor proved fatal. Executive producer Veber originally envisioned a box-office bonanza with Clint Eastwood and Woody Allen in the leads. R-rated for its gayness, *Partners* got much more publicity than *Deathtrap*, which was rated PG (the ratings board considered it only incidentally gay), but it boomeranged. Stephen Harvey wrote in *American Film*, "Picture this: A lot of Jews have been murdered and a gentile cop is teamed with a Jewish cop who's fixed his nose and changed his name. They go into this mysterious Jewish community and every Jew they find is pushy, foul-mouthed, vulgar, greasy, aggressive, and a gold digger." He added that no group other than gays could be so vilified or silently tolerate such vilification.

The Alliance of Gay and Lesbian Artists, founded in 1979, had sought to provide input to *Partners*, via a meeting with the filmmakers. AGLA later sent a letter to producer Aaron Russo, reprinted in several gay papers: "*Partners* is a cruel, insensitive 'fag joke.' . . . Had our ideas been given consideration, at least it would have given the project what it lacked from the beginning: integrity and honesty."

Making Love aired on CBS on January 21, 1984—partly because of Kate Jackson's popular series "Scarecrow & Mrs. King." The print ads gave the impression that she was the film's sole star. Her likeness was about ten times the size of "also" stars Ontkean and Hamlin. The film penetrated the so-called heartland and reached many more millions than in theatrical release. Interestingly, *TV Guide* offered different synopses for cable and network television. Respectively: "Story of a married doctor who becomes involved in a homosexual affair" and "*Making Love* centers on a doctor who comes to terms with his homosexuality after nine years of marriage."

The CBS ad read: "What does a woman do when the man who has loved her for eight years needs something no woman can give him?" The gayness was downplayed, and the disclaimer "due to the mature theme, parental discretion is advised" was run.

TV Guide's Judith Crist wrote that "Ontkean suddenly finds his sexual predilections changing." Despite CBS's censorship of Bart in bed with the slightly younger Tim (their bedroom conversation was *heard* in voice-over while Bart ate at a restaurant), the showing was another first. Although the close-up kiss was deleted, the two handsome, manly lovers were seen kissing in a long-shot. The next scene found them *in bed together*, the first of two such scenes. The low ratings for the film belied its impact. One female viewer wrote to the *San Mateo Times*: "I have a cousin in his early forties. . . . Like the rest of my family, I always thought he never married because he hadn't found 'the right girl.' After watching *Making Love*, I realized that he's dropped several hints that he's gay and wants to be accepted as such. But until *Making Love*, I couldn't believe in that possibility, simply because my cousin

Gay writes: *Superman* sex symbol Christopher Reeve in his role as a gay playwright in *Deathtrap*.

Reeve and Michael Caine toast their
personal and professional relationship
in *Deathtrap*.

Short-time companions: John Hurt
and Ryan O'Neal as a homosexual and
a heterosexual pretending to be mates.

happens to be a normal, good-looking masculine
man. . . ."

CBS opened 1985 with the broadcast of *Victor/
Victoria* on New Year's night. The network cut only
two scenes: one in which Norma tells Toddy that
"the right woman could reform you" and he replies
"likewise", and the other in which Toddy and
Squash (Alex Karras of "Webster") are sitting in bed
together. Retained were the words *queer, fairy, fag,
faggot, gay,* and *homosexual*, as in "a homosexual" (It
was Gore Vidal who noted that "homosexual" is not
a person or a noun, it's a type of act.)

Victoria/Victoria was the number one-rated theatrical film shown on network television during the
1984–85 season. Less successful was the *Deathtrap*
television broadcast in September 1986. Four new
"explanatory" minutes were added by Lumet, but
the kiss was removed. Instead, Caine told Reeve,
"Get into bed—and stay there." Reeve grinned: "I'll
buy that." So the gayness was retained, but not the
PG-level homosexuality.

Playtime: Mariel Hemingway and Patrice Donnelly as athletes
in love in *Personal Best*.

32

DOPPELGÄNGER:

Querelle

Brad Davis as *Querelle* (1983), the alluring but lethal sailor of Jean Genet's cult novel, *Querelle de Brest*.

Querelle. Planet/Gaumont/Triumph, 1983.
Director-writer: Rainer Werner Fassbinder; producer: Dieter Schidor.
Starring: Brad Davis, Franco Nero, Jeanne Moreau, Laurent Malet, Hanno Pöschl, Günther Kaufmann, Burkhard Driest, Dieter Schidor.

Rainer Werner Fassbinder and editor Juliane Lorenz completed *Querelle* ten days before the director's fatal drug overdose at age thirty-six. Fassbinder's last film—his wild card—was perhaps his most unusual. But had he not died before its release, it probably wouldn't have received as much attention or such wide distribution. It premiered at the 1983 Venice Film Festival and was lauded by jury president Marcel Carné, director of the classic *Les Enfants du Paradis*: "Whether one wants it or not, whether one deplores it or not, this controversial film will one day have its place in the history of the cinema." Decades earlier, Carné had sought to bring Jean Genêt's oft-banned novel *Querelle de Brest* to the screen.

Another legendary artist, Salvador Dalí, viewed *Querelle* in the privacy of his castle in Spain and pronounced it "an authentic surrealist sex farce."

Querelle (Brad Davis), a sailor, plans to smuggle a cask of opium into the port of Brest. He seeks an accomplice at the Hotel Feria, a brothel owned by Mme. Lysiane (Jeanne Moreau), who is married to Nono (Günther Kaufmann), a burly, light-skinned black. Horny sailors at the Feria shake Nono's

dice—if they win, they get to have sex with Lysiane, mid-fiftyish and the only woman in town. If they lose, they get screwed by Nono. Querelle deliberately loses.

Aboard the *Vengeur*, Lieutenant Seblon (Franco Nero) tells his tape recorder about his passion for Querelle. On shore, he scrawls obscenities on bathroom walls.

Querelle finds a smuggling accomplice named Vic (Dieter Schidor), who has the hots for him. After the deal is consummated, Vic strips for Querelle, who slits his throat.

Back at the Feria, Lysiane's current lover is Robert (Hanno Pöschl), Querelle's supposedly "look-alike" (but they don't) brother. When Robert learns from Nono that Querelle allowed himself to be screwed, he fights his brother. Furious at his brother's reaction, Querelle replaces him in Lysiane's bed. She has no idea about Nono's bisexuality, but when Robert and then Querelle use her bed to masturbate in—each fantasizing about the other brother—Lysiane realizes that she's being used. So she goes down to the bar, leans against a post, and croons Oscar Wilde's line, "Each man kills the thing he loves."

Other characters include Mario (Burkhard Driest), the town cop. By day he wears leather and shades; by night he haunts the Feria bar in leather and chains. Mario, too, has a thing for Querelle. Gil, a sailor (also played by Hanno Pöschl), sidles up to handsome young Roger (Laurent Malet), who pimps for his own sister, and rasps, "If only you were a girl," before kissing Roger on the lips.

Querelle and Gil fall in lust. The former notices that Gil looks exactly like Robert, except for the latter's mustache—Querelle thoughtfully supplies a duplicate. At their secret trysting place, the men exchange philosophy and not one but three sizzling kisses. Querelle wants to screw Gil but only does so symbolically: He helps Gil, wanted for a recent murder, plan his escape and then betrays him to the police.

Angry with himself, Querelle returns to the Feria and informs Lysiane that he's a "fairy." Mario notes that the madam "despises gays," so Querelle adds that her husband's one, too. After some cathartic yelling, Lysiane returns to the allegedly straight Robert, who seems none too thrilled.

Out on the streets of Brest, Querelle is rescued from a savage fight by his lovelorn lieutenant. He now knows that his fate is to be loved by Lieutenant Seblon, and the pair glides off into the orange-blue night.

Brad Davis came close to stardom in *Midnight Express* (1978). Then, as he told *Us* magazine, he took two years off and wallowed in liquor and drugs. "I understand the energy of self-destruction," he admitted, "no matter how it's disguised. Querelle's instinct is for death rather than life." Davis, whose sailor costumes were so tight-fitting that they reveal what religion he isn't, at first shunned the explicit role. "Then I realized that if I let the fear of being persecuted by the industry stop me from doing something I felt was right, my whole life was a lie." However, after the film's completion, Davis—who in 1981 starred Off-Broadway in *Entertaining Mr. Sloane*—told the press that *Querelle* was *not* about homosexuality or crime. (The movie didn't hurt Davis's career; in 1984 he played the title role in the miniseries *Robert Kennedy and His Times*.) His death from AIDS in 1991 stunned Hollywood, which he called, in a posthumously published article, "hypocritical" in its attitude toward the disease.

Jeanne Moreau made a courageous choice in playing Lysiane. No stranger to gay lifestyles, Moreau lived for years with an allegedly homosexual fashion designer in Paris, before marrying and divorcing director William Friedkin. (In 1984 she played the lesbian Ines in a BBC production of Sartre's *Huis clos*, [*No Exit*]. Many reviewers commented on Moreau's fall from glamour. Lysiane often resembles Glenda Jackson as the aged *Elizabeth R*. In a scene with Pöschl, the center of attention is a large wrinkle on Lysiane's bare back, caused by the actor's ascending thumb. Another scene finds Lysiane bluntly comparing Querelle's and Robert's organs.

Best known for *Camelot* and his romance with Vanessa Redgrave, Franco Nero accepted Seblon but not his nature. *Querelle*'s press kit quoted him: "I cannot say anything about the homosexual aspect of Seblon. I don't see this as a film about homosexuality but, rather, about universal feelings, passions, and relationships." The more up-front Herr Pöschl declared, "Homosexuality is not a disease. Besides, this is a film about love, emotion, freedom, and death."

Some gays were fascinated by *Querelle*'s sailor beefcake and the abundant phallic imagery etched on glass, embroidered on lacy curtains, and painted on the seawalls. Other gay viewers decried the movie's seaminess. The same film's characters who demand "What's *normal?*" and "Why not, if it feels good?" recoil when suspected of bi- or homosexuality. Initially Querelle growls, "I'm no fairy!" By film's end he accepts his true nature and screams, "I'm a *fairy!*" His truer nature is psycopathic and sadomasochistic.

Querelle did poor business in America. The *Advocate* called it "a pretentious bore" and noted that it "opened and closed quicker than a gay bar in Jerry Falwell's neighborhood." On the positive side, *Querelle*'s gays are extremely masculine—some are downright frightening. But they're also corrupt and incapable of love or loyalty.

By most accounts, Fassbinder's low self-esteem was the cause of both his professional rise and his personal decline. Dieter Schidor, producer and costar of *Querelle*, made a documentary about his friend titled *The Wizard of Babylon*. In it he recounted: "His father was a doctor and very wealthy. He owned many apartment houses, in Cologne, for Turkish guestworkers, exploiting them, charging high rents. The boy, when he was twelve or thirteen, had to go and collect the money from these people."

Fassbinder's mother, Liselotte Eder, is the official German translator of Tennessee Williams and Truman Capote. Mother and son weren't close until his adult years, when she often appeared in his films using the name Lilo Pempeit. His parents divorced

Producer/costar Dieter Schidor as Querelle's accomplice and eventual victim, Vic.

before Rainer was a teen, and eventually he chose to live with his father. The shy youth's lonely hours were filled by movies, but, when he applied to Berlin's prestigious Film Institute, he was rejected. Insiders say he always regretted his lack of a higher education.

Fassbinder made his first feature-length movie in 1969. His first projects ranged in cost from twenty-five to forty thousand dollars, but in later years his name alone guaranteed major financing. *Lola*, his remake of *The Blue Angel*, cost $10 million, Germany's most expensive film until that time. And despite *Querelle*'s controversial subject matter, the project was cofinanced by the Berlin Senate, after Fassbinder signed to direct.

One of Fassbinder's first lovers, Swiss director Daniel Schmid, told *GQ*, "He was an unhappy man who hurled himself into his work but had a low personal opinion of himself." The workaholic almost single-handedly revitalized German cinema with the forty-three films he made between 1969 and 1982. Schmid accompanied Fassbinder on his honeymoon with the actress Ingrid Caven. The union was brief; Fassbinder didn't want a working wife and was especially jealous and possessive. When Schmid hired Caven for a film, Fassbinder felt betrayed and severed the friendship temporarily and the marriage permanently. He and Caven later made amends, and they costarred in

Shadow of Angels, written by Fassbinder and directed by Schmid.

"He could not believe people could love him," Schmid explained. "All his life Rainer thought he was ugly. . . . The basis for his new friendships was always the same: You are a pig and I am a pig; let's start our relationship there." Over time Fassbinder became more personally demanding. To many, he was sweet and considerate, but he could also be cruel and neglectful. His last two lovers ended their own lives by hanging themselves. One of them was Hedi ben Salim, to whom Fassbinder dedicated *Querelle*.

Schmid: "I ask myself, when did the turning point come? He was drinking all the time since the 1960s . . . and uppers, downers, LSD, cocaine. But he was a gambler, not a suicide. Even in his last year he didn't want to die. He wanted to see how far he could go."

Others felt that the slide accelerated after the

Querelle: A loner with an insatiable appetite for sex and violence.

City of brotherly love: Robert and Querelle embrace.

More than brotherly love: Robert and Querelle.

Jeanne Moreau as the Feria's madam, Lysiane, and Hanno Poeschl as Robert, Querelle's brother.

suicide of Fassbinder's lifemate, Armin Meier, an "ideal Aryan" born in a Nazi *Lebensborn* eugenics farm. The overly dependent Meier felt abandoned when Rainer journeyed to Paris without him, and he hanged himself in their Munich home. Fassbinder died four years to the day after Meier.

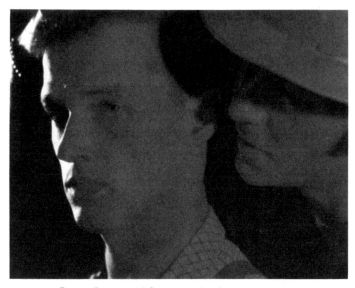

Roger (Laurent Malet), a youth of Brest, is coveted by much of its male population.

The seaport of Brest is base to an army of lusty sailors and midnight cowboys.

death, Brad Davis cried for two weeks, and Jeanne Moreau recalled, "He was devoted to those he knew genuinely liked him. But he couldn't verbalize it." At *Querelle*'s completion, "Everyone was so excited—and tired. Rainer sent me a box of white roses, and with them a lovely note that said simply, 'Until the next time.'"

Eight hours before his death on June 10, 1982, Fassbinder was interviewed by Schidor. He had several projects on the drawing board and had told friends that he wanted to become super-rich "like Steven Spielberg." The final night, Fassbinder called Daniel Schmid in Paris and informed him he'd flushed all his drugs down the toilet—except for one line of cocaine. Schmid remembered, "During those last telephone calls at three in the morning he would shout at me as if I had some secret of happiness, as if I were the lucky one and he was

Following Meier's death, Fassbinder immersed himself in film after film and in major television projects, including a fifteen-hour miniseries. In the last six months of his life he starred in Wolf Gremm's *Kamikaze '89* and made *Querelle*; the relative slowdown was due to escalating drug side effects.

During the making of *Querelle*, Fassbinder often arrived on the set at two in the afternoon, working his cast and crew for fourteen hours or more. Still, he retained his associates' support and affection. The cold, paranoid side he showed to his lovers was rarely exhibited to coworkers. After Fassbinder's

204

cursed by fate. He would shout: 'Why is it so simple for you to live? How can everybody else be so lucky?'

"Those who loved Rainer knew the good side. But within himself, the self-contempt, the low self-esteem, began to win."

His body was found with a cold cigarette between his fingers and notes on his next film under his head. His video machine was running *20,000 Years in Sing Sing*.

ABOUT *QUERELLE*

David Denby, *New York*: *Querelle* is a horrifying ending to Fassbinder's tumultuous, fascinating career. . . . Querelle is played by Brad Davis, whose short, muscular body and sweet, empty, all-American face bring the high-flying fantasies down with a thud. Davis reminds me of a Midwestern college wrestler; he's just bland. . . . As always in Fassbinder, characters stand stock-still and recite their lines as if drugged. . . . The material is overexplicit yet remote, florid yet unemotional, and we can't tell why the characters act the way they do.

Marianne Gray, *Photoplay* (U.K.): An extraordinary film for the select few—Fassbinder fans, gays heavily into cruising sailors, stylists in extremis, possibly Jeanne Moreau/Jean Genêt followers (although that's debatable). . . . We have sex, violence, guilt (loads of it), nihilism, brutality, weakness, murder, betrayal, and pain. At times it seems irrelevant which emotion it is; the film is such an intensely erotic and wonderfully overripe fruit that even when the watching begins to pall, it's almost impossible to drag one's eyes away. . . . I loved it, though millions won't!

Querelle's fantastic phallic sets captured the surreal homoeroticism of Genet's novel.

Wunderkind director Rainer Werner Fassbinder died from drugs in 1982, soon after completing *Querelle*.

Harold Fairbanks, *Stallion*: Behind the literary credentials of Genêt's 1947 novel and Fassbinder's reputation as a brilliant artist, *Querelle* is nothing more than a gay soap opera. There's definitely a cable television series in it, if anyone dares try . . . . What is the movie about? Physical beauty. Grand passion. A self-absorbed loner who won't admit to himself that he's homosexual. And heat.

Quentin Crisp *Christopher Street*: Presumably, M. Genêt endured a Catholic childhood. From this he seems never to have recovered. . . . M. Genêt keeps attempting to fling away his immortal soul, but in spite of all his farfetched efforts, it clings to his fingers like a toffee wrapper. M. Genêt's perpetual quest is for defilement, preferably at the hands of total masculinity— symbolized by vast sexual organs. He seems never to have known anyone of normal proportions.

Apart from spurious philosophizing and the operatic plot, *Querelle* has very considerable virtues. It is photographed through a gauzy twilight chiefly in shades of mauve and yellowish brown and is beautiful to watch. . . . But the ultimate message of this film is depressing. If you long for assurance that somebody really cares about you, being buggered can never be a patch on being stabbed.

By fadeout, Querelle (Brad Davis) belongs to his longtime admirer, Lieutenant Seblon (Franco Nero).

33

VAMPS:

The Hunger

David Bowie "came out" of the closet as a bisexual singer in the early 1970s.

The Hunger. MGM/UA, 1983. Director: Tony Scott; writers: Ivan Davis and Michael Thomas; producer: Richard A. Shepherd.
Starring: Catherine Deneuve, David Bowie, Susan Sarandon, Cliff De Young, Beth Ehlers, Dan Hedaya.

"I myself belong to Vampires Anonymous, and I can assure you that a vampire's life is not easy," joked gay reviewer Quentin Crisp. *The Hunger* was the first explicitly gay vampire film, boasting David Bowie as leading man to Catherine Deneuve and Susan Sarandon. To date, there has been no erotic gay male vampire movie—except *Gayracula*, a porno flick advertised with the line "He does *more* than suck *blood*!" But, as Crisp suggests, there is a long-standing parallel between vampires and movie homosexuality.

Since 1931's *Dracula*, the vampire has been a figure of loathsome fascination: sensual, immoral, well-mannered, but deadly. Eventually, vampires always die, gruesomely. But not before irresistibly drawing some weak souls under their evil spell, breakable *only* by a crucifix, wholesome sunlight, or a wooden stake. Bloodsucking—from either gender—is symbolic of oral sex, and blood bonds the transient predator and his or her victim. In the 1931 film, Bela Lugosi is mesmerized by Renfield's (Dwight Frye) pricked finger. The count approaches to suck the blood, but Renfield fends him off and sucks it himself. But soon, Renfield is the one mesmerized, by the suave Dracula, who eventu-

ally maddens him. The relationship is classic sado-masochism.

The gay overtones are stronger in *Dracula's Daughter* (1936). Eerie Gloria Holden's manservant stalks London's Chelsea to bring his mistress a virginal "model." Primarily lesbian, Countess Zaleska's private life is utterly private, and in public she must disguise her true nature. Her alienation from "decent" society causes her to prey upon it. She is a virtual parasite, who cannot breed, but adds to her ranks by seductive conscription. Her unions are "unholy"; she hates her life and would gladly trade it for a commonplace existence.

Since men write most novels and make most movies, the male vampire is still the norm, though less now than in the past. Lugosi remains the quintessential vampire; his insinuating charm toward women and men alike provides a bisexual subtext to his Dracula pictures. In the fifties and sixties feline Christopher Lee—slick yet commanding—reshaped the vampire-lover image. *Blood and Roses* (*Et Mourir de Plaisir*) (1961) reveals a chicly amorous relationship between Annette Vadim and Elsa Martinelli, courtesy of director Roger Vadim. Seventies variations included *Blacula* (1972), with a weak white faggot-victim. David Niven played *Old Dracula* (aka *Vampira*) in 1975, and in 1974, *Andy Warhol's Dracula* starred elfin Udo Kier. The 1979 *Dracula* remake starred Frank Langella (*Diary of a Mad Housewife*) as an exclusively straight vampire. His aggressive sex play shattered the mystery of earlier films, which merely hinted at or soft-pedaled the vampire's libido. (One assumes that the undead are functionally asexual, hence the surrogate bloodsucking.)

The first movie to include a gay male vampire was Roman Polanski's British film, *Dance of the Vampires*, better known by its American title, *The Fearless Vampire Killers* (1967). Polanski's friend Iain Quarrier played the vampire count's blond son, Herbert, who sports ruffled shirts and frilly behavior. MGM executives were taken aback at the notion of a gay vampire but acquiesced, since Herbert is a secondary, ludicrous, and doomed character (although vampirism in this film isn't destroyed). British censors noted in a production memo, "We ask that you avoid any physical advances on [Herbert's] part toward Alfred. This would refer to any embracing or fondling; his attack as a vampire would *not* prove objectionable."

By contrast, *The Hunger* treats its protagonists more casually. That Miriam (Deneuve), an ancient Egyptian vampire, alternates male and female lovers over the centuries seems only natural. (As Woody Allen once quipped, being bisexual automatically doubles one's choice of dates.) The movie initially plays on Miriam's relationship with John (Bowie), age about 200. The Blaylocks are fang-less vampires who slice their victims with razors concealed in the ankhs they wear around their necks; bats, stakes, and crucifixes are passé or politically incorrect. The pair are also classical-music lovers who give lessons to a fourteen-year-old named Alice (Beth Ehlers), whose manner calls to mind Bjorn Andresen's Tadzio.

John suddenly begins aging rapidly. Desperate for blood, he attacks Alice, then tosses her remains into an incinerator. Miriam is only moderately alarmed; Deneuve's frozen sparkle compares with ghoulish Gloria Holden's from 1936. John visits a top gerontological researcher, Dr. Sarah Roberts (Sarandon), who is fascinated, first by his condition, then by his wife. But, within hours, John is a mere wisp of a vampire, whom the quietly grieving Miriam stores in the attic next to her barely breathing ex-loves.

Whitley Strieber's novel, from which the film was made, has four main characters, including Tom, who functions as Sarah's lover and heterosexual conscience. In the film Tom (Cliff De Young) is a more casual boyfriend whose macho jealousy makes Miriam seem even more attractive. Although the film is more affirming of gayness than the book, Miriam is strictly straight in her husband's presence, and Sarah has a "man's" occupation but is employed chiefly for her physical qualities. (Charlotte Rampling, once described as "a necrophiliac's love goddess," was considered for the role.) As with *Personal Best*, many male critics fixated on the hungry love scenes, which *People* magazine deemed "visually dazzling and sensationally silly."

The expertly photographed scene of the two blond stars (Deneuve and Sarandon) using lips and tongues on each other's breasts and torsos was courageous. It's unlikely that a superstar American actress would have done such a frank scene, which also appealed to much of the female audience. A 1984 *Cosmopolitan* magazine article asked female readers, "What do women find erotic?" A college-age respondent said, "There's one scene in the vampire film *The Hunger* where Catherine Deneuve and Susan Sarandon are making love. Their necks are cricked in a strange way. It isn't until you look closely that you realize they're sucking each other's blood. It's arousing, though there's too much cutting away to curtains blowing in the wind. It's a very romantic film."

Most men, also, called it "decadent," "erotic," or "sexy," and the press kit noted, "Miriam's need to feed *The Hunger* draws both man and woman into her web and descent to a nightmare of erotic decadence and corruption." It described the doctor's lesbian affair (no doubt her first) thus: "Sarah, dazzled by Miriam's beauty, finds herself drawn into a saga of baroque horror, as she discovers that Miriam's perfection is an illusion barely concealing a corrupt and erotic decadence where death is the way to a sort of life."

The film is preeminently visual, thanks to award-winning-commercials-maker-turned-director Tony Scott, brother of Ridley (*Alien*, *Blade Runner*). The kit allowed that "*The Hunger* is a mood, a look, an ambience." It reeks with style: Deneuve in harlequin sunglasses, an attic filled with off-gray mummies and powder-blue pigeons, costumes by Milena Canonero, editing by MTV. It borrows from several predecessors. One reviewer compared it with *Cat People*. Another said it was an amalgam of *Making Love*, *The Birds*, and *Night of the Living Dead*. As in *Making Love*, the prelude to the big seduction is an awkward but riveting scene in which the women test each other and flirt. Miriam plays Delibes's *Lakmé*, explaining that it's the story of an Indian princess who falls in love with another girl.

Deneuve, apotheosized by publicists as "the depository of others' dreams," essentially played herself. Her elegant foreignness suits the exotic-emigré tradition of vampire movies. She observed, "I am not an obvious sex symbol. I create a certain reserve which is more attractive." The gutsy Sarandon told *Cosmopolitan*, "Why apologize? If you're going to go to bed with a woman, Catherine Deneuve is hardly difficult to take! I was supposed to be very drunk and under her spell; I kept wondering, Why are they giving me all these excuses and rationalizations? I mean, who wouldn't want to go to bed with Catherine Deneuve? She's incredible!"

It was Sarandon's first gay love scene. She said, "Luckily, I absolutely adored Catherine. . . . By the time we shot *the* scene, I sort of knew her. Still, it was pretty, well, *different*. . . . Naturally, it was all choreographed, so I can't say I actually lost my head." She told the less liberal *American Film* that it was "a relationship movie."

Director Scott rejected the lesbian aspect, telling one questioner, "It's *not* a love scene. It's a metamorphosis, an initiation into a new state of being. It's not real lesbianism; it's more of a school-girl crush." Inevitably, Sarandon was queried about her real-life love life. "I've never been to bed with a woman. I'm afraid another female would understand me too completely. . . . There's a certain amount of mystery that exists *between* the sexes. If you're with somebody of the same sex and they're onto all the tricks, that's *frightening*."

After Sarah becomes Miriam's lover-victim, she has second thoughts and stabs herself with the ankh. But *Sarah*, not Miriam, survives. By fade-out, Sarah is standing on a balcony wearing Miriam's clothes, makeup, and ankh; a male and a female lover are waiting inside. How did this come about? *The Hunger*'s illogical ending is its fatal flaw, lending credence to the accusation that the film is basically an extended stellar video. The ending is a major letdown that defies logic *and* all the rules of vampire movies. But then, the director contradicted himself more than once in "explaining" the film:

"It's not the traditional vampire genre movie. You really feel sorry for these people. They can't help being the creatures they are. They get sick and need extra vitamins and some juice; that's what justifies their eating human flesh. . . . The book was more hard-core horror. I've made more of a psychological study. When Susan wakes up after her

Wanna neck?: David Bowie appraises Ann Magnuson's neck prior to satisfaction in *The Hunger* (1983).

Ancient vampire Catherine Deneuve hypnotizes, then drains the life out of John Stephen Hill in *The Hunger*.

Old age is hell: Vampire Deneuve puts her younger but suddenly aged lover (Bowie) to sleep in her Manhattan mansion.

Susan Sarandon is the mortal whom Deneuve chooses as a lover and her latest centuries-long companion.

PHOTO: LOREY SEBASTIAN

Catherine Deneuve as the ageless Miriam dreams of a new lover—this time, a female.

PHOTO: DANA GILLESPIE

Once upon a mattress: In 1990, Bowie's ex-wife alleged that she'd once found her husband in bed with Mick Jagger!

I wanna suck your hand: Bela Lugosi as *Dracula* (1930) moves in on Renfield's (Dwight Frye) bloodied finger.

dingdong with Deneuve, she's real surprised. Deneuve is like Cassavetes in *Rosemary's Baby*. You weren't sure Mia Farrow was raped by the devil, and you think Deneuve's strong, but you don't know anything for sure. . . . The characters are sympathetic. You have these psychopaths for heroes. It's difficult to keep them sympathetic, but they are."

ABOUT *THE HUNGER*

Bart Mills, *San Francisco Examiner*: The last year or so has seen incestuous leopards, a backpacking werewolf, an ape-scientist, and a disembodied hand. It was inevitable that a drama about lesbian vampires should open at a theater near you. Now that the cinematic taboo versus lesbian hurdling has been smashed, it's time for bloodthirsty love scenes, and Deneuve and Sarandon deliver.

210

Merrill Shindler, *Los Angeles* magazine: There's a love scene between Deneuve and Sarandon during which the audience is so silent you can hear a metaphor drop. It may be the most sexually explicit scene in a major motion picture since *An Officer and a Gentleman*. It may be exploitive stylistic schlock, but it sure takes your breath away.

Guy Flatley, *Cosmopolitan*: Cast as a chic, lascivious Park Avenue clotheshorse old enough to be Dracula's mother, the dazzling Deneuve prowls Manhattan's tonier New Wave discos, on the watch for horny, red-blooded bedmates of all genders. . . . Standing androgynously by is the simpering sidekick she seduced centuries ago—David Bowie. . . . The tingles of the [sexual] encounter are spicily carnal. Concocted in the kitsch-en of Tony Scott, *The Hunger* is a yummy blend of caviar and Kool-Aid, a kinky feast sure to satisfy your lust for decadent delicacies. *Bon appetit!*

Quentin Crisp: It should have been called "The Glut." It drips with blood and oozes sex. . . . Miss Deneuve lives in a townhouse big enough to justify the installation of an elevator; presumably even fifty cents put into the capable hands of Mr. E.F. Hutton in the time of the Pharaohs would yield a considerable yearly income by 1983. . . . The film's only glimpse of reality is when Mr. Bowie sits all day in the hospital waiting room growing older by the minute. No one comes to his aid. In the next sequence we are back in our fantasy world; Dr. Sarandon calls on him without mentioning money! She meets Miss Deneuve, and they become lovers. . . . One fine day there is an earthquake. The house rocks, the coffins in the attic burst open, and the living dead arise from their crumbling inertia to revenge themselves upon their hostess, who lapses into instant decay. Why? How? What does it all mean?

Sapphic vampires à la mode: Elsa Martinelli (left) and Annette Vadim in Roger Vadim's *Blood and Roses* (1960).

Lesbian of the night: Gloria Holden as *Dracula's Daughter* (1936) with a new conquest (Nan Grey).

34

ONE IN EVERY CROWD

This chapter features secondary gay male characters; characters who likely would have been gay but for the quarter-century ban on gay and lesbian depictions; actors identified with gay roles; and certain gay films. . . .

• Missing Gays. A favorite movie-buff game is Guess Who's Really Gay in the old movies. The guessing can go on and on, because one can *read* any number of clues, some more substantial than others. For instance, 1933's *The Kennel Murder Case*, a Philo Vance mystery, has William Powell trying to solve "the murders of two *dog-fancier* brothers" (italics added to the *TV Guide* description). Mary Astor costarred, as in John Huston's 1941 *The Maltese Falcon*, with Peter Lorre as Joel Cairo. Cairo may be Sydney Greenstreet's lover; Hammett's novel pegged Cairo as "queer." Movie sensibilities being ten to twenty years behind those of books, the film's biggest clue is Spade's reaction to Cairo's scented hankie.

Sometimes the clue is role-reversal, as in *Lysistrata*—Ernest Truex as the househusband in *The Warrior's Wife* (1933). It was remade in 1955 as *The Second Greatest Sex*, starring George Nader. In the eighties Nader wrote one of the first gay sci-fi novels, *Chrome*. He was the major beneficiary of Rock Hudson's will, which some consider Hudson's recompense. According to *People* magazine, in the fifties Nader's career was cut short by homophobic publicity originally intended for bigger star Hudson.

Of course, resexualizing was the old Hollywood's simplest solution, and it survives. The gay alcoholic

The face that launched a thousand quips: Franklin Pangborn, gay comic actor supreme of the thirties and forties.

writer in *The Lost Weekend* (1945) became a straight with writer's block in the movie. Likewise, homophobia was "whitewashed," as it were, in *Crossfire* (1947). The movie's discrimination victim is black/straight rather than gay/white. (The source novel was written by Richard Brooks, who directed *Cat on a Hot Tin Roof*.) In 1972 gay love was turned to "straight like" in *The Mechanic*, with Charles Bronson and Jan-Michael Vincent as his "apprentice." The same was true for Roy Scheider and William Devane in John Schlesinger's *Marathon Man* (1976).

To many filmmakers, real people are as vulnerable to sexual reassignment as fictional characters. Thus Turkish-held prisoner Billy Hayes (Brad Davis) is heterosexual in 1978's *Midnight Express*. Director Alan Parker declared, "I couldn't afford to have my audience think my hero was a homosexual." Hayes, who revealed his gay experiences in a nonfiction book, told this author, "I had no control [over the movie portrayal]. But I don't know how anybody could measure how many viewers you might lose over that [gay] theme." Yet Parker's film includes masturbation, female exploitation, sadism, and racism. The film was a hit.

Another "missing" gay is the immortal Addison

Gay actor in *The Gay Divorcée* (1934, with Betty Grable): Veteran comic star Edward Everett Horton.

Front runner: Paul Newman played a crypto-gay Billy the Kid in Gore Vidal's *The Left-Handed Gun* (1958).

DeWitt (George Sanders) in *All About Eve*. Sanders won a Best Supporting Actor Oscar as the viper who uses and supposedly desires Eve Harrington (Anne Baxter). DeWitt is a worthy, more wicked successor to (gay) stooges like Franklin Pangborn, Eric Blore, Edward Everett Horton, and Monty Woolley. Rex Reed called Sanders (who married two Gabors) "the closest thing we have left to the bitchy memory of Clifton Webb and Monty Woolley." Sanders, whose autobiography was titled *Memoirs of a Professional Cad*, was to have starred in a Broadway musical based on *The Man Who Came to Dinner*, which had starred gay actor Woolley.

Trapeze (1956) is another expert-and-apprentice love story turned asexual—until Gina Lollobrigida comes along and causes friction between Burt Lancaster and Tony Curtis. Women were often the scapegoats in closeted plots, as with Truman Capote's *Breakfast at Tiffany's* (1961). Audrey Hepburn is Holly, a semi-hooker, and George Peppard is a gigolo to nasty Patricia Neal. When Peppard leaves her, he turns to Hepburn and conventional heterosexual manhood.

Like gigolos and "hustlers"—the Hollywood term for male hookers—any man in drag, however

briefly, was often suspect. For example, gay actor Paul Lynde's performance in *The Glass Bottom Boat* (1966). In an interview for *Talk* magazine, Lynde told this author, "My drag scene was a film highlight. But until it was decided I'd *dress up*, I had a bigger part. After I was in a dress, wig, and makeup, they wanted to shove my character under the stairs."

• Films that should have been gay include one based on the homoerotic fantasy-figure created by a gay man, the late Robert Ervin Howard. Instead, his *Conan the Barbarian* (1982) is a straight user. He befriends a gay Hyperborean priest then knocks him out to use his robes as a disguise. Conan's (Arnold Schwarzenegger) buddy, Subotai the Mongol (Gerry Lopez), is abandoned once Valeria (Sandahl Bergman) enters the picture. Asked by the *Advocate* about playing a gay man's creation, Schwarzenegger replied that he doesn't consider an author's sexual "preference" when accepting a role. Then he admitted that he hadn't known Conan's "father" was gay. The 1984 sequel, *Conan the Destroyer*, is nonhomophobic and features male bonding and a feminist Grace Jones.

Shampoo (1975) showcased Warren Beatty as a straight hairdresser. Even the beauty shop's proprietor, Norman (Jay Robinson), is straight, appearances to the contrary. Critic Wyatt Cooper wrote that the audience is relieved when Norman announces that he's lost his teenage son in a car accident. "The movie tells us, Don't jump to conclusions about homosexuals; some of them may be heterosexual." Like many of the general audience, Jack Warden mistakes everyone in the hair game for gay and is unaware that George (Beatty) has bedded his wife, girlfriend, and daughter. The script abounds with lines like "That boy couldn't get arrested as a boy" and "He's a fairy" (accompanied by a limp-wrist gesture).

Warden's daughter Carrie Fisher asks if George is a "fag" and questions his *thing* for older women: "That's sort of faggy, isn't it?" George replies that if a man's a Beverly Hills hairdresser, "You might as well be a faggot."

• Not-really-gays are sometimes read as gays by viewers and by other characters. Even today, most plays or films by gay authors are inspected for hidden messages and regendered characters, etc. A *New York Times* essay once "alleged" that three top unnamed American playwrights (reportedly Williams, Albee, and Inge) "hid" behind their female characters. Stanley Kauffmann felt that these gay writers created psychologically distorted portraits of women and marriage. He failed to point out how heterosexual male writers have traditionally been guilty of the same distortion. As writer Carlos Clarens said, "George Cukor never believed in victimizing women like, say, Hitchcock did, with women as prey. Cukor thought women were already victimized enough without making movies that brutalized them further." Actress Genevieve Page once noted that Ingmar Bergman—who told the press in 1984 that "women's lib has failed"—"is a heterosexual who hates women, and George Cukor is a homosexual who adores women."

In *Tea and Sympathy* (1956), John Kerr is a youth everyone assumes is homosexual. But he isn't, as his affair with Deborah Kerr shows. Sympathy is elicited precisely because the tormented Tom Lee *isn't* gay. There's little to indicate that Tom is gay, except for more aggressive males saying so. However, the *Advocate*'s Doug Edwards recalled, "It was thrilling just to see a character who was being accused of homosexuality despite the ending."

There's always the temptation to ascribe one's own sexuality to those one fancies or admires. Many gay men believed Pygar (John Phillip Law), the blind blond angel in *Barbarella*, to be gay. But until Jane Fonda lands in his nest, he gives no sign of being anything but asexual. On the other hand, the sadistic husband in *American Gigolo* (1980) was called bisexual by some gay and straight critics, on no more evidence than a scene implying anal sex with his wife. Likewise, the villain obsessed with Lauren Bacall in *The Fan* (1981) isn't gay. Michael Biehn goes to a gay bar, lures a man away, and murders him so that he can use the corpse to fake his own suicide. Only some very misguided critics called *that* character bisexual or gay.

Because 1978's *Moment by Moment* starred Lily Tomlin, was directed by her partner Jane Wagner, and featured a nonaggressive John Travolta, critics scanned the movie for gay intent. When it failed to attract audiences, the press trashed it and its stars. The film's financial failure discouraged any future older woman/younger man projects.

The 1984 hit *Footloose* was directed by Herbert Ross (*Funny Lady*, *The Last of Sheila*, and Goldie Hawn's nongay but pro-gay *Protocol*). In it Kevin Bacon teaches a male friend to dance and is told, "I thought only pansies wore ties," to which he responds, "I thought only assholes used words like *pansy*."

• *Gay deceivers* is the name sometimes given to straight, bisexual, or gay actors whose careers include several "gay" projects. (*The Gay Deceivers* also is the title of a 1969 film about young men pretending to be gay to avoid military service.) Among these is Roddy McDowall, who often costarred with friend Elizabeth Taylor—e.g., as an epicene Augustus Caesar in *Cleopatra*. McDowall played a female (a gypsy grandmother) in Joan Rivers's 1978 *Rabbit Test* and a gay female impersonator who teaches Mae West how to camp in the West television-movie biography with Ann Jillian. But his most flagrantly "gay" characterization (admittedly modeled on Tallulah Bankhead) was gossip columnist Rex Brewster in the 1982 Agatha Christie *Evil Under the Sun*. Brewster is another fag for audiences to laugh at. Referring to the possible murderer, Maggie Smith tells Poirot (Peter Ustinov), "*Cherchez le* fruit." A little girl tells the inquisitive Rex that her father told her "not to talk to *strange* men. . . ."

The most famous Christie-based film, *Murder on the Orient Express* (1974), costarred another actor in the gay-deceiver category, Anthony Perkins. He played Hector McQueen, who blurts to Poirot (Albert Finney), "Tell me I'm emotionally retarded—

214

that that's why I never married!" Of course, Perkins's most famous neurotic is mother-fixated Norman Bates in Hitchcock's *Psycho* (1960). In 1972's *Play It as It Lays* he's B. Z., " a suffering, self-destructive married homosexual" and Tuesday Weld's best friend. B. Z. takes an overdose of pills. . . . In 1975's *Mahogany* he's a fashion photographer who tries but fails to have sex with Diana Ross; then he wrestles Billy Dee Williams, who sticks a gun in Perkins's mouth but pulls out just in time.

Perkins, who took over the lead in *Tea and Sympathy* when John Kerr left the play to do the film, did not marry until 1973 (he wed Marisa Berenson's sister Berry). In a 1983 cover story he told *People* magazine that he'd had homosexual "encounters, but that kind of sex always felt unreal and unsatisfying." He was driven to visit a shrink four times weekly for nine years, until he wanted to try marriage. An early sixties *Photoplay* article, written with Perkins's cooperation, was titled "Wanted: A Wife. Apply: Desperate Tony Perkins." In 1984 the actor was arrested for drug possession in England, where he was undertaking the role of yet another ambiguous psycho. (Perkins died of AIDS in September of 1992.)

Clifton Webb was a more sophisticated version of Franklin Pangborn. Both actors were gay, though their publicity had it otherwise. Webb's most famous screen role is the possessive murderer in *Laura* (1944). Otto Preminger recalled that when he suggested Webb for Waldo Lydecker, Darryl Zanuck's casting assistant said, "He doesn't walk, he flies." Zanuck caught Webb onstage in Noël Coward's *Blithe Spirit* (the Rex Harrison role) and found him earthbound enough for the part. Two years later, Webb costarred in *The Razor's Edge*, directed by the gay Edmund Goulding, whose home was rumored to be a trysting ground for Tyrone Power and Errol Flynn. George Cukor had wanted to direct the story by Somerset Maugham, who worked on the screenplay in Cukor's home.

Paul Newman, a longtime gay-rights supporter, starred as a rather fey Billy the Kid in *The Left-Handed Gun* (1958), rewritten from a teleplay by Gore Vidal (godfather to one of Newman's daughters). The same year he also played the neutered Brick in *Cat on a Hot Tin Roof*. George Cukor was asked to direct *Cat on a Hot Tin Roof*, but he demurred: "The screenplay wouldn't hold up without that component of the plot." In 1962 Newman played a gigolo kept by Geraldine Page in Tennessee Williams's *Sweet Bird of Youth*. He went on to more commercial projects like *Harper* (1966), whose

Nuts: Anthony Perkins spent much of his post-*Psycho* (1960) career enacting gay stereotypes and/or murderers.

Warren Beatty as a secretly gay hooker argues with madam Lotte Lenya in Tennessee Williams's *The Roman Spring of Mrs. Stone* (1961).

215

ad read "This is a gun. It shoots straight. See Harper shoot straight. This is a fight. Harper has many fights. See the fights." Harper calls another character "you fish-eyed faggot." *Christopher Street's* Boyd McDonald wrote in 1984, "In light of Newman's offscreen life, it was an inappropriate word for him to use." *Harper* costarred Newman's friend Robert Wagner (who played a gay Brick in the 1976 British television production of *Cat*).

In *Slap Shot* (1977) Newman played an aging hockey player who at one point is called a "cocksucker." His response: "All I can get." The script was by Nancy Dowd, yet it includes a sexist sequence in which Newman confronts the female team owner. He advises her to get herself a man and lose her businesslike demeanor, or else her son will grow up to be a "faggot." As Pauline Kael noted (of the sexism, not the homophobia), "If Newman had refused to play the scene this way, what could the moviemakers have done? You can't blackball Paul Newman." The arch-macho movie also contains a partial strip in which Michael Ontkean ends up in his jockstrap. *Slap Shot* was Newman's first hit since *The Sting*.

In her long movie career Elizabeth Taylor worked with more bisexual or gay actors, writers, and directors than perhaps any other actress. Taylor, whom Norman Mailer accused (in *Marilyn*) of calling Marilyn Monroe a "dyke," has had several lengthy friendships with gay men. Her own favorites of her films are the ones with and by Montgomery Clift and Tennessee Williams, and Albee's *Who's Afraid of Virginia Woolf?* Favorite directors include George Cukor and Franco Zeffirelli. And she was friends with gay costars James Dean, Noël Coward, Rock Hudson, Van Johnson, Robert Taylor, and Laurence Harvey, her leading man in *Butterfield 8* (1960) and *Night Watch* (1973). Harvey never had a gay role, although he played a camp, stripping Hamlet in *The Magic Christian* (1969).

• True Brits. Daniel Day-Lewis costarred in two British films that were among the most popular foreign pictures to show on American screens in 1986. In Merchant-Ivory's *A Room With a View*, based on E. M. Forster's novel, he played a prissy heterosexual. In *My Beautiful Laundrette* he was a macho homosexual with a Pakistani lover played by Gordon Warnecke. *Laundrette* was originally made for British television but did so well at the Edinburgh Film Festival that it was rerouted from television into movie theaters.

The picture, which focused on the British Pakistani community, was called "a gay *West Side Story*

with a happy ending." When director Stephen Frears was asked why he didn't make *My Beautiful Laundrette* as a feature, he replied, "You couldn't seriously have gone out and said to a financier, 'I'm going to make a film about a gay Pakistani laundrette owner,' and confidently expect that there'd be an audience." That film, more than *A Room With a View*, helped make a star of the versatile and charismatic Day-Lewis, who'd also appeared in the play *Another Country*.

• Aliens. The only foreign gay film to really break through in America was the farcical *La Cage aux Folles*. More realistic films from other countries rarely reach even small gay audiences in the U.S. Their impact is greater in their home countries, where in some cases gay-themed films are a new phenomenon, due to past political oppression (Spain) or religious opposition (Israel, Italy). It's unlikely that any of these three nations would have produced 1981's sexually freewheeling German film, *Taxi zum Klo* (*Taxi to the John*), a minor hit which received surprisingly wide and favorable coverage by the media.

The *New York Post's* Archer Winsten declared, "Seeing it a second time, I was surprised by my own reaction. It seemed less shocking—its humanity and humor became more engaging." A virtual one-man show by actor-filmmaker Frank Ripploh, it cost fifty thousand dollars and received the 1981 Max Ophüls prize ("to the best film by a German director of the rising generation, in the tradition of Ophüls's erotic comedies"). The Catholic Film Commission condemned it, but word-of-mouth about its sexplicitness made it extremely profitable, inspiring several imitations.

Ripploh was a schoolteacher whose coming out in the weekly magazine *Stern* cost him his job. *Taxi* is largely autobiographical, with Ripploh as a teacher and his ex-lover Bernd Broaderup playing Bernd. The film depicts Ripploh shuttling between his workaday world and an obsessively sexual world. Sometimes the two merge, as when Ripploh corrects his students' school papers in unlikely cruising spots. With the theme of monogamy versus promiscuity, the latter wins hands down. The unapologetic movie crossed over to win sizeable straight audiences in Germany, but many gay U.S. critics felt it misrepresented gays. *Film Comment's* Elliott Stein called it "the best and brightest film made in Germany in the last few years," and the *Village Voice's* Stuart Byron raved, "It's the first masterpiece about the mainstream of male gay life." But Richard Dyer, the British editor of *Gays and Film*, stated, "It's all that macho-identified male culture, without irony. I feel oppressed by the film; it's telling me that I ought to do that."

Taxi includes a scene with Ripploh in drag—he's just returned from a costume ball—in front of his class. Dyer felt, "As an image of coming out, going into a class of school kids in drag is stupid and irresponsible." Vito Russo "liked the film but not the director's personal sensibility—he's just a shameless narcissist who can make a good, funny film. It's an advertisement for seeing people as meat."

Much less daring was *Ernesto* (1978), Italy's "first gay movie." It was not strongly gay, for it deals with people more in terms of class structure; its bisexual protagonist marries "well." The *Advocate* called it "a tame Junior League version of *Something for Everyone*." The film takes place in 1911 Trieste, where Ernesto's Christian father has abandoned him, and he's been raised by his orthodox Jewish mother (Virna Lisi). Like Daniel Hirsch in *Sunday, Bloody Sunday*, Ernesto (Martin Halm), seventeen, shuns orthodoxy. He conducts a relationship with a dockworker (Michele Placido) whom he later dumps and leaves with a token coin.

The independent British feature *Nighthawks* (1978) was also about a thirtyish schoolteacher who spends his off-hours cruising gay pubs and discos. Jim (Ken Robertson) is better dressed and less promiscuous than Ripploh; filmmakers Ron Peck and Paul Hallam were accused of too much gentility and not enough passion. Jim is not easily satisfied—his relationships fade without reason. When he is asked by a student, "Is it true that you're bent?" he answers their spiteful questions, provides information, and dispels their confusion. However, Jim is no longer an authority figure in class, and he almost loses his job. But he's also free of the fear of discovery and can reappraise his future. Critic David Denby declared, "*Nighthawks* may be the first movie about gay life made without fear, defensiveness, or show-off bravado."

Improper Conduct (*Mauvaise conduite*) was an internationally hailed documentary made in 1984 by Cuban emigrés Nestor Almendros and Orlando Jimenez-Leal (co-director of *El Super*). The most damning anti-Castro documentary yet, *Improper Conduct* focuses on the communist regime's harassment and internment of male homosexuals. It depicts Cuba's UMAP detention camps of the late 1960s and includes the on-camera participation of witnesses, members of Cuba's cultural elite, interviewed in Paris, New York, Miami, London, Rome, and Madrid. Another participant is former Castro supporter Susan Sontag, the American critic, who called Castro's campaign against gays part of a "puritan heritage." Witness Guillermo Cabrera-Infante, one of Cuba's greatest exiled writers, declares, "Persecution knows no boundaries; to win we must all be brothers and sisters, keeping only our commonality in mind."

Vincent Canby called *Improper Conduct* "the first legitimately provocative anti-Castro film I've seen." French President François Mitterand was moved to help effect the release of Armando Valladares, a poet who had spent twenty-two years in prison. The poet, one of the film's most eloquent witnesses, tells the story of a twelve-year-old boy, imprisoned for a minor offense, who was raped and tortured by guards and inmates of a Cuban prison. The documentary, shown on French television and cofunded by the left-wing government, won the grand prize at the Human Rights Festival in Strasbourg, France.

The filmmakers left Havana in 1962, two of over a million emigrants, including a large gay exodus in 1980. Almendros became an Oscar-winning cinematographer for *Days of Heaven*; he also shot *The Blue Lagoon*, *Kramer vs. Kramer*, and *Sophie's Choice*. He stated, "The subject of gay oppression is at the heart of *Improper Conduct*; it's a metaphor for a greater oppression in Cuba." *Improper Conduct* is one of the first films to elicit sympathy for an entire population via the plight of persecuted homosexuals. Almendros noted that the Cuban television broadcast of *Fame* in 1984 "expurgated, scene by scene, the homosexual character. The Cuban censors try to erase the humanity of gays by erasing them from depiction on the screen."

Almendros left Cuba "after I couldn't critique movies and in so doing try to reflect society's shortcomings." He had praised Jimenez-Leal's *P.M.*, a film about Havana nightlife, including the gay scene. "I decided to use my eye as the camera's eye and then hopefully move people to compassion and active interest."

• Boys Will Be . . . Tony Richardson's 1965 *The Loved One*, cowritten by Christopher Isherwood from Evelyn Waugh's novel, qualifies as the most lavender of "nongay" cult films. A satire about Southern California's funeral industry, it stars Robert Morse as the nephew of campy studio painter John Gielgud. When Gielgud takes his own life, Morse discovers Whispering Glades (read: Forest Lawn). The super-cemetery includes a "Damon and Pythias section, for loved ones who were very close." Also featured are Roddy McDowall as a studio executive, Tab Hunter as a cemetery guide, Liber-

Fanatic: Michael Biehn as a homophobic fan
who turns against Lauren Bacall in *The Fan* (1981).

The Loved One (1965): Openly gay Sir John
Gielgud as painter Sir Francis Hinsley in Evelyn
Waugh's macabre satire.

In *W.W. & the Dixie Dance Kings* (1975), Burt Reynolds
proclaims he'd gladly "go queer" for his screen idol, Errol
Flynn!

Roddy McDowall based his portrayal of gossip columnist Rex
Brewster in *Evil Under the Sun* (1982) on Tallulah Bankhead!

ace as a gay casket salesman, and Rod Steiger as Mr. Joyboy, a mincing embalmer. (Director Richardson succumbed to AIDS in 1991.)

Other pre- and post-Stonewall films also kept gays on the farcical side. John Standing played a British queer-joke in *Walk, Don't Run* (1966), Cary Grant's last movie. Standing, who also played pouffy in *X, Y, and Zee*, "graduated" to straight in *Privates on Parade*, as Captain Sholto Savory. In *If It's Tuesday, This Must Be Belgium* (1969) Aubrey Morris is a kleptomaniacal queer-joke who steals everything but the picture. *The Last Married Couple in America* (1980) spotlights divorce. Natalie Wood expresses sympathy ("I know it's going to sound crazy," she says twice) over the breakup of friends Donald (Stewart Moss) and Reggie (Colby Chester), the film's token gays.

By the eighties most bisexual and gay characters were more visible and verbal. *Mass Appeal* (1984) deals sympathetically with an outspoken seminarian (Zeljko Ivanek) who stands up for two gay colleagues who fall victim to the church's homophobia. He is eventually aided by Jack Lemmon. Wrote Quentin Crisp, "When Mr. Ivanek admits his bisexuality, Father Lemmon seems to suggest that the life of a priest will be more difficult for him than it would have been had he merely been heterosexual. I can't see why. In movies made from the works of Mr. [Graham] Greene, straight priests fall from grace like autumn leaves." Of course, there's no compromise, and Ivanek must leave the Church, while Lemmon puts his job on the line by opposing its antigay officialdom.

PHOTO: BARBARA WALZ

Openly gay actor-playwright Harvey Fierstein as a gay New Yorker (with Ron Silver) in *Garbo Talks* (1984).

Mass Appeal (1984): Jack Lemmon as a priest and Zeljko Ivanek as a bisexual seminarian fighting church homophobia.

St. Elmo's Fire was a 1985 ensemble hit whose publicity hid the implied homosexuality of Kevin (Andrew McCarthy), described by *Cosmopolitan* as "a not-so-happy journalist who fears himself to be gay." Unlike Ivanek, McCarthy is a stereotype in this picture about young people just out of college. Kevin's the lone gay, who socializes only with straights and has a crush on a female. This gay element is introduced—as in so many films aimed at younger audiences—only to milk laughs or appear relevant, and ultimately the issue is dropped.

The usual way of dealing with homo- or bisexuality is to ignore it altogether. The bigger the intended audience the more likely it will be ignored, as with NBC's lavish 1986 miniseries *Peter the Great*, "the turbulent love story between a man, a woman, and a nation." Press releases proclaimed, "His desire was to love only one woman." The show took major liberties with Peter's sexuality but comparatively minor liberties with other facts.

Far more truthful are the AIDS feature films, of which *Buddies* (1985) was the first. Written, produced, directed, and edited by Arthur J. Bressan, Jr., the movie depicts realities too harsh to ignore but was less than popular with gay and straight audiences (unlike television's sensationally advertised but ambivalent *An Early Frost*). Subsequent features include *Parting Glances*, the West German *AIDS, The AIDS Show Documentary* (from the makers of the Oscar-winning *The Times of Harvey Milk*), and German filmmaker Rosa von Praunheim's *A Virus Has No Morals*. Incidentally, the 1985 Western send-up *Rustlers' Rhapsody*, featuring Andy Griffith as a fey gay lawman, has the dubious distinction of including the big screen's first AIDS joke.

Television also contributed *Our Sons*, starring Julie Andrews and Ann-Margret and directed by *An Early Frost*'s John Erman, labeled "the George Cukor of the small screen." There were also ABC "Afterschool" and CBS "Schoolbreak" afternoon specials about AIDS aimed at teenage audiences.

The quite adult, British-made (shown in the U.S. on PBS) *Intimate Contact*, starred Claire Bloom as the wife of socially prominent British politician Daniel Massey, who contracts AIDS from a female prostitute while on a weekend business trip in Paris.

Such features, as well as the telefilms which, though moralistic, reach mass audiences, are the key to AIDS education, felt Arthur Bressan:

"Americans learn basically through stories. To humanize the issue is crucial. Without humanization, education is thwarted." He added, "Gay people have been characterized for years as being only gay, only for glitter, only for party. The AIDS crisis has shown that gay people have a strong, hard, solid underside that can deal with the ultimate issue in life, which is death—strongly, powerfully, heroically."

Buddies (1985): The first AIDS feature starred Geoff Edholm and David Schachter and was written and directed by Arthur J. Bressan Jr.

35

ALL-AMERICAN BOYS:

Streamers

Mitchell Lichtenstein as Richie, the gay protagonist of the grim barracks drama, *Streamers* (1983).

Streamers. United Artists Classics, 1983. Director: Robert Altman; writer: David Rabe; producers: Altman and Nick J. Mileti.
Starring: Matthew Modine, Michael Wright, Mitchell Lichtenstein, David Alan Grier, Guy Boyd, George Dzundza.

One observer of *Streamers* compared Mitchell Lichtenstein's Richie—gay and rich, like the comics' Richie the Rich Kid—to Tallulah Bankhead. Perhaps the military milieu underlines Richie's differentness—"sexual confusion," said one critic—for his femininity is less than that of many straight pop/rock singers. But men-in-uniform themes tend to force sexual individuality to a head, as in *The Sergeant* and *Reflections in a Golden Eye*.

Director Robert Altman broke through with the hit *M*A*S*H*, a tittering comedy bristling with jock humor. *Streamers*s marked Altman's return to Army turf, but with a difference. He said, "*M*A*S*H* was 1969. I'm telling the same war story now, but it isn't funny anymore." *Streamers*'s jocks don't laugh, except to relieve tension. The better they get to know each other and their likely fates in 1965 Vietnam, the more tense and afraid they become. "To synopsize the plot," said Altman, "isn't impossible, but it's inadvisable. The story line is one thing, its meaning quite another.

"Men, no, boys, from different walks of life thrown together cause enough trauma for any story. Billy, Roger, and Richie; all different, yet

Matthew Modine as the heterosexual protagonist—and therefore hero.

forced to live as if they were the same. Then Carlyle, the intruder, enters their world and declares it is not *his* world. He eventually proves it is not a world for any of them. The two old sergeants, Cokes and Rooney, having lived the same lie many times before, only prove the futility of all their endeavors."

Few critics categorized *Streamers* as an antiwar film, but it is that, and more. *Streamers* is about differences: white versus black, straight versus gay, repression versus self-expression. Outsiders Richie and Carlyle are catalysts to conflict—the gay white and bisexual black eventually come together, sparking homophobic violence. It doesn't matter that "all-American" Billy (Matthew Modine) may himself be gay (or "latent," in the critics' vernacular). Billy has swallowed every truth he's been spoon-fed since infancy, including that "deviant" sexuality is "sinful," America fights only just wars, whites are superior to blacks, and males are superior to females.

Outwardly easygoing, Billy is chummily tolerant of Richie and Roger (David Alan Grier). Roger is a black homophobic heterosexual who doggedly avoids controversy. Billy periodically asks Roger if Richie really means all the "outrageous" things he says. Roger reassures Billy that Richie's a good kid and "don't mean none of it." Roger tolerates celibate, silent gays, but not aggressive ones who believe (like Mae West!) that every man can be had. Thus, after Richie accepts Carlyle's crude advances, Roger hurls antigay epithets at the kid.

Roger is at least more practical than Billy. When the horny and angry Carlyle—from another barracks—demands privacy so he can be alone with the blond Richie, Roger is willing to comply and suggests to Billy that they [Roger and Billy] turn over on their cots and ignore the male couple making love. Billy, who's recently visited a whorehouse with Roger and Carlyle, won't hear of it. He refuses to countenance what he feels will demean *his* barracks.

The inevitable clash erupts between Billy and Carlyle. During a respite in the fight, Billy throws a shoe at Carlyle. But Carlyle has been ill-treated once too often and with his switchblade fatally stabs Billy. A drunken sergeant (Guy Boyd) happens into the barracks and is also murdered. When Richie fetches help, the white MPs assume that the cowering Roger is an accomplice, until Richie explains and saves him.

Earlier Billy had told Richie about a "straight" friend who went to gay bars (ostensibly for the free drinks bought by admirers) until he discovered he was gay himself and couldn't "change." Richie

asked if the story was really about Billy, who reacted angrily. The crucial difference between the self-accepting Richie and the less mature Billy is the degree of the latter's need to conform. His rigid intolerance—of himself and of others—destroys him.

The movie had begun with Richie tending to the slashed wrists of a fellow soldier (Albert Macklin). But Richie is no model gay. He later lets slip to Billy the noble act he's just performed and uses Carlyle to make Billy—the one he really desires—jealous. Semi-closeted, he uses a female pinup to camouflage his locker. But it doesn't work, for Roger—who hypocritically denies Richie's gayness in front of Billy—sneeringly informs Carlyle, "This here's the locker of a faggot."

The two sergeants—World War II and Korea vets—booze and bluster their way through the film and army life, united by shared memories. They alcoholically recall male camaraderie and war victories and warble "Beautiful Dreamer" (composed by gay Stephen Foster), substituting the word *streamers* for *dreamer*. At film's end, the surviving sergeant (George Dzundza) comforts the weeping Richie—though Richie is weeping for Billy and Carlyle, not himself—by insisting that there are worse things than being "queer," counting off war, disease, and death.

Richie is the first person besides his late buddy to whom Sergeant Cokes can sympathetically relate. But although Cokes has never wed or bred, in 1965 America he shares straight society's official view of a gay young man's lot.

That a 1983 interviewer would question an actor about playing "a homosexual" indicates persistent ignorance about gay characters and real-life gays and presupposes an interviewee's sexuality. Mitchell Lichtenstein's response: "I think the character is so well written that it doesn't matter. It's definitely a gay character but not a clichéd one. . . . I had no qualms."

Lichtenstein's only prior movie was *The Lords of Discipline*. However, he shared the Venice Film Festival award for Best Actor with his five *Streamer* costars. Despite the popularity of military-themed movies like *Taps* and *An Officer and a Gentleman*, Altman's film did puny business. The Vietnam and race angles, plus the grim ending, discouraged most potential viewers. Not even rear nudity and a blurred frontal of Modine (who later tormented the "queer" brother in *Hotel New Hampshire*) could attract many gay viewers.

The film's language is consistently harsh, and the

two sergeants provide only brief comic relief. Except for the opening—a crack drill team performing the manual of arms in shifting, hazy light—military life is deglamorized. The nearly two-hour film emphasizes the boredom, aimlessness, and despair of most newcomers to the military. Altman stated, "I don't like young men today being sent off in political armies; I don't think I would have made this film had the African and Central American situation not been what it is."

None of the characters in *Streamers* is heroic or dominates the film. The acting is ensemble work at its best. United Artists reportedly wanted a major star to play Billy and later shunted the film into its Classics division when Altman went with a cast of "unknowns." The director explained, "I took the point of view that there should be no lead, that each of those four boys was as important as the other.

"I was trying to not focus on one person's problems and attitudes but on the homogenization. . . . It's about each of them individually." And about intolerance of personal differences, and how a bigoted society can, and is bound to, backfire on itself.

ABOUT *STREAMERS*

Rex Reed, the *New York Post*: In the oppressive maze of bunk beds three roommates share each other's frustrations [including] Richie, a delicate lad who amuses, then disturbs the others with his fey, campy jokes. . . . By the end of the movie I felt like I knew these men, had lived with them, smelled their sweat and talcum, listened to their snores, touched their souls, and learned their secrets.

It is Richie, the prissy, sensitive one, whose homosexuality becomes the fuse that blows the other boys' masks to smithereens. The most intelligent and wordly one, he flirts and teases. . . . The others use Richie as a symbol of their masculine territorial imperative. . . . Richie grabs the audience by the heart with his wit, knowledge, and suffering, but his charisma is due to Mitchell Lichtenstein, who suggests defiled innocence masquerading as prep-school purity.

Richard Corliss, *Time*: *Streamers* takes place in a boot camp on the border of national psychosis. Set in 1965, *Streamers* was written after the 1975 fall of Saigon, and David Rabe's dialogue glows with the white heat of hindsight. . . . Men don't need a war to touch their heart of darkness; the threat of human intimacy is provocation enough. . . . When the crisis comes, they will be as surprised as the

paratrooper whose chute just wouldn't open.

Michael Wright's is the star presence. . . . He curls his lips around Carlyle's jive slurs until they are twisted into madhouse poetry. He glides through the barracks like a hipster on a death mission. Charlie Parker, meet Charlie Manson. Carlyle is the creepily irresistible spirit of all wars, hot and cold, global and interior, war without end, amen.

Richie is paid persistent court by Michael Wright as the bisexual Carlyle.

Carlyle and Roger (David Alan Grier) both feel themselves outsiders, but Carlyle is the angry rebel.

Carlyle kills Billy (Modine) and is arrested.

36

BRITS:

Privates on Parade and *Another Country*

The Andrews Sisters ride again, via S.A.D.U.S.E.A. (Song and Dance Unit, Southeast Asia).

Privates on Parade. Orion Classics, 1982. Director: Michael Blakemore; writer: Peter Nichols; producer: Simon Relph.
Starring: John Cleese, Denis Quilley, Michael Elphick, Simon Jones, Joe Melia, John Standing, Nicola Pagett, Patrick Pearson.

Another Country. Orion Classics, 1984. Director: Marek Kanievska; writer: Julian Mitchell; producer: Alan Marshall.
Starring: Rupert Everett, Colin Firth, Tristan Oliver, Cary Elwes, Robert Addie, Adrian Ross-Magenty, Philip Dupuy, Anna Massey.

"Mention England and homosexuality," said Peter Finch in 1975, "and people think of two things: drag and boys' schools. We seem to have more of both than anywhere else." Drag, from stage "pantos" to television's Benny Hill and Monty Python, has been little explored in British films. A Pinewood studio official once noted, "Our pictures are rather image-conscious. . . . We try and keep the la-la at home." Not so the film of the 1977 stage hit *Privates on Parade*. Both starred Denis Quilley (*Murder on the Orient Express, Evil Under the Sun*) and were written by Peter Nichols, who as an RAF member toured Southeast Asia in an entertainment unit similar to S.A.D.U.S.E.A. (Song and Dance Unit, Southeast Asia) after World War II.

With references like "the Middlesex regiment"

and "privates swelling with pride," the movie is often self-consciously funny. Its byzantine plot includes a mixed bag of soldiers. Sergeant Steven Flowers (Patrick Pearsons) is the naive, straight newcomer and audience surrogate. He falls in love with Anglo-Indian Sylvia Morgan (Nicola Pagett), a sometime hooker. She's pregnant by traitorous officer Reg Drummond (Michael Elphick), but after she and Flowers make love (in the film's only sex scene), Flowers thinks *he's* the father.

Major Giles Flack (John Cleese) is an ultraconservative imperialist and devout christian, who abhors sexual divergence but doesn't recognize a "fairy" when he sees one. Acting Captain Terri Dennis (Quilley) is the drag empress who calls all the "dears" by female names and supplies most of the film's humor. Rounding out the gay contingent are the gruff Sergeant Len Bonny (Joe Melia), who falls in love with mild Sergeant Charles Bishop (David Bamber).

The pop-eyed Terri is reprimanded by Bishop for *always* camping and acting like a woman. Terri responds that he camps to keep up morale and to forget his own dead lover, killed in the war by a torpedo. Bishop and Bonny's friendship grows into love, and they sing a touching and heartfelt paean to their camaraderie. Suddenly the Malaysian jungle erupts with guerrillas. Several unit members are killed or wounded. The survivors return to England, where they're reminded that it's an honor to die in battle. Bishop, who's lost Bonny, says, "Nothing is worth dying for."

The ad for the U.S. version, which omitted several drag numbers, including imitations of Dietrich and Vera Lynn, read: "Malaysia, 1947. Some fought. Some danced." The homemade blend of comedy, drag, straight romance, and song-and-dance (including a memorable black-and-white Astaire-Rogers number) fared better in Britain than in the States, though American reviewers gave *Privates on Parade* high marks. The U.S. audience was predominantly gay, but Quilley told British *Photoplay,* "Women *love* seeing men in drag. They think it's very funny and maybe exciting, in a curious way. I've played many butch parts—bearded kings and the like—and I used to get fan mail from men! But with *Privates on Parade,* I got more fan letters from women than ever before."

He added, "The British have always done drag. Don't ask me why." He explained that he'd based Terri's mannerisms and appearance (both extremely exaggerated) on "old friends I've known and loved for years" in the theater. But Terri's command of most situations and his joie de vivre save him from becoming a caricature. When conservative Eric Young-Love (Simon Jones) protests being called Erica—"But I'm not a homosexual!"—Terri reassures him, "Don't worry, love. It doesn't

show up front." Stumbling upon a grim native, Terri coos, "*Love* the blowpipe, very *you.*"

Playboy noted that *Privates on Parade* "outcamps *La Cage aux Folles.*" One reason is that the soldiers shift back and forth—uneasily, because of Major Flack—between military and female drag. Their roles are more fluid than Albin's, who has chosen his niche and remains there. But because even Terri can *pass,* he eventually does the "proper" thing and pretends to be the father of Morgan's baby. As Quilley put it, "I get the girl."

A versatile theatrical actor, Quilley told the American press, "The English theater is about the most tolerant society, accepting the lower class, the Jewish, the upper class, the black, the bisexual, and the homosexual." He revealed that "*Privates on Parade* isn't a gay movie in any sense. The gayness is neither underlined nor backed away from. . . . If there had been a character like Captain Dennis twenty years ago, it would probably have been howled down by critics and the public. They would either have said it was 'disgusting' or 'How dare you make fun of a poor, twisted homosexual.' Whereas nowadays, it's perfectly possible to be a heterosexual and play a homosexual just as you would play a banker, without sending anyone up."

ABOUT *PRIVATES ON PARADE*

Vincent Canby, the *New York Times*: Acting Captain Terri Dennis, recruited to put "Jungle Jamboree" together, is the role of a lifetime, and Denis Quilley never lets us forget it. His Terri is a camp figure of heroic proportions. . . . A hilarious, show-bizzy performance, sentimental, wise, and as broad as Asia, especially in drag. . . . A pricelessly coquettish Carmen Miranda, when he puts on a blond wig to impersonate Patti Andrews singing something side-splitting called "Pistol-Packing Deputy of Okinawa," he looks like—and has the dignity of—Rose Kennedy. . . . Joe Melia and David Bamber, fellow soldiers and lovers, sing and dance a soft-shoe that stops the show.

Quentin Crisp, *Christopher Street*: I am averse to "drag" shows. To me, there is always a pathetic, self-wounding element in this kind of entertainment, often performed by people who wish they were glamourous actresses but who, not daring to give sincere expression to those yearnings, deliberately make themselves grotesque. . . . The author's view of homosexuality seems ambiguous. Everyone has been coyly given a female first name. Everywhere there is a parade of the least lovable at-

Cuanto le gusta!: Captain Terri Dennis (Quilley) as Brazilian bombshell Carmen Miranda, with chorus boys, Sergeants Len Bonny (Joe Melia, left) and Eric Young-Love (Simon Jones).

John Cleese (left) and Denis Quilley as opposite sides of the same army in *Privates on Parade* (1984).

Quilley prepares Joe Melia for a show to entertain British troops in wartime.

tributes of camp. But toward the end, two of the men, neither dressed as a girl, sing a song of friendship which we are expected to take seriously.

Over the years, a small army of distinguished Britons from Churchill to Olivier has admitted to schoolboy homosexuality. Yet few British films have explored its prevalence in public (private) boys' schools. The protagonists of *Another Country*, set in the 1930s and based on British spies Guy Burgess and Donald McLean, are opposites united by their mutual outcast status. Self-indulgent, irresponsible Guy (Rupert Everett) fervently desires to become one of the "gods," the student elite who rule the school. Like everyone except egalitarian Tommy Judd (Colin Firth), all Guy really wants is to be "top of the whole stinking heap," to lord it over juniors and "inferiors." An idealistic Marxist, Tommy seeks to better society by ridding England—and eventually its schools—of cruel elitism. ("Faggot" derives from the public school term *to fag*, meaning to slavishly serve an upperclassman.)

Although homo-sex permeates the school, two commandments govern its existence: It must be merely a phase leading to girls and procreation (for the Empire), and it must never be found out. Guy, who dreams of a diplomatic career, breaks both rules. (When a younger student was discovered to be homosexual, his shame led him to hang himself in the school chapel.)

But Guy refuses to hide his "awesome" love for the blond Harcourt (Cary Elwes). He longs to "pour honey at the base of his throat" but comes up against the conservative christian Fowler (Tristan Oliver).

Fowler tries to purge the school of "sinfulness" by leading prayer sessions that quote paternalistic, homophobic passages from the Bible. The plot thickens as Fowler threatens to become Head of House, but his bid is thwarted by a more moderate student politico.

Guy's superficial mother (Anna Massey), a widow engaged to a "colonel person"—Guy's phrase—is also sadly deluded. Because her son isn't an extreme stereotype, she assumes he couldn't be anything but heterosexual. Speaking of the student suicide, she smugly states that she has known "one or two of *those*" in her time, and they are "never very happy."

Fowler catches Guy sending a love note to Harcourt. In front of the school prefects, Guy is severely caned. He bitterly realizes that his career is doomed and says to Tommy, "I'm never going to love women. This is my true nature."

Guy turns to the ideology of his fellow pariah, but Tommy's idealism has a major loophole. Guy tells him, "In spite of your talk of equality and fraternity, you still believe some people are better than others because of the way they make love." (Tommy is based on Donald Maclean, who, unlike Tommy, was gay; Tommy dies in Spain fighting Franco's fascists.)

226

Another Country does oversimplify. Homophobia and his desire for "stardom" in the diplomatic arena are the sole reasons Guy Bennett becomes a spy. But Richard Kaye has pointed out that "Marxist thought was central to many young men of Guy Burgess's generation. Becoming spies was as much an intellectual decision as a reaction to England's system of rigid class and social relations." Yet nearly all the film's critics equated political conversion with what they viewed as sexual conversion.

How, then, to explain John Schlesinger's 1985 film *The Falcon and the Snowman*? Its real-life young American spies, who sold satellite secrets to the Soviets in the seventies, were both heterosexual and Catholic. One was a Republican who dealt drugs "for the money." Most spies aren't gay, but *Vanity Fair*'s Stephen Schiff could only note that "these spies weren't the usual tweedy British fussbudgets. They were Mustang drivers, LP buyers—every American mother's sons."

Unlike *Falcon*'s Timothy Hutton and Sean Penn, *Another Country*'s Rupert Everett isn't likable or amusing in the role. In fact, there's hardly a likable character in the picture. Guy is needlessly petulant and self-destructive. By contrast, the chaste-seeming Harcourt is less mannered and later puts homosexuality aside (in the filmmakers's fictional biography) to become a successful breeder and banker. Everett, who originated the role of Guy in Julian

Rupert Everett (left) and Colin Firth as a heterosexual with Marxist leanings.

The English "public" school, traditional setting for upper-class gay love affairs, as in *Another Country* (1984).

Rupert Everett as Guy, a gay student whose betrayal by his own country propels him to defect to another country.

Guy's sexuality is discovered, and school rules mandate his punishment for it.

Mitchell's play *Another Country*, is best known to Americans as the incestuous Ram from television's *Princess Daisy*.

This beautifully photographed picture further compromises its integrity by not including a single kiss between the male lovers. Director Marek Kanievska felt, "It would be superfluous to get involved in heavy-petting scenes, since they wouldn't have added to an understanding of the relationship." (Do kissing and petting in heterosexual love stories add to an understanding?) Instead, Kanievska opted for "a great feeling of romance and longing and desire." The men cuddle discreetly in a docked rowboat in two moonlit scenes which the *San Francisco Chronicle* called "one of the frankest depictions of homosexual love on film."

The *Chronicle*'s Judy Stone felt that the film "doesn't do much to illuminate why one of British society's illustrious members finally chose another country." Even the publicity kit wondered what could cause a young man with "all the advantages" to turn against his own country. But was it ever his own country? Geography alone doesn't create loyalty, and membership in any country or society entails basic rights—not mere advantages—such as the freedom to be different, the freedom to love, freedom to live one's natural life. What *Another Country* fails to illuminate is that more can be gained if a Guy turns, not to another, more harshly prejudicial country, but to fighting, with the other Guys, to improve what should and can be his own country.

ABOUT *ANOTHER COUNTRY*

David Ansen, *Newsweek*: Seeds of treason cannot have been planted on more beautiful lawns than Eton and Gresham, where privileged schoolboys of the twenties and thirties Guy Burgess and Donald Maclean—later Soviet spies—took their first taste of Marxism before going on to Cambridge and a full meal. Burgess, the dandy and flamboyant homosexual, serves as the model for Guy Bennett—a sharp-tongued sybarite openly ambitious for status. . . . The feudally oppressive educational system, the budding idealism, and the realization that to choose homosexuality openly is to choose social ostracism were the first steps toward Bennett's rejection of his country.

Michael Boodro, *Harper's Bazaar*: English schoolboys hold a place in Americans' hearts. We cheered *Chariots of Fire*'s Olympians but still welcomed into our homes *Brideshead Revisited*'s increasingly drunken, self-destructive Sebastian. . . . A story of suicide, hypocrisy, and hidden perversion, *Another Country* is a plausible recounting of dramatic events that altered the lives and attitudes of these young men, leading them to embrace Communism and betray their country. . . . A romantic exercise in nostalgia, even as it points out the evils—bigotry and small-mindedness—of the English caste system.

37

EXOTICS:

Kiss of the Spider Woman and *Mishima*

Hurt as the stereotypical window dresser Molina, in jail because of his sexual orientation.

Kiss of the Spider Woman. Island Alive, 1985. Director: Hector Babenco; writer: Leonard Schrader; producer: David Weisman.
Starring: William Hurt, Raul Julia, Sonia Braga, José Lewgoy, Milton Gonçalves, Miriam Pires.

Mishima: A Life in Four Chapters. Warner Bros., 1985. Director: Paul Schrader; writers: Paul and Leonard Schrader; producers: Mata Yamamoto and Tom Luddy.
Starring: Ken Ogata, Kenji Sawada, Yasosuke Bando, Toshiyuki Nagashima, Mashayuki Shionoya, Junkichi Orimoto.

Kiss of the Spider Woman proves that in movies, as in everything else, people mostly see what they *want* to see. Some saw a powerful film about bonding, trust, and politicization. Others saw one more embarrassing gay stereotype who is ennobled only by servicing heterosexuality, yet is sacrificed in the end. Like *La Cage aux Folles*, the semidrag *Kiss of the Spider Woman* was a surprise crossover hit. It earned four major Academy Award nominations, including Best Picture and Director, and revitalized William Hurt's career with an historic Oscar as Molina, the gay window-dresser.

The 1976 novel by openly gay Manuel Puig is a two-man story told in dialogue and set mainly in an Argentine jail cell. Said Puig, "It's very much about the ideological and social repression of Argentina in 1973, but I primarily wanted to talk about the possibility of people changing." Puig's best-seller has been made into a play in Britain, an opera in Germany, and a musical in the U.S. Like all his novels, it was greatly influenced by movies Puig had seen (though *The Cat People* was dropped from the film, and neither book nor film includes *The Spider Woman*). Other Puig titles—most of them banned in his homeland—include *Betrayed by Rita Hayworth*, *Heartbreak Tango*, *The Buenos Aires Affair*, and *Eternal Curse on the Reader of These Pages*.

Puig, like director Hector Babenco, is Argentine-born but resides in Rio de Janeiro. The film *Kiss of the Spider Woman* is more politicized than the novel, due to the vision of Babenco, a son of Jewish immigrants, who had been a political prisoner. Babenco's second picture, *Lucio Flavio*, about a thief in cahoots with the police, caused his home to be machine-gunned. His third, *Pixote*, about abandoned children who become thieves (it starred real street children), won international acclaim and featured an unforgettable gay adolescent character.

For his fourth feature, Babenco felt compelled to make *Kiss of the Spider Woman* after reading the novel and feeling "invaded" by it. Other filmmakers, including Fassbinder and Liliana Cavani, had approached Puig for the film rights and been turned down. Seventy-ish Burt Lancaster asked to play the thirty-nine-year-old Molina, but reconsidered and then decided to coproduce instead. (After a heart attack, he was out of the project.) Richard Gere was in the running, then became unavailable.

229

Valentín and Molina: In the novel, Valentín was blond and Molina brunet, and both Hispanic.

Oscar-winner William Hurt, director Hector Babenco, and costar Raul Julia of *Kiss of the Spider Woman* (1985).

Once William Hurt (*Body Heat, The Big Chill*) was signed, Babenco expected ready funding and distribution for his $1.8 million production. It wasn't forthcoming, due to the grim setting, the homosexuality, and the bleak ending. Enter David Weisman, a former poster designer best known for producing a recycled Japanese B-movie that he retitled *Shogun Assassin*. Weisman secured international distribution via CBS Theatrical, but no U.S. distribution. The project stalled. Babenco's close friend Nestor Almendros was almost set as cinematographer until scheduling intervened.

Leonard Schrader (*Blue Collar, The Yakuza*) was hired to adapt the novel, and *Kiss of the Spider Woman* was heterosexualized to include Sonia Braga, a box-office star in Brazil (*Doña Flor and Her Two Husbands*). Braga took on most of the film's female roles, including the girlfriend of Molina's revolutionary cellmate Valentín (Raul Julia).

The script cut references to time and setting, presumably to attract non-Latin audiences, and Valentín's Marxism was eliminated to make him more sympathetic to American audiences. On the one hand, Babenco declared, "My movie aims to destroy the myths of what makes a man a man . . . and that is respect for himself and the capacity to give something to another person." But he also told the press, "I'm making a movie about something I consider more deep, more humanitarian than just a gay relationship."

Once full financing was raised (mostly in Brazil),

production began in late 1983 in Saō Paulo. Hurt later admitted that he would have played Molina more stereotypically but for his director. Hurt first showed up, according to Babenco, "looking like a witch, with a ponytail wig, heavy makeup, and a beauty mark. I said, 'No-no-no!'"

Julia was coached by a choreographer on how to convey the physical tenseness of a torture victim. According to the publicity, the same choreographer "assisted Hurt in portraying femininity."

Kiss of the Spider Woman had been completed for over a year before a small U.S. distributor was found. When the film opened in Manhattan, it broke the weekend record held by *On Golden Pond* and the first-week peak established by *Chariots of Fire*. It eventually reached 150 screens. Movie critics exulted in the departure from escapist summer fare. Most of the kudos went to the "daring" Hurt (who'd played gay onstage in *The Fifth of July*), and *People* magazine contradicted itself by calling his "surely the best gay performance ever by a major actor, looking and acting like the queen he says he is, but never resorting to cliché or camp."

The film's title and poster art were heterosexual lures, and *Kiss of the Spider Woman* received a barrage of publicity praising the picture and confirming negative stereotypes. Photos and capsule descriptions of Julia/Valentín and Hurt/Molina labeled one "the revolutionary" (not "the heterosexual") and the other "the homosexual," as though it were a profession. Virtually every review noted that

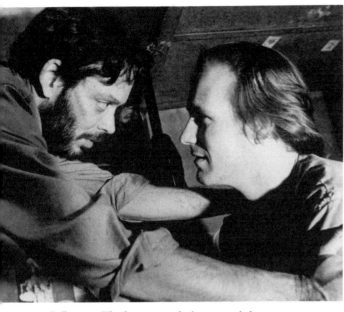

Cellmates: The hetero revolutionary and the gay
bourgeois come to love and even understand
each other.

Molina is imprisoned for "child molestation," "corrupting a minor," etc. This detail is a glaring and inflammatory contradiction: The gay stereotype who's only interested in "real" men—"I always take it like a woman," he says—goes for "little boys."

Wrote Quentin Crisp, "To increase the confusion, this character has been accused of pederasty. This makes it very hard for us to feel that he could become romantically attached to a full-grown man. Either the film should have made it clear that Mr. Hurt had been falsely charged or that his physical interest in Mr. Julia is a last resort."

Molina loathes being a male; this candidate for transsexual surgery says he would cut off his penis if he "had the courage." He is mother-fixated—much of the audience titters when he's shown watching television with his mom (Miriam Pires). He's masochistic and only desires a relationship with a man (preferably nongay) in which he can play a sexist female role. (Molina's lovelorn musings inspired derisive titters among many straight males in the audience.) Molina's outlook is totally superficial; he's blithely unaware of the vicious anti-Semitism in one of his favorite German movies, which he recounts to an infuriated Valentín.

Of course, the men do have an effect on each other. Molina gives Valentín creature comforts and a sense of humor, while Valentín instills courage in Molina, who carries out a fatal mission after being released (the prison authorities believe he will betray Valentín; he doesn't). But the two men have kissed and made love, and they must pay the Hollywood price: Molina dies amid garbage and savage verbal abuse, and the film ends with a final heterosexual dream-fantasy for the hospitalized Valentín.

Unfortunately, the noble sentiments and progressive declarations are overshadowed in most audiences' memories by the aimlessness, loneliness, and feminized looks and behavior of Molina. Yet Hurt informed interviewers that he wasn't interested in doing a stereotypical portrayal. Again, because and in spite of its stereotypes, *Kiss of the Spider Woman* was a solid hit. Producer Weisman theorized, "*La Cage* [the play] helped pave the way. It made middle-of-the-road audiences ready. They said, 'Now give us some more.'"

For his depiction of an edge-of-the-road gay man, Hurt became the fourth Best Actor Oscar-nominee in a gay role and the first to win. Yet consider the quality and integrity of these four actors' performances: the first two stars, Peter Finch and Marcello Mastroianni, played complex men who happened to be gay. Tom Courtenay and William Hurt played characters whose sexually-derived personalities overwhelmed and needlessly limited their lives.

ABOUT *KISS OF THE SPIDER WOMAN*

Tom Hutchinson, *Photoplay* (U.K.): A film which reaches parts of the human heart that others don't—or daren't—attempt. It shows how lust becomes love becomes loyalty becomes self-sacrifice. *Kiss of the Spider Woman* has two astonishing performances and bids fair to be one of 1986's most remarkable movies. . . . We feel that both men's are equally valid existences. Love between them grows, is consummated, and then moves beyond the deaths of one, or both, of them. The ending is one of the most moving—with a quietude that affirms like a fanfare—I have seen for a very long time. [The film] embraces big concepts of how human beings live and relate to each other. A very rare movie indeed.

David Denby, *New York*: Hurt wears his hair long and dyed orangy blond; preparing to entertain, he puts on a touch of lipstick, a dressing gown, and a towel turban. His large, soft hands caress the air; his shoulders move languorously up and down like a ship. . . . Hurt lets his big body go slack and discreetly flirts with the camera. He's feminine, all right, but he doesn't overdo the queenly poses.

Sellout: Ken Ogata in *Mishima* (1985), a highly fictionalized
and revisionist screen biography of Yukio Mishima.

Mishima's fanatical nationalism finds an outlet in right-wing
militarism and his own private army.

Mishima was a $5 million aesthetic experience that
appealed to just about nobody. It was too "alien" for
Western tastes, too westernized for the Japanese,
too nongay for gay audiences, and too complex for
fun-seekers. The semibiography is divided into
four parts—Beauty, Art, Action, and the Harmony
of the Pen and Sword. Shot partly in color and
graced by Eiko Ishioka's sets, it won Best Artistic
Contribution at the 1985 Cannes Film Festival.

Mishima's Japanese dialogue alternates with first-
person English narration delivered in monotone,
and excerpts from three of Mishima's less-distin-
guished (and least-gay) novels are dazzlingly but
hollowly visualized. The film tells little about the
subject. *Mishima* is more like a collection of trailers
for an upcoming movie than a movie itself. Several
filmmakers—Roman Polanski and Elia Kazan,
among them—tried to film Mishima's story. As with
the Nijinsky film, the major barrier was a widow.

Yoko Mishima prohibited depiction of her mate's
homosexuality or violent death. Mishima (forty-
seven-year-old Ken Ogata) died at forty-five in
1970, in a *shinji*, or double-death pact, with his lover
Morita (Mashayuki Shionoya). Mishima, who wrote
twenty-five plays and two hundred short stories,

starred in and directed the 1965 hit *The Rite of Love and Death*, which graphically depicted the *seppuku* of a young army officer and his wife. After Mishima's death, Yoko destroyed the negative and burned every print of the movie she could find.

Born in 1925, Mishima (né Kimitake Hiraoka) published a groundbreaking gay-themed novel, *Confessions of a Mask*, in 1948. In Japan or abroad, Yukio Mishima was never in the closet. He posed for suggestive photographs as St. Sebastian and established friendships with Isherwood, Capote, and Williams. Mishima's father, a bureaucrat who hadn't wanted his son to become a writer, destroyed his early manuscripts, ordering him to read only books about the Nazis.

Mishima's father pressured him into marriage by pretending that Mishima's mother had cancer and was on her deathbed. After the marriage, Mishima's mother "recovered" completely. Mishima fathered two children. As Mishima's celebrity grew (he would become the "Japanese Hemingway"), he became disillusioned with Japanese materialism and the fact that his personal statements had a larger circulation in the media than through his books. He turned to politics and advocated a return to the values of the samurai (who were often lovers). He not only wrote

about defending the emperor from communism but created his own small army.

A full year before his death, Mishima—who believed beauty should never wither—planned his suicide and set the date. On the chosen day, he handed in the last installment of his *Sea of Fertility* series of novels. Mishima drove to an army base where he was allowed to drill by head of the defense department Yasuhiro Nakasone. A general was taken hostage, and Mishima exhorted the nation's troops to rise up, march on the Diet (parliament) and demand a revocation of the U.S.-mandated constitution.

The plot failed, and Mishima killed himself and was disowned by many of his countrypeople. Attempts to film his story were quashed by his widow and by members of the political right, who threatened violence. Writer-director Paul Schrader (*American Gigolo*, *The Cat People*) agreed to Yoko Mishima's demands. However, she later sued, for Schrader included the *seppuku* and minimal homosexuality.

Distribution outside Japan was undertaken by Warners because of the prominence of executive producers George Lucas and Francis Ford Coppola. Schrader's brother Leonard cowrote the

Student extremists vow to rid Japan of foreign influences in a stylized movie segment.

Mishima exhorts military troops, shortly before carrying out his ritualized suicide.

screenplay with his Japanese wife Chieko, who received no credit. Possible Japanese government obstacles never materialized; Prime Minister Nakasone didn't wish to help the film by creating publicity. Right-wing death threats during production came to nothing.

Mishima's U.S. reception was dismal. It has not been released in Japan, despite the popularity of Ken Ogata, whose *The Ballad of Narayama* won the 1983 Cannes Film Festival's Golden Palm. Rather than casting a younger actor or one more closely resembling Mishima, Schrader chose "the best actor working in Japan." He added, "Ogata tried to school himself in acting more feminine, but he really didn't have the physical equipment to make that crossover."

Schrader and his films have often been accused of homophobia, which he denies. But *Mishima*'s credits include this disclaimer: "Yukio Mishima is acknowledged to have been a real person, but his acts have been fictionalized by writers." For *fictionalized*, read *de-gayed*. (Warners' press kit described Morita as merely a "close friend" and alluded to Mishima's "latent homosexuality.")

Incredibly, Schrader told the Japanese press, "The only way to be true to Mishima is to be true to ourselves." When this first Japanese-American co-production was rejected by the first Tokyo International Film Festival board, Schrader called for a boycott of the festival. The *Advocate*'s Elliott Stein wrote, "The producers of *Mishima* called for a boycott against a film festival that did not choose to show their misguided movie. How about a boycott against theaters that *do* show it?"

The consensus in Japan was that if *Mishima* proved popular enough in America, it would finally be released there, too. But it was a resounding flop. Production designer Ishioka declared, "It's a big disappointment for me that the Japanese people can't judge what I did with *Mishima*. I wanted to show the film myself, secretly, but right-wing groups threatened me. . . . The controversy from Mrs. Mishima is ridiculous. She is not a logical or an intellectual woman. She's like a housewife, so her statements are all emotional. She doesn't want people to think she was married to a homosexual man. It's so stupid. Recently I spoke with a literature consultant, and he said before Mishima's suicide, his wife never read his novels."

Stereotype or silence, which is preferable? Neither is ideal, but more fearful and strangulated is the unmentionable *other*. *Kiss of the Spider Woman* indicates that some truth may be wrung even from easy stereotypes. *Mishima* proves that when the truth is hidden, nobody is satisfied. Visibility and a voice are required for understanding and acceptance of the love (and lust) that once dared not speak its name.

ABOUT *MISHIMA*

Molly Haskell, *Vogue*: A near Mishima. . . . A self-created man, he changed his name in his youth and his body in middle age. He pumped iron, posed in the nude, formed his own army, dedicated himself to male purity while remaining married and a father, and in between wrote thirty-five novels and directed and acted in several films. Was there a "real" Mishima behind the many Mishimas? Paul Schrader evidently doesn't think so, for *Mishima* is a glittering pageant of surfaces, an avant-garde "This Is Your Life."

The idea is that Mishima's childhood, his writings, his flamboyant homosexuality, and his doomed emperor-worship were pieces of a puzzle that foretold his suicide. . . . What finally emerges is a psychological drama without a Rosebud, a puzzle that, when all the pieces fall neatly into place, leaves us cold.

Tom Hutchinson: Never the twain shall meet? . . . Schrader has a brave stab at a Western assessment of one of Japan's greatest writers. "Stab" is the right word, for after a lifetime of trying to reconcile art and action, pen and sword, Mishima committed ritual suicide. . . . Schrader's account is never very probing, but he creates a very scrutable world of mental illness and reveals someone searching for a spiritual gratification his bisexuality was never physically able to fulfill. A rare movie: to try to understand alien ideas.

38

NEW WOMEN:

Lianna and *Desert Hearts*

Lianna realizes her innate lesbianism via friends and lovers like Ruth (Jane Hallaren).

Lianna. United Artists Classics, 1983. Director-writer: John Sayles; producers: Jeffrey Nelson and Maggie Renzi. Starring: Linda Griffiths, Jane Hallaren, Jon DeVries, Jo Henderson, Jesse Solomon, John Sayles, Maggie Renzi.

Desert Hearts. Samuel Goldwyn, 1985. Director-producer: Donna Deitch; writer: Natalie Cooper. Starring: Helen Shaver, Patricia Charbonneau, Audra Lindley, Andra Akers, Gwen Welles, Dean Butler, James Staley.

Some critics compared *Lianna* with the previous year's *Making Love*, also about a repressed individual who exchanges a contractual mate for a partner of the same gender. The new relationship, which doesn't continue happily ever after, is nonetheless an introduction to the gay love that the character had avoided while fulfilling a traditional role. *Lianna* depicts how one wife-mother's coming out affects her and those around her; the "gay world" is almost as alien to Lianna (Linda Griffiths) as to her baffled family and friends.

Lianna fell in love with and married the domineering Dick (Jon DeVries), her professor. Now she is in love with her night-school teacher Ruth (Jane Hallaren). When philandering Dick finds out, he ejects Lianna from "his" home and away from "his" children, claiming she is an unfit role model. Lianna's best friend Sandy (Jo Henderson) also rejects her and paranoically reexamines their relationship (they reconcile in the end).

Lianna takes a new job and lifestyle and, like many lesbians, finds herself drifting toward poverty. She makes new friends and looks at and relates to women differently. Newly assertive, she informs one tenant in her apartment building, "I'm gay." The woman responds, "I'm Sheila."

Lianna goes with the otherwise closeted Ruth to a gay bar—one whose female patrons are far more joyful than those in *The Killing of Sister George*. At the bar, Lianna espies another PTA mom. Dick eventually offers Lianna joint custody, but only because single-parenting interferes with his work and sex life. John Sayles's slice-of-life has no pat happy ending—the tribulations don't suddenly cease—but Lianna's gay life is not a hopeless butch-femme obstacle course, either.

Lacking a Hollywood formula or star, *Lianna* didn't reach as wide an audience as it deserved. Rex Reed felt, "It's one hundred times better than *Personal Best*." One reason is its sexual honesty. Said Sayles, "Lianna's discovery of the side of her that's always been attracted to women is *part* of her growing up, not an adolescent phase."

Originally Sayles had an $800,000 budget for *Lianna*, which was to star Brooke Adams (*Days of Heaven*). But Adams backed out with "cold feet about the material." It took eighteen months to raise $300,000 from twenty-four first-time movie investors. The money was raised by Sayles's coproducer Maggie Renzi. (Both have small roles in *Lianna*; Sayles is an affable jock who's amazed when Lianna turns him down for sex.) At thirty-two, Sayles had already made the acclaimed *Return of the Secaucus Seven* and written the features *Alligator* and *The Howling*. But when he first approached the studios with *Lianna*, about a wife and mother whose teenaged son says, "It's okay with me if my old lady's a dyke," they all turned him down, "unless I could get Jane Fonda or whoever was hot at the moment."

Because Sayles "wanted to do *my* story, not theirs," he forsook the studio system and sought lesbian financing. He encountered two problems. First, gay women naturally prefer to fund projects *by* gay women, who have an even harder time obtaining funding and distribution, and second, "A lot of wealthy gay women can't get at their money, because it's in trust and they can only get at it when they marry."

Sayles's persistence paid off: *Lianna* broke all house records in its first two days in Manhattan. The tide ebbed quickly, and *Lianna* did little business in mid-America, but the movie earned a respectable profit. Sayles said, "I hope this will make it easier for the women who are trying to raise money

Poolside companion: Lianna and Ruth enjoy a quiet moment.

Fun with Dick and Lianna?: Dick (Jon DeVries) is an oppressive husband to Linda Griffiths as *Lianna* (1983).

to make gay films." Moreover, the R-rated picture (X in Britain and therefore banned to under-eighteens) won the Los Angeles Film Critics award for Best Screenplay and made several Ten Best Films lists.

Sayles said, "I thought it was really important when Maggie and I went around the country promoting *Lianna* that we'd never do the number, 'Oh, this isn't a movie about homosexuality—it's about people.' I heard that a lot after *Personal Best* and *Making Love*. It may be good advertising for a general audience, but if you're not proud of what you do, why do it in the first place?"

While trying to raise money from nongay sources, Sayles kept hearing, "Oh, another one of those?" (even before the wave of '82 films). "It was really frustrating. Then I would realize that they'd only seen maybe one other movie, and all of a sudden there's 'another one of *those*,' as if there weren't a hundred other kinds of movies out there. . . . It gave me all the more reason to make one of *these*."

ABOUT *LIANNA*

Catherine R. Stimpson, *Ms.*: John Sayles dislikes bullying men and admires courageous women. Some of *Lianna*'s most tender and touching images are of women caring for each other. . . . But it

237

Lianna's writer-director, John Sayles.

Desert Hearts (1985): Professor Vivian Bell (Helen Shaver in suit and hat) and Reno locals Alex McArthur, Patricia Charbonneau, and Gwen Welles.

evades the deeper feelings a "real" Lianna would experience. Sayles avoids the "Well of Loneliness" syndrome, but Lianna's overnight passage into gay life is comparatively free from sexual fumbling, qualms, and guilt. Although she pins their drawings on her refrigerator, she thinks of her children with odd infrequency.

Sayles's erotic lesbian scenes are discreet, attractive, and witty but lack energy and passion. The camera stares benignly at the lovers in their muted rapture. . . . *Lianna* is too well-meaning to be voyeuristic or exploitive. However, it's too gawky to be exemplary, and too slight to be the iconoclastic, rich exploration of families and of lesbians that might shatter a shallow familiarity with both.

Sue Zemel, *Bay Area Reporter*: Sayles's story avoids romanticizing lesbianism, while making a positive statement about its validity. Sayles is particularly adept at presenting the responses of non-Gay people. . . . Husband Dick is the most problematic, least likable character. Although a bona fide jerk, he explains Lianna's relationship to the children with surprising sensitivity.

Ruth, Lianna's first woman lover, is too stiff and chooses to stay in control rather than express her strong feelings about Lianna. . . . *Lianna* is an important addition to the collection of films that explore lesbianism. Sayles proves himself right-on and respectful.

Lesbian filmmaker Donna Deitch, asked to compare *Desert Hearts* to some other film, described it as "a remake of *The Misfits* [John Huston's 1961 movie], with a twist. I'm not really serious—it's not a remake of anything. But it takes place in Reno, where Marilyn Monroe went to get a divorce and got involved with Clark Gable. Vivian Bell goes to Reno to get a divorce, too, and gets involved with this young woman who works in the casinos."

Like John Sayles, Deitch spent time—almost three years—raising funds (a "low" budget of $1.5 million) for a picture of supposedly limited interest. But, unlike *Lianna, Desert Hearts* became a surprisingly substantial crossover hit. Above all, its frank and airy depictions, and the fact that it was made—and made well, like *Maedchen in Uniform*—by women, delighted lesbian audiences. Heterosexual audiences could take comfort in the 1950s setting that predated women's rights and the gay movement. For feminist and gay audiences, the setting heightened awareness of how little women's roles have changed and of the degree to which homophobia is still with us.

Less housebound than *Lianna, Desert Hearts* benefits from the sunny, exotic desert setting and a colorful supporting cast: a salty and homophobic rancher, a vivacious blonde bisexual, and a lesbian-baiting divorcée staying at the ranch. The male

Desert Hearts's producer-director, Donna Deitch.

Walter (McArthur) tries to welcome Vivian, a divorcée-to-be, to the Dude Ranch.

characters are minor, mostly meant as distractions, alternatives, or relatives.

Though short on plot or action, *Desert Hearts* is long on engaging actors and characterizations. At the film's core is the uptight Vivian (Helen Shaver), who travels from a childless, in-name-only marriage to a warm, loving lesbian relationship. Cay (Patricia Charbonneau) is open and free-spirited sexually but has no permanent love object. Frances (Audra Lindley) is Cay's adoptive mother and sparring partner.

Since Vivian is the central character but a stranger to the scene, it is Cay's relationships that are described. At first, she and Frances seem more than relatives; there is a hint of obsessive, possibly sapphic love on Frances's part. But Frances turns nasty once it's clear that Cay has found Vivian and helped Vivian find herself. At film's end, Frances grudgingly accepts Cay but not her orientation. When Cay pecks her on the cheek, Frances self-consciously wonders aloud if *she*'ll be taken for "queer." Yet such is Lindley's vibrant, ingratiating performance (so different from her Mrs. Roper on television's "Three's Company") that Frances is merely pitiable, never detestable.

Also close to the point of intimacy is Cay's friend-

Happy ending: Vivian and Cay (Charbonneau) have an affair which blossoms into love, then ride off toward an urban sunset.

ship with fellow casino-worker Sylvia, nicknamed Silver (Andra Akers). The women even bathe together, to the delight of Silver's older fiancé! Cay has a fiancé of her own, her boss Darrell (Dean Butler), who knows of Cay's gay ways but has no doubt that a wedding will change all that. Cay dumps Darrell and explains to Vivian that they were never truly engaged: "I just allowed myself to become attracted to his attraction to me."

Vivian is herself briefly pursued by Frances's son Walter (Alex McArthur), an English literature professor. Vivian explains to Cay that her long-standing marriage was largely a matter of form. Form is important to Vivian, at least until the end of the movie when she may lose Cay (she doesn't).

Donna Deitch makes a cameo appearance as the "Hungarian gambler." Playing two slot machines at once, she informs Cay—and so delivers the film's theme—"You have to play to win." This goes for love as well as gambling, and the lovingly persistent Cay finally teaches Vivian how to gamble and win at love.

When asked if doing the lesbian love scene in *Desert Hearts* was difficult, Patricia Charbonneau replied that it was easier than doing such a scene with a man, which would have impinged on her relationship with her husband. In the old days, if well-known actresses did lesbian projects at all, they were only discreetly asexual ones. Those actresses who did lesbian love scenes were either European or didn't expect to subsequently appear in Hollywood studio projects. In a refreshing change from that, *Desert Hearts*'s principals went into major projects afterward. Charbonneau starred for William Friedkin, and Helen Shaver for Martin Scorsese (opposite Paul Newman in *The Color of Money*).

Since the seventies, the studios—seeking bigger and younger audiences—have stopped doing lesbian- and gay-themed motion pictures. This is just as well, for such pictures are now made by independent producers passionately commited to quality and integrity on the screen. The source material is often by gay writers and is often brought to the screen by gay scenarists, directors, and/or producers.

In the words of Christopher Isherwood, "Each homosexual-themed film is an ambassador, and it's much too important to put into the hands of hack moviemakers who aren't willing to exercise their minds, their taste, or their goodwill."

ABOUT *DESERT HEARTS*

Michael Musto, *Saturday Review: Desert Hearts*, based on Canadian Jane Rule's 1964 novel *Desert of the Heart*, confronts its lesbian theme like few films before it, with unflinching integrity, not dark lighting and fade-outs. . . . Lesbianism isn't exploited for angst à la *Children's Hour* or touched upon then dropped as in *Personal Best*; it's handled tenderly and optimistically, if not with a lot of levity and wit. The mood is so heavy that it's almost a shock when Vivian Bell (Helen Shaver) unpurses her lips for a minute and actually lightens up. . . . Patricia Charbonneau as the young kook Cay Rivvers is simply winning.

Neil Norman, *Photoplay* (U.K.): I urge you to make the effort to see *Desert Hearts*, not because it will have a limited release (it will), nor because it is a low-budget film that deserves your support (it does), but because to miss it would be to deprive yourselves of one of the most exhilarating and truthful experiences you are likely to have in the cinema for years. . . . *Desert Hearts* is quite simply the most brilliant exploration of the way women relate to each other that I have ever seen—less self-conscious than John Sayles' *Lianna*. Set in 1959, its period ambience in no way detracts from its current relevance.

Candid, beautiful, funny, truthful, and, in one particular scene, breathtakingly erotic, *Desert Hearts* is a film to write home about. You'll be putting your soul in peril to miss it!

39

LOVE STORIES:

Prick Up Your Ears and *Maurice*

Prick Up Your Ears. Civilhand Zenith/Samuel Goldwyn, 1987. Director: Stephen Frears; producer: Andrew Brown; writer: Alan Bennett.
Starring: Gary Oldman, Alfred Molina, Vanessa Redgrave, Wallace Shawn, Lindsay Duncan, Julie Walters, James Grant.

Maurice. Merchant Ivory/Cinecom/Film Four International, 1987. Director: James Ivory; producer: Ismail Merchant; writers: Kit Hesketh-Harvey and Ivory.
Starring: James Wilby, Hugh Grant, Rupert Graves, Denholm Elliott, Simon Callow, Billie Whitelaw, Ben Kingsley, Phoebe Nicholls.

Two Hollywood traditions haven't changed much over the years: the preference for casting gay roles with straight actors, and the propensity of such actors for making stereotypical public statements about their roles. One example is Gary Oldman, who played Joe Orton in *Prick Up Your Ears*: "To play Orton, you just think about cock a lot. I went off sex; Lesley and I didn't make love, and Fred [Alfred Molina, as Kenneth Halliwell] went through the same thing with his wife, and we both became very camp. It's fun for eight weeks to be a gay man; we were like these two screaming queens by the end. That's the Method."

Before *Prick Up Your Ears*, Oldman had played Sid Vicious in another tale of a doomed couple, *Sid and Nancy*. The role of Orton's lifemate of sixteen years, Halliwell, was to have been played by openly gay Ian McKellen, who left the production at the

Gary Oldman as iconoclastic gay playwright Joe Orton in *Prick Up Your Ears* (1987).

last minute. Insiders said McKellen felt he was too old for the seven-years-older Halliwell.

Alfred Molina, an actor of Spanish-Italian extraction, was cast, though he was considered by many as both too tall (Orton and Halliwell were the same size and wore each other's clothes) and too unusual-looking.

Vanessa Redgrave costarred as Orton's high-powered literary agent (not long after playing male/female in the telefilm *Second Serve, The Renée Richards Story*), and Julie Walters (*Educating Rita*) played a virtually unrecognizable cameo role as Orton's shrewish mother, locked in a long, loud, and loveless marriage. When his mother dies, Orton tells his family that at least he and Kenneth have had a better time in the sack than his folks did. His father nods glumly.

Prick Up Your Ears (often referred to in the press as just *Prick*) is, like most recent gay films, not shy about sexuality. The highly suggestive sex scenes start early and occur in a variety of settings—in bed,

Scenes from a marriage: As Orton's career eclipses Halliwell's, problems arise in the relationship.

Alfred Molina as Kenneth Halliwell, Orton's mate of sixteen years, vacationing in Morocco.

in lavatories, in Morocco. The film heralded a new physical frankness for gay love stories on-screen; *Maurice* soon followed with monogamous sex scenes plus frontal male nudity. Both pictures were sizeable hits.

Prick Up Your Ears was the most in-depth look at a relationship between two men until that time. As *American Film* put it, "The first wave [of gay films] treated gays like Problems. The new wave treats them like people with problems."

The movie, set in the 1960s, was able to sidestep AIDS and current social politics. But in its consciousness of gay bonding, *Prick Up Your Ears* is very much a modern film. Another 1987 film spotlighting a real-life homosexual pair was *Waiting for the Moon*. Apparently for commercial reasons, *Moon* completely eschewed sexuality, while *Prick Up Your Ears* included it (and was much more commercially successful). Director Stephen Frears had already shocked some audiences (but pleased most) by including gay and straight love scenes in his previous picture about a gay relationship, *My Beautiful Laundrette*.

Of course, with as promiscuous a character as Orton, *Prick Up Your Ears* had to be carnal to maintain integrity. Despite their gay-marriage sub-

ject matter, neither *Waiting for the Moon* nor *Prick Up Your Ears* was exhibited at gay film festivals. Their releasing companies felt this might diminish their fiscal futures or negatively "label" them. The "problem" of poor reviews after a gay or lesbian film-festival screening had been solved by the AIDS love story *Parting Glances*, screened under condition that it not be reviewed until its official release.

Written by Alan Bennett (*An Englishman Abroad*) from the Joe Orton biography by John Lahr (son of actor Bert), the film is sensationalistic by the very nature of its ending. In this case the ending overshadowed the life and relationships of the London theater's gay white hope, and received more publicity—often homophobic and cautionary—than the movie itself.

Director Frears noted: "Orton and Halliwell's life together was as natural to them as a more conventional heterosexual life is to others. This is the way it was—no excuses or explanations. But the fact that they were gay is secondary to their story. It's about marriage, with many of the same problems as any other marriage that goes wrong, except between two men."

In fact, Bennett and Frears paralleled one marriage with another. Anthea (Lindsay Duncan), the wife of Lahr (Wallace Shawn) is seen in the same powerless, underrated position as Halliwell. When Halliwell is referred to as a "wife," the implications aren't sexual but political and professional. Anthea

Lahr is contrasted with Orton's agent Peggy Ramsay (Vanessa Redgrave), who has little time for "unimportant" wives.

The central relationship becomes sorely strained by the characters' changes in fortune. When they met in 1951, Halliwell was the smarter, more affluent, and more ambitious of the pair. He was the writer. Later, in frustration, he gives up writing. But he shares ideas, titles, even plot lines with John—who takes the name "Joe" as part of his hip new image. The egocentric Joe won't publicly share bed *or* literary credit, and he won't move into the newer lodgings that Kenneth urges for them. And in spite of his ambisexual plays, Orton prefers to be thought of as a heterosexual, even while criticizing the media and other British institutions as hypocritical.

As in Bob Fosse's *Star 80*, about *Playboy* Playmate-turned-actress Dorothy Stratten—murdered by her ambitious boyfriend-manager—*Prick Up Your Ears* describes more than one relationship. It is a microcosm of its time and place, of society's yearnings; ultimately it is about people being seduced—by fame, greed, and public expectations.

ABOUT *PRICK UP YOUR EARS*

Richard Corliss, *Time*: By your example you spread the word: Art is supposed to show us how to live, and artists are supposed to show us how not to.

Stanley Kauffmann, the *New Republic*: *Entertaining Mr. Sloane*, by Joe Orton, may be the only work in history dedicated to a person who later murdered its author.

Brad Harris, *New York Native*: Essentially the story of *A Star Is Born*, with Norman Maine dragging Vicki Lester with him into the ocean. . . . I can't help feeling the missing piece [of the movie] is already there in the facts. Orton and Halliwell were alone with each other for almost a decade. They concocted collages together. They wrote novels together. In *The Boy Hairdresser* they imagined themselves dying together, Orton killed in a car wreck and Halliwell so alone and grief-stricken he has no alternative but to commit suicide.

Such isolated intimacy is some people's ideal of domestic happiness (and others' ideal of hell). . . . All it would have taken would be one scene, perhaps of the two working together, to show that Orton and Halliwell were, for a long time, genuinely happy with each other.

Gay writer W. Somerset Maugham once said, "I learned a lot from E. M. Forster—from his mis-

Homosexual Clive (Hugh Grant) takes a wife (Phoebe Nicholls) for socioeconomic reasons in *Maurice* (1987).

After splitting with Clive, Maurice (blond James Wilby) befriends the working-class Alec (Rupert Graves).

takes." The prolific Maugham's heterosexual-themed stories were frequently made into motion pictures, from *Rain* and *The Letter* to *The Razor's Edge* and *The Moon and Sixpence*.

In his day Forster was thought by at least one critic to be "crippled [as a writer] by his condition." Being gay, he supposedly couldn't write of the love between men and women, yet he couldn't publish about the love between men. So he stopped writing, accursed by both integrity and over-sensitivity to criticism. His last novel was *A Passage to India* in 1924, though he lived to be ninety-one and died in 1970. He lived long enough to read about the Stonewall riots in 1969 that gave birth to the Gay Rights movement, and to read Susan Sontag's avowal that two minorities were making the only significant postwar contributions to culture: Jews and gays.

Forster might also have read Theodore Solotaroff's essay about "the homosexual imagination having the most decisive effect in defining the moral as well as the aesthetic character of the age. . . . The darkest truths about drug addiction come from William Burroughs, about Negro-white relations from Genet and Baldwin, about modern marriage from Albee and Tennesee Williams, about the disaffected young from Allen Ginsberg."

Maurice (pronounced Morris), Forster's 1914 gay novel dedicated "to a Happier Year," wasn't pub-

Despite their differing classes and mutual gender, Maurice and Alec become lifemates in "merry" olde England.

Laurence Olivier (a gay dress designer in *The Collection*, 1976): "If you're British, Hollywood casts you in lavender."

lished until 1971. In the late 1980s there was a filmic rediscovery of Forster, with David Lean's *A Passage to India* and Merchant Ivory's *A Room With a View* and *Maurice*.

Much as John Schlesinger's hit *Midnight Cowboy* spurred *Sunday, Bloody Sunday*, so *A Room With a View* made *Maurice* possible. The posthumously published gay novel had long been a pet project of producer Ismail Merchant and director James Ivory, filmmaking partners and lifemates. In twenty-five years as "collaborators in art and in life," as *People* magazine said, it was the first time the media revealed that the pair lived together.

Maurice, like *Prick Up Your Ears*, is set in the past and so harks back to a simpler, though harsher, time. Still ruled by Victorian morality, British law made homosexuality a crime—as it still was in Orton's day. The "queer" tag could ruin a career and make one an outcast within one's class (particularly the upper class). This explains the panic that envelops Maurice (James Wilby) and Cambridge classmate Clive (Hugh Grant) when they discover that they're in love.

The introspective Maurice takes a while to accept his gayness, and by the time he does, the ambitious Clive has decided to wear a straight mask in public *and* in private. Clive gives in to pressure from his mother to wed when a friend is ruined after arrest on a "morals charge." The rising barrister rejects the man's appeal for help and warns Maurice that they must forget the past and respect the boundaries of friendship.

Maurice seeks "treatment" from a quack American hypnotist (Ben Kingsley) and tries to resume a platonic relationship with Clive, now married to Anne (Phoebe Nicholls) and even less happy than before. Maurice imagines he is the only one of his kind in the world until he meets and slowly befriends Alec (Rupert Graves), a handsome, easygoing gamekeeper. The two have secret trysts, to the delight of Clive, who believes Maurice has a girlfriend he hasn't told anyone about.

But as his relationship with Alec deepens, Maurice becomes concerned about their class differences and about the possibility that Alec might blackmail him. When Clive discovers that Maurice's paramour is male, he is appalled—especially by Alec's working-class background—and more than a little jealous.

John Gielgud (with Roddy McDowall in *The Loved One*, 1965): "I am an actor. Of *course* I can play a heterosexual!"

Alec tries to reconcile with Maurice, but to no avail. So he chooses to emigrate. At the last moment he decides to stay in England and goes to their usual trysting place, where Maurice and their new life together await him.

Simon Callow, who played a small role in *Maurice*, proclaimed, "The public has embraced *Maurice*, and women in particular have found it a very moving and touching love story that they can relate to. Some people have groaned that this is 'just another coming-out story.' What they forget is that,

Britisher David Hemmings played "a notorious Hollywood gay" in Jacqueline Susann's *The Love Machine* (1971).

245

to a younger generation growing up in the era of AIDS, coming out is just as difficult as it was before Stonewall. . . . This movie is really for young gay people about the same age as Maurice and Clive and Alec."

Like Sir Ian McKellen, Callow—who also appeared in *A Room With a View*—is one of Britain's openly gay and regularly working actors, a phenomenon that still has no counterpart in Hollywood.

ABOUT *MAURICE*

Dale Winogura, *Frontiers*: Passionate yet civilized, candid yet dignified, *Maurice* is among the few genuinely romantic gay films ever made and a landmark of the genre. . . . Avoiding the stuffy cultural pomposity and surface calendar-art of *A Room With a View*, James Ivory has cowritten and directed with subtle elegance his finest effort to date.

The tasteful, discreet sexuality and brief nudity have a matter-of-fact approach toward male desire that's positively refreshing and unpatronizing. The emotional connection among the characters is related with strength and compassion. The virtues and flaws of each person and idea are explored with enriching truth and intelligence. . . . *Maurice* explores old terrain with wide, fresh eyes. It's the Mount Everest of the gay cinema.

Bonnie Rtockwell, *Entertainment This Week*: You've come a long way, boy! In *Suddenly, Last Summer* you were a phantom, a sinister shadow, a corpse. In *Reflections in a Golden Eye* you were Marlon Brando, no less, but repressed, self-loathing, stuck in a travesty marriage but too cowardly to get out. . . . In *Making Love*, you did get up and out. It was a revolutionary film — positive and real and compassionate. But baffling. How did you get into that marriage in the first place? *Maurice* explains all that; this time out you discover yourself, your loving and sexual nature, and you find out how unfair Society is. You almost make the mistake of marriage for appearances' sake—as your friend Clive does. Clive, who is no friend to you, to your kind, to society, or to himself or his poor, duped wife.

Linda Fresia, *Time Out*: Times change in the gay or lesbian film, for today, even when the setting is Edwardian, the sensitivity is Late-'80s, or Gay-'90s. No longer is the homosexual character asea in a heterosexuals-only universe. No longer is that character a villain—in fact, there are no individual villains, the only near-villain being the self-deceiving sort who harms only himself and his intimates. . . . No longer are temporary "conversion" or death the only outs.

Maurice is a thoroughly modern look at a hopeless time. In underlining the foibles and cruelties of the past, *Maurice* provides stately but lively entertainment, a few emotional and visual thrills, and more importantly points the way back to the present and on into a hopeful future where courage and love and self-worth are their own rich rewards.

246

40

SURVIVORS:

Torch Song Trilogy and Longtime Companion

Harvey Fierstein as Arnold Beckoff in *Torch Song Trilogy* (1988): All he wants is a little respect.

Torch Song Trilogy. New Line Cinema, 1988. Director: Paul Bogart; writer: Harvey Fierstein; producer: Howard Gottfried.
Starring: Anne Bancroft, Matthew Broderick, Harvey Fierstein, Brian Kerwin, Karen Young, Eddie Castrodad, Charles Pierce.

Longtime Companion. Samuel Goldwyn, 1990. Director: Norman René; writer: Craig Lucas; producer: Stan Wlodkowski.
Starring: Stephen Caffrey, Patrick Cassidy, Bruce Davison, John Dossett, Mark Lamos, Dermot Mulroney, Campbell Scott.

The last major gay-themed feature of the eighties and the first of the nineties both depict survivors living in New York City. The center of the gay universe—the world's most influential metropolis—has been ravaged by AIDS. The city was and remains the hardest-hit site outside the Third World. But the first of these films doesn't deal with the modern plague, for it's set in the seventies, a time of emerging liberation and promiscuity. *Torch Song Trilogy*, of course, began as a four-hour, three-part play by Harvey Fierstein. It was born Off-Broadway at La Mama in 1978, moved to Broadway (for over twelve hundred performances), and earned Tony Awards for Best Play and Best Actor.

When Harvey Fierstein first played the role of Arnold Beckoff, he was twenty-four and an un-

known Brooklyn playwright and actor. A decade later, when his play came to the screen (his brother Ronald served as executive producer), Harvey was rich, famous, and America's best-known openly gay actor.

Despite *Torch Song Trilogy*'s flamboyant onstage success, Hollywood showed only a wary interest and with provisos: if Arnold were played by a film star—and if the screenplay focused on Arnold adopting a son rather than on his love life. The gravel-voiced Fierstein chose to retain artistic control and present Arnold his way, himself. But the question was still asked—wasn't he too old to play the younger Arnold?

He said, "It's not a matter of playing younger. It's remembering what it's like. . . . As you get older, you learn to cover up better and better. To be that naked again is the hard part."

As an actor, Fierstein had long since abandoned drag performances, but in *Torch Song Trilogy*'s opening scene he's a professional drag artist named Virginia Hamm (working with Ken Page as Marcia Dimes and Charles Pierce as Bertha Venation). The decision was made to drastically trim a clothed, but suggestively explicit, sex scene at the beginning of the film. Another notable change was casting Ma with film star Anne Bancroft, instead of Estelle

Ma (Bancroft) finds out that she's a grandmother to Arnold's adopted son David (Eddie Castrodad).

Ma refuses to equate Arnold's grief over Alan with her own; her homophobia causes a rift between mother and son.

Getty, who had played the part onstage and gained fame on television's "Golden Girls."

Film star Matthew Broderick was cast as Alan, Arnold's mate of five years. Broderick had made his stage debut in *Trilogy*, at nineteen, as David, the teen adopted by Arnold. Brian Kerwin was cast as Arnold's ex-lover Ed, a role he's perfected in the West

Coast stage run. The film version was a labor of love, and all its participants played for less than their usual salaries.

Said Bancroft: "The world is full of people afraid of what they don't understand or know. There is nothing you can do except try and educate them. . . . My role epitomizes the parent who wants to control their [sic] children into becoming what they dream them to be, rather than what they want and who they are. I can only hope some people will see the film and notice themselves in this person, and learn to love and support and not to control."

Fierstein, who in 1984 earned a third Tony for writing *La Cage aux Folles* and who narrated the Oscar-winning *The Times of Harvey Milk*, wondered: "When did heterosexuals get the patent on the values of home and hearth and family and commitment? How can straights possibly think we don't have families?" He defended *Trilogy*'s timing: "This is the perfect time to do the film, because it's all too easy for people to think of gays as a high-risk group and nothing else. I mean, aren't you a little sick of every time seeing a gay person on-screen with an I.V. in his arm?"

About his playing Arnold rather than casting an officially heterosexual star, he declared, "You may not mind watching heterosexuals play gays, but I do!" As to the film's box-office prospects: "Listen, if every gay person in this country went to see it, it'd be the largest-grossing movie ever. We forget how many of us there are. . . ."

Torch Song Trilogy concerns Arnold Beckoff, a nice Jewish boy who simply wants to be loved and accepted on his own terms. At a gay bar, he meets Ed (Brian Kerwin), a schoolteacher who becomes his lover but can't accept his own gayness and chooses to marry.

When Arnold meets Alan, a young model, the two become lovers, then lifemates. They adopt David, a disadvantaged gay teen. But Alan is fatally beaten by an antigay gang, and Arnold is left to raise David on his own.

Arnold's mother comes to visit and creates conflict by refusing to accept that Arnold's relationship with Alan was as valid as hers with her late husband, as are his parenthood and sexuality. Arnold informs his mother that if by now she can't accept him as he is, she should get out of his life.

A partial reconciliation occurs, and, more definitively, Ed comes to terms with his true sexuality—he leaves his wife to live with Arnold, and they raise David together.

ABOUT *TORCH SONG TRILOGY*

Peter Miller, *New York Native*: The famous gay-bashing death of Alan, only referred to in passing in the stage version, is here portrayed in one short, shocking scene. . . . At the end, Ma does come to understand what his late lover meant to him, and that his homosexuality is not a passing phase. However, she leaves him once his back is turned, so there is the suggestion she has not come fully to terms with him even yet.

To Life! (Israel): It wasn't predictable that *Torch Song Trilogy* would become a hit play with homo- and heterosexual alike. Why? Because it's the unique story of a homosexual Jew who's also a female impersonator whose goal is a monogamous union and a child by adoption. But the universal message of Beckoff's search for dignity and fulfillment, and his enduring hope in the face of adversity, propelled the tale into a human interest and humane classic.

The film accomplishes the same. . . . The cast is ideal, excepting Ms. Bancroft's awkward striving toward Jewish caricature. The Jewish Ms. Getty of the stage version made no such efforts and was far more believable. . . . Here finally is a film in which the characters' homosexuality isn't meant to make them better or worse, just themselves.

Like AIDS itself, *Longtime Companion* brought out the best in some people and the worst in others. An example is the soft-drink company that often supplies film productions with free refreshments insisting that their product not be seen on-screen, for fear of its identification with the disease. By contrast, Panavision, DuArt Film Labs, and Sound One donated hundreds of thousands of dollars of goods and services, and the cast and crew worked for scale.

Norman René (left) and Craig Lucas, director and writer of *Longtime Companion* (1990).

Some of the news that's fit to print: Howard (Patrick Cassidy) shares a 1981 article about a new disease called AIDS.

Writer Craig Lucas said his film would have been more political if he'd known that the play *The Normal Heart* and the book *And the Band Played On*—both optioned for films—wouldn't reach the big screen. "This isn't a movie about how the system has failed us—which it has. It's about how a community became heroic."

Critic Vito Russo affirmed, "These [characters] are shocked out of their 'This is our beach house, these are our cocktails, and these are our magnificent pecs' life-style. By the end of the film they're talking about sit-ins outside city hall, wearing ACT-UP buttons and T-shirts, and working the phones at the Gay Men's Health Crisis. That's the way it happened." (Russo, author of *The Celluloid Closet*, died of AIDS in late 1990.)

The movie's format is to show one day per year, from 1981 to 1989. Each segment details the mounting impact of AIDS on the loves, lives, and careers of the principals. The couples are: Allan (Stephen Caffrey), an entertainment attorney, and gym instructor Willy (Campbell Scott); Howard (Patrick Cassidy, Shirley Jones's son), an actor on a soap, and Paul (John Dossett), an office worker; and Sean (Mark Lamos), who writes Howard's soap, and David (Bruce Davison), an independently wealthy

Radical right-wing bigots blasted PBS and the National Endowment for the Arts for sponsoring a true and nonjudgmental film about gay people and their struggles. But *Rolling Stone*—not a liberal publication where gays are concerned—deemed *Longtime Companion* "the best American movie this year."

On the other hand, *People* magazine, which unofficially ignores gays' existence in and out of Hollywood, criticized the film as "too" gay, therefore alienating mainstream audiences. *People*-reader Keith Hoffman responded, "I have yet to read a review of a movie that was criticized for being inaccessible to a gay audience." And although *Longtime Companion* included no sex scenes, merely casual affection between gay couples of the sort shown between hetero couples on G-rated television, it was rated a severe R—merely for demonstrating affection between gay men, as opposed to the propagandistic loathing of movies like *Staircase* and *Cruising*.

One Goldwyn executive called the film and its cast "courageous." Costar Stephen Caffrey ("All My Children," "Tour of Duty") told the gay paper *Frontiers*, "It's the people in the gay community who have been courageous. If we captured a piece of that, then we did our job." Oscar nominee Bruce Davison explained, "*Longtime Companion* is not about suffering, it's about survival."

Willy (Campbell Scott) and Fuzzy (Stephen Caffrey) become friends, then lovers, on Fire Island.

Sean (Mark Lamos), John (Dermot Mulroney), and David
(Bruce Davison) share the good times in the early 1980s.

party-giver. Involved in the story are gay friend
John (Dermot Mulroney) and female friend Lisa
(Mary-Louise Parker).

In a naturalistic way *Longtime Companion* charts
these New Yorkers' fear, denial, anger, sadness,
and loss, but also their life-affirming humor and
mutual support. It reflects the slow or nonexistent
sympathy of employers, the media, and men afraid
they themselves may be afflicted. Distressingly in-
sightful is the deterioration of Sean (enacted by
Tony Award-winning director Mark Lamos) from
brilliant writer to wizened infant to gasping skeleton.

The cast's standout is Bruce Davison. He had
already played gay characters on-stage and television, i.e., the soldier in *Steambath*, Barbara Hutton's
cousin Jimmy in *Poor Little Rich Girl*, and the lover in
the L.A. production of Larry Kramer's *The Normal
Heart*, opposite Richard Dreyfuss.

Davison didn't hesitate to accept another gay role.
"When I was doing *The Normal Heart*, my agent, my
manager, and my commercial agent all died within
a year. The agent I have now wasn't thrilled about
my doing *Longtime Companion*, but it's a part that
comes by once in a lifetime." The film's dramatic
zenith is the death scene in which David urges Sean
to release himself from his misery and pain. The
formerly self-centered lover reins in his own shat-

At the hospital, David and Willy anxiously await news of a
loved one's condition.

251

tered emotions and thinks solely of his companion's good. "It's okay," he sweetly tells Sean, "you can let go. Let go, my baby. It's all right. Let go. *Let go.* . . ."

Davison's performance earned the New York Film Critics award, a Golden Globe, and the National Society of Film Critics award for Best Supporting Actor. Yet he said he had mixed feelings: "It's what actors dream of, but at the same time I feel the fraud of portraying the people who are really living this." In the Oscar race Davison was up against Al Pacino in *Dick Tracy* and Andy Garcia in *Godfather III* but lost to Joe Pesci, who played a violent hood in *GoodFellas*.

Longtime Companion ends with a fantasy that was misunderstood by some critics. Three survivors—two gays and a female friend—stroll a deserted beach and wonder aloud what it will be like when AIDS is finally conquered. They're suddenly encircled by a jubilant crowd rushing onto the beach—a crowd including their deceased, now blissfully alive friends, whom they embrace. It is a heartbreaking illusion, but a symbol of hope and a tribute to the departed who are alive in memory.

The film also pays tribute to the survivors, said writer Craig Lucas. "What hadn't been told was the purely human story—who buys the groceries, who changes the diapers, who holds the dying man's hand, who calls the mortician. . . . I believe that was the most universal thing about AIDS." Lucas pointed out however that "the gay community has not supported AIDS-themed movies. *Parting Glances* lost money, so did *Buddies*. It wasn't like you could assume that the twenty-five to thirty million gay and lesbian Americans would go to see this movie. They go to *Batman*, like everyone else."

Although over twenty distributors declined *Longtime Companion*, it garnered raves *and* satisfied packed houses in larger cities. At the Sundance Film Festival, it won the Audience Favorite award. At the American Film Market, it sold widely internationally, and Hollywood nominated it for the Best Picture Academy Award. Even *TV Guide* commended Lindsay Law, executive producer of *American Playhouse*, for pushing through the 100 percent financing of the film. (Profits from *Longtime Companion* were earmarked for AIDS organizations such as Gay Men's Health Crisis and AIDS Films.)

Vito Russo concluded, "Look back over those dozens of gay-themed motion pictures. Most are negative, to say the least. Because they were made mostly by heterosexuals. Usually homophobic ones. Today we have fewer films built around gay themes. But these few are better, because they're made mostly by gay people for gay people and for enlightened heterosexuals. Quality signifies more than quantity—this is what gay people have felt all along and what is increasingly being reflected on the lavender screen."

ABOUT *LONGTIME COMPANION*

Aviva Haddad, *Oregon Jewish Times*: *Longtime Companion* offers the riveting and wrenching stories of a group of eight gay friends from the day when one reads an article in the *New York Times* about a 'rare cancer' in the gay community—Karposi's Sarcoma, previously affecting mostly elderly Jewish European men. . . . The title is the euphemism used in many obituaries to describe the surviving intimates of those claimed by AIDS. . . . The nine intense years covered here are a testament to the spirit and resilience of the Aching '80s.

Gay-Pied (France): Hollywood studio films go out of their way to salute the gay presence with a gratuitous slap in the face, further magnifying their cruelty by the complete lack of AIDS themes or compassion. . . . It took openly gay writer Craig Lucas and openly gay director Norman René, longtime Broadway collaborators, to create this fascinating, funny, compassionate, and irresistible AIDS saga.

Maenneraktuell (Germany): As relevant as the stories of three male couples through the 1980s is the story of every studio in Hollywood refusing to make or even distribute *Longtime Companion*. It was financed entirely by America's educational television channel [PBS's *American Playhouse*] for $1.5 million and eventually picked up by Goldwyn. . . . The splendid cast features unknowns, though rising star Alec Baldwin planned to appear until his schedule intervened. . . . Particularly memorable is Campbell Scott, son of actors Colleen Dewhurst and George C. Scott.

BIBLIOGRAPHY

Anger, Kenneth. *Hollywood Babylon*. San Francisco: Straight Arrow Books, 1975.

———. *Hollywood Babylon II*. New York: E.P. Dutton, 1984.

Bogarde, Dirk. *An Orderly Man*. New York: Alfred A. Knopf, 1983.

———. *A Postillion Struck by Lightning*. New York: Holt, Rinehart and Winston, 1977.

———. *Snakes and Ladders*. New York: Holt, Rinehart and Winston, 1978.

Bosworth, Patricia. *Montgomery Clift*. New York: Harcourt Brace Jovanovich, 1978.

Box, Betty. *Odd Woman Out*. London: Frewin, 1974.

Brandreth, Gyles. *John Gielgud: A Celebration*. Boston: Little, Brown & Co., 1984.

Brode, Douglas. *The Films of the Fifties*. Secaucus, N.J.: Citadel Press, 1976.

Bronski, Michael. *Culture Clash: The Making of Gay Sensibility*. Boston: South End Press, 1984.

Carr, Virginia Spencer. *Lonely Hunter, a Biography of Carson McCullers*. Garden City, N.Y.: Doubleday, 1975.

Collins, Joan. *Past Imperfect*. London: W.H. Allen, 1978.

Cook, Bruce. *Dalton Trumbo*. New York: Scribner's, 1977.

Core, Philip. *Camp: The Lie That Tells the Truth*. New York: Delilah Books, 1984.

Cottrell, John. *Laurence Olivier*. London: Weidenfeld & Nicolson, 1975.

——— and Fergus Cashin. *Richard Burton: Very Closeup*. Englewood Cliffs, N.J.: Prentice-Hall, 1971.

Crist, Judith. *Moviemakers on Moviemaking*. New York: Viking Penguin, 1984.

DeGrazia, Edward and Roger K. Newman. *Banned Films: Movies, Censors and the First Amendment*. New York: R.R. Bowker, 1982.

Delaney, Shelagh. *A Taste of Honey*. New York: Grove Press, 1959.

Dickens, Homer. *What a Drag: Men as Women and Women as Men in the Movies*. New York: Quill, 1984.

Dundy, Elaine. *Finch, Bloody Finch, A Life of Peter Finch*. New York: Holt, Rinehart and Winston, 1980.

Dyer, Charles. *Staircase*. New York: Grove Press, 1966.

Dyer, Richard, ed. *Gays and Film*. London: BFI Publishing, 1977.

Eells, George and Stanley Musgrove. *Mae West*. New York: Morrow, 1982.

Erens, Patricia. *Sexual Stratagems: The World of Women in Film*. New York: Horizon Press, 1979.

Everson, William K. *Love in the Film*. Secaucus, N.J.: Citadel Press, 1979.

Faulkner, Trader. *Peter Finch*. New York: Taplinger Publishing Co., 1979.

Ferris, Paul. *Richard Burton*. New York: Coward, McCann & Geoghegan, 1981.

Fitzgerald, Michael G. *Universal Pictures*. New Rochelle, N.Y.: Arlington House, 1977.

Frank, Alan. *Monsters and Vampires*. London: Octopus Books, 1976.

Friedman, Lester D. *Hollywood's Image of the Jew*. New York: Frederick K. Ungar, 1982.

Frischauer, Willi. *Behind the Scenes of Otto Preminger*. New York: Morrow, 1974.

Geist, Kenneth L. *Pictures Will Talk: The Life and Films of Joseph L. Mankiewicz*. New York: Charles Scribner's Sons, 1978.

Gilliatt, Penelope. *Sunday, Bloody Sunday*. New York: The Viking Press, 1971.

Godfrey, Lionel. *Paul Newman, Superstar*. New York: St. Martin's Press, 1978.

Goldstein, Norm. *Henry Fonda*. New York: Holt, Rinehart and Winston, 1982.

Goodman, Ezra. *The Fifty Year Decline and Fall of Hollywood*. New York: MacFadden Books, 1962.

Gray, Simon. *Butley*. New York: The Viking Press, 1971.

Greif, Martin. *The Gay Book of Days*. Secaucus, N.J.: Lyle Stuart, Inc., 1982.

———. *The Gay Engagement Calendar 1984*. Pittstown, N.J.: The Main Street Press, 1983.

Hall, William. *Raising Caine*. Englewood Cliffs, N.J.: Prentice-Hall, 1981.

Halliwell, Leslie. *The Filmgoer's Companion*. New York: Hill and Wang, 1977.

Hamblett, Charles. *Paul Newman*. Chicago: Henry Regnery, 1975.

Harrison, Rex. *Rex: An Autobiography*. New York: Morrow, 1975.

Hayman, Ronald. *John Gielgud*. London: Heinemann, 1971.

Herbert, John. *Fortune and Men's Eyes*. New York: Grove Press, 1967.

Herlihy, James Leo. *Midnight Cowboy*. New York: Simon and Schuster, 1965.

Herndon, Venable. *James Dean: A Short Life*. New York: NAL, 1973.

Higham, Charles. *Kate, The Life of Katharine Hepburn*. New York: Norton, 1974.

——— and Roy Moseley. *Princess Merle: The Romantic Life of Merle Oberon*. New York: Putnam, 1983.

Hirschhorn, Clive. *The Films of James Mason*. Secaucus, N.J.: Citadel Press, 1977.

———. *The Warner Brothers Story*. New York: Crown, 1979.

Hoberman, J. and Jonathan Rosenbaum. *Midnight Movies*. New York: Harper & Row, 1983.

Hodges, Andrew. *Alan Turing, The Enigma*. New York: Simon and Schuster, 1983.

Hughes, Eileen Lanouette. *On the Set of 'Fellini Satyricon.'* New York: Morrow, 1971.

Insdorf, Annette. *Indelible Shadows—Film and the Holocaust*. New York: Random House, 1983.

Isherwood, Christopher. *The Berlin Stories*. New York: New Directions, 1945.

Kael, Pauline. *Deeper Into Movies*. Boston: Atlantic-Little, Brown, 1973.

———. *Going Steady*. New York: Warner Books, 1979.

———. *I Lost It at the Movies*. Boston: Little, Brown, 1965.

Kanin, Garson. *Tracy and Hepburn*. New York: The Viking Press, 1971.

Kelley, Kitty. *Elizabeth Taylor: The Last Star*. New York: Simon and Schuster, 1981.

Kiernan, Robert F. *Gore Vidal*. New York: Frederick K. Ungar, 1982.

Klapp, Orrin E. *Heroes, Villains and Fools*. Englewood Cliffs, N.J.: Prentice-Hall, 1962.

LaGuardia, Robert. *Monty: A Biography of Montgomery Clift*. New York: Arbor House, 1977.

Lambert, Gavin. *On Cukor*. New York: G.P. Putnam's Sons, 1972.

Lanchester, Elsa. *Elsa Lanchester, Herself*. New York: St. Martin's Press, 1983.

Lehman, Peter and William Luhr. *Blake Edwards*. Athens: Ohio University Press, 1981.

Levin, Meyer. *Compulsion*. New York: Simon and Schuster, 1956.

McCambridge, Mercedes. *The Quality of Mercy*. New York: Times Books, 1981.

McCullers, Carson. *Reflections in a Golden Eye*. Cambridge, Mass.: Riverside Press, 1941.

MacDonald, Dwight. *On Movies*. Englewood Cliffs, N.J.: Prentice-Hall, 1969.

Madsen, Axel. *John Huston*. Garden City, N.Y.: Doubleday, 1978.

Mann, Thomas. *Stories from Three Decades*. New York: Alfred A. Knopf, 1936.

Medved, Harry and Michael. *The Golden Turkey Awards*. New York: Perigee, 1980.

———. *The Hollywood Hall of Shame—The Most Expensive Flops in Movie History*. New York: Perigee, 1984.

Minnelli, Vincente. *I Remember It Well*. Garden City, N.Y.: Doubleday, 1974.

Mordden, Ethan. *The Hollywood Musical*. New York: St. Martin's Press, 1981.

———. *Movie Star: A Look at the Women Who Made Hollywood*. New York: St. Martin's Press, 1984.

Morley, Robert and Sewell Stokes. *Robert Morley*. New York: Simon and Schuster, 1967.

Newquist, Roy. *Conversations With Joan Crawford*. Secaucus, N.J.: Citadel Press, 1980.

Orton, Joe. *The Complete Plays*. New York: Grove Press, 1976.

Peary, Danny. *Cult Movies*. New York: Delta, 1981.

Perry, George. *The Great British Picture Show*. New York: Hill and Wang, 1974.

———. *Movies From the Mansion: A History of Pinewood Studios*. New York: American Zoetrope, 1982.

Phillips, Gene D. *The Films of Tennessee Williams*. Berkeley, Cal.: Art Alliance Press, 1980.

Prawer, S. S. *Caligari's Children: The Film as Tale of Terror*. New York: Oxford University Press, 1980.

Preminger, Otto. *Otto Preminger, an Autobiography*. Garden City, N.Y.: Doubleday, 1977.

Quirk, Lawrence J. *The Films of Paul Newman*. Secaucus, N.J.: Citadel Press, 1971.

Randall, Richard S. *Censorship of the Movies*. Madison: University of Wisconsin Press, 1970.

Reed, Rex. *Big Screen, Little Screen*. New York: MacMillan, 1971.

———. *Conversations in the Raw*. New York: World Publishing, 1969.

———. *Do You Sleep in the Nude?* New York: NAL, 1968.

Rotha, Paul. *The Film Till Now*. London: Spring Books, 1967.

Rovin, Jeff. *The Films of Charlton Heston*. Secaucus, N.J.: Citadel Press, 1977.

Russo, Vito. *The Celluloid Closet: Homosexuality in the Movies*. New York: Harper & Row, 1981.

Samuels, Stuart. *Midnight Movies*. New York: MacMillan, 1983.

Sayre, Nora. *Running Time: The Films of the Cold War*. New York: Dial Press, 1982.

Simon, John. *Acid Test*. New York: Stein and Day, 1963.

———. *Reverse Angle*. New York: Clarkson N. Potter, 1982.

———. *Something to Declare: Twelve Years of Film From Abroad*. New York: Clarkson N. Potter, 1983.

Simon, Randy and Harold Benjamin. *Edward D. Wood Jr.: A Man and His Films*. Los Angeles: Edward D. Wood Jr. Film Appreciation Society, 1981.

Sontag, Susan. *Against Interpretation and Other Essays*. New York: Delta, 1966.

Spada, James. *The Films of Robert Redford*. Secaucus, N.J.: Citadel Press, 1977.

——— and Karen Swenson. *Judy and Liza*. Garden City, N.Y.: Doubleday, 1983.

Springer, John. *The Fondas*. Secaucus, N.J.: Citadel Press, 1970.

Steinem, Gloria. *Outrageous Acts and Everyday Rebellions*. New York: Holt, Rinehart and Winston, 1983.

Stirling, Monica. *A Screen of Time: A Study of Luchino Visconti*. New York: Harcourt Brace Jovanovich, 1979.

Strieber, Whitley. *The Hunger*. New York: Morrow, 1981.

Stuart, Sandra Lee. *The Pink Palace: Behind Closed Doors at the Beverly Hills Hotel*. Secaucus, N.J.: Lyle Stuart, Inc., 1978.

Taylor, John Russell. *Hitch, the Life and Times of Afred Hitchcock*. New York: Pantheon Books, 1978.

Thomas, Tony. *The Films of Marlon Brando*. Secaucus, N.J.: Citadel Press, 1973.

——— and Aubrey Solomon. *The Films of Twentieth Century-Fox*. Secaucus, N.J.: Citadel Press, 1979.

Truffaut, François and Helen G. Scott. *Hitchcock*. New York: Simon and Schuster, 1967.

Turan, Kenneth and Stephen F. Zito. *American Pornographic Films and the People Who Make Them*. New York: Praeger, 1974.

Tyler, Parker. *Screening the Sexes: Homosexuality in the Movies*. New York: Holt, Rinehart and Winston, 1972.

Vermilye, Jerry and Mark Ricci. *The Films of Elizabeth Taylor*. Secaucus, N.J.: Citadel Press, 1976.

———. *The Great British Films*. Secaucus, N.J.: Citadel Press, 1978.

Vidal, Gore. *Myra Breckinridge*. New York: Bantam Books, 1968.

Walker, Alexander. *Hollywood, UK; the British Film Industry in the Sixties*. New York: Stein and Day, 1974.

Williams, Tennessee. *Memoirs*. Garden City, N.Y.: Doubleday, 1975.

———. *The Night of the Iguana*. New York: NAL, 1961.

———. *Suddenly, Last Summer*. New York: New Directions Books, 1958.

Windeler, Robert. *Julie Andrews*. New York: St. Martin's Press, 1983.

Wood, Robin. *Hitchcock's Films*. Cranbury, N.J.: A.S. Barnes, 1977.

Woodward, Ian. *Audrey Hepburn*. London: W.H. Allen, 1984.

ORDER NOW!
More Citadel Film Books

If you like this book, you'll love the other titles in the award-winning Citadel Film Series. From James Stewart to Moe Howard and The Three Stooges, Woody Allen to John Wayne, The Citadel Film Series is America's largest and oldest film book library.

With more than 150 titles--and more on the way!--Citadel Film Books make perfect gifts for a loved one, a friend, or best of all, yourself!

A complete listing of the Citadel Film Series appears below.
If you know what books you want, why not order now!
It's easy! Just call 1-800-447-BOOK and have your MasterCard or Visa ready.

STARS
Alan Ladd
Barbra Streisand: First Decade
Barbra Streisand: Second
  Decade
Bela Lugosi
Bette Davis
Boris Karloff
The Bowery Boys
Buster Keaton
Carole Lombard
Cary Grant
Charles Bronson
Charlie Chaplin
Clark Gable
Clint Eastwood
Curly
Dustin Hoffman
Edward G. Robinson
Elizabeth Taylor
Elvis Presley
Errol Flynn
Frank Sinatra
Gary Cooper
Gene Kelly
Gina Lollobrigida
Gloria Swanson
Gregory Peck
Greta Garbo
Henry Fonda
Humphrey Bogart
Ingrid Bergman
Jack Lemmon
Jack Nicholson
James Cagney
James Dean: Behind the Scene
Jane Fonda
Jeanette MacDonald & Nelson
  Eddy
Joan Crawford

John Wayne Films
John Wayne Reference Book
John Wayne Scrapbook
Judy Garland
Katharine Hepburn
Kirk Douglas
Laurel & Hardy
Lauren Bacall
Laurence Olivier
Mae West
Marilyn Monroe
Marlene Dietrich
Marlon Brando
Marx Brothers
Moe Howard & the Three
  Stooges
Norma Shearer
Olivia de Havilland
Orson Welles
Paul Newman
Peter Lorre
Rita Hayworth
Robert De Niro
Robert Redford
Sean Connery
Sexbomb: Jayne Mansfield
Shirley MacLaine
Shirley Temple
The Sinatra Scrapbook
Spencer Tracy
Steve McQueen
Three Stooges Scrapbook
Warren Beatty
W.C. Fields
William Holden
William Powell
A Wonderful Life: James Stewart
DIRECTORS
Alfred Hitchcock
Cecil B. DeMille

Federico Fellini
Frank Capra
John Ford
John Huston
Woody Allen
GENRE
Bad Guys
Black Hollywood
Black Hollywood: From 1970 to
  Today
Classics of the Gangster Film
Classics of the Horror Film
Divine Images: Jesus on Screen
Early Classics of Foreign Film
Great French Films
Great German Films
Great Romantic Films
Great Science Fiction Films
Harry Warren & the Hollywood
  Musical
Hispanic Hollywood: The Latins
  in Motion Pictures
The Hollywood Western
The Incredible World of 007
The Jewish Image in American
  Film
The Lavender Screen: The Gay
  and Lesbian Films
Martial Arts Movies
The Modern Horror Film
More Classics of the Horror Film
Movie Psychos & Madmen
Our Huckleberry Friend: Johnny
  Mercer
Second Feature: "B" Films
They Sang! They Danced! They
  Romanced!: Hollywood
  Musicals
Thrillers
The West That Never Was

Words and Shadows: Literature
  on the Screen
DECADE
Classics of the Silent Screen
Films of the Twenties
Films of the Thirties
More Films of the 30's
Films of the Forties
Films of the Fifties
Lost Films of the 50's
Films of the Sixties
Films of the Seventies
Films of the Eighties
SPECIAL INTEREST
America on the Rerun
Bugsy (Illustrated screenplay)
Comic Support
Dick Tracy
Favorite Families of TV
Film Flubs
Film Flubs: The Sequel
First Films
Forgotten Films to Remember
Hollywood Cheesecake
Hollywood's Hollywood
Howard Hughes in Hollywood
More Character People
The Nightmare Never Ends:
  Freddy Krueger & "A Night-
  mare on Elm Street"
The "Northern Exposure" Book
The "Quantum Leap" Book
Sex In the Movies
Sherlock Holmes
Son of Film Flubs
Those Glorious Glamour Years
Who Is That?: Familiar Faces and
  Forgotten Names
"You Ain't Heard Nothin' Yet!"

For a free full-color brochure describing the Citadel Film Series in depth, call 1-800-447-BOOK; or send your name and address to Citadel Film Books, Dept. 1341, 120 Enterprise Ave., Secaucus, NJ 07094.